Social Work and Restorative Justice

Social Work and Restorative Justice

Skills for Dialogue, Peacemaking, and Reconciliation

Edited by
Elizabeth Beck
Nancy P. Kropf
Pamela Blume Leonard

OXFORD
UNIVERSITY PRESS
2011

OXFORD
UNIVERSITY PRESS

Oxford University Press, Inc., publishes works that further
Oxford University's objective of excellence
in research, scholarship, and education.

Oxford   New York
Auckland   Cape Town   Dar es Salaam   Hong Kong   Karachi
Kuala Lumpur   Madrid   Melbourne   Mexico City   Nairobi
New Delhi   Shanghai   Taipei   Toronto

With offices in
Argentina   Austria   Brazil   Chile   Czech Republic   France   Greece
Guatemala   Hungary   Italy   Japan   Poland   Portugal   Singapore
South Korea   Switzerland   Thailand   Turkey   Ukraine   Vietnam

Published by Oxford University Press, Inc.
198 Madison Avenue, New York, New York 10016
www.oup.com

Library of Congress Cataloging-in-Publication Data
Social work and restorative justice: skills for dialogue, peacemaking,
and reconciliation / edited by Elizabeth Beck, Nancy Kropf, Pamela Blume Leonard.
   p. cm.
Includes bibliographical references and index.
ISBN 978-0-19-539464-1
1. Restorative justice.   2. Social service.   3. Social work with criminals.
4. Victims of crime–Services for.   I. Beck, Elizabeth.   II. Kropf, Nancy P.
III. Leonard, Pamela Blume.
HV8688.S67 2011
364.6'8—dc22
2010016619

This book is dedicated to all victims of homicide, especially Gregory Rodriguez and Meleia Starbuck. Despite their deaths, Meleia and Gregory inspire us, their families, and friends to seek peace and justice in their names.

Contents

SETTINGS

Contributors

Lauren Abramson, PhD
Licensed Psychologist (Maryland)
Founder, Executive Director
Community Conferencing Center

Lorraine Stutzman Amstutz, MSW
Co-Director, Office on Justice & Peacebuilding
Mennonite Central Committee U.S.

Elizabeth Beck, PhD
Associate Professor, School of Social Work
Director, Center for Collaborative Social Work
Georgia State University

Alexandra Lee Crampton, MSW, PhD
Assistant Professor, Marquette University

David S. Crampton, PhD
Associate Professor of Social Work
Mandel School of Applied Social Sciences
Case Western Reserve University

Thomas K. Crick, B.Sc M.S.Sc.
Associate Director, Conflict Resolution Program,
The Carter Center
Emory University

Nancy J. Good, PhD, LCSW
Associate Professor of Trauma and Conflict Studies,
Eastern Mennonite University
Founding Partner, Mediator, Psychotherapist
Newman Avenue Associates

David L. Gustafson, MA, RCC Registered Clinical Counselor
Co-Director, Fraser Region Community Justice Initiatives Association
Langley, British Columbia, Canada
Adjunct Professor, School of Criminology
Simon Fraser University

Michele V. Hamilton, EdD
Research & Professional Development Specialist
UC Davis School of Education-CRESS Center

M. Kay Harris, MA
Administration, School of Social Service
University of Chicago
Associate Professor, Department of Criminal Justice,
Temple University

Lesa Nitcy Hope, LMSW, PhD
Director of Community Services
AADD—All About Developmental Disabilities

Mary P. Koss, PhD
Regents' Professor of Public Health and Licensed Clinical Psychologist,
Mel and Enid Zuckerman College of Public Health
University of Arizona

Nancy P. Kropf, PhD
Professor & Director, School of Social Work
Georgia State University

Pamela Blume Leonard, MA
Executive Director, Council for Restorative Justice
School of Social Work
Georgia State University

Joan Pennell, MSW, PhD
Professor and Director, Center for Family and Community Engagement
North Carolina State University

Patricia L. Rideout, BA, JD
Senior Consultant, Child Welfare Strategy Group
The Annie E. Casey Foundation

Barb Toews, MA
PhD Candidate, Graduate School of Social Work and Social Research
Bryn Mawr College

Mark Umbreit, PhD
Director, Center for Restorative Justice and Peacemaking
Professor, School of Social Work
University of Minnesota

Nancy Rothenberg Williams, PhD, LCSW
Associate Professor of Social Work, School of Social Work
University of Georgia

Andrea Wood
Emory University School of Law
Robert W. Woodruff Fellow

Howard Zehr, PhD
Professor of Restorative Justice,
Center for Justice & Peacebuilding
Eastern Mennonite University

Foreword

From the humble beginnings of restorative justice in the 1970s, to its current status as a social movement in the global community endorsed by the United Nations, social workers have played a critical role, as program managers, volunteers, board members, community organizers, trainers, and mediators. Despite this early participation in the development of restorative justice by key social workers, the relationship of the restorative justice movement to the field of social work is marked by paradox. On the one hand, individual social work practitioners and faculty have been actively involved in the restorative justice movement from its inception. The first flowchart describing the Victim–Offender Reconciliation Process (VORP), a precursor of the restorative justice movement, was prepared by a recent MSW graduate who was on the staff of the first VORP program in the United States. A social work faculty member played a leadership role on the board of directors of the first community-based organization to fully develop and promote victim–offender reconciliation in the United States. Social workers served as volunteer mediators in several of the initial victim–offender mediation programs in the Midwest.

On the other hand, restorative justice has not been widely recognized or claimed within the social work profession. This is despite the historical impact of social workers in corrections and criminal justice issues, including Jane Addams's work in the development of the first juvenile court in the country, as well as the later frequent service by social work practitioners as probation officers in communities throughout America.

However, there are two notable exceptions. The first is Dr. Katherine van Wormer, social work practitioner and scholar at the University of Northern Iowa, a strong advocate for the inclusion of restorative justice in social work education and practice. Her many articles and books persuasively articulate the linkages between restorative and social justice, and between restorative justice and the strengths perspective of social work. Dr. van Wormer has been a lone voice over many years for the marriage of social work and restorative justice.

The second example is the full-page article in the 2005 issue of the publication of the National Association of Social Workers (NASW), *NASW NEWS*, entitled "Restorative Justice: A Model of Healing: Philosophy Consistent with Social Work Values." The article quotes NASW member and former colleague, Mark Chupp, who played a critical leadership role in the first victim–offender reconciliation program in the U.S.: "[R]estorative justice and social work are a match made in heaven. . . . the values of both are very consistent."

The *NASW NEWS* article also highlights the work of my colleagues at the Center for Restorative Justice & Peacemaking in the School of Social Work at the University of Minnesota, which was founded in 1995 and represents the first and most widely recognized academic-based restorative justice center in the world. The Center has trained thousands of practitioners in more than 23 countries, and its numerous publications, training manuals, books, DVDs, and videotapes have been distributed throughout the world and translated into many languages.

The fact remains, however, that despite the widely recognized work of the Center for Restorative Justice & Peacemaking and the more recent develop and impact of the Council for Restorative Justice at the School of Social Work at Georgia State University and the Institute for Restorative Justice and Restorative Justice Dialogue in the School of Social Work at the University of Texas in Austin, restorative justice is essentially marginalized within the social work profession.

Social Work and Restorative Justice: Skills for Dialogue, Peacemaking, and Reconciliation makes a significant contribution to changing this reality. Elizabeth Beck and her coauthors do a fine job of highlighting the interface between the restorative justice movement and the field of social work. In this very well-written and well-organized book, which contains many rich case examples, a new dialogue between social work students and practitioners and the growing restorative justice community has now been initiated.

Mark Umbreit, PhD
Professor and Founding Director
Center for Restorative Justice & Peacemaking
School of Social Work, University of Minnesota
Coauthor of *Restorative Justice Dialogue: An Essential
Guide for Research & Practice*

Acknowledgments

This book developed from a strong desire to have more social workers understand the field of restorative justice. In achieving our goal, we are deeply grateful to several leaders in the restorative justice field, including Mark Umbreit, Lorraine Stutzman Amstutz, and Howard Zehr, who all supported the idea and the writing of this book. They, along with Katherine van Wormer and other social workers who saw and shared the value of incorporating restorative justice into their work, paved the way through their careers and commitment to healing, peacemaking, and reconciliation.

More locally, at our own university, there were several sources of encouragement and support. Our colleagues Doug Yarn and Carolyn Benne have encouraged all aspects of our practice and research as they work to strengthen the restorative justice community throughout the southeastern United States. Graduate research assistant Leah Tioxin's wisdom, cheer, and knowledge of APA style simplified the project. We are grateful to student intern Marybeth Britton for industriously identifying restorative justice programs and resources.

We are also grateful to the staff at Oxford University Press who took an early interest in this book. Many thanks to Maura Roessner and Nicholas Liu at OUP. We appreciate their support, particularly their creativity in assembling a wise team of reviewers whose critiques, ideas, and suggestions strengthened our book.

Most importantly, the *genesis* of this book came from the experiences and stories of the people who have been part of the restorative justice process. We have met many people whose courage and commitment to peacemaking and reconciliation has transformed our understanding of healing. In particular, we have been deeply affected by the humanity of Phyllis and Orlando Rodriguez, whose son Gregory was killed on 9/11; Tina Walker, whose father and stepmother were murdered; and Kimberly, John, and Zachary Starbuck, the family of Meleia, a homicide victim. All of these victim–survivors strongly support restorative justice and work for its implementation in their cases and as an option for all victim–survivors of homicide.

Social Work and Restorative Justice

Chapter One

Introduction

ELIZABETH BECK

In the 1990s, Howard Zehr asked his readers to rethink the retributive lens through which American society tended to view crime and justice, by thinking about crime in terms of people and relationships. Specifically, he explained that, rather than understanding crime as a violation of the state, it might be more beneficial to those directly involved and to society as a whole to view crime as a violation of people and relationships which needed to be put right (Zehr, 2005). The restorative lens he proposed shifted the attention from what needed to be done *to* the offender to *how* the needs of victims, offenders, and communities harmed by the crime could be addressed (Leonard, 2006; Zehr, 2005). This way of thinking about and dealing with the effects of crime is called *restorative justice*.

Today, restorative justice is described not only as an alternative or complement to punishment, but as a strategy designed to promote healing for victims, offenders, and communities after a crime has occurred. It also has been referred to as an international social movement and a method of human interaction that can transform the power imbalances that support oppression, violence, and counterviolence (Sullivan and Tifft, 2005; van Wormer, 2004). In order to actualize these aims, restorative justice proponents and practitioners have developed a host of practices, including Victim Offender Dialogue, Peacemaking Circles, Family Group Conferences, and Community Justice. These practices (which are described in detail in Chapter 4) are found in a variety of settings inside and outside the criminal justice system that are familiar terrain to social workers and include death-penalty trials, the juvenile justice system, prisons, child welfare offices, and schools.

In 2004, Katherine van Wormer wrote that social work needed to be at the head (rather than the back) of the restorative justice movement, and predicted that such a reorientation was likely. In 2009, Gumz and Grant undertook a systematic review of the social work literature and found that, while a smattering of articles and even a special edition of the *Journal of Sociology and Social Welfare* have been devoted to restorative justice, the role of social work in the theory and practice of restorative justice remains small. This book seeks to encourage and strengthen the relationship of social work and restorative justice.

As part of this introduction, I examine the fit between social work and restorative justice by recounting my own entry into restorative justice. The theme of fit is visited in each of the subsequent chapters and examined in the conclusion as well. I also consider some explanations for why restorative justice may be slow in coming to social work and the ways we—the authors—believe this book can support a partnership between social work and the restorative justice movement.

MY STORY

I started working as a community organizer and activist well before I entered an academic social work program, so it is not surprising that I identified as a community based or macro social worker. I moved from Pennsylvania to Georgia in the mid-1990s. Due to a variety of coincidences, I became a volunteer with the Office of the Georgia Capital Defender, where I provided clinical rather than organizing support. The first capital case I worked on was that of a mentally ill man, Marcus. Not long before the murder and his subsequent trial, Marcus began displaying visible signs of mental illness. Sarah, his mother, did everything she could to try to get him help, but Marcus, like many people with mental illness, did not accept it. About 2 years after Sarah's failed attempts to obtain treatment for her son, she was called as a witness in her son's death-penalty trial. She provided eloquent and moving testimony about her efforts to help Marcus and the numerous ways in which community-based institutions, ranging from the local mental health center to the school system, had failed Marcus. She asked the jury to show mercy and spare her son from execution. After Sarah completed her testimony, she rose and walked out of the courtroom. When the heavy doors closed behind her, Sarah let out a deep wail. Everyone in the courtroom understood that her cry was rooted in a mother's pain.

From that experience, two things shifted for me. First, as I thought about Marcus's story, I began to see the nexus between micro and macro practice through a new lens and developed a strong *person in the environment* approach to social change. Specifically, this insight led me to revisit the intersection of social justice and violence. I reread Gandhi, Martin Luther King, Jr., and Bayard Rustin. Additionally, as someone who had studied community practice, I began to expand my analysis of community issues beyond those traditionally identified with community practice approaches—economic and social justice, neighborhood supports, and thoughtful planning—to include strategies designed to address neighborhood violence, and I began to search for ways to provide alternatives to youth who have been caught up in violence or witness its harm. I became engaged with the idea of building neighborhood relationships as a way of stemming crime (which is described in Chapter 7). After I learned about restorative justice, I saw the significance of restorative processes in supporting that aim.

I also realized that, because there was so little information regarding the collateral damage done to family members of the offender, the full story of capital punishment had not been told. Pamela Leonard, who was then Chief Investigator and Chief Death Penalty Mitigation Specialist for the Multi-County Public Defender Office in Georgia, and I began a research initiative that resulted in my interviewing more than 50 family members of men and women on death row. Criminologist Sarah Britto joined with Pamela and me. She and Pamela shared an interest in restorative justice and introduced me to the concept. Together we made an intentional decision to root our interview protocol in principles associated with restorative justice, which included listening nonjudgmentally, providing space for storytelling, and affirming the relationship between the individual on death row and his or her family members. While conducting the interviews, I began to see in many cases the importance and, in some cases, the transformative nature, of storytelling (Beck & Britto, 2006).

Sarah and I joined with professor of social work Arlene Andrews and turned our investigation into a book, *In the Shadow of Death: Restorative Justice and Death Row Families* (Beck, Britto, and Andrews, 2007). With Sarah as a guide on the academic side of restorative justice and Pamela as a guide on the practice side, we began to envision an alternative to the harm of capital trials. On Pamela's advice, I participated in a restorative justice training session at Eastern Mennonite University's Summer Peacebuilding Institute in 2006. I heard faculty member Tammy Krause say something to the effect that, when people's needs for being heard, acquiring information, and obtaining validation begin to be met, their need for vengeance tends to diminish (though this does not mean apology or forgiveness necessarily occurs), and things began to click for me. I had seen the shift Tammy described occur with the family members I had interviewed. Further, I began to see the intersection between individual and societal transformation and how providing information, enabling storytelling, and encouraging dialogue are important components that support critical consciousness.

In 2006, Pamela Leonard and I received funding to support Georgia, our home state, in developing infrastructure to make the restorative justice practice of Defense-Initiated Victim Outreach[i] available to interested victim–survivors in death penalty cases. At about the same time, Nancy Kropf became director of the Georgia State University School of Social Work. Nancy was finishing a project on grandparents who were raising their grandchildren (because the parents were incarcerated) and had a strong interest in the concept of forgiveness. As she learned more about restorative justice and our project, Nancy became keenly interested in both restorative justice as a concept and restorative practices as a skill set that can support social work practice, and her ardent support for exploring the areas for interaction led us to writing this particular book.

Together, Pamela, Nancy, and I have helped to develop a number of bridges between social work and restorative justice. We at Georgia State University are proud to host the Council for Restorative Justice, which received funding from the Bureau of Justice Assistance to support infrastructure development for Defense-Initiated Victim Outreach in two additional states, Texas and Louisiana.

As an activist, social worker, researcher, and social work faculty member, restorative justice has enlightened my understanding of social problems. It plays an important role in helping me envision how we can grow and support more just and caring communities throughout the world.

RESTORATIVE JUSTICE AND SOCIAL WORK: BARRIERS AND OPPORTUNITIES TO RECOGNIZING THE FIT

Given the significant overlap of principles and goals between restorative justice and social work, the relationship between them has been slow to develop. We postulate three conditions that will jump-start this relationship: 1. increased reciprocal awareness between the two fields; 2. knowledge: and 3. collaboration. In this section, we look at the ways in which the absence of these conditions may have hampered a partnership between restorative justice and social work, how progress is being made to overcome these potential obstacles, and how the structure of this book seeks to address each topic.

Increased Reciprocal Awareness

Social worker Katherine van Wormer suggests that restorative justice is a new model for the 21st century but she acknowledges that the integration of the restorative justice model with social work has been slow (van Wormer, 2006). Indeed, one problem van Wormer identified was the lack of an entry for restorative justice in the *Encyclopedia of Social Work*, an omission that was remedied in 2008 (van Wormer, 2008). In van Wormer's view, it is in the interest of social work to take a leadership position in advancing restorative justice principles and restorative processes. Her prediction that the application of restorative justice in social work would grow was based on several factors, including the success of restorative justice in addressing the needs of victims, offenders, and communities; the fit between social work and restorative justice; positive media attention to restorative justice; and social work's "search for innovative remedies to social problems" (van Wormer, 2006)

In contrast, restorative justice theory includes a critique of the power of institutions to take control of social problems (especially those problems that involve conflict), hire professionals who offer few or no solutions, and sideline the individuals who are directly involved. The implementation of restorative justice within the criminal justice system belies the reservations that restorative justice practitioners have about working with institutionalized professionals who are pushed to reach resolution of a conflict, rather than use the conflict to support growth, transformation, and build stronger relationships.

Greater knowledge about the overlapping principles and goals shared by social work and restorative justice, particularly the goal of social justice, is needed. Otherwise, the idea of collaborating with the strongly institutionalized field of social work may present more risks and compromises than benefits to restorative justice practitioners. Conversely, the field of social work, which has achieved professional and academic credibility, may not feel comfortable with close association with a discipline that has previously eschewed professionalization and is a subject that is studied by other disciplines but has not, as yet, established itself as a discreet area of academic study.

There may be moments where the constraints of social work as a profession guided by ethics and norms of practice may bump up against restorative justice which, as Howard Zehr states, "embraces mystery and ambiguity" (Zehr, 2009). However, these sore spots will be soothed when both social work and restorative justice acknowledge their potential vulnerabilities and gain understanding and respect for each other's cultures, goals, and norms. Further, as in any collaboration, there is a need to view fit as a subject for ongoing evaluation

Knowledge

Restorative justice practitioners must be well-grounded in the theory and principles of restorative justice and well-trained in the discipline's practice skills. For most social workers, gaining this information requires a serious commitment of time and effort beyond their workplace, college or university, or field placement setting.

Learning a new literature is always a daunting task, and teasing out a broad literature to fit the needs and interests of social workers requires an extra layer of sifting. The current body of literature on social work and restorative justice, though small, is an important orienting step. However, the student of restorative justice will have to go well beyond that to gain a sense of the theory, principles, debates, and areas of practice involved. The student may find him- or herself overwhelmed by conflicting definitions of restorative justice in the literature and disheartened by the small number of empirical evaluations.

Because social work is theoretical as well as practical, social workers seeking to learn more about restorative justice may also want to gain skills in restorative processes. To support skill development, several excellent practice institutes have developed. Courses range from multi-day intensive training sessions on a particular practice, to accredited programs leading to a master's degree.

Additionally, at the time of this writing, only a few schools of social work in the United States have restorative justice components. The University of Minnesota School of Social Work's Center for Restorative Justice and Peacemaking, the Georgia State University School of Social Work (which is home to the Council for Restorative Justice), and the Institute for Restorative Justice and Restorative Dialogue at the University of Texas at Austin are the most visible. The existence of these programs potentially eases the burden for social workers seeking to obtain training in restorative justice. Further, at the 2008 Council of Social Work Education's Annual Program Meeting, Beck, East, and Toews offered a skills workshop, "Restorative Justice and Its Application in the Social Environment," which provided an overview of restorative justice, its practices and application to social work.

Interdisciplinary Collaboration

Interdisciplinary collaboration is challenging across many sectors, and several obstacles may affect interdisciplinary collaboration between social workers and restorative justice practitioners. The first factor is knowledge. Until introductory social work textbooks include information about restorative justice, the discipline will remain a mystery to many social work students, practitioners, and faculty. A second problem area concerns the issue of interaction among scholars. The number of restorative justice theorists across the globe is relatively small, and many of these individuals are international experts located outside the United States, whereas American writers tend to dominate social work literature. In addition to social workers, criminologists, sociologists, and law school faculty are teaming up with restorative justice practitioners to explore the theory, efficacy, and implications of restorative practices. Though this development sets the stage for some important interdisciplinary collaborations, it also diffuses restorative justice research across the academy and limits interactions in discipline-related professional conferences and other professional organizations.

While interdisciplinary collaborations can be difficult to form, the results can be exciting and very strong. Not only are the two collaborators expanding their own knowledge and field by building on the work of another discipline, but these collaborations also can lead to new ways of seeing phenomena, which can support new theory and practices.

STRENGTHENING THE FIT: THE STRUCTURE OF THIS BOOK

Goals

We hope that this book will increase the traction of the restorative justice movement and jump-start the introduction of restorative justice into social work. Equally important, we want this book to aid efforts to promote dialogue, peacemaking, and reconciliation that support wellbeing, justice, and conflict transformation.

The book's structure is meant to provide knowledge and skills and promote interdisciplinary collaboration. The initial chapters afford social workers and restorative justice practitioners a glimpse into the history, theory, and practice settings of each other's work, while presenting an introduction for individuals who seek to learn more about the current literature of social work or restorative justice. Because skills cannot be built from a text alone, we sought to supply readers with a picture of restorative justice and social work skills with the hope that practitioners of one discipline might participate in skills-based trainings offered by the other.

The following chapters further support interdisciplinary collaboration as each is coauthored by a social worker and a restorative justice theorist, researcher, or practitioner. In some cases, we suggested teams, and in others, individuals found each other or worked with longtime collaborators. We asked each team to provide a literature review of social work and restorative justice initiatives centered on the chapter topic. The literature review is followed by a case study that involved one of the authors. Although, for the purposes of publication, the content of the case studies have not been changed the names of the participants have. The purpose of the case studies is to provide social workers with descriptions of restorative processes and examples of some of the various contexts in which restorative justice skills and principles can be implemented. Next, we asked the teams to provide a critical analysis of the fit between social work and restorative justice and to explore ways in which the fit might be strengthened.

Chapter Review

The first four chapters of this book, including this one, are designed to introduce the reader to social work and restorative justice as theories as well as areas of practice and research. These chapters are foundational, providing readers with an overview of restorative justice and social work.

In Chapter 2, "Justice, Restoration, and Social Work," Nancy Kropf traces the history of the social work profession. In particular, she explores the diverse beginnings of social work including the so-called friendly visitors, with their more individual perspectives, and the community-focused practice of the settlement houses. In moving to the present, she examines trends and social work practices as related to each of the areas found in Part 2 of this book, and beginning with chapter 5 "Settings." Her review reveals social work as an evolving field whose recent approaches are based on a belief that individuals and communities have the capacity to grow, develop, and change, and to do so by building on existing strengths.

As author of Chapter 3, "An Introduction to Restorative Justice," Pamela Leonard admits that it is not easy to write a literature review of an idea that does not yet have a fully agreed-upon definition, not to mention a field that is burgeoning in such important areas as applications, methods of evaluation, and ethics. Leonard sifts through these challenges and explores restorative justice from three important perspectives in her chapter. First she seeks to address what restorative justice means, how it came to being, and its present applications. Next she moves to its foundation, which are values and principles. Finally, she views the processes that make an encounter restorative. She does not shy away from debates in the field, and she recognizes that restorative justice is in need of a greater evidence base. Her cautions, however, are tempered by her enthusiasm for the potential of restorative justice.

In Chapter 4, "Restorative Justice Practice," Andrea Wood and I seek to give readers a picture of the restorative practices discussed in future chapters. Specifically we want to offer individuals who have not participated in a restorative encounter the opportunity to envision one from preparation through follow-up. Echoing some of Pamela Leonard's thoughts, not all restorative justice practitioners would choose to focus on the four practices that we do in this chapter (Victim–Offender Dialogue, Circles, Family Group Conferencing, and Truth and Reconciliation Commissions); however, we selected practices that we believe social workers and human service providers might choose to make use of in their work. Additionally, it is important to note that several models exist of each of the practices described, for example, the model of Victim–Offender Dialogue found in this chapter is different than a similar one found in the chapter on severe crime. Our goal is not to advocate for a particular model, but to encourage readers to explore the variations that may exist between practice institutes, countries, and localities.

Part 2, "Settings," is the body of this book, and the case studies are its heart. Each chapter is centered on a case study and coauthored by a restorative justice practitioner and a social worker. Schools provide the setting in Chapter 5 for Michele Hamilton and Lesa Hope's "Social Work and Restorative Justice: Implications for School System Practice." The authors quickly point out a major contradiction in the North American public school system. Ideally, schools are places where children acquire intellectual and social skills that support their capacity to develop into productive individuals and citizens. However, when behavioral problems occur, too often students are addressed from a deficit-based approach, and opportunities for them to learn from mistakes are lost. This contradiction, they add, has forced some school social workers into needing to support students who have experienced detrimental effects associated with social discipline. Restorative process then provides an alternative strategy for resolving conflict and remediating difficult situations. In the literature review, the authors explore the use of restorative processes in extreme punishment scenarios such as as expulsion, but the case study focuses on a restorative process called because of an ordinary and routine issue—miscommunication between a school staff member and student. However, the case study does more than just explore a resolution to a disagreement; it also examines issues of power and provides an opportunity for a school social worker to assist a student with legitimate and large needs. The case study clearly shows that a power struggle between those individuals who are part of a restorative justice intervention needs to be handled sensitively and effectively.

As authors Barb Toews and Kay Harris note in Chapter 6, "Restorative Justice in Prisons," social work's presence in prisons has decreased significantly over recent decades. This decline, they argue, is shortsighted. The authors point out that the effects of incarceration and reentry into the greater community affect social work's role with individuals, families, and communities, and that social workers need to take an active role in stemming mass incarceration through prevention strategies and policy change. Both Toews and Harris have made significant contributions to the study of restorative justice. Therefore, not surprisingly, their examination of restorative justice includes the critical tenets of accountability, repair, and dialogue. Toews and Harris have examined and participated in a number of restorative justice initiatives within the prison setting, including the development of restorative dorms, a practice that is gaining support. For their case study, they choose to focus on a unique event: incarcerated men watching a live theatrical performance of a series of vignettes dramatizing victims' experiences with crime and its aftermath. The case study demonstrates the transformative nature of art, shows the necessity for preparation and debriefing, and provides a model for bringing together unlikely partners, such as a prison advocacy organization, victim services, and the state Department of Corrections, around the issues of accountability, repair, and dialogue.

As we will see, a number of chapters discuss how the community factors into both problems and resolutions, as well as the stress and opportunities experienced by individuals and families. In this regard, communities can be victims, offenders, or the providers of a restorative resolution. In Chapter 7, "Using Conflict to Build Community: Community Conferencing," the community was the victim, offender, and provider of a restorative resolution, as it was the subject of a restorative process. The chapter, written by Lauren Abrahamson and me, describes how, by working together, restorative processes and social work's community practice can transform a neighborhood.

Child welfare is one of the oldest and most difficult aspects of social work. Having to remove a child from a home can be a heart-wrenching and disruptive process for the child, family, and community. In Chapter 8, David Crampton and Patricia Rideout show how a process called Team Decision-Making set the tone for an out-of-home placement, in which a cooperative relationship was built between the birth and foster families to support the child. In "Restorative Justice and Child Welfare: Engaging Families and Communities in the Care and Protection of Children," the authors view restorative justice as a practice that does not stand alone, but rather complements child welfare. They describe how, with Team Decision–Making, restorative justice provides a set of values, principles, practices, and skills that enhance child welfare strategies designed to support the care and protection of children who are at risk for abuse and neglect.

Feminist practice also has meaning both to social work and restorative justice. In Chapter 9, "Feminist Perspective on Family Rights: Social Work and Restorative Practices for Stopping Abuse of Women," Joan Pennell and Mary Koss expand the discourse on feminist practice in each of the arenas. The authors examine how restorative processes and social work can combine to fashion a feminist solution for addressing domestic violence. In an interesting twist, the authors analyze the term *family rights* and argue that this concept must encompass respect for diverse family cultures and uphold universal human rights such as safety. In their case study, the authors show how restorative processes can render moot what they call the paradox of family rights—which is based on diversity and universality—by providing a space in which all are respected and rights are safeguarded. While the authors see clearly the potential of restorative process in cases of domestic violence, they do not shy away from the multiple cautions that are associated with restorative practices in cases of family violence.

Nancy Good and David Gustafson take us to Canada to explore healing following severe violent crime in Chapter 10, "Coming Together After Violence: Social Work and Restorative Practices." These authors provide a case study of a Victim–Offender Mediation Program (VOMP), a form of Victim–Offender Dialogue. They show how the Canadian process of VOMP, which is supported at the national level, stretches beyond existing restorative justice models in the United States. Further, in the VOMP program, extensive therapeutic support is provided to participants. Including this model gives social workers and restorative justice practitioners the opportunity to view what the authors call "deep trauma healing," while learning lessons from Canada's First Nations elders.

Healing in the aftermath of war and within an emerging democracy form the backdrop to Nancy Williams's and Thomas Crick's Chapter 11, "Social Work and Restorative Justice in an International Context: The Case of Liberia." Their chapter examines both the restorative processes used to support the country as it moves forward, and the role of social work within that context. The Liberian case is particularly interesting as it involves state support for ingenious and community-based approaches to resolve disputes, and the authors pull significant insights from this partnership. They include an interview with a Liberian social worker to highlight the issues facing the country as it seeks to recover from poverty, conflict, trauma, and the issues related to rape and sexual violence. The Liberian case shows an opportunity for restorative justice and social work to develop as both individual and related practices.

In the final setting chapter, Chapter 12, "Restorative Justice and Aging: Promise for Integrated Practice," Alex Crampton and Nancy Kropf explore a new area for restorative justice. The authors note that, while restorative justice has only been applied in limited situations with older adults, gerontology is an area where restorative justice holds a great deal of promise. With advanced age, older adults may need to rely on others for support and assistance. Restorative justice practices seem to have potential within family situations of care and settings that have responsibility to provide care (e.g., home health aide care, assisted living residences). Rather than describing a restorative response, the authors' case study explores the limitations of current strategies while suggesting opportunities for implementing restorative justice.

We recognize that the case studies presented in this book have positive endings. While we want readers to walk away from the examples excited about the possibilities, we know that a collection of selected case studies does not comprise an evidence-based body of work. Throughout the book a number of authors point to the need for empirical studies regarding interaction between social work and restorative justice. In Chapter 13,"Concluding Thoughts and Next Steps," we examine the intersection between restorative justice and social work and begin to describe an accompanying research and practice agenda.

Collectively, the chapters offer insight into collaboration between restorative justice and social work in various contexts and client populations. The types of situations represented in the case studies are extremely broad and illuminate vast differences in the level of integration and applications among the settings. Some of the chapters reveal a defined literature and well-established practices that have begun to be evaluated in terms of effectiveness and efficacy. The book contains examples of multilevel interventions where restorative justice is used to prevent conflict, as well as remediate situations where harm has already occurred. In these cases, an evidence base has determined best practices and validates additional, carefully planned efforts to integrate restorative justice into social work interventions. In other chapters, however, restorative justice clearly is just beginning to be utilized, let alone partnered with social work.

Each of the case studies portrays methods of incorporating restorative justice practices to work through conflict, harm, or wrongdoing, ranging from small conflicts of everyday life (e.g., a "falling-out" between a student and a teacher) to examples of severe violence, including rape and homicide.

We hope that the variation in contexts, settings, type of conflicts, and experiences of participants in each of the practice areas will encourage readers to envision additional areas where collaboration between social work and restorative justice will lead to improved skills among practitioners and increased well-being among the people and institutions they serve.

NOTES

i Defense-Initiated Victim Outreach is a relatively new practice that seeks to address the needs of victims and their families throughout the legal process by providing a bridge of communication between victims and the defense, especially in capital cases. Defense attorneys who represent the accused in criminal cases increasingly are recognizing the potential of the adversarial process to further traumatize victims/survivors. In an attempt to ameliorate this trauma and to address the harms to and needs of victims/survivors, defense attorneys seek the assistance of trained Victim Outreach Specialists, who provide an opportunity for victims to have access to the defense team, which historically has not been available.

REFERENCES

Beck, E., & Britto, S. (2006). Using feminist methods and restorative justice to interview capital offenders' family members. *AFFILIA, 21*, 59–70.

Beck, E., Britto, S., & Andrews, A. (2007). *In the shadow of death: Restorative justice and death row families*. New York: Oxford University Press.

Beck, E., East, C., & Toews, B. (2008). Restorative Justice and Its Application in the Social Environment. Council of Social Work Education Annual Program Meeting. Philadelphia, PA.

Gumz, E., & Grant, C. (2009). Restorative justice: A systematic review of the social work literature. *Families in Society, 90*, 119–126.

Herman, J. (1992). *Trauma and recovery: The aftermath of violence—From domestic abuse to political terror*. New York: Basic Books.

Leonard, P. (2006, December). All but death can be adjusted. *The Champion, 40*.

Sullivan, D., & Tifft, L. (2005). *Restorative justice: Healing the foundations of our everyday lives* (2nd ed.). Monsey, NY: Willow Tree Press.

van Wormer, K. (2004). *Confronting oppression, restoring justice: From policy analysis to social action*. Alexandria, VA: Council of Social Work Education.

van Wormer, K. (2006). A case for restorative justice: A critical adjunct to the social work curriculum. *Journal of Teaching Social Work, 26*, 57–69.

van Wormer, K. (2008). Restorative Justice. In T. Mizrahi and L. Davis (Eds.), *Encyclopedia of Social Work* (20th ed., pp. 531–533). New York: Oxford University Press.

Zehr, H. (2005). *Changing lenses: A new focus for crime and justice* (3rd ed.). Scottdale, PA: Herald Press.

Zehr, H. (2009). Restorative Justice: What is That? Presentation at the International Institute for Restorative Practices. Bethlehem, PA.

Chapter Two

Justice, Restoration, and Social Work

NANCY P. KROPF

Both restorative justice and social work seek to promote positive change for individuals and society. This chapter specifically focuses on the profession of social work. Although social work is a relatively young profession compared to others (e.g., medicine, education), it has a rich history of working to improve the lives of individuals and to create a more equitable and just society. This focus is a primary reason why people from diverse backgrounds, belief systems, and life experiences choose social work as a career.

This chapter has three primary sections. The first section is an historical summary of some of the major events that have shaped the profession. While numerous social work reformers and pioneers have been part of our history, the major contributions of the Charitable Organization Societies (COS) and the Settlement House Movement will be examined in detail. From these beginnings, the progression of ethics and values as the foundation of social work practice is traced, along with the proliferation of various social work contexts and roles. The second section briefly reviews some of the major concepts key to social work today. Although not an exhaustive list, the concepts of empowerment, social justice, and resilience provide a foundation for understanding many of the current approaches in social work. The final section looks to the future of social work and some of the issues that will shape the profession in coming years. The brief analysis provided in this chapter offers a better opportunity to appreciate how social work and restorative justice practices share some common ground, while maintaining unique practice positions.

THE BEGINNINGS AND EVOLUTION OF SOCIAL WORK

The beginnings of social work are rooted in the late 1800s, mainly as a response to the problems which stemmed from the Industrial Revolution. Against the backdrop of mass immigration and urbanization, numerous problems emerged such as poverty, disease, illiteracy, and mental health challenges (Garvin & Cox, 2001). In addition, migration to large urban centers created stratifications within society, from the wealthy industrialists to the unemployed or low-wage worker. These second-order changes increased the need for physical and social assistance for many Americans. As McNutt (2008) states, "Social work is a profession that began its life as a call to help the poor, the destitute, and the disenfranchised of a rapidly changing social order" (p. 138).

Initial Social Movements

The formalization of social work as a profession evolved from two major social movements, both of which were prominent during the late 1800s and early 1900s. These were the Charity Organization Society and the Settlement House Movement (Haynes & White, 1999; Schneider & Lester, 2001). The Charity Organization Society (COS) stressed the concepts of morality and personal responsibility, while the Settlement House Movement was founded upon social responsibility and focused more heavily upon the individual as part of a unique neighborhood and community context. The different philosophical perspectives of these two move- ments led to different emphases on intervention approaches and desired outcomes. Even today, the profession maintains divisions in practice approaches that are founded upon fundamental differences in the attributes of problems in human functioning.

In the mid-1800s, a model of providing aid to "the disadvantaged" was cen- tered on volunteers who served as a moral compass. These "friendly visitors" were typically women of wealth who volunteered to help those in need, and were the foundation of the Charity Organization Societies. The premise of the COS was that the purposeful mixing of the social classes would provide those in lower strata the opportunity to learn and gain spiritual guidance, and therefore establish a "more functional" social order.

Over the course of working with very complex dynamics and situations, friendly visiting became more systematic and informed. "Scientific charity" had the goal of moving beyond the good intentions of the friendly visitors to incorpo- rating a more systematic and rational method to deal with the individual's prob- lems in functioning (Trattner, 1999). In addition, an understanding grew that volunteering was not enough, and that there needed to be a more educated and systematic way of dealing with the problems in functioning and deficiencies within the environment.

From this more methodological perspective, a new orientation to "the helping profession" emerged. Mary Richmond, one of the pioneers in the profession, advanced the practice of social work through her groundbreaking work, *Social Diagnosis* (1917). Her early work evolved into the social casework tradition of social work, which focused on problems in functioning at the individual level.

The overall goal of COS was to create a more caring and compassionate soci- ety. Justice and restoration outcomes would be a result of the shared goal of ser- vice, which both the rich and poor would espouse. The more rational approach to philanthropy yielded a hope that poverty would be eradicated (Haynes & White, 1999). These social dynamics would link people of all social classes in a community where service and compassion would prevail. Sadly, this outcome was not actualized to any significant degree, and continues to be an important goal within our profession today.

Similar to the COS, the Settlement House Movement had goals of eradicating urban poverty and associated social ills. However, the approach of the Settlement House Movement was markedly different from the one which evolved through the COS, and subsequently, social casework. Settlement house pioneers, including Jane Addams and Lillian Wald, did not have the same beliefs as the COS about the source of problems in human functioning. These reformers believed that the problems experienced by immigrants and the poor stemmed from a poor fit between these individuals and families, and the social environment (Haynes & White, 1999).

The intervention approaches of the Settlement House Movement were to enhance individual or family and environmental congruence. This approach was a comprehensive and holistic one. The settlement houses were places where the families lived and learned skills to help them integrate into the community and labor force. Classes included language acquisition, literature, arts and crafts, and other social, educational, and cultural programs.

Settlement houses were also home to neighborhood health clinics and other service provision activities, such as child care centers. Settlement houses had a neighborhood focus and were an integral and embedded institution within the lives of the neighborhood and community. However, they also sought to eliminate the causes of poverty, which they identified as stemming from the conditions of individuals and the surrounding neighborhood. In this way, the workers engaged in what has been coined the three "R's" strategy: residence, research, and reform. Specifically, the settlement house workers provided direct service through the residence programs and identified the social conditions which led to the problems they were seeking to address. Once a social condition was identified as problematic, the settlement house workers researched the causes and consequences of the problem, and then developed an advocacy strategy designed to reform laws.

Unlike the friendly visitors, who had marked distinctions between themselves and the people that they served, these workers lived in the neighborhood, which decreased the sense of separation and hierarchy between the staffers and the people they served. In fact, this principle was the foundation of the movement as stated in this quote about Jane Addams and her ideology about the relationship of members within the settlement house community: "The give-and-take interactions among Hull-House residents and neighbors revealed the reciprocity at the heart of a community of equals as Addams understood the settlement house to be" (Klosterman & Stratton, 2006 p. 160).

As a result of these differences, the profession of social work continues to define restoration differently within our intervention and professional value system.

Depending on the philosophical principles upon which each of the various prac-tice foundations were established, there is a varied approach to helping individu-als, families, and communities restore and enhance functioning. Both of these major social movements contributed to our current conceptualization of person-in-environment as an underlying framework for social work practice.

Policy Practice

A central part of the dialogue about the orientation and focus of social work was the concern about the "cause–function" debate of the profession. At the founda-tion of this division was the issue of whether social workers should help their cli-ents accept or adapt to their conditions, or whether efforts should be focused on changing the social conditions that created the problems experienced by clients (Wyers, 1991). Direct practice methods were construed as promoting the status quo within society and therefore, keeping unjust social conditions unchanged.

In the 1980s, the term *policy practice* started to emerge within social work (Jansson, 1984; Pierce, 1984; Schorr, 1985). During this era, neoconservative fiscal policies were eliminating social welfare programs and dismantling govern-mental protections for those in need. The pervasive philosophy was one of indi-vidual success or failure; the government was not responsible for creating safe and humane alternatives for individuals. This mentality led some in the social work community to be more actively involved in the public policy agenda and to move away from the more individual-level responses of direct practice. As Iatridis (1983) stated, "Uncoordinated individual interventions are fruitless and represent false promises unless accompanied by concerted efforts to restructure the institutions that perpetuate the injustice and inequality that foster the personal and commu-nity problems of the profession's clients" (p. 106). Within policy practice, the goal of the social worker is to be an agent of change in transforming public policy to be equitable and just for all members of society.

Over the ensuing decades, policy practice has emerged to support social work goals of system change. Various methods have been identified with policy practice, including legislative advocacy, litigation, social action, and policy analysis (Figueira-McDonough, 1993; Schneider & Lester, 2001; Wyers, 1991). In fact, some social workers have taken the invitation seriously to shape social policy and have successfully run for elected office. At this point, the National Association of Social Workers (NASW) reports that 7 members of Congress and 71 state elected officials have social work degrees (National Association of Social Workers, 2008a).

Ethics and Values

Social work is founded upon a set of values that influence and guide direct practice with clients. The mission of the social work profession is rooted in a set of core values that have been embraced by social workers throughout the profession's history, and form the foundation of social work's unique purpose and perspective. These values are:

1. service
2. social justice
3. dignity and worth of the person
4. importance of human relationships
5. integrity
6. competence.

This constellation of core values reflects what is unique to the social work profession (National Association of Social Workers, 2008b).

Although values have a central place in social work, ethics guide social workers in transforming professional values into practice activities (Dolgoff, Loewenberg, & Harrington, 2005). While related terms, "the distinction between ethics and values is that values relate to what is good and desirable, whereas ethics pertain to what is right and correct" (Greene, Cohen, Galambos, & Kropf, 2008, pp. 100–101). Although this statement may seem to imply that ethics are absolutes, different periods in the history of our profession have defined ethical issues in various terms. Frederic Reamer (2006), an expert on ethics and social work, has identified four distinct periods in the progression of ethics within the profession. The first, termed the *morality period,* was at the beginning stage of the social work profession. During this period, the dominant attitude toward clients was paternalistic and the emphasis was more on the morality of the client (versus the actions of the practitioner). This orientation is clearly evident in the COS movement, where the objective was the reform of individual clients. The social reforms movements, evidenced by the settlement house and related movements, also were founded on a morality perspective. The shift, however, was the belief that society had a moral imperative to be more responsive to individuals and families through the amelioration of poverty and structural problems within society.

With social conditions that stemmed from World War I and the Great Depression, a shift occurred that focused more on social reform efforts. These changes heralded the second phase, the *values period,* which existed until the 1970s. During this time, greater emphasis was placed on the primary values of the profession and codifying the major values that are central to social work practice (Pumphrey, 1959; Teicher, 1967). In 1960, for example, NASW constructed its initial Code of Ethics. In addition, there was more emphasis on the intersection of the practitioners' and clients' personal values and belief systems during this time period. Partially, this was an artifact of the growth of the profession, which had expanded across the spectrum of practice with individuals, families, groups, communities, organizations, and society as a whole.

Ethical theory and decision-making was the third period and was focused upon ethics as both theory and application. The events that occurred during the 1960s and 1970s (e.g., the Civil Rights movement, the Vietnam War, Watergate) contributed to the national and professional consciousness about the importance of ethics and values. Theories and models of decision-making were integrated into social work practice, research, and education. During this period, ethics became a more integrated component of the profession, with an emphasis on theoretical understanding that should be incorporated into professional practice across client situations and contexts.

Reamer (2008 terms the current period as *ethical standards and risk management*. At this point, liability, malpractice, and professional accountability are all paramount within our practice. One reason is the dramatic change in the provision of healthcare services, especially managed care practice (Strom-Gottfried, 1998). With the recent passage of the healthcare legislation, there is hope that situation might change in a positive directions. It is clear that professional ethics have evolved over time, and reflect the predominant social and practice issues that social workers face during particular time periods.

SOCIAL WORK IN THE PRESENT DAY

As the previous section describes, social work is a profession that started from divergent social movements. Even today, the term "social work" stands for numerous forms of intervention (e.g., work with individuals, groups, organizations, communities, or at the legislative level) and contexts (e.g., child welfare, aging, labor, health, etc). In spite of the continued line of questioning, there are unifying aspects of the social work practice. One is *empowerment*, which is a "central concept in the practice of social work within the United States" (Woodcock, 2008, p. 579). A second primary concept is *social justice*, which is "the core value . . . based on the ethical principal [sic] that social workers challenge injustice at the individual, group, and institutional levels" (Gumz & Grant, 2009, p. 119). An additional principle is *resilience*, which is defined as the "unpredicted or markedly successful adaptations to negative life events, trauma, stress and other forms of risk" (Fraser, Richman, & Galansky, 1999, p. 136). While different forms and methods of social work emphasize these principles differently, the focus on working with clients to preserve and enhance functioning is a common outcome across interventions and methodologies. At the core of social work is a belief that individuals have the capacity to grow, develop, and change. Each of these concepts are relevant to social work practice across the spectrum of client populations and intervention methodologies.

Empowerment

Throughout the profession, social work has a long history of working toward client empowerment. In the mid-twentieth century, social movements such as civil rights, feminism, gay rights, and awareness of the disability community fueled the efforts to work to empower clients who were consumers of social welfare services (Simon, 1994). As a practice construct, empowerment "is a process through which individuals become strong enough to participate in, share in the control of, and influence their own lives . . . [as such] it cannot be viewed as an end state or a plateau at which they arrive. Rather, it is the engagement of individuals in actions that challenge or change the personal, interpersonal, or political aspect of their life situations" (Cox, 1994, pp. 36–37). As this definition implies, empowerment practice involves working across multiple systems levels and providing social work clients with knowledge and skills to make positive change within their own lives.

Today, the concept of empowerment is particularly emphasized in practice approaches with those populations that demonstrate limited degrees of efficacy. For example, empowerment-oriented programs have been successfully delivered to parents that are experiencing challenges in caregiving because of limited resources, or functional limitations of their child (Graves & Shelton, 2007; Palmer-House, 2008; Xu, 2007; Zeman & Buila, 2007). Elements of these programs provide education and skill training to develop greater levels of effectiveness in their care provision roles. In addition to desired family-related outcomes, the impact of these interventions provides additional resources within the community. An example is the custodial grandparent empowerment program that helps grandparents become more effective in childrearing, and serve as peer mentors for other grandparents within their communities (Cox, 2002).

In particular, what are the hallmarks or characteristics of an empowerment model of practice? In her book on empowerment practice, Cox (1994) outlines several aspects of practice that are part of this approach. These are redefining the relationship between practitioner and client to maximize collaboration and mutual responsibility; assisting the client to feel a personal sense of power as part of the helping process; raising consciousness about structural issues that impact problems in functioning such as class and power; and accepting (versus challenging) the client's definition of his/her problem. Within empowerment practice, the goal is to help clients make positive changes, but also to feel a sense of agency and self-efficacy in creating the change process.

Social Justice

As a professional value, social justice has been embedded in practice approaches and work with clients since the beginnings of our profession. In the *Encyclopedia of Social Work* entry on social justice, Flynn and Jacobson (2008) state, "Social justice is one of the core values guiding social work, a hallmark of its uniqueness among the helping professions" (p. 44). Beyond a professional value, social justice is an appropriate goal for an equitable and fair society overall.

While client empowerment tends to be a value that focuses on work directly with clients, social justice seeks to realign social institutes, laws and regulations, and resource allocations in efforts to decrease inequities that exist. In particular, social justice goals seek to advance the outcomes for groups that are marginalized or experience barriers to full societal participation. Social justice interventions can take numerous forms such as policy practice, social advocacy, feminist models which place an emphasis on both individual and social change goals (White, 2006), and reconfiguration of organizations to stay more related to real-life issues faced by consumers and clients (Mulroy, 2004).

Multicultural and culturally competent practice are also part of social justice. The earliest social work practices tended to reflect the sociocultural values of those times and thus focused on assisting clients in assimilating to the dominant American culture. The belief was that immigrants should modify their cultural perspective and become part of the "melting pot" of society (Martinez-Brawley & Brawley, 1999). In addition, the major outreach at this point was to white, European populations, excluding groups that represented other races/ethnicities (e.g., African-Americans, Central American persons), and groups that shared common cultural characteristics (e.g., religious affiliation, sexual orientation).

Today, multiculturalism is a central theme in social work practice. The beginning part of this process is to make practitioners aware of their own cultural heritage, and how this worldview impacts their narrative and belief systems about others (Lum, Zuñiga, & Gutiérrez, 2004). A multicultural approach enhances the practitioner's ability to look beyond the problems facing an individual to transforming social policies to eradicate forms of social oppressions and socioeconomic injustice (Van Soest & Garcia, 2003). In this way, it enhances the effectiveness of social work interventions across all levels of systems, from work with individuals to changes in social policies.

Within social work, there is a growing interest in ways that social justice issues are part of global and international social work initiatives. Moving beyond the borders of the U.S., our profession has become involved in human rights issues in many countries. In addition, many international efforts focus on trauma work, such as the international chapter in this book that describes the degree to which women and girls have been victimized by sexual violence in a war-ravaged country.

Resilience

As a theoretical concept, resilience was initially associated with the reduction of risk situations. Risk situations are those where a potential to experience negative outcomes exists, such as experiencing abuse, conflict, natural or human-made disasters and other types of physical, social, and emotional trauma. Unfortunately, these situations typically do not exist independently, so risk situations have a synergic impact. In an article on resilience and American Indian youth, Gilgun (2002) defines this additive effect as *cumulative risk*. Resilience-enhancing practice models are in their infancy, but predictions are that these efforts will continue to proliferate and additional models of practice will be constructed and evaluated (Greene, 2007; Leitch, Vanslyke, & Allen, 2009).

Definitions of resilience promote this concept as being more complex than the absence of pathology in response to stress life situations. For example, Greene (2008) outlines a number of factors that have been included in multiple definitions of resilience. These include the variation in individual responses to risk situations; the identification of coping strategies to address adversity and stress; the ability to maintain a stable sense of self and personal narrative following a traumatic event; and the philosophy that resilience is a normal and healthy process under the experience of difficulty. As these definitions suggestion, the concept of resilience involves a client's ability to handle stress and adversity, and involves coping and integrating elements from the experience to form a new level of identity and functioning.

Resilience is not simply a quality associated with individuals. Client systems of multiple levels, including families, neighborhoods, organizations, and communities, also show evidence of resiliency and adaptation. An example is the community resilience model that was developed to work with refugees (Doron, 2005). In this model, social work intervention is multifaceted and focuses on both the individuals who have been displaced, as well as the receiving community. Resilient communities have several characteristics, which include understanding and employing the talents and skills of all community members; enacting social policies and structures that take into account the unique life experiences of various community members; setting priorities on interpersonal relationships within the community; and understanding the various sociocultural narratives that exist within the community and shape community members' behaviors and values (Greene, Cohen, Gonzalez, Lee, & Evans, 2007).

As members of a dynamic profession, social workers fill numerous roles and work with diverse client populations. While there are common shared concepts that permeate all types of practice, social work continues to change and respond to social issues. Looking toward the future, there is a current emphasis on working to reinvest in our profession and provide a foundation for social work to flourish in coming years (National Association of Social Workers, 2009). Clearly, the future will bring the profession many challenges and decision-making points.

THE FUTURE OF THE PROFESSION: SOCIAL WORK AT THE CROSSROADS

There is a legend about the great blues musician Robert Johnson, in which a crossroads figures prominently.

Robert Johnson (1911–1938) was a gifted singer, guitarist and songwriter whose life story is wrapped in mystery and legend. Only two photographs are known to exist of him and he recorded only 29 songs before his death in 1938 at the age of 27. Many of his contemporaries believed that he met the Devil at a lonely crossroads in Clarksdale Mississippi at midnight and made a deal to sell his soul in return for becoming the greatest blues musician of all time. (http://www.robertjohnsonbluesfoundation.org/Bio.html)

Like Robert Johnson, social work is also at a crossroads. As professional social workers, we have evolved and hold a more central (and some would argue comfortable) place in providing health and human services. For example, we are currently one of the main providers of health and mental health services in the United States (National Association of Social Workers, 2009). The Bureau of Labor Statistics (2008–09) reports that employment of social workers is expected to increase by 22% during the 2006–16 decade, which is much faster than the average for all occupations. Since the pioneering work of Mary Richmond, Jane Addams, and other founders of our profession, social work has become a broad and diverse profession.

Yet, some within our profession have wondered whether we are making the same choice as Robert Johnson did back in the Delta. That is, is social work foregoing its professional roots in social change and justice for greater professional status and prestige? Harry Specht and Mark Courtney (1995) argue this point in a controversial book titled *Unfaithful Angels: How Social Work Has Abandoned Its Mission*, which decries the changes that are taking place in the focus and emphasis of social work. Specht describes the changes in the profession over time in the introduction to the book:

When I came to know social workers a half a century ago, they had a mission that was to me, appealing and significant: to help poor people, improve community life, and to solve difficult social problems. But times have changed . . . It is our intention within this book to stir debate about social work's purpose in American life . . . and to persuade Americans to chart a new course for social work. (pp. ix–x)

As this quote highlights, this book argues strongly that social work needs to reclaim and rebuild its professional mission.

Due to the breadth of our profession, it is difficult to chart a single course for social work that covers the various roles held by social workers. In an article on the future of social work practice, Ginsberg (2005) states that, "it is one of the unfortunate truths about social work that we do not always have accurate or comprehensive ideas about where we are going" (p. 7). Yet some of the sociodemographic trends indicate that our profession must consciously and prudently consider how to position itself within this changing context. With our shifting society and social conditions, social work must analyze these emerging trends and continue to consider how the core values of the profession can shape the agenda for the future.

This book is an exciting opportunity to look at some of the issues within our society and consider how to make decisions about going forward within our profession. In the various chapters of this book, leading authors in restorative justice and social work discuss practice in a variety of contexts. From a social work perspective, what are some of the trends that will impact social work practice in future years in these areas? To conclude this chapter, some of the major issues that we will face in coming years are summarized in the areas that will be described in greater detail in the rest of this book.

Schools

Schools are a primary social institution providing both education and socialization to children and teens. Yet several issues are currently facing school systems that compromise their ability to effectively carry out these missions. Most school social workers practice within public school systems, which increasingly have to deal with decentralized authority and diminishing resources, increasing disparities in student performance due to inequities such as technological resources and teacher quality, and a de-emphasis on learning for learning's sake and more emphasis on particular outcome indicators such as standardized tests (Franklin, 2005).

Along with the learning process, socialization also happens in schools. Challenges exist in dealing with the interpersonal situations associated with developmental changes. One example is a tragedy that happened in a school district in Atlanta. In the spring of 2009, Jaheem Herrerra, a fifth-grader in DeKalb County, hung himself in the bedroom of his family's apartment. His family stated that this 11-year-boy took his own life because he was relentlessly bullied at his school and called "gay" (Rankin and Torres, 2009). Bullying and school violence are two growing problems in schools that are increasingly more diverse in population.

Criminal Justice

Criminal justice settings are not places where many social workers practice. A gauge of interest in this setting is the number of students who are placed in internship sites in criminal justice settings, which represents less than 3% of internships nationally at both the undergraduate and graduate levels (Lennon, 2005). Of note, however, is the entry about criminal justice in the *Encyclopedia of Social Work*, which discusses the importance of social work in the growing trend toward restorative justice in this field (Alexander, 2008). This trend seems to signify the importance of transforming the penal system to one that has a greater connection to professional social work values.

What are some of the trends in criminal justice currently? There are several areas where social work can have a significant role in reversing the troubling trends in criminal justice (Sarri & Shook, 2005). These include reducing incarceration rates by providing community-based alternative options for diversion; working to reverse the troubling trend of trying juveniles as adults; working with families of incarcerated parents to reduce trauma and promote family unification; creating more humane environments within jails and prisons; working to decrease the overrepresentation of persons of color within the prison populations through unfair policies and practice; having responsive gender programs for women and girls; and providing mental health services as part of the justice system. Although this area of practice does not attract many social work practitioners currently, there are numerous opportunities to be part of the change process in the future.

Child Welfare

Social work has a rich history in work with children and their families. Although the main focus is on reducing the risk and incidence of abuse and neglect, social work practitioners who practice in this area may work in a variety of settings. Unfortunately, a disconcerting myth about social work practice is that we are a profession of "baby snatchers" who take children away from their families. In fact, the goals of child welfare are to help families function more effectively so they can stay together, and to reunify children with parents in situations if at all possible. Although this field is termed *child* welfare, much of the work performed by practitioners in this field involves working with parents and other caretakers, and community agencies to identify cases of suspected maltreatment.

Over time, several trends have emerged that have affected current child welfare practice. One is the changing structure of the contemporary family. As families become more diverse (e.g, grandparents who are primary caregivers for grandchildren, same-sex parents, interfaith families), there is a potential for practitioners to become involved in new areas of practice. For example, families where grandparents are raising grandchildren may create questions of who retains legal authority of the children, or disputes between dysfunctional or incapacitated biological parents and grandparents. Involvement in these various family situations indicate that practitioners within child welfare will be involved in working to enhance family functioning, and decreasing conflicts that occur as a result.

Violence

Although violence toward women has existed throughout the years, social work only became involved in this area of practice in the late 1960s. Currently, various approaches are used to help women and families who are experiencing violence. These include temporary safe shelters, relocation assistance, case management, help with employment, as well as referral to appropriate medical and mental health services. In addition, social work has become involved in global initiatives to reduce violence and torture of women internationally. In a discussion on global perspectives, Morgaine (2007) describes the emergence of a transnational agenda of combating violence against women and the importance of framing this type of violence as a human rights issue.

There has been a call for additional restorative justice initiatives addressing violence against women. The tension between the criminal justice system and social work perspective within this practice context has been discussed widely. van Wormer (2009) discusses the solution-based and inclusive perspective of restorative justice as a way toward reconciliation in this process. Like other situations described in other chapters, domestic violence is an area where restorative justice has a great deal to lend to social work practice.

Aging

As baby boomers age, our population will include a greater number of older adults and more people who are living longer lives than previously. For example, our society is aging and we expect that one quarter of the population will be over the age of 65 by 2050, when the baby boomers reach late life (National Center for Health Statistics, 2009). With this projected increase, there have been numerous debates about the social and economic impact of age-related changes such as increasing healthcare costs, the impact on family life (especially care provision), and the preparedness of social workers to work with older clients. Additional ways to practice with the challenges of later life are sorely needed. Although some of the challenges of aging can be remediated (e.g. geriatric depression), other situations cannot be reversed and require interventions that transform attitudes about the older population in general (e.g., ageism).

Global and International Contexts

As a social work pioneer, Jane Addams was very involved in international issues, including peace movements and immigration support. Since the earliest days of our profession, international social work efforts have expanded dramatically. However, consensus about what constitutes *international* or *global* social work continues to evolve and has been defined differently during different eras (Healy & Thomas, 2007). Some international efforts focus on social conditions that are barriers to quality social conditions, such as inadequate health care or poverty. Other efforts work to decrease the trauma of a catastrophic event such as war, genocide, or a large-scale natural disaster. International efforts at improving global conditions are increasing as the interconnections between people and their environments are construed as professional imperatives.

In summary, the beginnings of social work were a result of the industrialization of society and the concomitant social and cultural changes that were taking place. As a consequence, the early social work pioneers focused on helping their clients to enact functional changes to decrease problems that they were experiencing. Over time, social work grew into a broad and comprehensive profession, and work with various types of client situations was established. Future trends in social work that fit with the various contexts that are covered in this book were also discussed.

As you review the various settings for social work and restorative justice, there are numerous references to the early roots of the profession. Across the chapters, there are both similarities and differences in the ways that social work practice has evolved and emerged in the different contexts and with varied populations.

The historical and summative content contained within this chapter provides an important backdrop and foundation for understanding the social work practice that is described throughout the chapters of this book.

REFERENCES

Alexander, R. (2008). Criminal justice: An overview. In T. Mizrahi & L. E. Davis, (Eds.), *Encyclopedia of Social Work* (20th ed., Vol. 1, pp. 470–476). New York: Oxford University Press.

Bureau of Labor Statistics. (2008–09). *Occupational outlook handbook.* Retrieved May 22, 2009, from http://www.bls.gov/oco/ocos060.htm#outlook

Cox, C. B. (2002). Empowering African American custodial grandparents. *Social Work, 47*(1), 45–54.

Cox, E. O. (1994). *Empowerment-oriented social work practice with the elderly.* Pacific Grove, CA: Brookes/Cole Publishing.

Dolgoff, R., Loewenberg, F.M., & Harrington, D. (2005). *Ethical decisions for social work practice* (7th ed.). Belmont, CA: Brooks/Cole–Thomson Learning.

Doron, E. (2005). Working with Lebanese refugees in a community resilience model. *Community Development Journal, 40,* 182–191.

Figueira-McDonough, J. (1993). Policy practice: The neglected side of social work intervention. *Social Work, 38,* 179–188.

Flynn, J. L., & Jacobson, M. (2008). Social justice. In T. Mizrahi & L. E. Davis, (Eds.), *Encyclopedia of Social Work* (20th ed., Vol. 4, pp. 44–52). New York: Oxford University Press.

Franklin, C. (2005). The future of school social work practice: Current trends and opportunities. *Advances in Social Work, 6,* 167–181.

Fraser, M. W., Richman, J. M., & Galinsky, M. J. (1999). Risk, protection, and resilience: Toward a conceptual framework for social work practice. *Social Work Research, 23,* 129–208.

Garvin, C., & Cox, F. (2001). A history of community organization since the Civil War with special reference to oppressed communities. In J. Rothman, J. Erlich, & J. Tropman (Eds.), *Strategies of community intervention* (pp. 65–100). Itasca, MN: Peacock.

Gilgun, J. F. (2002). Completing the circle: American Indian medicine wheel and the promotion of resilience in children and youth care. *Journal of Human Behavior in the Social Environment, 6,* 65–84.

Ginsberg, L. (2005). The future of social work as a profession. *Advances in Social Work, 6*(1), 7–16.

Graves, K. N., & Shelton, T. L. (2007). Family empowerment as a mediator between family-centered systems of care and changes in child functioning: Identifying an important mechanism of change. *Journal of Child and Family Studies, 16*(4), 556–566.

Greene, R. R. (Ed.). (2007). *Social work practice: A risk and resilience perspective.* Belmont, CA: Wadsworth.

Greene, R. R. (2008). Resilience. In T. Mizrahi & L. E. Davis, (Eds.), *Encyclopedia of Social Work* (20th ed., Vol. 3, pp. 526–530). New York: Oxford University Press.

Greene, R. R., Cohen, H. L., Galambos, C. M., & Kropf, N. P. (2008). *Foundations of social work practice in the field of aging*. Washington, DC: NASW Press.

Greene, R. R., Cohen, H. L., Gonzalez, J., Lee, Y. & Evans, M. (2007). Cultural narratives, older adults, and resilient communities. In R. R. Greene (Ed.), *Social work practice: A risk and resilience perspective* (pp. 219–237). Belmont, CA: Thomson Brooks/Cole.

Gumz, E. J., & Grant, C. L. (2009). Restorative justice: A systematic review of the social work literature. *Families in Society, 90*, 119–126.

Haynes, D. T., & White, B. W. (1999). Will the "real" social work please stand up? A call to stand for professional unity. *Social Work, 44*(4), 385–391.

Healy, L. M., & Thomas, R. L. (2007). International social work: A retrospective in the 50th year. *International Social Work, 50*, 581–596.

Iatridis, D. (1983). Neoconservatism reviewed. *Social Work, 28*, 101–107.

Jansson, B. (1984). *Theory and practice of social welfare policy: Analysis, process and current issues*. Belmont, CA: Wadsorth.

Klosterman, E. M., & Stratton, D. C. (2006). Speaking truth to power: Jane Addams value basis for peacemaking. *Affilia: Journal of Women & Social Work, 21*(2), 158–168.

Lasch-Quinn, E. (1993). *Black neighbors: Race and the limits of reform in the American settlement house movement, 1890–1945*. Durham, NC: UNC Press.

Leitch, M. L., Vanslyke, J., & Allen, M. (2009). Somatic experiencing treatment with social service workers following Hurricanes Katrina and Rita. *Social Work, 54*, 9–18.

Lennon, T. (2005). *Statistics on social work education in the United States*. Alexandria, VA: Council on Social Work Education.

Lum, D., Zuñiga, M., & Gutiérrez, L. (2004). Multicultural social work education: Themes and recommendations. In L. Gutiérrez, M. Zuñiga, & D. Lum (Eds.), *Education for multicultural social work practice: Critical viewpoints and future directions* (pp. 319–325). Alexandria, VA: Council on Social Work Education.

Martinez-Brawley, E., & Brawley, E. (1999). Diversity in a changing world: Cultural enrichment or social fragmentation. *Journal of Multicultural Social Work, 7*(1/2), 19–35.

National Center for Health Statistics. (2009). *Health, United States, 2008*. Retrieved MONTH March 22, 2010 http://www.cdc.gov/nchs/hus.htm

McNutt, J. (2008). Social work practice: History and evolution. In T. Mizrahi & L. E. Davis, (Eds.), *Encyclopedia of Social Work* (20th ed., Vol. 4, pp. 138–141). New York: Oxford University Press.

Morgaine, K. (2007). Domestic violence and human rights: Local challenges to a universal framework. *Journal of Sociology and Social Welfare, 34*(1), 109–129.

Mulroy, E. (2004). Theoretical perspectives on the social environment to guide management and community practice: An organization-in-environment approach. *Administration in Social Work, 28*(1), 77–96.

National Association of Social Workers. (2008a). *Social workers in elected office*. Retrieved May 21, 2009, from https://www.socialworkers.org/pace/state_swers.asp

National Association of Social Workers. (2008b). *Code of Ethics*. Retrieved May 21, 2009, from http://www.socialworkers.org/pubs/code/code.asp

National Association of Social Workers. (2009). *Social work reinvestment: A national agenda for the profession of social work*. Retrieved May 22, 2009, from http://www.socialworkers.org/advocacy/resources/TransitionBook.pdf

Palmer-House, K. E. (2008). The perceived impact of strengths-based family worker training: Workers' learning that helped empower families. *Families in Society, 89*(3), 429–438.

Pierce, D. (1984). *Policy for the social welfare practitioner.* New York: Longman.

Pumphrey, M. W. (1959). *The teaching of values and ethics in social work education.* New York: Council on Social Work Education.

Rankin, B., & Torres, K. (2009, April 23). DeKalb DA to investigate fifth-grader's suicide. *The Atlanta Journal Constitution.* Retrieved April 21, 2010, from http://www.ajc.com/metro/content/metro/dekalb/stories/2009/04/23/dekalb_bully_investigation.html

Reamer, F. G. (2006). *Social work values and ethics* (3rd ed.). New York: Columbia University Press.

Reamer, F. G. (2008). Ethics and values. In T. Mizrahi & L. E. Davis, (Eds.), *Encyclopedia of Social Work* (20th ed., Vol. 2, pp. 143–151). New York: Oxford University Press.

Richmond, M. (1917). *Social diagnosis.* New York: Russell Sage.

Robert Johnson Blues Foundation. Biography. http://www.robertjohnsonbluesfoundation.org/Bio.html Retrieved on March 2, 2010

Sarri, R. C., & Shook, J. J. (2005). The future for social work in juvenile and adult criminal justice. *Advances in Social Work, 6,* 210–220.

Schneider, R. L., & Lester, L. (2001). *Social work advocacy: A new framework for action.* Belmont, CA: Brookes/Cole.

Schorr, A. (1985). Professional practice as policy. *Social Service Review, 59,* 178–196.

Simon, B. L. (1994). *Empowerment traditions: History of empowerment in social work.* New York: Columbia University Press.

Specht, H., & Courtney, M. (1995). *Unfaithful angels: How social work has abandoned its mission.* New York: Simon & Schuster.

Strom-Gottfried, K. (1998). Is "ethical managed care" an oxymoron? *Families in Society, 23,* 25–33.

Teicher, M. (1967). *Values in social work: A re-examination.* New York: National Association of Social Workers.

Trattner, W. (1999). *From poor law to welfare state: A history of social welfare in America* (6th ed.). New York: The Free Press.

Van Soest, D., & Garcia, B. (2003). *Diversity education for social work justice: Mastering teaching skills.* Alexandria, VA: Council on Social Work Education.

van Wormer, K. (2009). Restorative justice as social justice for victims of gendered violence: A standpoint feminist perspective. *Social Work, 54*(2), 107–115.

White, V. (2006). *The state of feminist social work.* New York: Routledge.

Woodcock, R. (2008). Preamble, purpose and ethical principles sections of the NASW Code of Ethics: A preliminary analysis. *Families in Society, 89,* 578–586.

Wyers, N. L. (1991). Policy-practice in social work: Models and issues. *Journal of Social Work Education, 27,* 241–250.

Xu, Y. (2007). Empowering culturally diverse families of young children with disabilities: The double ABCX model. *Early Childhood Education Journal, 34*(6), 431–437.

Zeman, L. D., & Buila, S. (2007). Practice wisdom on custodial parenting with mental illness: A strengths view. *Journal of Family Social Work, 10*(3), 51–65.

Chapter Three

An Introduction to Restorative Justice

PAMELA BLUME LEONARD

In this chapter I look at the major recurring themes in restorative justice literature that you will come across as you work and study in this field. I highlight significant contributors to the theories and foundational values and beliefs that are included under the "large tent" (Sharpe, 2004) of restorative justice. However, new applications, methods of evaluation, ethical considerations, and questions arise daily, and scholarship in the field is burgeoning. As a result, I can claim to offer no more than summaries of some of the current definitions (yes, there is more than one definition of restorative justice), values, principles, practices, evaluations, and debates within the field. For those who seek further reading, milestone works, significant anthologies and articles, and several texts are cited in this chapter.

WHAT IS RESTORATIVE JUSTICE?

There are many answers to the question, "What is restorative justice?" This discipline is still developing and the definitions, theories, and practices of restorative justice continue to expand and adapt to our ever-changing world. At the same time, there is a consistent, strongly held understanding that restorative justice emphasizes responding to the harms done to and the needs of victims, rather than the offense and punishment of an offender (Table 3.1). It is instructive to consider the driving questions asked by restorative justice in comparison to the questions asked by the criminal justice system in response to an offense. Criminal justice focuses on wrongdoing by an offender and asks,

Was a law broken?
If so, who did it?
What punishment will be put upon the offender? (Zehr, 2002, p. 21)

Table 3.1

Two Different Views	
Criminal Justice	*Restorative Justice*
• Crime is a violation of the law and the state.	• Crime is a violation of people and relationships.
• Violations create guilt.	• Violations create obligations.
• Justice requires the state to determine blame (guilt) and impose pain (punishment).	• Justice involves victims, offenders, and community members in an effort to put things right.
Central focus: Offenders get what they deserve.	**Central focus:** Victim needs and offender responsibility for repairing harm.
Three Different Questions	
Criminal Justice	*Restorative Justice*
• What laws have been broken?	• Who has been hurt?
• Who did it?	• What are their needs?
• What do they deserve?	• Whose obligations are these?

In contrast, restorative justice focuses on the victim and reframes the response to harm this way:

> *Who was harmed?*
> *What are their needs?*
> *Whose obligations are these needs? (Zehr, 2002, p. 21)*

As restorative justice practitioners put it, the major concern in the aftermath of harm, whether criminal or not, shifts from the more punishment-oriented question, "What should be done *with the offender?*" toward a more restorative concern expressed as, "What should be done *for the victim?*" [emphasis added] (Johnstone, 2002, p.12). Using that simple description, let's look at the emergence of restorative justice in North America, while keeping in mind that there are exemplary restorative justice programs across much of the globe, particularly in Europe, Australia, and New Zealand.

Beginnings of Restorative Justice

Restorative justice developed in the 1970s as an alternative framework for thinking about crime and justice (Zehr, 2002). At the time there was growing concern about deficiencies in the criminal justice system (Braithwaite, 1989; King, 2007; Munford, 2007; O'Hear, 2007; Van Ness & Strong, 2006), dissatisfaction with the juvenile justice system (Miller, 2008), disappointment with the penal system's inability to rehabilitate offenders (Archibald, 2008; Barker, 2007) and calls from crime victims for greater voice and restitution (Achilles & Stutzman-Amstutz, 2008; Acker, 2008; Barker, 2007; Danieli, 2008; Dignan, 2005). These were among the restive thoughts that fueled early restorative justice efforts in the 1960s and early 1970s.

Around 1970, the rise of local mediation programs, particularly in Minnesota, New York, and Ohio, brought victim and offender together; they were among the first buds of restorative justice practices (McCold, 2008). In May 1974, two teen-age vandals in Elmira, Ontario pleaded guilty to 22 counts of vandalism. They expected to return in a few months for customary sentencing. During the intervening time, their probation officer, a Mennonite[i], attended a meeting about how church members could become more involved in the criminal justice system. There he learned about the gains made in mediation programs, and he decided that it might be more effective for the young offenders to meet the victims and hear firsthand the effects of their drunken spree. By the end of the year, the young men had spoken directly to 21 victims, and subsequently paid them for damages. At the time, none of the people involved—victims, offenders, or court officials—had any idea that they were participating in "The Elmira Case," which has come to be regarded as a leap forward in the victim–offender mediation movement (Peachey, 2003).

Over the next ten years, the experiment in Elmira evolved into a small program known as the Victim–Offender Reconciliation Program (VORP)[ii] and other experimental programs, mostly mediation or community justice centers, grew in communities in North America and Europe (Umbreit, Vos, Coates, & Lightfoot, 2007; McCold, 2008). By the mid-1980s, restorative justice was beginning to get traction as a "viable option for interested crime victims and offenders" (Umbreit et al., p. 519). During that time, Howard Zehr, one of the early and important theorists of restorative justice, was writing his book *Changing Lenses*, which was an early articulation of restorative justice theory. Looking back in awe at the development of restorative justice, he wrote:

When I was writing Changing Lenses *in the mid-1980s I sometimes wondered whether it would be the object of laughter and derision. To be sure, victim–offender conferencing was being practiced in several countries by that time but it was not widely known and the conceptual framework of restorative justice was new and seemed a little crazy. (2005a, p. 263)*

Reflecting further on restorative justice two decades later, he added,

[R]estorative justice is well established internationally as a movement and as a field of study and practice. . . . [A]wareness of it is widespread and growing throughout the world. Academics now study and debate it at conferences and in a rapidly growing literature in various languages; governments sometimes finance and even advocate it; a growing number of communities and countries throughout the world are implementing it; and increasing numbers of people are seeking to make careers of the field. (2005a, p. 263)

A Constructive Community-Based Response to Conflict

According to John Paul Lederach, a renowned scholar of conflict studies, "Conflict is normal in human relationships" (2003, p. 4). Moreover, "conflict flows from life" and "offers opportunities to grow and to increase our understanding of ourselves, of others, of our social structures" (p. 18). This view places the primary responsibility for constructively addressing conflict on people who are engaged in the conflict.

In Western culture, however, conflicts that can be subjected to court jurisdiction often become lawsuits, which are, by definition, dominated by lawyers. This happens too often, according to Norwegian criminologist Nils Christie (1977), who, in the 1970s, pointed the finger at the legal system for "stealing conflicts" (p. 4) away from the people involved in a specific conflict. Christie, like Lederach, described conflict as "a potential for activity, for participation" (p. 7). However, he cautioned that when the state assumes the role of injured party in the prosecution of crime (e.g., the name of the court case carries the name of the prosecuting entity versus the defendant, not the victim versus the defendant, as in *State of Georgia v. Defendant*), the most interested participant—the victim—is sidelined and the broader community is deprived of "opportunities for norm–clarification" (p. 8), which provide invaluable teaching moments to illuminate and stimulate discussions among citizens about "what represents the law of the land" (p. 8).

This view is an important tenet of restorative justice, where victim, offender, and community—the primary stakeholders[iii]—come together to address conflict and harm. In this context, the form of community involvement is flexible. It could consist of the family or community of support for a victim of crime as well as for the offender. In a neighborhood or workplace dispute, the people directly involved and affected by the outcome would likely compose the community. Former prosecutor Ronnie Earle relies on relationships to define community as "a network of relationships where members share joy and pain" (Earle in Bazemore & Schiff, 2005, p. 277). A "community of care" (a term often used in restorative justice), "includes anyone who feels connected, either indirectly or directly in the crime or the event itself" (Schiff, 2007, p. 235).

Restorative justice recognizes the many ways that people conceptualize community as social resources, and it responds to harm and injustice by harnessing positive individual empowerment and social resources to support healing. This "bottom up" approach (Braithwaite, 2003, pp.14–15; Walgrave, 2002, p. 208) offers an alternative, and sometimes a complement, to the "top down approach in traditional criminal justice (and other fields of problem-solving as well), where decisions are imposed according to strict rules leaving little room, if any, for the views and interests of those directly concerned" (Walgrave, 2002, p. 209).

Restorative Justice Today

Over the last three decades, restorative justice has developed beyond a practice concerned almost exclusively with responding to lesser offenses committed by juveniles into one that also offers effective responses to crimes of severe violence, from homicides to mass atrocities. Further, restorative justice, while still deeply embedded in the criminal justice system, has evolved into a social movement (Johnstone, 2008) that, according to Pranis, provides social processes for citizens "to demonstrate mutual accountability—the collective responsibility of citizens to care about and take care of one another" (as cited in Wachtel & McCold, 2001, p. 114).

There are restorative justice initiatives around the globe, in multiple settings. From Oprah Winfrey (Rakieten, 2004) to the United Nations (Johnstone, 2003; Van Ness, 2003), powerful individuals and institutions are highlighting restorative justice as a constructive and potentially transformative response to harm that can benefit victims, offenders, communities, and societies. This rich variety of situations, motives, and applications has led to differing, and sometime competing, perspectives about the definition, values, principles, and purpose of restorative justice, which is variously described as a set of specific practices (Umbreit et al., 2007), a philosophy (Zehr, 2002), a social movement (Johnstone, 2008), a way of life (Abramson et al., 2003; Pranis, 2007a), a form of conflict transformation (Ellison & Shirlow, 2008; McEvoy & Eriksson, 2008), a tool for moving toward just and nonviolent societies (Gil, 2008), and a misplaced effort to achieve universal justice (Pavlich, 2003).

DEFINITIONS OF RESTORATIVE JUSTICE

Kathleen Daly asserts, "There is no agreed-upon definition" (2008a, p.135) of restorative justice. Indeed, the array of definitions used by scholars and practitioners of restorative justice makes it worthwhile to review those that are most enduring, and to consider the hazards of attempting to define this broad and evolving field.

A Response to Crime

When Howard Zehr's book *Changing Lenses* was published in 1990, Zehr, a Mennonite and a social historian, had been involved in the Victim–Offender Reconciliation Program (VORP). Drawing on his training, experiences, and faith, he described the restorative justice perspective this way: "Crime is a violation of people and relationships. It creates obligations to make things right. Justice involves the victim, the offender, and the community in a search for solutions that promote repair, reconciliation, and reassurance" (1995, p. 181).

Tony Marshall composed a frequently cited and still useful definition of restorative justice in 1999: "Restorative justice is a process whereby parties with a stake in a specific offence collectively resolve how to deal with the aftermath of the offence and its implications for the future" (Marshall, 2008, p. 28)." This elegant and influential definition is frequently relied upon to impart the essence of restorative justice as a compassionate and effective response to crime (Daly, 2008b; Umbreit, et al., 2007; Zehr, 2002).

By 2000, the proliferation of programs conceived and implemented without the benefit of a uniform definition of restorative justice prompted calls for a uniform definition of restorative justice (Roche, 2001) and clear boundaries regarding the scope of restorative justice (McCold, 2008). Roche found the emphasis on process in the Marshall definition too vague to guard against non-restorative undesirable outcomes (e.g., overly severe punishment). In response, he proposed that the distinctiveness of restorative justice "lies in the combination of a deliberative process and the core values of repairing harm" (Roche, 2001, p. 351).

As early as 1990, the participants at the United Nations Congress on Crime Prevention and the Treatment of Offenders ("Crime Congress") began breakout discussions about restorative justice. A lengthy process followed as NGOs, experts in the field of restorative justice, and representatives from the Crime Congress worked to build international awareness of restorative justice and promulgate guidelines and standards for its implementation. In 2002, this body produced a document formally endorsing the use of restorative processes in criminal cases and laying out basic principles on its use[iv]. Of note is the avoidance within the document of defining restorative justice. Van Ness attributes this "intentional omission" (2003, p. 166) to two factors. First, the guidelines address "programmatic expressions of restorative justice" rather than those at the level of "vision, public policy or a comprehensive system" (Van Ness, 2003, p. 166). Secondly, and more relevant to our discussion of definitions, "*there is no general agreement on a definition of restorative justice* [emphasis added] and it seemed unwise to embed a particular definition into a United Nations document not likely to change significantly in future years" (Van Ness, 2003, p. 166). However, adapting Tony Marshall's process-oriented definition, the United Nations document does define restorative *process*.

"Restorative Process" means any process in which the victim, the offender, and/or any other individuals or community members affected by a crime actively participate together in the resolution of matters arising from crime, often with the help of a fair and impartial third party. Examples of restorative processes include mediation, conferencing and sentencing circles. (Van Ness, 2003, p. 167)

In his *Little Book of Restorative Justice*, Howard Zehr (2002) acknowledged and modified Marshall's 1999 definition as follows: "Restorative justice is a process to involve, to the extent possible, those who have a stake in a specific offense and to collectively identify and address harms, needs, and obligations, in order to heal and put things as right as possible" (p. 37).

Several years later, Zehr sought to further clarify and articulate his understanding of the key concepts of restorative justice in the afterword of the third edition of *Changing Lenses* (2005a), where he wrote,

Restorative Justice . . .

1. *Focuses on harms and consequent needs. (Of victims, but also communities and offenders)*
2. *Addresses obligations resulting from those harms. (Offenders' but also communities' and society's)*
3. *Uses inclusive, collaborative processes.*
4. *Involves those with a stake in the situation. (Victims, offenders, community members, society)*
5. *Seeks to put right the wrongs. (p. 270)*

Consistent with his earlier definition of restorative justice, Zehr emphasized individual wrongdoing and restorative processes as a response. In addition, he expanded his vision of restorative justice to include the call of transformative justice to take seriously the "harms and obligations inherent in social, economic, and political systems" (2005a, p. 274).

Beyond a Response to Crime

Zehr's work in restorative justice grew out of his work for the Mennonite Central Committee, and *Changing Lenses* contains many references to his faith. Eventually, various faith leaders began to see a connection between their own work and restorative justice. Michael L. Hadley (2001) explored the relationship between justice and spirituality in his book, *The Spiritual Roots of Restorative Justice*. He included Marshall's 1999 definition and went further in describing restorative justice: "It is about doing justice as if people really mattered [Employing a phrase used by Virginia Mackey in 1990, p. 28 in *Restorative Justice: Toward Nonviolence*]; it addresses the need for a vision of the good life, and the Common Good" (p. 9). Hadley returned to this theme in 2008, when he wrote,

> *[R]estorative justice is at its root a deeply spiritual process of transformation: of persons, situations, and even institutions. Drawing on spiritual values, it responds to human needs holistically in order to restore the moral bond of community. It involves recognizing justice not solely in terms of forensic and adversarial legal processes alone, but in terms of restoration, healing, and peace. (Hadley, 2008, p. 174)*

Also pushing against the trend to limit the theory and practice of restorative justice as solely a response to crime, Sullivan and Tifft (2005) offered a radical understanding of restorative justice as a peacemaking force that extends far beyond the justice system and into relationships at all levels, including relationships of individuals with institutions and governments. Although not growing out of a particular faith, their views have a spiritual tone. Rather than defining restorative justice, they "explore the possibilities of a restorative justice that is transformative, a justice that allows us to rebuild from the ground up, not only the way we relate to others but also the social arrangements through which we live with and among others in our everyday lives" (2005, p. 196).

John Braithwaite distinguished the transformative approach this way:

> *Restorative justice, conceived as an intellectual tradition or as an approach to political practice, involves radical transformation. On this radical view restorative justice is not simply a way of reforming the criminal justice system, it is a way of transforming the entire legal system, our family lives, our conduct in the workplace, our practice of politics.* Its vision is of a holistic change in the way we do justice in the world. *[emphasis added] (2003, p. 1)*

There are efforts by some proponents who view restorative justice primarily as a response to crime to consider, and sometimes incorporate, the perspective of transformative justice. Bradt, a Flemish social worker, argues that even in the context of adult Victim–Offender Mediation, it is important "to let an individual change-focus go hand-in-hand with social change-focus. If social work focuses only on the individual level . . . it limits its role to humanizing the criminal justice system . . . and loses a lot of its potential to influence and reorient the criminal justice system itself towards a more restorative approach" (Bradt & Bouverne-De Bie, 2009, p. 188). In their book *Restoring Justice: An Introduction to Restorative Justice*, Van Ness and Strong (2006) acknowledge that there is no authoritative body with the responsibility or credibility to make determinations concerning what is or is not restorative. After discussing a variety of views on its meaning and embracing the challenges presented by transformative justice, they exercised a preference for "specificity" when presenting their own definition of restorative justice as a "theory of justice that emphasizes repairing the harm caused or revealed by criminal behavior. It is best accomplished through cooperative processes that include all stakeholders" (p. 43).

Conversely, Sullivan and Tifft (2008) include a wide range of perspectives about the practices, promises, and limits of restorative justice in their edited *Handbook of Restorative Justice*. They also reiterate their belief in the necessity for *transformative* restorative justice, because "responding to crime and social harms [with] intervention strategies and the processing of individuals is confusing the iceberg with its tip" (p. 13). They add, "We know that restorative justice conferencing and similar modes of restoration will be limited in what they can achieve if we do not work toward creating a social reality, that is, social institutions that reflect a one world body of relatives" (p. 13).

Transformative theory, then, argues that restorative justice can be used to prevent and address all manner of harm in all manner of settings. In this book, we explore a variety of creative restorative justice applications, and there are many more, including using Peacemaking Circles (for a description of this restorative process, see Chapter 4) to reduce staff conflict among corrections officers (Pranis, 2007b); incorporating victim–offender mediation when disciplining doctors (Farbiarz, 2008); using restorative justice to resolve environmental law cases (Strickland & Miller, 2007); urging museum personnel to think restoratively about returning cultural artifacts to indigenous communities (Simpson, 2009); and encouraging defense attorneys to reach out to families of homicide victims (Beck, Britto, & Andrews, 2007).

Synthesizing Definitions

Currently there are attempts to create a definition of restorative justice that acknowledges the discipline's various interests and agendas. A succinct effort to incorporate the various definitions of restorative justice in use can be found at restorativejustice.org:

> Restorative justice is a theory of justice that emphasizes repairing the harm caused by criminal behavior. When this is done using cooperative processes that include all stakeholders, transformation is possible (Prison Fellowship International, n.d.).

However, synthesis of the many extant definitions of restorative justice remains a challenge. The website for the United States Department of Justice Office of Justice Programs addresses the array of definitions currently in use by offering at least nine "working definitions" of restorative justice in the criminal justice context (National Institute of Justice, 2007).

We end this section where we began: "There is no agreed upon definition of restorative justice" (Daly, 2008a, p. 135). However, among the wide range of definitions we reviewed, all of them reflect recurring underlying values and principles, which we will look at next.

FOUNDATIONAL VALUES AND PRINCIPLES THAT GUIDE THE PRACTICE OF RESTORATIVE JUSTICE

The Need for Clearly Articulated Values and Principles

The inchoate state of restorative justice provides rich opportunities for creative and compassionate responses to harm, but the task of moving restorative justice beyond theory and into effective practices and processes must be approached with caution. Since the early 1980s, Howard Zehr has warned restorative justice practitioners about the numerous pressures that "threaten the integrity and future of the field" (Zehr, 2006, p. 1). Two obvious pressures are the powerful "culture of punishment" that thrives not only in the United States but also throughout much of the world, and the persistence of structural injustices including racism, poverty, and privilege (Zehr, 2005c). To counter these pressures, Zehr contends, "the field is most likely to stay on track if we articulate and are guided by clear principles and values" (Zehr, 2005c, p. 3). He describes the link between clear values and principles and principled practice: "Principled practice requires a limited and clearly articulated set of principles and values, in easily accessible form, without layers of interpretation that obscure them. In my view, they should allow flexibility and go beyond a specific model of practice such as conferencing in order to allow situations to be shaped to the needs of the situation" (Zehr, 2005c).

"Values" and "principles" are central concepts in restorative justice. Although they may seem to have similar meanings, they are related yet fundamentally distinct. Values are understood to be the fundamental aspirations of the movement; for example, respect is a key value of restorative justice. Principles, on the other hand, tend to describe pathways for putting values into action; for example, a principle of restorative justice is to show respect to all parties—victim, offender, justice colleagues. Values and principles often are entwined in the restorative justice literature, making it difficult to examine values without considering principles, or to examine principles without understanding values. However, values are the most fundamental components of restorative justice so I will focus on them first, and will then look at principles.

Values

The fluid nature of restorative justice, a relatively new, fast-growing, and evolving field, leads to variability of characteristics and emphases within the "lists" of the most basic restorative values. Just as there are multiple definitions of restorative justice, there is no uniform set of restorative justice values. However, non-domination, empowerment, respect for all stakeholders, accountability of the offender, and concern for the harm and needs of stakeholders—at least victim, offender, and community—recur as bedrock values. Further, a number of scholars and practitioners have underscored the need for restorative justice to affirm fundamental human rights (Braithwaite, 2000; Mackay, 2006; Skelton & Sekhonyane, 2007) with the *Declaration of Human Rights* by the United Nations (United Nations, 1948) as a universal starting place (Skelton & Sekhonyane, 2007) followed by its sequels (Dorne, 2008).

Despite the many efforts to name and describe restorative justice values, these efforts have been criticized by scholars within and without the field for being vague (Hudson, 2003) and unbounded (Shapland, 2003). Some scholars see restorative justice as offender-centered (Mika, Achilles, Halbert, Amstutz, & Zehr, 2004; Herman, 2004); others say it jeopardizes the rights of offenders (Skelton & Frank, 2004) and favors victims' needs (Hudson, 2003). There are concerns that restorative justice conceals race and class bias underneath an overlay of humanitarian concern (Daly, 2008b; Delgado, 2000), has inaccurately appropriated feminist theory (Daly, 2003b), and encourages an easily faked ritual of apology (Acorn, 2004).

Nevertheless, in her recent analysis of restorative justice values, Kay Pranis found that "restorative values are emerging as a unifying concept that grounds theory and guides practice" (2007b, p. 59). She identified two categories of restorative values: process values and individual values. Process values are "essential aspects of restorative justice" (p. 61) that "guide practice, including the design and implementation of the structure and operation of specific processes" (p.61). Among the recurring process values that Pranis—who leans toward a transformative conception of restorative justice—found in her review are respect, maintaining individual dignity, inclusion, responsibility, humility, mutual care, reparation, and non-domination (p. 62). Pranis's distinction between process and individual restorative values does not imply a belief that either stands alone. Rather, she argues that restorative process values support individual restorative values of "respect, honesty, taking responsibility, compassion, patience" (p. 63) and contribute to a safe environment in which participants "are more likely to access their best self" (p. 63). Shifting from the effects of restorative values in a single case, Pranis attributes more far-reaching effects for restorative justice values: "To a large degree our beliefs shape the world we create with our actions and our energy. Choosing a positive vision expressed through values contributes to creating a more positive world" (p. 73).

Predictably, restorative justice practitioners and critics tend to emphasize specific values according to their various contexts, experiences, and conceptions of restorative justice. For example, Pranis, Stuart, & Wedge (2003) list general values, which they describe as "universal," "individual" "core values," including respect, honesty, trust, humility, sharing, inclusivity, empathy, courage, forgiveness, and love (pp. 33–47), which "help us work through our differences" (p. 33) in a Peacemaking Circle process. John Braithwaite acknowledges the core "general" values, such as accountability, (2003, p. 8) of restorative justice and recognizes that specific values are just as important. For example, the value of educational development would be equally as important as restorative justice values in a school setting.

The most widely agreed upon restorative value was articulated by Howard Zehr, who believes that, above all, restorative justice is about respect for all, and that such respect requires deep humility, which prohibits taking undue credit or assuming that one's own way of knowing is the "right" way (Zehr, 2005b).

> Respect reminds us of our interconnectedness but also our differences. Respect insists that we balance concern for all parties. If we pursue justice as respect, we will do justice restoratively. If we do not respect others, we will not do justice restoratively, no matter how earnestly we adopt the principles [of restorative justice]. The value of respect underlies restorative justice principles and must guide and shape their application. (Zehr, 2002, p. 36)

Next, we will examine how, as Zehr insists, restorative justice values shape and inform principles of practice.

Principles

Principles establish shared standards and provide ethical guidelines for restorative justice practice. Because they tend to be general in nature, principles can be applied to the wide variety of settings, situations, and ethical questions that arise in restorative processes. At the same time, restorative justice principles provide values-based boundaries that support and promote healing.

Restorative justice has gained a valid place in the justice system of New Zealand, where the process of establishing values-based principled practice offers a blueprint for collaborative systemic change (Bowen, Boyack, & Marshall, 2004). Following a proliferation of restorative justice service providers and funding for an extensive pilot restorative justice program, the government was poised to set standards of practice and distributed draft principles for review. The Restorative Justice Network (RJN), a group of providers, was engaged in an internal series of discussions (Bowen et al., 2004) that culminated in *Restorative Justice Values and Processes*. In 2004, the New Zealand Ministry of Justice published *Restorative Justice in New Zealand: Best Practice* (Ministry of Justice, 2004). This document contains both the RJN document and the principles developed by the Ministry, because the collaborative process resulted in the two documents having "internal consistency about the values and principles of restorative justice" (p. 6). The practitioners' need to "protect the inherent flexibility of restorative justice processes" (p. 6; see also p. 22) and the government's responsibility to provide "clear guidance about the use of these processes in a safe and appropriate way" (p. 10) were achieved. As a result, *Restorative Justice in New Zealand: Best Practice* sets out a useful description of the spirit and process of conducting principled, values-based restorative justice services when embedded in the criminal justice system. This is so, in part, because the values and principles articulated in the document are thoroughly entwined.

The core restorative justice values identified by the RJN correspond to those identified in the section above by Zehr and Pranis. The eight principles emphasize voluntariness, participation, preparation and information, emotional and physical safety of the participants, and accountability of the offender. The restorative justice process must be flexible and responsive, effective (with high quality facilitators) and evaluated, and only undertaken in appropriate cases, with careful consideration given to the seriousness and classification of the crime and the suitability of the participants for a restorative process (Ministry of Justice, 2004). In the United States, an example of clearly and succinctly articulated principles is *Signposts of Restorative Justice*, written by Harry Mika and Howard Zehr in 2001. Unlike the New Zealand example above, Mika and Zehr were not writing principles for a specific setting. Rather, they offer general guidelines, or as they call them, signposts, meant to be easily understood, recalled, and put into practice by a variety of practitioners in a myriad of settings:

Signposts of restorative justice

1. *Focus on the harms of crime rather than the rules that have been broken.*
2. *Show equal concern and commitment to the victims and offenders, involving both in the process of justice.*

3. *Work toward the restoration of victims, empowering them and responding to their needs as they see them.*

4. *Support offenders, while encouraging them to understand, accept, and carry out their obligations.*

5. *Recognize that while obligations may be difficult for offenders, those obligations should not be intended as harms, and they must be achievable.*

6. *Provide opportunities for dialogue, direct or indirect, between victim and offender as appropriate.*

7. *Find meaningful ways to involve the community and to respond to the community bases of crime.*

8. *Encourage collaboration and reintegration of both victims and offenders, rather than coercion and isolation.*

9. *Give attention to the unintended consequences of your actions and program.*

10. *Show respect to all parties – victims, offenders, justice colleagues. (Dorne, 2008, pp. 12–13)*

Values-based principles offer necessary guidelines, but it is important to recognize that no single set of guidelines can address the myriad situations that arise in the practice of restorative justice. As Wachtel and McCold (2001) advise, "see every instance of wrong-doing and conflict as an opportunity for learning" (p. 128). It is important to establish a diverse circle of colleagues who appreciate the context of the work, understand the values and principles of restorative justice, and are willing to share time and insights to help a fellow practitioner analyze confusing instances in past or present work. This is a vital step in learning to apply restorative justice values and principles consistently.

THEORETICAL CONCEPTIONS OF RESTORATIVE JUSTICE

Given the various emphases appearing in the definitions and characterizations of restorative justice, it is no wonder that Johnstone and Van Ness describe restorative justice as "a deeply contested concept" (2007, p. 9) that does not now, and may not ever, fit into a single conception. They do see in current theories and practices several overlapping themes, which they identify as the encounter conception, the reparative conception, and the transformative conception (Johnstone and Van Ness, 2007).

The Encounter Conception

The encounter conception is associated with restorative justice processes that respond to crime by providing an opportunity for restorative dialogue (Johnstone & Van Ness, 2007; Umbreit et al., 2007), including Victim–Offender Mediation, conferencing, and circles, which occur in cooperation with the criminal justice system. These practices (described in detail in Chapter 4) are distinctive because they provide the option of one or more face-to-face, facilitated meetings between victim, offender, and perhaps their supporters, to address what happened and its impact on the participants. These meetings consist of structured dialogue based on restorative justice values. It is the structure and values that inform the process upon which proponents of the encounter concept rely, in order to establish, conduct, and maintain a restorative justice process.

The Reparative Conception

The reparative conception rejects the notion that punishment reflecting the severity of a crime (often called "just desserts") is the most appropriate response to crime, because a punishment solution is offender-focused, tends to sideline victims, and does not address the circumstances that contributed to the crime. While voluntary encounters are positive and may result in the offender offering an apology, the reparative conception provides a framework that requires attention to the needs of victims and obligations of offenders. Further, the reparative conception seeks alternative approaches to addressing harms and needs when an encounter is not possible (Van Ness & Strong, 2006). Some examples are shuttle facilitation, in the form of videotaped sessions and/or letters shuttled back and forth between victim and offender, as well as indirect communication through attorneys, facilitators, and family members. The reparative concept also would seek restorative responses to cases in which the offender had not been apprehended, and cases of wrongful conviction.

The Transformative Conception

The transformative conception addresses "broken relationships at multiple levels of society" (Van Ness & Strong, 2006, p. 42). Some theorists and practitioners believe that restorative justice is a transformative way of life that not only could, but also must, begin with understanding ourselves and our own relationships (Sullivan & Tifft, 2005). This conception of restorative justice emphasizes the worth and interconnectedness of all people and stresses needs-based rather than rights-based justice (Sullivan & Tifft, 2005).

David Gil believes that too many restorative justice practitioners fail "to confront social-structural violence, injustice, and privilege" (2008, p. 499). He urges the transformative conception to stretch toward a "'radical' paradigm shift" so that restorative justice practitioners "function as agents of fundamental social change," expanding their knowledge to include a deeper understanding of human needs and development (p. 508). Further, at every level, restorative justice should consider sociological implications, including "social organizations, social values, and social justice" (p. 508). Discarding neutrality, deviating from system-reinforcing behavior, fighting oppression and violence, and implementing social strategies through nonviolent dialogical methods would be part of this radical shift (Gil, 2008).

RECURRING THEMES OF RESTORATIVE PRACTICES

According to Mark Umbreit, a prominent scholar and practitioner who teaches and facilitates restorative dialogue as a response to severe violent crime and conflict around the world, "Restorative justice is not a list of specific programs or a clear blueprint for systemic change" (Umbreit et al., 2007, p. 518). Howard Zehr observed that restorative justice practices originally developed for use within the Western criminal justice field are in use today in settings and situations ranging from schools and workplaces to large-scale societal conflicts and wrongdoing (2002).

There are many sources for the current array of restorative practices. Community mediation centers and the Victim–Offender Reconciliation Project, which emerged in the 1970s, were especially influential in launching Victim–Offender Mediation. Two specific practices, Peacemaking Circles and Family Group Conferences, reflect older traditional forms of justice. Peacemaking Circles have been adapted to our contemporary cultural context by combining the ancient impulse to sit in a circle and talk, the North American First Nations' tradition of passing a "talking piece" that empowers only the person holding the talking piece to speak, and current Western ideals of democracy diversity, and inclusion (Pranis, 2005). The model for Family Group Conferences was influenced by culturally adapted methods developed in Australia and New Zealand (McRae & Zehr, 2004).

A word of caution: Rightly, restorative justice has been taken to task for appropriating, mischaracterizing, and romanticizing "indigenous" practices and failing to acknowledge the effects of colonization and attempts to eradicate traditional culture and justice modes (Daly, 2008b; Daly, 2003b; Pratt, 2006; Cunneen, 2004; Zehr, 2002). It is likely that the complex simplicity of the adapted indigenous practices drew restorative justice practitioners to them. Likewise, the task of current practitioners is both simple and complex: how to acknowledge and thank the traditions from which these practices were taken without condescension, cover-up, or hubris.

CORNERPOSTS OF RESTORATIVE JUSTICE

As Van Ness and Strong (2006) remind us, "restorative processes and practices retain their restorative character as they reflect the values and principles of restorative justice. If these values and principles are lost or violated, the result may not only be less restorative, it may be destructive" (p. 58). They identify four values as "cornerposts" (p. 58) of restorative justice: encounter, amends, reintegration, and inclusion. They then explicate them in a criminal context (although they are applicable in less formal, non-criminal settings as well). We will look at these cornerposts as recurring themes of restorative justice, which blend and distill the restorative justice values and principles examined.

Encounter

Direct involvement of stakeholders is at the heart of restorative justice philosophy and practice. When possible, there is "an encounter between key stakeholders–victim and offender [with a facilitator] at minimum, and perhaps other community and justice people as well" (Zehr, 2002, pp. 44–45). The purpose is to allow "an opportunity for participants to explore facts, feelings, and resolutions" (p. 45) and encourage the victim and offender "to tell their stories, to ask questions, to express their feelings, and to work toward mutually acceptable outcomes" (p. 45).

Participation by victims in any restorative justice process is always completely voluntary, but some judicial processes require (or strongly encourage) offenders to participate. If both the victim and offender of a specific incident cannot or will not participate in a face-to-face meeting, a representative of either or both stakeholders might attend, or letters or videotapes might be exchanged; video-letters, created with the assistance of filmmakers, are another method of communication that is emerging (Raye & Warner Roberts, 2007), as is the option of a surrogate victim offender meeting (VOCARE, n.d.; Domestic Violence Surrogate Dialogue, n.d.).

Strong and Van Ness (2006) identified these signature elements of encounter: meeting, narrative, emotion, understanding, and agreement. In his description of the "most restorative" aspects of Victim–Offender Dialogue, Umbreit (2001) illuminated these critical elements of encounter:

- Primary focus on providing an opportunity for victim and offender to talk directly to each other
- Allows victims to express the full impact of the crime on their lives and to receive answers to important questions they have
- Allows offenders to learn the real human impact of their behavior
- Allows offenders to take direct responsibility for seeking to make things right
- Victims are continually given choices throughout the process: where to meet, whom they would like to have present, and so on
- Separate preparation meetings with victim and offender prior to bringing them together, with emphasis on identifying their needs and preparing them for dialogue
- Parties do most of the talking, high tolerance for silence
- High tolerance for expression of feelings and full impact of crime
- Emphasis on direct dialogue between the involved parties and with the facilitator saying little
- Voluntary for victim and offender.

(Adapted from Umbreit, 2001, p.xli)[v]

Restorative encounters are voluntary, and deciding whether to participate or not can contribute to the empowerment of victims. A restorative encounter allows victims and offenders to engage in a safe, structured dialogue in order to discuss the offense in terms that matter to them, and to understand the impact and after-math of the offense. Sometimes this encounter results in healing for both parties. In contrast, court proceedings are not voluntary for the victim or the offender. Facts are more important than feelings in court proceedings, and this tends to "flatten" the story of the offense and its aftermath. In addition, lawyers do most of the talking in court proceedings, thus diminishing the participation of both the victim and the offender. It is rare for offenders to speak in court, and when they do, their speech is likely to be proscribed by their lawyers. The legal system achieves closure when the case is resolved; this closure does not extend to victims and their families or, in many cases, to offenders and their families. Therefore, restorative encounters offer potential benefits to victims and offenders alike that generally are not offered by the legal system.

Amends

In the context of restorative justice, committing harm is a violation that requires the offender to repair the harm done to the victim to the extent possible. Restorative encounters provide a direct way for offenders to comprehend and internalize the full impact of the harm they have caused. It also offers offenders a direct, struc-tured, and supported way to redress the harm they committed.

Sharpe (2007) points out three common ways that humans redress injustice: vengeance, retribution, and repair. Whereas the victim takes vengeance, a respon-sible authority (the criminal justice system in most Western countries) claims ret-ribution. But it is the offender alone who can initiate repair. As Walgrave (2003) describes it, the offender's role in restorative justice—that of paying back and put-ting things right—is active rather than passive and, therefore, may be more genu-ine than punitive retributivism, where harm is balanced through pain suffered by the offender.

Radzik sees the making of amends "as a form of reconciliation, or the restora-tion of relationships" (2007, p. 194). Reconciliation does not require the victim and offender to have a positive relationship, but it does mean that the relationship can be less marked by the indignity and imbalance of power held by the offender in the victim–wrongdoer dyad (Radzik, 2007)[vi]. By making amends, the offender has an opportunity to earn reconciliation through his own right action, as well as reclaim some sense of self-worth and shed some debilitating guilt (Radzik, 2007).

Reparations can take either material or symbolic form, with the offender's apology and remorse a component in either form. A sincere apology by the offender, offered as directly as possible to the victim, sends a message that acknowl-edges wrongdoing, expresses remorse, provides vindication to the victim, makes assurances that the wrongdoing will not recur, and offers symbolic reparations.[vii]

Material reparation includes concrete compensation, such as financial restitu-tion, or the performing of specific services for the victim, such as carpentry and painting to repair damaged property. Offenders who are incarcerated may be unable to provide material reparation. In such cases, victims have to rely on state-funded restitution for monetary loss. Offenders can still offer amends by providing information about the crime to the victim, or making an apology or offering other forms of reparation, such as making and keeping a pledge to develop work and life skills while in prison and thus avoid recidivism, or perhaps making a work of art for the victim.

Reintegration

Restorative justice puts great emphasis on offenders taking responsibility for the harm they have caused, and the subsequent obligation to put things as right as possible. The community, too, has responsibilities—both to the victim and to the offender. Safety is the first need of crime victims. They also need access to ongoing support and information as they interact with the criminal justice system, even when a perpetrator is not apprehended. The criminal justice system has its own set of rules and procedures, which are sometime discouraging and disempowering for victims. Additionally, it is not unusual for victims, especially victims and victim–survivors of severe violent crime, to feel that their closest communities of support—namely, faith, social, and family groups—withdraw after a short time, sensing that the well of their sympathy and responses has run dry. These circumstances can contribute to the traumatizing effects of being a crime victim, and may hinder victim–survivors' return to participation in work, family interactions, and social events (Zehr, 2001).

Offenders, whether or not they have participated in restorative justice processes, certainly will need guidance and resources during both their incarceration and reentry back into society, in order to change their behavior and avoid future wrongdoing (Maruna, 2001). These are reparative tasks that call upon individuals and institutions in a given community to respond with reintegrative interventions so that "the parties are given the means and opportunity to rejoin their communities as whole, contributing members" (Van Ness & Strong, 2006, p. 50).

Remorse is a culturally expected response of people who have committed an offense, especially a crime (Murphy, 2007). In this vein, scholar John Braithwaite considers it beneficial for society to express its moral sense of right and wrong to a degree that instills shame in an offender. Importantly, this expression needs to be regulated to avoid overuse or destructive use of shaming. He calls this process "reintegrative shaming" (Braithwaite, 1989). The purpose is to entwine and transform both the shame of the offender and the moral authority of the community into a mutual commitment that results in support for an offender's reintegration into the community. This theory influenced the Wagga Wagga (Australia) model, a form of police cautioning[viii], which was loosely based on New Zealand's style of family group conferencing (Moore & O'Connell, 2003). This model was introduced in North America in the 1990s. It has met with criticism from a number of restorative justice practitioners, who recognize the potency of shame, and practitioners' concern about exploiting this emotion runs deep (Maxwell and Morris, 2004; Matthews, 2006, Harris & Maruna, 2008). However, the value of constructive, non-stigmatizing management of shame is a valued component of restorative justice processes (Harris & Maruna, 2008) and a necessary step in the successful reentry of offenders into the community (Van Ness & Strong, 2006).

Inclusion

In addition to reintegration of offenders, restorative justice seeks greater voice for victims. However, the formal criminal justice system tends to be preoccupied with questions of law-breaking and the punishment of the offender, which tends to sideline, if not exclude, victims and victim–survivors. In criminal contexts, practitioners of restorative justice work with all justice professionals to make a place for victims' voices to be heard—perhaps through a victim impact statement or testimony—and, at the same time, to respect the rights of defendants. Defendants have legal representation to advise them, but there is also a need for victims, victim–survivors, defendants' families, and the community to understand the legal process that is taking place and the status of the case. Victims and victim–survivors may choose to be present in court throughout the proceedings, but they should never be pressured into attending against their will.

In a broader sense, inclusion means welcoming the diversity of stakeholders—their race, gender, social status, culture, and spiritual beliefs—and attempting to understand how these identity issues affect their decision of whether or how to participate in restorative processes (for a discussion of culture, class, and gender effects in restorative justice, see Raye, 2004). Inclusion also stands for inviting *all* victims and offenders to participate in appropriate restorative processes—not just the "ideal victim," who wants to sincerely forgive, and the "ideal offender" (Dignan, 2005, pp. 97–102), who wants to authentically repent. The needs and perspectives of victims change over time, and these changes are invited and supported in restorative justice processes. Changing the behavior of an offender to that of non-offender is one of the goals of restorative justice, as is supporting the resilience and healing journey of victims—however bumpy it may be.

EFFICACY OF PRACTICES

The diversity of practices, as well as new forms of practice, can be accommodated within restorative justice (Bowen et al., 2004). However, the very broad, loosely constructed net of restorative justice raises concerns that, as programs become incorporated into the mainstream justice machine, they will be made routine, diluted, or repackaged so that they are "restorative" in name only (Johnstone, 2002). von Hirsch noted that there are "[d]angling standards for evaluation" because evaluation criteria are based on imprecise goals (von Hirsch, Roberts, Bottoms, Roach, & Schiff, 2003, p. 23).

Such demands by scholars and practitioners for accountability of programs and practitioners in the field have resulted in an array of calls for clarity, ethics, and standards. These include the meaning and means of accountability of restorative justice (Bowen et al., 2004; Roche, 2003; Braithwaite, 2000; Leverton, 2008; Doolin, 2007; the degree of restorative justice in actions and outcomes (Claasen, 1996 as cited in Dorne, 2008; Zehr, 2002); statements of purpose and ethics from practitioners (Abramson, et al., 2003; Dyck, 2004); extensive internal dialogue regarding values-based practice (Coben & Harley, 2004; Ministry of Justice, 2004; Umbreit et al., 2007); the appropriation of indigenous practices (Daly, 2003b Maxwell, 2008); practitioner competency and training (Gustafson, 2004; Bussler, 2004); accreditation of practitioners (Bussler, 2004); clearer means of assessing and evaluating restorative justice in practice (Mika, 2002; Strang, 2002; Poulson, 2003; Sherman & Strang, 2007; Bazemore & Ellis, 2007); and the role and capacity of communities to respond to crime (Moore, 2002; Walgrave, 2003; Takagi & Shank, 2004; McCold, 2008; Walklate, 2008).

Daly (2003a) further cautions against concentrating on studies with positive outcomes and argues, "By making variation [of outcome] explicit and expectable, we are able to test the theory of restorative justice and its limits" (p. 48). Mika (2002) argues that the process of evaluation itself should be a collaborative peacemaking process employing multiple methods, both qualitative as well as quantitative, rather than a "disembodied practice . . . cloaked in its mantel of science" (p. 349).

Numerous scholars have echoed Braithwaite's lament that since restorative justice is only around 30 years old, "evaluation research . . . is at such a rudimentary state, our claims about what is good practice and what is bad practice can rarely be evidence-based" (Braithwaite, 2003, p. 1; see also, Daly, 2003b; Miller, 2008).

Bazemore and Schiff (2005) conducted an impressive 5-year study of restorative programs in juvenile justice in the United States. The goals of the study were to quantify and characterize existing programs, determine how restorative these programs were, and look at how these programs interacted with the larger juvenile justice reforms taking place across the country at the time. In addition, they sought to determine what makes a practice "restorative," and why some restorative approaches work, while some do not. They identified 773 programs, locating in nearly every state at least a few programs, and in a few states, robust statewide initiatives. Victim–offender mediation was by far the most prevalent practice. Among the 25 programs from which they collected qualitative data, they found a strong focus on restorative justice versus traditional juvenile justice practices, due to concern by staff and volunteers for victims' needs, offender support, and stakeholder involvement. However, commitment to community and government role transformation, which Bazemore and Schiff considered a basic principle of restorative justice, had as yet found little traction. In addition to findings, the authors relied on their data and various restorative justice theories to propose a visionary research agenda that has yet to be realized.

In a review of restorative justice programs in the United States, Umbreit et al. (2007) found growing implementation of restorative justice, with 29 states providing support for restorative justice dialogue. This expansion underscores the urgent need for comprehensive evaluation of state level restorative justice initiatives. Umbreit et al. sought to analyze evaluation data from scores of programs, but their overview reveals the difficulty of gleaning meaningful evidence that can be used to inform best practices, due to the variety of individual applications and evaluation measures.

Also in 2007, Sherman and Strang released their study *Restorative Justice: The Evidence*, a systematic search for and analysis of literature from 1986 to 2005 regarding the impact of restorative justice in the United Kingdom and internationally (Sherman & Strang, 2007). Using sophisticated methods to select and weigh data from 36 studies, they found promising evidence that, even in cases when participants had little or no choice between the criminal justice system and restorative justice and the self selection bias was removed, "restorative justice is at least as effective in producing desired results of justice as C[riminal] J[ustice], often more so, and only rarely (if powerfully) counterproductive" (p.13). There are also indications of possible cost savings due at least in part to "substantial reductions in repeat offending for both violence and property crime" (p. 8). Somewhat unexpectedly, they found that restorative justice "seems to reduce crime more effectively with more, rather than less, serious crimes . . . suggest[ing] that it works better with crimes involving personal victims than for crimes without them" (p. 8). However, Waldman (2007) found that victim satisfaction is related to the distress level of the victim. She compared several studies that looked at restorative responses to crimes ranging in seriousness from genocide in three war zones— Rwanda, Bosnia and Herzegovina, and Croatia—to juvenile offenses in Australia, and New Zealand. She found that even when crimes were less egregious, "victims whose distress level remains high and who continue to suffer psychological fallout of intense trauma may be unable to benefit from [restorative] interactions" (p. 93). Waldman agrees with data from the Australian youth conferences (mediation-style meetings attended by victim, offender, parents, and police officers) suggesting that "victims who are 'lightly touched' by crime orient themselves more readily to the ideal R[estorative] J[ustice] script" (Daly (2005) p. 162). She urges restorative justice practitioners and theorists to give more thought to screening victims prior to restorative justice encounters and to offering material and emotional assistance to those who are depressed and traumatized.

The Sherman and Strang study is a significant step forward in research in restorative justice because the researchers were able to combine data from a number of studies. This allowed them to address a methodological barrier that in the past had prevented a comprehensive meta analysis because of the ambiguity of the term "restorative," as well as findings among various studies that are often relevant to the effectiveness of a specific programmatic model rather than a general, theoretically informed intervention (Bazemore & Schiff, 2005).

Miller, Gibson, and Byrd (2008) have broadly criticized the state of research on restorative justice. They have complained that restorative justice puts too little emphasis on accountability and too much reliance on "liberal feel good" (p. 271), which is accomplished by "doing the right thing" (p. 271). They assert that scholarship regarding accountability is primarily "commentaries, literature reviews, and, at best, meta analyses" (p. 263) that point out the lack of and need for accountability. Instead, they argue, there is urgent need for a theoretically based research agenda stressing accountability, which is a necessary step in achieving programmatic soundness and credible data upon which to base future development of restorative justice. They acknowledge the risks of seeking empirical confirmation for the assumptions, practices, and theories of restorative justice in comparison to those of traditional criminal justice, but insist it is a necessary risk because "in American society, to be scientific is to be highly valued" (p. 277). The view that science can make or break restorative justice is a point to be debated. However, being responsive to the questions that social science raises and willing to encounter the difficult data that has come from research is a crucial test for the values and development of restorative justice.

QUESTIONS, LIMITS, AND CAUTIONS

The rapid growth of restorative justice programs is the source of most of the significant questions, limits, and cautions in this section. From its beginnings in juvenile justice, we now see restorative justice in a range of legal arenas, from child protective services to death penalty cases. Courts and public services at all levels, foundations and faith-based funders, nonprofits, allied fields, universities, and scholars see the great promise of this work. Restorative justice is still developing and finding places to grow into. A recurring question asks how the field can respond to the broad interest in restorative justice theories and practices yet remain centered on its own values and principles.

Yet, the public at large, including many victims, offenders, and community leaders, are not aware of restorative justice. Moreover, the adversarial culture in the U. S. stands in stark contrast to the peacemaking purpose, processes, and outcomes of restorative justice. This leads a number of people to mistakenly reject restorative justice as just another naïve, "Kumbaya" concept which, in turn, makes it easy for them to ignore the growing evidence that restorative justice offers a voluntary, cost-effective, community-capacity-building means of addressing conflict.

Restorative justice can address harm and provide opportunities for healing in these and other settings only if there is adherence to values-based practice and there is a strategic effort to persuasively and accurately impart the values, goals, and benefits the field of restorative justice offers to a broader audience.

Addressing Adherence to Values-Based Practice by Individuals

It is an exhilarating time to work in this field, but it is also time for all restorative justice practitioners, including those from allied fields, to take a sober inventory of their preparedness to work in restorative justice, and to take steps to support values-based practice. Here are a few ideas that have helped me work toward consistent values-based practice and stay within the limits of my knowledge, skills, and readiness to take on new challenges:

- Write out your own version of restorative values and principles, along with helpful guidelines, and keep them at hand for reference.
- Approach all stakeholders with deep humility. Respect their individuality and strengths. Collaborate with them to create responsive and unhurried restorative processes that work for them.
- Deeply and constantly consider issues of privilege and power, particularly as they pertain to race, gender, age, culture, and economic status. Actively seek and support diverse colleagues to join the field of restorative justice.
- Write a brief introductory description of your work in restorative justice; take the time to learn to deliver it so you can effectively and consistently explain restorative justice and your role in it.
- Grow diverse alliances in your community and model restorative justice values.
- Honestly assess your skills and obtain more training when it is needed.
- When entering a new arena or a new level of practice, find a mentor.
- Develop a diverse circle of colleagues who serve as a "circle of accountability" for each other, bringing practice questions to the group for advice and cautions.
- Keep up with the contemporary restorative justice literature and attend national and international conferences when possible.

Reaching a Broader Audience

Some countries seem to be moving toward collaboratively building systems that incorporate (but do not co-opt) restorative justice (Ministry of Justice, 2004; Bazemore & Schiff, 2005) but the U. S. lags behind, perhaps due to the widely disbursed independent programs here and the lack of nationwide federal programs (Bazemore & Schiff, 2005). But there is also a need to reexamine the benefits and disadvantages of the "outsider" role of restorative justice in relation to the criminal justice system, which makes many criminal justice professionals uncomfortable with the field, and hence less willing to support implementation of restorative justice programs (Robinson, 2003; see also Miller, Gibson, and Byrd, 2008), arguing that classifying restorative justice as a conflict theory is inaccurate and misguided. This leads to the broader question of what role professionals will occupy in the field of restorative justice, where volunteer facilitators from the community often carry the bulk of the load (Erbe, 2004).

So far, restorative justice is not an independent academic discipline. There is no PhD program in restorative justice in the United States (although there are some terminal degree programs in the making in Europe) and there are very few Master's-level programs, so restorative justice must rely on academics from other disciplines to develop theories and conduct research. Therefore, the lack of time and training that people on the ground have to effect theory and research is limited. This may contribute to the heavy emphasis on program evaluation rather than theoretical research. In turn, the absence of evidence demonstrating the effectiveness of values-based restorative processes may contribute to the risk of dilution of restorative justice, particularly in the criminal justice system, where officials have the power of credentials, authority, and customary adversarial rules for settling cases. This has led to concern that restorative justice processes imbedded in the criminal justice system will be streamlined without sufficient preparation to support restorative dialogue or be otherwise misused, perhaps through over-shaming (see Umbreit et al., 2007 for a discussion of some of the potential pitfalls facing restorative justice). All of this is to underscore the overdue need for restorative justice proponents to assess the many steps that must be accomplished if restorative justice is to move beyond the scattering of programs that currently exist in the United States.

First, restorative justice must mature into a movement that is capable of developing a definition, principles, and goals that are credible, comprehensive, comprehensible, and consistent to the public at large. In the absence of a cohesive restorative justice community that is able and willing to take on this task internally, the field risks dilution, co-optation, misrepresentation, the eclipse of its signature values, and a loss of the capacity to transform conflict into a healing opportunity for individuals, families, communities, and our legal and social systems.

Growth has outstripped research, and practitioners of restorative justice are increasingly being challenged to show evidence that it works for victims, offenders, and communities. So far, the willingness of those in the field and adequate resources have not joined hands to develop and implement a comprehensive research agenda. At a time when the major social systems in the United States emphasize the importance of evidence-based practice, this void puts restorative justice at risk to lose favor, funding, and influence among the healing and problem-solving professions.

Navigating the challenges of rapid growth, maintaining values-based practice, developing a comprehensive strategy to earn public support, and designing an effective research program are necessary steps in overcoming the current limitations of restorative justice, answering recurring questions about the field, and effecting policy changes that seek to transform conflict into an opportunity for learning, healing, and diminishing future harm.

CONCLUSION

In the United States, we are badly in need of improved ways to address conflict, harm, and healing. Restorative justice has developed knowledge and skills that provide an effective, and arguably more desirable and sustainable, response than we have come to expect in our individual disputes, government interventions, and legal system. As Bazemore and Schiff (2005) point out, in the hotly adversarial legal system, "a healed victim is not a success" (p. 245). Nor is a remorseful and transformed offender considered a success, regardless of the current concern about reducing recidivism.

However, there are individuals within the most contested public arenas and professions who recognize the promise of addressing harm with more than punishment. For example, there are judges, prosecutors, defense attorneys, and law school faculty members who have actively supported restorative justice (Geske, 2005; Geske & McCanse, 2008; Cutting Edge Law, n.d.; Bazemore and Schiff, 2005; Burr, 2003). There are judges, prosecutors, defense attorneys, law enforcement officers, and court administrators who seek and are willing to listen to new ideas. Bazemore and Schiff (2005) advocate "building insider allies" in the criminal justice system (p. 247). Support for restorative justice could also come from public agencies that value and support well-being, particularly social services, public health, mental health, victim services, prison ministry and, perhaps unexpectedly, corrections. Further, scholars in all of these fields could contribute to the development of a comprehensive restorative justice research agenda. No doubt, potential allies for policy changes that support values-based implementation of restorative justice reside among these people and agencies. Strategic outreach to all of these sources is long overdue.

The variety of approaches, practices, and goals held by restorative justice scholars and practitioners has been a creative source of healing and transformation for everyone who participates in the processes. The greatest challenge for restorative justice today is to gain sufficient legitimacy to provide services in a wider range of settings without compromising the values-based strengths of its practices. Whether the field will resolve its internal questions regarding the definition, scope, and efficacy of the restorative justice movement remains to be seen. Failing to do so will leave the unanswered questions about the capacity of restorative justice to set its own boundaries to fester. This would almost surely cap the growth and development of this powerful tool for peacebuilding.

NOTES

i The Christian Mennonite faith is deeply pacifist and traditionally reluctant to interact with government systems. Mennonites perhaps are best known for their commitment to nonviolence and peacemaking. For a discussion of the role and significance of Mennonites in the development of restorative justice, see Dorne, C. K. (2008).

Restorative justice in the United States (pp. 164–174) .Upper Saddle River, NJ: Prentice Hall.

ii For a more detailed description of the birth and growth of VORP, see Peachey, in Johnstone (2003), pp. 178–186.

iii The term "stakeholder" is a commonly used term in restorative justice. However, there are concerns about the ambiguity of the word, because it has meaning as to who should be included in a restorative process (Schiff, 2003, p. 328). Further, Zehr finds it problematic because the origins of the word relate to white settlers using stakes to claim land belonging to First Nations people (Zehr, 2002, p. 70).

iv For a detailed description of the development of Basic principles on the use of restorative justice, including the vital role played by NGOs, see Vann Ness (2003) .

v In keeping with current preferred terms, "dialogue" was substituted for mediation and "facilitator" for mediator.

vi For a discussion of evolutionary aspects of forgiveness, see McCullogh, 2008; For a biological understanding of resistance to apology, forgiveness, and reconciliation, see Yarn & Jones (in press).

vii Contrast Murphy (2007), regarding the cheapening of apology through overuse and insincerity, particularly by public figures. Also see Duff (2003) for numerous questions about the form of an apology; Daly (2008a) regarding the difficulty of achieving a sincere apology; Radzik (2007) on the acceptance or rejection of apology; and Strang (2003) regarding the healing effect of apology in a restorative justice encounter.

viii Dignan describes a caution as "[a] formal disposal of a criminal case, consisting of a warning that is administered to an offender in person by a senior police officer in uniform, usually in a police station. The measure is an alternative to further criminal proceedings and therefore does not involve either prosecution or the courts" (2005, p. 196).

REFERENCES

Abramson, A., et al. (2003). *A charter for practice of restorative justice.* Retrieved September 17, 2009, from www.sfu.ca/cfrj/fulltext/charter.pdf

Achilles, M., & Stutzman-Amstutz, L. (2008). Responding to the needs of victims: What was promised, what has been delivered. In D. Sullivan & L. Tifft (Eds.), *Handbook of restorative justice* (pp. 211–220). London: Routledge.

Acker, J. R. (2008). Hearing the victim's voice amidst the cry for capital punishment. In D. Sullivan & L. Tifft (Eds.), *Handbook of restorative justice* (pp. 246–260). London: Routledge.

Acorn, A. (2004). *Compulsory compassion: A critique of restorative justice.* Vancouver, BC: The UBC Press.

Archibald, B. (2008). Let my people go: Human capital investment and community capacity building via meta/regulation in a deliberative democracy—a modest contribution for criminal law and restorative justice. *Cardozo Journal of International and Corporate Law, 16,* 1–53.

Barker, V. (2007). The politics of pain: A political institutionalist analysis of crime victims' moral protests. *Law and Society Review, 41,* 619–647.

Bazemore, G., & Ellis, L. (2007). Evaluation of restorative justice. In G. Johnstone and D. W. Van Ness (Eds.), *Handbook of restorative justice* (pp. 397–425). Cullumpton, Devon, UK: Willan Publishing.

Bazemore, G. & Schiff, M. (2005). *Juvenile justice reform and restorative justice: Building theory and policy from practice*. Cullumpton, Devon, UK: Willan Publishing.

Beck, E., Britto, S., & Andrews, A. (2007). *In the shadow of death*. Oxford: Oxford University Press.

Bowen, H., Boyack, J., & Marshall, C. (2004). How does restorative justice ensure good practice? In H. Zehr & B. Toews (Eds.), *Critical issues in restorative justice* (pp. 265–276). Monsey, NY: Criminal Justice Press.

Bradt, L., & Bouverne-De Bie, M. (2009). Victim offender mediation as a social work practice. *International Social Work, 52*(2), 181–193.

Braithwaite, J. (1989). *Crime, shame, and reintegration*. Cambridge, UK: Cambridge University Press.

Braithwaite, J. (2000). *Standards for restorative justice*. United Nations Crime Congress. Ancillary meeting. Vienna, Austria. Retrieved May 12, 2010, from http://www.restorativejustice.org/10fulltext/braithwaite

Braithwaite, J. (2003). Principles of restorative justice. In A. von Hirsch, J. Roberts, A. E. Bottoms, K. Roach, & M. Schiff (Eds.), *Restorative justice & criminal justice: Competing or reconcilable paradigms?* (pp. 157–176). Oxford: Hart Publishing.

Burr, R. (2003). Litigating with victim impact testimony: The serendipity that has come from Payne v. Tennessee. *Cornell Law Review, 88*(2), p. 517.

Bussler, D. (2004). Are 98.6 degrees enough?: Reflections on restorative justice training credentialing. *Hamline Journal of Public Law & Policy, 25*, 335–346.

Christie, N. (1977). Conflicts as property. *The British Journal of Criminology, 17*, 1–15.

Coben, J. & Harley, P. (2004). Intentional conversations about restorative justice, mediation, and the practice of law. *Hamline Journal of Public Law & Policy, 25*, 235–334.

Cunneen, C. (2004). What are the implications of restorative justice's use of indigenous traditions? In H. Zehr & B. Toews (Eds.), *Critical issues in restorative justice* (pp. 345–354). Monsey, NY: Criminal Justice Press.

Cutting Edge Law. (n.d.) Judge Tracy McCooey: Maverick in problem-solving courts and restorative justice. Retrieved September 17, 2009, from http://cuttingedgelaw.com/video/judge-tracy-mccooey-maverick-problem-solving-courts-and-restorative-justice

Daly, K. (2003a). Making variation a virtue: Evaluating the potential and limits of restorative justice. In E. Weitkamp & H. Kerner (Eds.), *Restorative justice in context: International practice and directions* (pp. 23–50). Cullumpton, Devon, UK: Willan Publishing.

Daly, K. (2003b). Restorative justice: The real story. In G. Johnstone (Ed.), *A restorative justice reader: Texts, sources, context* (pp. 363–397). Cullumpton, Devon, UK: Willan Publishing.

Daly, K. 2005. A tale of two studies: restorative justice from a victim's perspective. In Elliott, E. & Gordon, R. (Eds.) (pp. 153–174). Cullumpton, Devon, UK: Willan Publishing.

Daly, K. (2008a). The limits of restorative justice. In D. Sullivan & L. Tifft (Eds.), *Handbook of restorative justice* (pp. 134–145). London: Routledge.

Daly, K. (2008b). Seeking justice in the 21st century: Towards an intersectional politics of justice. In H. V. Miller (Ed.), *Restorative justice: From theory to practice: Vol. 11. Sociology of crime, law and deviance* (pp. 3–30). Bingley, UK: JAI Press.

Danieli, Y. (2008). Essential elements of healing after massive trauma: Complex needs voiced by victims/survivors. In D. Sullivan & L. Tifft (Eds.), *Handbook of restorative justice* (pp. 343–354). London: Routledge.

Delgado, R. (2000). Prosecuting violence: A colloquy on race, community, and justice. *Stanford Law Review, 52,* 751–775.

Dignan, J. (2005). *Understanding victims and restorative justice.* New York: Open University Press.

Domestic Violence Surrogate Dialogue. (n.d.) Retrieved September 3, 2009, from http://www.dvsdprogram.com/

Doolin, K. (2007). But what does it mean? Seeking definitional clarity in restorative justice. *Journal of Criminal Law, 71*(5), 427–440.

Dorne, C. K. (2008). *Restorative justice in the United States.* Upper Saddle River, NJ: Pearson Prentice Hall.

Duff, R. A. (2003). Restorative punishment and punitive restoration. In G. Johnstone (Ed.), *A restorative justice reader: Texts, sources, context* (pp. 382–397). Cullumpton, Devon, UK: Willan Publishing.

Dyck, D. (2004). Are we—practitioners, advocates—practicing what we preach? In H. Zehr & B. Toews (Eds.), *Critical issues in restorative justice* (pp. 277–292). Monsey, NY: Criminal Justice Press.

Ellison, G. and Shirlow, P. (2008). From war to peace: Informalism, restorative justice and conflict transformation in Northern Ireland. In H. V. Miller (Ed.), *Restorative justice: From theory to practice: Vol. 11. Sociology of crime, law and deviance* (pp. 31–58). Bingley, UK: JAI Press.

Erbe, C. (2004). What is the role of professionals in restorative justice? In H. Zehr & B. Toews (Eds.), *Critical issues in restorative justice* (pp. 293–302). Monsey, NY: Criminal Justice Press.

Farbiarz, R. E. (2008). Victim-offender mediation: A new way of disciplining America's doctors. *Journal of Medicine and Law, 12,* 359–386.

Geske, J. (2005). Why do I teach restorative justice to law students? *Marquette Law Review, 89*(2), 327–334.

Geske, J. and McCanse, I. (2008). Neighborhoods healed through restorative justice. *American Bar Association Dispute Resolution Magazine, 15,* 16–17.

Gil, D. G. (2008). Toward a "radical" paradigm of restorative justice. In D. Sullivan & L. Tifft (Eds.), *Handbook of restorative justice* (pp. 499–511). London: Routledge.

Gustafson, D. (2004). Is restorative justice taking too few, or too many risks? In H. Zehr & B. Toews (Eds.), *Critical issues in restorative justice* (pp. 303–314). Monsey, NY: Criminal Justice Press.

Hadley, M. L. (Ed.). (2001). *The spiritual roots of restorative justice.* Albany, NY: State University of New York Press.

Hadley, M. L. (2008). Spiritual foundations of restorative justice. In D. Sullivan & L. Tifft (Eds.), *Handbook of restorative justice* (pp. 174–187). London: Routledge.

Harris, N. & Maruna, S. (2008). Shame, sharing and restorative justice: A critical appraisal. In D. Sullivan & L. Tifft (Eds.), *Handbook of restorative justice* (pp. 452–462). London: Routledge.

Herman, S. (2004). Is restorative justice possible without a parallel system for victims? In H. Zehr & B. Toews (Eds.), *Critical issues in restorative justice* (pp. 75–84). Monsey, NY: Criminal Justice Press.

Hudson, B. (2003). Victims and offenders. In A. von Hirsch, J. Roberts, A. E. Bottoms, K. Roach, & M. Schiff (Eds.), *Restorative justice & criminal justice: Competing or reconcilable paradigms?* (pp. 177–194). Oxford: Hart Publishing.

Johnstone, G. (2002). *Restorative justice: Ideas, values, debates.* Cullumpton, Devon, UK: Willan Publishing.

Johnstone, G. (2003). (Ed.). *A restorative justice reader: Texts, sources, context.* Cullumpton, Devon, UK: Willan Publishing.

Johnstone, G. (2004). How, and in what terms, should restorative justice be conceived? In H. Zehr & B. Toews (Eds.), *Critical issues in restorative justice* (pp. 5–16). Monsey, NY: Criminal Justice Press.

Johnstone, G. (2008). The agendas of the restorative justice movement. In H. V. Miller (Ed.), *Restorative justice: From theory to practice: Vol. 11. Sociology of crime, law and deviance* (pp. 59–80). Bingley, UK: JAI Press.

Johnstone, G., & Van Ness, D. W. (Eds.). (2007). *Handbook of restorative justice.* Cullumpton, Devon, UK: Willan Publishing.

King, R. (2007). Restorative justice: How law schools can help heal their communities. *Fordham Urban Law Journal, 34,* 1285–1298.

Lederach, J. P. (2003). *The little book of conflict transformation.* Intercourse, PA: Good Books.

Leverton, W. R. (2008). The case for best practice standards in restorative justice processes. *American Journal of Trial Advocacy, 31,* 501–521.

Mackay, R. E. (2006). The institutionalization of principles in restorative justice—a case study from the UK. In I. Aertsen, T. Daems, & L. Robert (Eds.), *Institutionalizing restorative justice* (pp. 194–215). Cullumpton, Devon, UK: Willan Publishing.

Marshall, T. F. (2008). Restorative justice: An overview. In G. Johnstone (Ed.), *A restorative justice reader: Texts, sources, context* (pp. 28–45). Cullumpton, Devon, UK: Willan Publishing.

Maruna, S. (2001). *Making good: How ex-convicts reform and rebuild their lives.* Washington, D.C.: American Psychological Association.

Matthews, R. (2006). Reintegrative shaming and restorative justice: Reconciliation or divorce? In I. Aertsen, T. Daems, & L. Robert (Eds.), *Institutionalizing restorative justice* (pp. 237–260). Cullumpton, Devon, UK: Willan Publishing.

Maxwell, G. (2008). Crossing cultural boundaries: Implementing restorative justice in international and indigenous contexts. In H. V. Miller (Ed.), *Restorative justice: From theory to practice: Vol. 11. Sociology of crime, law and deviance* (pp. 81–98). Bingley, UK: JAI Press.

Maxwell, G., & Morris, A. (2004). What is the place of shame in restorative justice? In H. Zehr & B. Toews (Eds.), *Critical issues in restorative justice* (pp. 133–142). Monsey, NY: Criminal Justice Press.

McCold, P. (2008). The recent history of restorative justice: Mediation, circles, and conferencing. In D. Sullivan & L. Tifft (Eds.), *Handbook of restorative justice* (pp. 23–51). London: Routledge.

McCullough, M. (2008). *Beyond revenge: The evolution of the forgiveness instinct.* San Francisco, CA: Jossey Bass.

McEvoy, K., & Eriksson, A. (2008). Restorative justice in transition: Ownership, leadership and "bottom-up" human rights. In D. Sullivan & L. Tifft (Eds.), *Handbook of restorative justice* (pp. 321–335). London: Routledge.

McRae, A., & Zehr, H. (2004). *The little book of family group conferences: New Zealand style.* Intercourse, PA: Good Books.

Mika, H. and Zehr, H. (2001). Restorative justice sign posts. *Conciliation Quarterly 20*(3): 11.

Mika, H. (2002). Evaluation as peacebuilding?: Transformative values, processes, and outcomes. *Contemporary Justice Review, 5*(4), 339–349.

Mika, H., Achilles, M., Halbert, E., Amstutz, L. S., & Zehr, H. (2004). *Taking victims and their advocates seriously: A listening project.* Akron, PA: Mennonite Central Committee Office on Crime and Justice.

Miller, H. V. (2008). Restorative justice and youth courts: A new approach to delinquency prevention. In H. V. Miller (Ed.), *Restorative justice: From theory to practice: Vol. 11. Sociology of crime, law and deviance* (pp. 189–208). Bingley, UK: JAI Press.

Miller, J. M., Gibson, C. L., and Byrd, J. (2008). Getting beyond the liberal feel-good: Toward and accountability-based theoretical research program for restorative justice. In H. V. Miller (Ed.), *Restorative justice: From theory to practice: Vol. 11. Sociology of crime, law and deviance* (pp. 261–277). Bingley, UK: JAI Press.

Ministry of Justice. (2004, May). *Restorative justice in New Zealand: Best practice.* Issue Brief No. 0-478-20189-3. Wellington, New Zealand.

Moore, C. (2002). Restorative justice when the system is the offender. *Conciliation Quarterly, 20,* 4–6.

Moore, D. B., & O'Connell, T. A. (2003). Family conferencing in Wagga Wagga: A communitarian model of justice. In G. Johnstone (Ed.), *A restorative justice reader: Texts, sources, context* (pp. 212–224). Cullumpton, Devon, UK: Willan Publishing.

Munford, L. T. (2007). The peacemaker test: Designing legal rights to reduce legal warfare. *Harvard Negotiation Law Review, 12,* 377–403.

Murphy, J. G. (2007). Mercy and clemency: Remorse, apology, and mercy. *The Ohio State Journal of Criminal Law, 4,* 423–442.

National Institute of Justice. (2007). Working definitions of restorative justice. In *Restorative justice.* Retrieved September 10, 2009, from http://www.ojp.usdoj.gov/nij/topics/courts/restorative-justice/definitions1.htm

O'Hear, M. M. (2007). Bargaining in the shadow of the law—The relationship between plea bargaining and criminal code structure: Victims, apology, and restorative justice in criminal procedure: Plea bargaining and victims: From consultation to guidelines. *Marquette Law Review, 91,* 323–388.

Pavlich, G. (2003). Deconstructing restoration: The promise of restorative justice. In G. Johnstone (Ed.), *A restorative justice reader: Texts, sources, context* (pp. 451–460). Cullumpton, Devon, UK: Willan Publishing.

Peachey, D. E. (2003). The Kitchener experiment. In G. Johnstone (Ed.), *A restorative justice reader: Texts, sources, context* (pp. 178–186). Cullumpton, Devon, UK: Willan Publishing.

Poulson, B. (2003). A third voice: A review of empirical research on the psychological outcomes of restorative justice. *Utah Law Review, 1,* 167–203.

Pranis, K. (2005). *The little book of circle processes.* Intercourse, PA: Good Books.

Pranis, K. (2007a). Healing and accountability in the criminal justice system: Applying restorative justice processes in the workplace. *Cardozo Journal of Conflict Resolution, 8,* 659–668.

Pranis, K. (2007b). Restorative values. In G. Johnstone and D. W. Van Ness (Eds.), *Handbook of restorative justice* (pp. 59–74). Cullumpton, Devon, UK: Willan Publishing.

Pranis, K., Stuart, B., and Wedge, M. (2003). *Peacemaking circles: From crime to community.* St. Paul, MN: Living Justice Press.

Pratt, J. (2006). Beyond evangelical criminology: The meaning and significance of restorative justice. In I. Aertsen, T. Daems, & L. Robert (Eds.), *Institutionalizing restorative justice* (pp. 44–67). Cullumpton, Devon, UK: Willan Publishing.

Prison Fellowship International. (n.d.). Definition of restorative justice. In Restorative Justice Online. Retrieved May 12, 2010, from www.restorativejustice.org/university-classroom/01introduction/tutorial-introduction-to-restorative-justice/lesson-1-definition/lesson-1-definition

Radzik, L. (2007). Making amends. In G. Johnstone and D.W. Van Ness (Eds.), *Handbook of restorative justice* (pp. 192–208). Cullumpton, Devon, UK: Willan Publishing.

Rakieten, E. (Executive Producer). (2004, October 25). *The Oprah Winfrey Show* [Television broadcast]. Chicago: American Broadcasting Company.

Raye, B. (2004). How do culture, class, and gender affect the practice of restorative justice? In H. Zehr & B. Toews (Eds.), *Critical issues in restorative justice* (pp. 329–340). Monsey, NY: Criminal Justice Press.

Raye, B. E., & Warner Roberts, A. (2007). Restorative processes. In G. Johnstone and D.W. Van Ness (Eds.), *Handbook of restorative justice* (pp. 211–227). Cullumpton, Devon, UK: Willan Publishing.

Robinson, P. H. (2003). The virtues of restorative processes, the vices of "restorative justice." *Utah Law Review, 1,* 375–388.

Roche, D. (2001). The evolving definition of restorative justice. *Contemporary Justice Review, 4,* 3–4, 341–353.

Roche, D. (2003). *Accountability in restorative justice.* New York: Oxford University Press.

Schiff, M. (2003). Models, challenges and the promise of restorative conferencing strategies. In A. von Hirsch, J. Roberts, A. E. Bottoms, K. Roach, & M. Schiff (Eds.), *Restorative justice & criminal justice: Competing or reconcilable paradigms?* (pp. 315–338). Oxford: Hart Publishing.

Schiff, M. (2007). Satisfying the needs and interests of stakeholders. In G. Johnstone and D.W. Van Ness (Eds.), *Handbook of restorative justice* (pp. 228–246). Cullumpton, Devon, UK: Willan Publishing.

Shapland, J. (2003). Restorative justice and criminal justice: Just responses to crime? In A. von Hirsch, J. Roberts, A. E. Bottoms, K. Roach, & M. Schiff (Eds.), *Restorative justice & criminal justice: Competing or reconcilable paradigms?* (pp. 195–218). Oxford: Hart Publishing.

Sharpe, S. (2004). How large should the restorative justice "tent" be? In H. Zehr & B. Toews (Eds.), *Critical issues in restorative justice* (pp. 17–32). Monsey, NY: Criminal Justice Press.

Sharpe, S. (2007). The idea of reparation. In G. Johnstone and D. W. Van Ness (Eds.), *Handbook of restorative justice* (pp. 24–40). Cullumpton, Devon, UK: Willan Publishing.

Sherman, L. W., & Strang, H. (2007). *Restorative justice: The evidence.* London: The Smith Institute.

Simpson, M. (2009). Museums and restorative justice: Heritage, repatriation and cultural education. *Museums International, 61*(1–2), 121–129.

Skelton, A., & Frank, C. (2004). How does restorative justice address human rights and due process issues? In H. Zehr & B. Toews (Eds.), *Critical issues in restorative justice* (pp. 203–214). Monsey, NY: Criminal Justice Press.

Skelton, A., & Sekhonyane, M. (2007). Human rights and restorative justice. In G. Johnstone and D. W. Van Ness (Eds.), *Handbook of restorative justice* (pp. 580–597). Cullumpton, Devon, UK: Willan Publishing.

Strang, H. (2002). *Repair or revenge: Victims and restorative justice.* New York: Oxford University Press.

Strang, H. (2003). Justice for victims of young offenders: The centrality of emotional harm and restoration. In G. Johnstone (Ed.), *A restorative justice reader: Texts, sources, context* (pp. 286–293). Cullumpton, Devon, UK: Willan Publishing.

Strickland, C. Y., & Miller, S. (2007). Creative sentencing, restorative justice and environmental law: Responding to the Terra Nova FPSO oil spill. *Dalhousie Law Journal, 30,* 547–564.

Suffolk University. (2009). Center for restorative justice. Retrieved September 9, 2009, from http://www.suffolk.edu/college/1496.html

Sullivan, D., & Tifft, L. (2005). *Restorative justice: Healing the foundations of our everyday lives* (2nd ed.). Monsey, NY: Willow Tree Press.

Sullivan, D., & Tifft, L. (Eds.). (2008). *Handbook of restorative justice.* London: Routledge.

Takagi, P., & Shank, G. (2004). Critique of restorative justice. *Social Justice, 31*(3), 147–163.

Umbreit, M. (2001). *The handbook of victim offender mediation: An essential guide to practice and research.* San Francisco: Jossey-Bass.

Umbreit, M., Vos, B., Coates, R. B., & Lightfoot, E. (2007). Restorative justice: An empirically grounded movement facing many opportunities and pitfalls. *Cardozo Journal of Conflict Resolution, 8,* 511–551.

United Nations' Universal Declaration of Human Rights. (1948). Retrieved September 3, 2009, from http://www.un.org/en/documents/udhr/

Van Ness, D. W. (2003). Proposed basic principles on the use of restorative justice. In A. von Hirsch, J. Roberts, A. E. Bottoms, K. Roach, & M. Schiff (Eds.), *Restorative justice & criminal justice: Competing or reconcilable paradigms?* (pp. 157–176). Oxford: Hart Publishing.

Van Ness, D. W., & Strong, K. H. (2006). *Restoring justice: An introduction to restorative justice* (3rd ed.). Cincinnati, OH: Anderson Publishing Co.

VOCARE. (n.d.) *Victims, offenders, and communities—A restorative experience.* Retrieved September 17, 2009, from http://www.doc.state.mn.us/crimevictim/documents/VOCARE%20Brochure.pdf

von Hirsch, A., Roberts, J., Bottoms, A. E., Roach, K., & Schiff, M. (Eds.). (2003). *Restorative justice & criminal justice: Competing or reconcilable paradigms?* Oxford: Hart Publishing.

Wachtel, T., & McCold, P. (2001). Restorative justice in everyday life. In H. Strang & J. Braithwaite (Eds.), *Restorative justice and civil society* (pp. 114–129). Cambridge, UK: Cambridge University Press.

Waldman, E. (2007). Restorative justice and the pre-conditions for grace: Taking victim's needs seriously. *Cardozo Journal of Conflict Resolution, 9,* 91–244.

Walgrave, L. (Ed.). (2002). *Restorative justice and the law.* Cullumpton, Devon, UK: Willan Publishing.

Walgrave, L. (2003). Imposing restoration instead of inflicting pain. In A. von Hirsch, J. Roberts, A. E. Bottoms, K. Roach, & M. Schiff (Eds.), *Restorative justice & criminal justice: Competing or reconcilable paradigms?* (pp. 61–78). Oxford: Hart Publishing.

Walklate, S. (2008). Changing boundaries of the "victim" in restorative justice: So who is the victim now? In D. Sullivan & L. Tifft (Eds.), *Handbook of restorative justice* (pp. 273–285). London: Routledge.

Yarn, D., & Jones, G. (in press). A biological approach to understanding resistance to apology, forgiveness, and reconciliation in group conflict. *Law and Contemporary Problems.*

Zehr, H. (1995). *Changing lenses: A new focus for crime and justice* (1st ed.). Scottdale, PA: Herald Press.

Zehr, H. (2001). *Transcending: Reflections of crime victims.* Intercourse, PA: Good Books.

Zehr, H. (2002). *The little book of restorative justice.* Intercourse, PA: Good Books.

Zehr, H. (2005a). *Changing lenses: A new focus for crime and justice* (3rd ed.). Scottdale, PA: Herald Press.

Zehr, H. (2005b). Evaluation and restorative justice principles. In E. Elliot & R. Gordon (Eds.), *New directions in restorative justice.* Cullumpton, Devon, UK: Willan Publishing.

Zehr, H. (2006). Signposts and markers on a circuitous road: Standards and value in restorative justice. In Tie, W., Jülich, S., & Walters, V. (Eds.), *New frontiers in restorative justice: A reviewed selection of conference papers.* Auckland: Center for Justice and Peace Development.

Chapter Four

Restorative Justice Practice

ELIZABETH BECK AND ANDREA WOOD

Restorative justice proposes the possibility of healing, transcendence, and transformation following crime, and in order to support such outcomes, a restorative approach to crime introduces new questions. How can healing occur for victims and offenders? How might the community take a more active role in addressing the issues of its members? How can communities heal from crime? These questions require more than a change of perspective; they also necessitate the development and use of new processes and forms of interaction.

This chapter will describe four processes used in restorative justice efforts: Victim–Offender Dialogues, Family Group Conferences, Circles, and Truth Commissions. While these processes are often used in the aftermath of crime, all of them can be adapted to address wrongdoing in a number of other contexts. In this chapter, we explore restorative justice practices and their foundational principles in order to assist social workers and other human service providers, peacemakers, and individuals in incorporating these techniques and values into their work. As seen in Chapter 3, the discussion of what constitutes restorative justice has yet to be solidified. For example, Truth and Reconciliation Commissions are not often included in discussions of restorative justice initiatives, but we decided to include them in this chapter because of a desire to provide a broad range of practices. Moreover, we support restorative justice theorist and practitioner Jenifer Llewellyn's claim that Truth and Reconciliation Commissions offer an important restorative response to violations of human rights (Llewllyn, 2006).

VICTIM–OFFENDER DIALOGUE[i]

Victim–Offender Dialogue is the most common and most publicly recognized restorative justice practice used in North America. It allows interested victims and offenders to meet in the presence of a trained facilitator to discuss a crime, its impact on their lives, and possibilities for repairing harm. It should be noted that the practice we are terming "Victim–Offender Dialogue" also may be referred to as a "meeting" or "mediation" (Umbreit, 2001; Wallis & Tudor, 2008).

During the dialogue, both the victim and offender share thoughts and feelings in an attempt to materially and symbolically address some of the harm caused by the criminal act. Victim–Offender Dialogue relies on engagement and interaction between the participants. The process generally consists of three distinct phases: pre-dialogue preparation, the dialogue, and follow-up. In all of these phases the victim and offender assume active roles—something not generally afforded them in criminal justice proceedings (Dzur, 2003; Leverton, 2007–2008). Since crime strips a victim of a sense of power and safety, the entire Victim–Offender Dialogue process works to support and empower the victim. Therefore, victims make decisions that guide the process and agenda of the dialogue (Umbreit, 2001; Umbreit, Coates, & Vos, 2007).

Although the process is victim-focused, an offender's needs also must be respected (Umbreit & Greenwood, 2000). David Doerfler (2003), an experienced facilitator of Victim–Offender Dialogues, uses the terms "victim-centered" and "offender-sensitive" to describe his work. During the dialogue, offenders have the opportunity to accept responsibility after learning the full impact of their actions, and they may agree to enter into a restitution plan, through which they work to repair the harm caused (Umbreit, 2001). While not necessary, forgiveness and reconciliation may occur between the parties (Zehr, 2002). Although positive outcomes are common, Victim–Offender Dialogues do have the potential to raise painful issues and thereby create retraumatization and, therefore, may pose risks to the victim or offender (Daly, 2002).

This examination of Victim–Offender Dialogue relies heavily on the evidence-based work of Dr. Mark Umbreit, the founding director of the Center for Restorative Justice & Peacemaking and a professor at the University of Minnesota's School of Social Work. Umbreit's work includes analysis of existing Victim–Offender Dialogue programs, as well as the creation of guidelines for conducting effective and appropriate dialogues. This section also draws upon the guidelines and suggestions offered by Barbara Tudor, a victim-offender development officer at West Midlands Probation Service, and Peter Wallis, a senior practitioner with Oxfordshire Youth Offending Service.

The Victim-Offender Dialogue Process

Pre-dialogue preparation

Programs that conduct Victim–Offender Dialogues are usually sponsored by community-based agencies, although they may also be run out of probation departments, churches, victim services agencies, or prosecuting attorneys' offices (Umbreit, 2001). The process begins when a case is referred to a program. A referral generally comes from a judge, probation officer, prosecutor, defense attorney, police officer, or victim advocate.[ii] Although particularly appropriate for crimes involving juvenile offenders, Victim–Offender Dialogue programs can also be effective in cases involving adult offenders (Umbreit, 2001). Each program has its own specific criteria for case selection, which often include the type of crime, age of the offender, and criminal history of the offender (Umbreit, 2001). Once the case has been accepted, a facilitator is assigned.

The facilitator first gathers all relevant and available information about the case, the offense, and the participants. This information may include a pre-sentence report, other relevant reports, any available assessment of the offender, the victim's personal statement, all referral information, and the participants' contact information, as well as any details regarding their culture, languages, or disabilities (Wallis & Tudor, 2008).

The facilitator initiates contact with the referred participants through an introductory letter. This letter allows the facilitator to indicate the referral source, introduce the program, and briefly describe restorative justice and the Victim–Offender Dialogue process. Through a follow-up phone call, the facilitator arranges individual meetings with the victim and offender. During these meetings, the facilitator further explains the dialogue process, learns more about the incident, identifies needs, and builds rapport with the participants (Umbreit, 2001). By showing interest in each participant's background and family and sharing basic personal information, the facilitator can create a relaxed atmosphere conducive to the positive exchange of information. When dealing with either a juvenile offender or victim, that individual's parents must be consulted prior to initiating contact (Bazemore & Schiff, 2001).

If the victim and offender express interest in participating in a dialogue, the facilitator begins preparing them for the meeting and brainstorming potential restitution options (Wallis & Tudor, 2008). The facilitator explains rules of confidentiality, and reminds the victim and offender that participation is voluntary (Leverton, 2007–2008; Umbreit, 2001; Victim Offender Mediation Association, 2006; Wallis & Tudor, 2008).[iii] Prior to meeting the victim, the offender must assume personal accountability for the offense and understand that the dialogue process will not benefit him or her in the court system (Umbreit, 2001; Wallis & Tudor, 2008).

The Dialogue

If both parties express a desire to meet and the facilitator believes that a face-to-face meeting will not be harmful for either participant, the facilitator schedules the dialogue (Umbreit et al., 2007).[iv] Although both parties need to agree on a neutral venue, the victim ultimately determines the dialogue's location, time, and date (Umbreit & Greenwood, 2000).

Both parties can choose to have support persons present during the dialogue, such as a family member, friend, neighbor, community leader, minister, teacher, or probation officer (Umbreit, 2001). Although these individuals may be given an opportunity to express their thoughts during the dialogue, they must understand their role as supportive observers. Optimally, each side would have roughly the same number of support persons present (Wallis & Tudor, 2008). Prior to the dialogue, the facilitator determines the seating arrangement to ensure that the victim and offender can directly communicate (Umbreit, 2001; Wallis & Tudor, 2008).

After all parties arrive, the facilitator begins with introductions, a brief welcome, and an opening statement. The opening statement allows the facilitator to set a positive tone for the dialogue through his or her language and words of encouragement for the participants (Szmania, 2006). The facilitator reviews the ground rules and basic structure of the meeting. Common ground rules include those that promote respectful communication, prohibit interruption, and permit participants to request a break at any point in the meeting (Umbreit, 2001; Umbreit et al., 2007). Next, the facilitator restates that everyone is present voluntarily and that the offender accepts responsibility for the crime. The facilitator also reinforces his or her participation as a neutral party. Following these remarks, the facilitator shifts to an active listening role, which demands "sensitive checking and an exploration of meanings, with care and consideration given to responses and options" (Wallis & Tudor, 2008, p. 17). The facilitator remains ready to intervene or offer guidance when necessary (Umbreit, 2001).

Following the introduction, both parties have the opportunity to describe their personal thoughts and feelings about the crime and its effect on their lives. Experts generally agree that the victim begins, although he or she must be given the choice of whether to speak first (Umbreit, 2001). After both parties have spoken, the facilitator ensures that neither party has any additional questions or comments before the support persons are given an opportunity to speak.

Following the exchange of descriptive information, the parties discuss possible actions or steps needed to address the harm and losses created by the crime. In this stage, the victim has the opportunity to summarize the loss, and each party shares ideas for repairing harm. Possible restitution options include monetary restitution (which cannot be more than the victim's material loss), community service hours, personal service activities (such as mowing a lawn or doing other yard work or housework), a donation to a charity, a written or verbal apology, attending a class or treatment program, or a form of creative restitution that might draw on the special skills or interests of the offender, such as creating a work of art (Umbreit, 2001).

Some Victim–Offender Dialogues generate a written contract or agreement that summarizes the restitution plan settled upon by both parties. The agreement includes details of the restitution arrangement and designates who will monitor the offender's progress in completing the agreement. Clear and concise, the agreement includes a note that both parties have contributed to the creation of the document and have agreed to its contents (Umbreit, 2001).

Follow-Up

Following the creation of the agreement, participants have an opportunity to speak again or ask further questions before the dialogue's conclusion. The facilitator may offer the possibility of a follow-up meeting if all issues have not been resolved, or to assess the fulfillment of the agreement (Umbreit, 2001). Whether or not another meeting occurs, the facilitator contacts each party soon after the dialogue to gauge participant satisfaction and answer any new questions. The agreement is monitored, and the facilitator notifies both parties at its completion (Umbreit, 2001).

Facilitation

A Victim–Offender Dialogue may be conducted by a single facilitator or a team of facilitators.[v] A trained facilitator plays a key role throughout an effective Victim–Offender Dialogue (Szmania, 2006). The facilitator does not take an active, settlement-driven approach, but rather assumes a nondirective role and works to provide information, facilitate discussion, and protect against further harm and revictimization (Leverton, 2007–2008; Umbreit, 2001). By maintaining impartiality—or what some restorative justice practitioners refer to as "balanced partiality"—and actively listening to each party, the facilitator works to promote a safe environment that allows for constructive communication between victim and offender (Bradt & Bouverne-De Bie, 2009; Victim Offender Mediation Association, 2006).

Because a mishandled dialogue can have serious consequences, restorative justice practitioners recommend extensive training for facilitators before they participate in any portion of the process. Umbreit (2001) recommends 32 to 40 hours of facilitator training, including working with an experienced facilitator in Victim–Offender Dialogue settings through a case apprenticeship. When Victim–Offender Dialogue is used in cases that involve more serious and violent offenses, advanced training is necessary. Cases involving domestic violence present unique obstacles and hazards, and facilitators working with these types of cases also require additional instruction (Zehr, 2002).

Training allows a facilitator to develop skills in communication, problem-solving, and negotiation. An effective facilitator communicates simply and avoids jargon. He or she works with participants to strengthen their communication skills. During the dialogue, the facilitator utilizes body language to promote eye contact and direct communication between the parties. Differences in the cultural backgrounds of the victim, offender, and facilitator could lead to miscommunication, feelings of being misunderstood, or even revictimization. The facilitator must be aware of these differences and prepare the participants by helping them understand the viewpoints and different communication styles of the other involved parties (Victim Offender Mediation Association, 2006). The facilitator must also offer equal opportunities for communicating to all parties, including those who might not speak English as a first language, those with literacy challenges, and those with disabilities (Umbreit, 2001; Wallis & Tudor, 2008).

An effective facilitator allows participants to express emotion as long as their communication does not become disrespectful or involve a personal attack. Given the nature of the meeting, silences should be expected, and strong facilitators do not try to fill gaps in conversation (Szmania, 2006). An experienced facilitator calls for appropriate breaks to address issues as they arise, but also understands that conflicts may not be fully resolved during the meeting (Wallis & Tudor, 2008).

Victim–Offender Dialogue offers important opportunities for victims, offenders, and connected support persons to face the harm created by a crime. By encouraging direct engagement and the honest sharing of thoughts and feelings between victim and offender, the dialogue process may begin to repair some harm (Bradt & Bouverne-De Bie, 2009; Umbreit, 2001).

FAMILY GROUP CONFERENCE

Family Group Conference is a restorative process that supports families in decision-making and interaction. It is generally used in what may appear to be two dissimilar situations: when a youth has committed a crime, and in cases of child protection. In both cases, a Family Group Conference brings together juveniles, parents/guardians, extended family members (kin or otherwise), social service professionals, community members, and other stakeholders to make decisions with and about the family (Bazemore & Schiff, 2001; Bazemore & Schiff, 2005; Holland & O'Neill, 2006; Johnstone, 2002; Lubin, 2009; MacRae & Zehr, 2004; Merkel-Holguin, 2000; Pennell & Burford, 1994).

Although Family Group Conference occurs throughout the world, it is primarily associated with New Zealand and that country's passage of the Children, Young Persons, and Their Families Act in 1989. This act sought to redress the overrepresentation of the Maori as offenders in New Zealand's criminal justice system by incorporating Maori values and beliefs into that system. These values include: 1) recognizing the importance of why a crime occurred; 2) valuing the extended family as part of a system of care that holds responsibility for its members; 3) supporting healing following an offense, and; 4) acknowledging that the Western system of justice undermines the young people who pass through it. The Children, Young Persons, and Their Families Act legislated the use of Family Group Conference in cases of juvenile crime and child protection and created the new positions of Care and Protection Coordinator and Youth Justice Coordinator (Chandler & Giovannucci, 2004; Connolly, 2006; Love, 2000; MacRae & Zehr, 2004).

In this section, we describe the process of the Family Group Conference in criminal and child welfare matters. For criminal matters, we examine the New Zealand process and rely on the writings of Allan MacRae and Howard Zehr (2004). We also incorporate the practice models associated with the International Institute for Restorative Practices, which has developed practice techniques and training modules for Family Group Conference based on work begun in Wagga Wagga, New South Wales (Moore & McDonald, 2000; O'Connell, Wachtel, & Wachtel, 1999).

The Family Group Conference is being used in child protective cases in communities across North America, and several academics have played important roles in developing and examining these models. An early pioneer is Joan Pennell, director of the North Carolina State School of Social Work, who wrote Chapter 9. Casey Family Programs, the American Humane Association, and the Annie E. Casey Foundation support Family Group Conference in child welfare cases through research, funding, training, or programmatic assistance (Adams & Chandler, 2002; Chandler & Giovannucci, 2004; Connolly, 2006; Merkel-Holguin, Nixon, & Burford, 2003; Pennell, 2006; Waites, Macgowan, Pennell, Carlton-LaNey, & Weil, 2004).

Conference Process

When a Family Group Conference is initiated, a coordinator is assigned. Whether in cases of crime or child welfare, prior to the conference, the coordinator meets with family members to ensure that a conference is an appropriate next step and then works to prepare them for it.[vi] The coordinator also arranges the conference, which involves inviting participants, informing them about the process, and selecting a site. During this preparation phase, the coordinator asks the family if they would like to include an opening ceremony or prayer in the conference and, if they do, asks them to select the content (MacRae & Zehr, 2004).

The actual conference is broken into four stages: an opening, information sharing, deliberations and agreement, and a closing. When the Family Group Conference commences, the coordinator thanks everyone for coming, makes introductions, reviews the agenda, and establishes guidelines (Baffour, 2006; MacRae & Zehr, 2004; Moore & McDonald, 2000; Olson, 2009; Pennell, 2006).

Information sharing is the second stage of the conference. In a New Zealand-style case in which a crime has been committed, a police officer reads a summary of the facts of the case, and the offender must acknowledge responsibility. In other nations, the summary may be read by an official other than a police officer. Following the summary, victims who have chosen to participate speak, and if other victims have submitted written statements, these are then read aloud.[vii] Victims generally discuss the impact of the crime on their lives. The coordinator then summarizes the victim's initial comments. Next the offender explains *why* he or she committed the crime. The victim can ask questions of the offender and his or her family members (Baffour, 2006; MacRae & Zehr, 2004; Moore & McDonald, 2000; Olson, 2009).

Once the exchange is complete, the coordinator proceeds to the third phase of the family group conference, providing the group with information about their deliberations and the formation of a plan to address the issue and move forward. After this explanation, a break is taken for refreshments before the family begins private deliberations. In a New Zealand-style conference, the family can invite anyone they choose to participate in these deliberations. Following the private deliberations, the family presents an initial draft of an agreement, which often includes an apology, community service, restitution, a plan for treatment or support (such as drug or alcohol rehabilitation), an agreement to seek training, or a commitment to complete school. The initial agreement is negotiated by the participants until a consensus forms regarding the content of the agreement, which is then recorded. The Family Group Conference concludes with a closing ceremony and an evaluation of the process by the participants (Baffour, 2006; Connolly, 2006; MacRae & Zehr, 2004; Moore & McDonald, 2000; Olson, 2009).

Conference Process and Considerations for Child Welfare

When a Family Group Conference is held in response to a child welfare matter, it tends to follow the general procedures described above. However, because the safety of the child is the first consideration in all cases of abuse and neglect, additional procedures are implemented. In New Zealand, upon an accusation of abuse or neglect, a social worker is assigned to the case. The social worker determines if the child is in danger and if his or her immediate needs, such as medical care and education, are being met (Adams & Chandler, 2004; Pennell & Burford, 2000; Pennell, 2006; O'Connell, Wachtel, & Wachtel, 2009).

In order to ensure the safety of children, some programs in the United States have chosen to use Family Group Conference as part of a comprehensive child abuse and neglect *prevention* strategy. In these cases, a Family Group Conference is not called in cases of child abuse and neglect, but rather is called for the purpose of garnering additional supports for children. For example, many child welfare agencies employ family team meetings, which resemble conferences, but are called to support struggling families by formalizing a strategy in which extended family members, the community, or service providers offer resources to a family. These meetings also can be called to address a specific problem. Sometimes, the meeting may address an issue stemming from the child's behavior, such as truancy; other times, the problem may relate to parental behavior, such as absence. The family team decision-making model may be used by child protective service workers to make decisions about child placement, including permanency planning in cases of termination of parental rights (Adams & Chandler, 2004; Pennell, 2006; Pennell & Burford, 2000).

Coordinator Role and Skills

The coordinator's skills are critical to the outcome of a Family Group Conference (Merkel-Holguin et al., 2003). All coordinators must have received instruction in Family Group Conference, and many hold degrees in social work. It is important that coordinators be skilled mediators, have strong listening skills, and be able to juggle logistics. Additionally, coordinators will need to know how to develop additional resources with the family and forge partnerships with agencies and individuals within the community and the family (Connolly, 2006; Hudson & Burford, 2000; MacRae & Zehr, 2004; Olson, 2009).

Prior to convening the Family Group Conference, the coordinator will have spent time working with the offenders, the victims, and the community. In cases where a crime was committed, the coordinator will ensure that the offender admits his or her wrongdoing and explore options for repair. The coordinator will also encourage the offender to understand the reasons for his or her actions. When working with victims, the coordinator emphasizes the voluntary nature of participation and encourages them to bring a support person to the conference. The coordinator also will let victims know that they can send a representative, submit a letter, or talk by phone if they prefer not to participate in person. The coordinator will make sure victims understand they can freely express their emotions, including anger, to offenders (Hudson & Burford, 2000; MacRae & Zehr, 2004; Olson, 2009).

In cases of family violence, the coordinator must ensure that all participants are safe, and that all family members are able to speak about their experience and needs without coercion from other members (Pennell, 2006). Additionally, the coordinator works with children to help them determine if they would like to participate (Holland & O'Neill, 2006). Although Family Group Conference may be used differently in cases involving child welfare and crime, at all times coordinators adhere to shared principles.

Core Commonalities of Family Group Conferencing

Numerous authors have identified common characteristics of the Family Group Conference (see for example, Chandler & Giovannucci, 2004; MacRae & Zehr, 2004; Merkel-Holguin, 2000; Olson, 2009; Pennell, 2006; O'Connell, Wachtel, & Wachtel, 2009; Waites et al., 2004). The following outlines many of these shared traits:

- Family Group Conference builds on the existing strengths that families have, and the process should further strengthen the family by building skills and resources.
- Partnerships and new types of relationships are built between professionals and the family.
- Family Group Conference supports democratic principles, as families and communities have a voice in decisions that affect them; decision-making power rests with individuals rather than official organizations.

- Family Group Conference is inclusive, as it encourages the attendance of extended family members and anyone else who has an interest in the child or the outcome of the conference.
- Family Group Conference is responsive to the culture of the family.
- The family has private time for deliberations.
- Consensus decision-making is encouraged.
- A coordinator is appointed who works with the family in organizing the conference. The coordinator does not represent an entity, such as the prosecutor or child welfare services, that might have a specific interest in the outcome of the conference.

In cases of crime, MacRae and Zehr (2004) have identified two additional principles that guide Family Group Conference procedures. The first is to develop agreements that avoid criminal proceedings whenever possible. The second is to craft an agreement that is not unduly restrictive. MacRae and Zehr (2004) believe restrictive or unfair sanctions undermine a youth's ability to see the consequences of his or her behavior. This belief is reflected in the New Zealand statute, which requires that the least restrictive option be used.

Drawing on existing strengths and resources within families and communities, Family Group Conference provides a space where issues can be constructively addressed, often resulting in positive changes for participants. MacRae attests to the potential impact of a Family Group Conference: "I have come to believe in family group conferencing because I have witnessed offenders having to face the impact that they have had on people. I have seen healing come when they acknowledge the hurt they have caused, and when they struggle to correct what they can and take responsibility for what they cannot" (p. 3–4).

Additional Applications

The use of Family Group Conference is moving beyond child protective services and juvenile crime. In this book, we look at two specific applications, with domestic violence cases and with aging, although the options for additional use are many. For example, the National Center on Addiction and Substance Abuse's CASA Safe Haven program is using family group conference as the basis for determining treatment plans for clients (O'Connor, Morgenstern, Gibson, & Nakashian, 2005).

CIRCLES

Like a Family Group Conference, the Circle can bring together an unlikely mix of people. A Circle involves listening and being heard, often with transforming results: "People who come in polarized and angry . . . find themselves working through problems in ways they couldn't anticipate" (Pranis, Stuart, & Wedge, 2003, p. 79). Circles are used to end disputes, address conflict, foster relationships, and strengthen community. Sometimes the Circle is designed to end in an agreement on a specific topic, while other times it is used only for purposes of discussion (Abramson & Moore, 2000; Bazemore & Umbreit, 1999; Pranis et al., 2003, Ross, 1996).

In this section, we explore the Circle process, and in so doing, we rely on Kay Pranis, a restorative justice practitioner and internationally recognized teacher; Judge Barry Stuart, who brought the Circle to courtrooms across Canada; and Mark Wedge, a mediator and circle keeper born into the Carcross/Tagish First Nation in the Yukon in Canada. These individuals, their First Nations teachers and mentors, and individuals like Robert Yazzie, a law professor and retired Chief Justice of the Navajo Nation, deserve much of the credit for bringing circles and indigenous processes to public consciousness, courtrooms, and the fields of criminal justice and social services.

Key Components

Pranis, Stuart, and Wedge believe that the Circle is effective because it is based on a specific process, held together by shared values, and guided by specific principles. In this section we explore each of the components of an effective Circle.

The Circle Process

Pranis et al. (2003) identified five components used in the Circle process: 1) ceremonies; 2) the talking piece; 3) the circle keeper; 4) guidelines; 5) and consensus decision-making.

A Circle is bookended by opening and closing ceremonies. The opening ceremony allows participants to shake off the day and become present in the circle. It can include reading a poem, listening to a drum, or sharing personal information. The closing ceremony is used to transition out of the Circle and honor the work that was done in the Circle (Pranis et al., 2003). While opening and closing ceremonies are always used, other ceremonies may be added during the Circle to mark a moment or to remind participants of specific values and goals.

Although the purpose of the Circle is to promote interaction, conventional dialogue seldom takes place. Rather than exchanging ideas and feelings through unstructured dialogue, the Circle uses a more directed method based on a *talking piece*. A talking piece is a designated secular object that holds meaning such as a feather, rock, or flower. Sitting in a circle, participants pass the talking piece in one direction, and only the person holding the talking piece is permitted to speak. This structure facilitates equality by creating an environment in which everyone has the opportunity to speak if desired (the talking piece can be passed without comment) and reminds individuals to limit their speaking time (Baldwin, 1994; Pranis et al., 2003). By eliminating distractions such as side jokes or conversations, debate, and tangents, the use of a talking piece supports deep listening and authentic responses; it sets a stage where individuals speak with intention and listen with attention (Baldwin, 1994).

The opening ceremony, the introduction of the talking piece, and the operation of the Circle are the responsibilities of the circle keeper. Rather than being facilitated, a Circle is *kept* by a trained circle keeper. Ideally circle keepers have participated in at least one multi-day training. During circle training, keepers learn skills and participate in a number of circle processes. By experiencing circle activities, participants see the rhythm and power of the Circle and have an opportunity to observe a practiced circle keeper.

During the Circle, circle keepers raise topics for discussion and pose questions for group members to explore. Keepers arrange and set up the space and summarize decisions. While they may intervene on rare occasions, keepers more often let the participants address any problems that arise. If a Circle is dealing with a difficult or painful issue, it is important that the Circle include more than one keeper (Pranis et al., 2003; Pranis, 2005).

Following the opening ceremony, the introduction of the talking piece, and steps like check-ins and introductions, the group takes on its first task, which is to identify guidelines. Using the talking piece, participants reach consensus on a set of guidelines that will govern their interactions. Typical guidelines include requests for respect, honesty, and confidentiality (Pranis et al., 2003).

Because a Circle moves decision-making from traditional holders of authority to community members and seeks to meet the needs of multiple stakeholders, including victims and offenders, consensus decision-making is critical. In a diverse group, reaching consensus will generally require that the talking piece be passed for several rounds of discussion. Pranis (2005) argues that this time is well spent, as consensus creates stronger and more effective resolution.

Shared Values

An effective Circle depends on respect for personal and shared values, and time to explore those values (Stuart, 2001). Participants may be asked to reach consensus about values that they both bring to the Circle themselves and seek from others in the Circle. Thalhuber and Thompson (2007) offer additional suggestions for this discussion. For example, participants may be asked to identify values they care about, explore why those values are important to them, and discuss their experiences with those values.

After talking with numerous people from many walks of life about their values, Pranis et al. (2003) identified 10 values they believe are universally respected: honesty, trust, humility, sharing, respect, inclusivity, empathy, courage, forgiveness, and love. It is not surprising that when circle participants explore the values that are important to them, many of these 10 values are included.

Principles

Pranis et al. (2003) also identified 13 principles that are important to creating a meaningful circle experience. These principles, which also reflect the values, ideas, and skills that the circle keeper brings to the Circle, are used by the circle keeper both in organizing the Circle and setting its tone. It is important to note that the principles are suggestions, and the keeper assesses whether and how to implement them. The principles include:

1) The facilitator brings circle values to his or her work (i.e. respect and humility);
2) The Circle includes representatives of all perspectives;
3) The Circle must be physically and otherwise accessible;
4) Everyone has an equal opportunity to participate;
5) Involvement in a Circle is voluntary;
6) Each person in the Circle speaks for him- or herself;
7) The Circle is guided by a shared vision;
8) A Circle is designed by its participants;
9) A Circle is flexible enough to honor the uniqueness of a situation;
10) A Circle takes a holistic approach that includes asking participants to engage with the physical, mental, emotional, and spiritual parts of themselves;
11) Respect for all is maintained;
12) The Circle includes a secular spiritual foundation defined as "connecting with the heart and embracing our shared human condition without denomination" (p. 66);
13) Accountability is fostered in the Circle (Pranis et al., 2003; Pranis, 2005).

While the principles initially provide guidance to the circle keeper, they also can become part of the shared values of the group. Bazemore (2000) explains that these circle principles have the additional benefit of fostering self-reliance and self-governance among participants.

Types of Circles

Circles are used in a variety of settings to achieve a range of objectives. The following sections explore an assortment of circle applications.

At least five types of circles aim to facilitate a focused interaction rather than address a problem. *Talking Circles* explore a particular topic. *Understanding Circles* are used to develop an appreciation of parts of a conflict or difficult situation. *Healing Circles* and *Celebration Circles* focus on a particular event or individual for the purpose of collectively exploring pain and accomplishment. *Support Circles* offer a collective method to assist an individual who is experiencing a difficult time (Pranis, 2005; Pranis et al., 2003).

Four types of circles seek to make a decision or address a problem by reaching an agreement (we introduce all four here but discuss Sentencing Circles in more detail). *Conflict Circles* seek to reconcile conflict between disputing parties by creating an agreement. *Community-Building Circle* strengthen community development by bringing together neighbors for the purpose of reaching an agreement on community-building activities. *Reintegration Circles* support individuals who have become estranged from the community, often as a result of incarceration.[viii] *Sentencing Circles* are used following a crime.

Sentencing Circles, the most widely used circles, are used in locations as disparate as Montgomery, Alabama, the Yukon in Canada, and New South Wales, New Zealand to address crime. In many cases, Sentencing Circles are a joint effort between the community and the criminal justice system (Pranis et al., 2003; Pranis, 2005)[ix].

Generally present in the Circle are the victim(s) and the offender(s), as well as their family members and actors from the criminal justice system such as the judge, prosecutor, defense attorney, and law enforcement representative. During a Sentencing Circle, many questions are explored, including what happened, why it happened, what impact it had, and what can be done to repair the harm and prevent further harm. Following the discussion, the group creates an agreement through consensus decision-making to address the issues. The agreement may include how to support the victim, criminal sentencing for the offender, and methods to support the offender (Bazemore & Schiff, 2005; Pranis, 2005). If consensus is not reached or if the agreement is not kept, the case returns to the criminal process. However, more often than not, agreements are reached and kept.

The effectiveness of a Circle in accomplishing its purpose is largely based on preparation. The first step is to determine which type of Circle is suitable for addressing the specific issue. Adequate time must be devoted to circle preparation; sometimes weeks or even months go into planning a specific Circle. Planning includes ensuring that all stakeholders are invited to the Circle, that they have received information about the circle process, and that the circle keeper understands the background of the case (Pranis, 2005; Pranis et al., 2003). The significance of preparation cannot be overstated. Bazemore and Schiff (2001) found instances of negative outcome following a circle process where preparation was inadequate (see also Van Ness & Strong, 2006).

Circles draw on Aboriginal values of harmony, balance, and peace in the community, as well as the Navajo peacemaking ceremony, as a means to address crime or harm. Zion and Yazzie (2006) explain that Navajo thought involves *nahat'a*, or planning, so questions following a crime or a misdeed include, "Where do we go from here?" By melding ancient customs with newer practices, the modern Circle allows individuals, families, and communities to address issues effectively in a collective manner[x] (Pranis, 2005; Winfree, 2002).

TRUTH COMMISSIONS

The Truth Commission is a way some countries have chosen to respond to their own histories of mass violence and abuse. A Truth Commission is a temporary, officially authorized body created to research and report on past violations of human rights within a particular country or related to a particular conflict.[xi] A Truth Commission works to uncover and publicize truth. By taking statements and testimony from victims, surviving family members, and perpetrators, a Truth Commission seeks to paint an accurate picture of events and offer a formal acknowledgement of abuses that may have been long silenced (Hayner, 1994).

Although not initially connected with restorative justice efforts, the number of truth commissions has grown dramatically since their initial appearance in the 1970s. Recently, a number of them have incorporated the principles and language of restorative justice into their work (Llewellyn, 2006; Zehr, 2002).[xii] This shift has illuminated the potential for restorative justice to make an impact in situations of mass violence and abuse (Llewellyn, 2006).

After the successful and widely publicized United Nations Truth Commission for El Salvador published its report in 1993, many countries undergoing political transitions began to consider truth commissions a viable tool to address previous abuses (Hayner, 1994). At present count, over 20 truth commissions have been established, with many of the earliest occurring in Latin America (Truth Commissions Project, n. d.). Although differing in sponsorship, organization, funding, procedure, and perceptions of success, truth commissions have occurred in numerous locations, including (but not limited to), Argentina, Chile, Uruguay, the Philippines, Chad, Bolivia, Zimbabwe, Ethiopia, Germany, Uganda, Rwanda, Guatemala, Malawi, and East Timor (Christie, 2000).

In this section, we offer an overview of the Truth Commission in general and a closer examination of the specific truth commissions established in South Africa and Greensboro, North Carolina. This section draws on the research and writing of Priscilla B. Hayner, an expert on truth commissions who cofounded the International Center for Transitional Justice (ICTJ), a human rights organization based in New York City which offers tools and support to countries and communities looking to confront large-scale atrocities or human rights abuse. Since its founding in 2001, the ICTJ has supported justice and truth-seeking institutions, governments, civil organizations, and international nongovernmental organizations in over 30 countries. Hayner serves as the Director of the ICTJ's Geneva office and its Peace and Justice Program (International Center for Transitional Justice, n. d.). We also make use of the writings of Archbishop Desmond Tutu, who chaired the South African Truth and Reconciliation Commission, perhaps the most public and internationally recognized of all the truth commissions.

Defining Truth Commissions

Hayner (1994) identifies four basic features of the Truth Commission. First, a Truth Commission only examines past events. Second, it seeks to address a larger picture of human rights abuses that occurred during a set period of time, rather than focusing on a specific event. Third, a Truth Commission exists only for a predetermined period of time, and it dissolves once it has submitted a final report on its findings. Finally, a Truth Commission is granted authority through which it can access information, have protection to delve into sensitive topics, and publish its report with credibility.[xiii]

Although Hayner's criteria outline some basic components, truth commissions often vary from this model. Hayner (1994) acknowledges that different circumstances allow for different forms of truth commissions and states that one "fixed model" does not exist for truth commissions. Rather, the unique circumstances of each country may call for "other new and innovative models" (p. 607).

A Truth Commission is charged with the monumental tasks of uncovering and acknowledging truth and building collective memory through investigation, collecting victim and perpetrator testimony, and publishing a report. As Christie (2000) explains, truth commissions "have the task of seeing the unseeable, revealing the concealed, and finding and remembering the obliterated" (p. 5). Many advocates of truth commissions believe that this establishment of truth plays an important role in preventing future abuses. By ensuring that an accurate history is remembered, a Truth Commission "allow[s] a society to learn from its past in order to prevent a repetition of such violence in the future" (Hayner, 1994, p. 607). Some truth commissions even provide specific recommendations for preventing similar abuses, which may include reforms of the military and police, judicial reform, or measures for victim reparation (Hayner, 1994). Beyond preventing future human rights abuses, a Truth Commission can also help heal rifts between groups of people, promote reconciliation, and even lead to forgiveness (Hayner, 1996).

Two Examples of Truth Commissions

South Africa

South Africa's Truth and Reconciliation Commission (TRC) investigated the atrocities that occurred during apartheid, a period of government-sanctioned segregation and concentration of power in the hands of the white elite (Christie, 2000). The South African government established the Truth and Reconciliation Commission in 1996 through the Promotion of National Unity and Reconciliation Act, as part of the negotiated settlement that ended apartheid and led to the election of Nelson Mandela as president. Mandated with investigating human rights abuses committed between 1960 and 1994, the Truth and Reconciliation Commission sought to paint a complete picture of the past abuse in order to "try to rehabilitate the civil and human dignity of the victims who had suffered as a result of that conflict" (Tutu, 1999, p. 91).

Guided by the principle of *ubuntu*, a term from the Nguni group of languages that refers to the core essence of humanity and the interconnectedness of all people, the South African Truth and Reconciliation Commission (TRC) emphasized healing and forgiveness. Archbishop Tutu described the purpose of the TRC thusly: "Our nation sought to rehabilitate and affirm the dignity and personhood of those who for so long had been silenced, had been turned into anonymous, marginalized ones. Now they would be able to tell their stories, they would remember, and in remembering would be acknowledged to be persons with an inalienable personhood" (Tutu, 1999, p. 30). To fulfill their mandate, the Commission created three committees composed of politically, religiously, ethnically, and professionally diverse individuals: the Human Rights Violations Committee, to investigate human rights abuses; the Amnesty Committee, to review amnesty applications; and the Reparation and Rehabilitation Committee, to propose recommendations for victim reparations to the government (Allan & Allan, 2000).

The Human Rights Violations Committee collected victim statements from approximately 22,000 individuals. About 10% of those who offered statements had the opportunity to testify in one of the public hearings (Graybill, 2002). During these hearings, the committee strove to be sensitive to the needs of the victims. For example, witnesses sat on the same level as the panel and could have a relative or other support person directly beside them during their testimony. Additionally, victims could offer their testimony in any of South Africa's official languages (Tutu, 1999). With an emphasis on openness and transparency, all hearings were filmed and broadcast in 11 languages by the South African Broadcasting Company (Tutu, 1999).

Rather than offer general or blanket amnesty like most earlier truth commissions, the TRC granted perpetrators of acts of violence amnesty in exchange for full disclosure of the act for which they requested amnesty (Llewellyn, 2006; Tutu, 1999). In instances of gross violations of human rights, applicants for amnesty had to appear at a public hearing and be cross-examined by a lawyer for the victim (Ntsebeza, 2000; Tutu, 1999). The Committee on Amnesty processed over 7,000 amnesty applications (Tutu, 1999). Once amnesty had been granted, no criminal proceedings could be brought against the offender and no further civil cases could be pursued (Allan & Allan, 2000). Although Tutu acknowledges that this procedure for granting amnesty "was not perfect," it did offer the best solution "that could be had in the circumstances—the truth in exchange for the freedom of the perpetrators" (Tutu, 1999, p. 58).

Although perpetrators of violence did not have to pay restitution, the act that established the TRC created a process whereby the South African government would offer reparations to victims (Tutu, 1999). The Reparation and Rehabilitation Committee made recommendations to the president concerning who should receive reparations and how much they should receive. Only after the president's proposals were approved by Parliament did the government present payment to the victims (Shea, 2000). The reparations process proved much slower than the speed at which perpetrators were granted amnesty, a troublesome fact for many victims and observers. Additionally, the amount of reparations paid was extraordinarily small, lower even than the committee's recommendations (Allan & Allan, 2000).

In October 1998, the Truth and Reconciliation Commission presented its main report to South African President Nelson Mandela. In his writings after the commission dissolved, Tutu indicated that the commission succeeded in affirming the human dignity of the victims, as "many bore witness to the fact that coming to talk to the commission had had a marked therapeutic effect on them" (Tutu, 1999, p. 27). Although not without legitimate criticism, many agree that the South African Truth and Reconciliation Commission was a remarkable effort that increased awareness about the use of the Truth Commission as a tool for countries moving away from periods of human rights abuse (Allan & Allan, 2000; Graybill, 2002). As a restorative effort, the South African TRC successfully incorporated values of restorative justice into some components of the work, while leaving much room for improvement in others (Llewellyn, 2006).

Greensboro, North Carolina

In June 2004, the first commission to call itself a truth and reconciliation commission was established in the United States.[xiv] The Greensboro Truth and Reconciliation Commission (GTRC) was charged with examining "the context, causes, sequence, and consequence" of the events that transpired in Greensboro, North Carolina on November 3, 1979, when five people were killed and 10 were wounded (Greensboro Truth And Reconciliation Commission, 2003). On that day, which came to be known as the "Greensboro Massacre," a racially mixed group of protesters, some of whom belonged to the Communist Workers Party (CWP), gathered in a public housing project primarily comprised of African-American residents to demonstrate against the Ku Klux Klan (KKK) and hold a forum on economic justice. Although the local police force knew that armed Klansmen and members of the Nazi Party intended to disrupt the forum and provoke the protesters, the police had no direct or visible presence at the scene. The KKK and Nazi Party members opened fire into the crowd of mostly unarmed protesters, killing five people and wounding 10 others. Some armed protesters did return fire, although no injuries were sustained as a result (Magarrell & Wesley, 2008).

In the aftermath of the event, the City of Greensboro and the Greensboro Police Department distanced themselves, refused accountability, and influenced an inaccurate depiction of events in the media (Magarrell & Wesley, 2008). In state and federal criminal trials, the accused KKK and Nazi Party members were acquitted by all-white juries (Magarrell & Wesley, 2008). At a later civil trial, participants in the march sued numerous defendants for damages in federal court on behalf of all those killed or wounded. In these federal civil proceedings, damages were awarded for the death of only one victim (Magarrell & Wesley, 2008). These factors contributed to existing feelings of confusion, vulnerability, and alarm among community members (Magarrell & Wesley, 2008).

The Greensboro Truth and Reconciliation Commission was formed over 20 years after this event, when a group of civic leaders, including some surviving former members of the CWP, called for the creation of an impartial commission to address the event and its aftermath. The GTRC's mandate described its reason for existence this way: "There comes a time in the life of every community when it must look humbly and seriously into its past in order to provide the best possible foundation for moving into a future based on healing and hope" (Greensboro Truth and Reconciliation Commission, 2006). The Commission sought to promote healing and community reconciliation, clear up the confusion surrounding the events of November third and their aftermath, acknowledge the feelings of community members and those involved, and encourage beneficial changes in social consciousness and community institutions (Magarrell & Wesley, 2008). To fulfill its mandate, the Commission pursued a course of research and community engagement.

The Commission collected statements from more than 150 involved parties.[xv] Over 30 individuals most affected by the events of November third offered statements: 17 demonstrators and 14 residents of the housing complex where the demonstration took place. The Commission also collected statements from six police officers and five current or former Nazis or Klansmen. Nine people involved in the various trials offered statements, including prosecutors, a judge, and other attorneys, including several of the defense attorneys for the Klan and Nazi members (Magarrell & Wesley, 2008). The Commission supplemented these statements with data gleaned from testimony in the three court cases stemming from the event, federal Grand Jury testimony, medical examiner's reports, depositions and pre-trial interviews from the civil and criminal suits, news photographs and footage, and discoveries from the civil suit, which included the internal records of the Greensboro Police Department, the Federal Bureau of Investigations, and the Bureau of Alcohol, Tobacco and Firearms (GTRC Final Report, 2006).

While collecting information and compiling its research, the Commission sought to initiate a dialogue in the Greensboro community about the facts and how the community should respond to them (Greensboro Truth and Reconciliation Commission, 2006). In their efforts to promote public awareness and involvement in the process, the Commission hosted three 2-day-long public hearings in July, August, and September of 2005. These hearings provided victims with a public forum to tell their stories, offered the public an open look at the Commission's work, encouraged support for the process, and disseminated accurate information about the events of November 3, 1979 and their aftermath (Magarrell & Wesley, 2008).

Sofia Macher, a commissioner for Peru's Truth and Reconciliation Commission, emphasized the importance of reaching out to the Greensboro community: "The fact that the Greensboro TRC does not have official status means that the legitimacy of its work depends solely on the community itself . . . Public hearings will be one of the principal tools by which to conduct this process in an open manner that can involve the society as a whole in an honest reflection on its past" (Magarrell & Wesley, 2008, p. 99). Between 300 and 500 people attended each hearing (Magarrell & Wesley, 2008).

In May 2006, the GTRC published its final report, which included conclusions and recommendations. The Commission saw its final report as "the beginning of a citizen effort toward investigation and dialogue, rather than the end" (Greensboro Truth and Reconciliation Commission, 2006). The Commission attributed blame for the violent events to several parties, including the Klan and Nazi Party members that approached the demonstrators on November 3, 1979 with "malicious intent" and a desire to provoke a violent confrontation. The Commission attributed less responsibility to the Communist Workers' Party, some of whom came armed and some of whom struck Klan and Nazi Party members' cars. The Commission found the absence of the police in the face of foreseeable violence to be "the single most important element that contributed to the violent outcome of the confrontation" (Greensboro Truth and Reconciliation Commission, 2006). For the purpose of promoting reconciliation, justice, and reparation, the Commission recommended an acknowledgement of the truth of the events of November third by a range of involved parties, institutional reforms to prevent future abuses, and continued citizen engagement (Greensboro Truth and Reconciliation Commission, 2006).

While its local scale and unofficial status differentiates it from most other truth commissions, the Greensboro Truth and Reconciliation Commission shows how the framework created by international truth commissions can be used to address community needs (GTRC Final Report, 2006). In the introduction to its *Final Report*, the GTRC argues for the appropriateness of the truth commission model to address the events that occurred in Greensboro in 1979: "While the GTRC recognizes the differences between Greensboro's history and the abuses addressed by other truth commissions, we share a common aspiration: that the truth about the past will help us build a better, more just and more inclusive future" (Greensboro Truth and Reconciliation Commission, 2006). The GTRC also "heartily recommend[ed]" the truth and reconciliation model to other communities throughout the United States "considering processes to seek the truth and work for reconciliation around tragic, unjust events in their own histories" (Greensboro Truth and Reconciliation Commission, 2006). With the goal of confronting the truth of the past and encouraging accountability and respect for all people, the GTRC demonstrates how the defining principles and methodologies of truth commissions can be successfully adapted in the United States (International Center for Transitional Justice).

PUTTING IT TOGETHER: EMOTIONS, STORYTELLING, AND HEALING

Restorative processes are based on the assumption that storytelling is healing (Tutu, 1999). Beck and Britto (2006) wrote about the positive effects of storytelling when interviewing individuals about a traumatic event. Thalhuber and Thompson (2007) argue that when "personal stories are heard, the process of healing and empowerment begins" (p. 19). Yoder (2005) explains how this healing and empowerment occurs: "When our story is acknowledged and mourned—the valor, heroism, sacrifice, pain, fear, resilience, betrayals, humiliations, shortcomings—atrocities and guilt then shame and humiliation can be shed, forgiveness sought, courage celebrated and reenactment ended" (p. 54). Through the process of repeated storytelling and expressing pain through storytelling, people can begin to create a new narrative that incorporates painful events into their larger life narratives. As described by Howard Zehr (2002), this "re-storying" process allows an individual to begin to reestablish lost meaning and identity by exerting control and power over the event and its aftermath.

The four processes described in this chapter introduce social workers to an additional set of tools that can aid them in supporting transformation in their clients and in the communities in which they work. All of these processes require training. At present, only training for Victim–Offender Dialogue is offered through a school of social work, but when we as a profession think about the future of our programs and our curriculum, these tools offer interesting possibilities.

NOTES

i Some experts recommend avoiding potentially stigmatizing terms like "victim" and "offender" when interacting with participants (Beck, Blackwell, Leonard, & Mears, 2003; Wallis & Tudor, 2008; Zehr, 2002).

ii When accepting referrals from the judicial system, programs generally accept cases either pre-adjudication, as a way to avoid or divert prosecution, or post-adjudication, after the offender formally enters a guilty plea to the court. In the United States, programs receive about one-third of their referrals pre-adjudication, one-third of their referrals post-adjudication but before disposition, and one-third of their referrals at the post-disposition level (Umbreit, 2001). The opportunity to participate in victim–offender dialogue also may be a condition of an offender's probation.

iii Although experts emphasize the importance of this voluntary participation, some programs require offender participation. In his research, Leverton (2007–2008) found mandatory offender participation in programs in California, Kansas, Montana, North Carolina, Ohio, Washington, and Wisconsin.

iv If the victim does not desire to directly participate in the dialogue, the victim may choose to work through a third party, known as a "secondary" or "surrogate" victim, who can represent the victim's views in the dialogue. If the victim declines these options but would like to indirectly communicate with the offender, a form of "shuttle mediation" can occur, in which the facilitator transfers information between the parties as they work toward the formation of an agreement. "Shuttle mediation" can be an effective alternative to a face-to-face meeting (Wallis & Tudor, 2008; Umbreit, 2001).

v The number of facilitators involved in a case introduces different benefits and challenges. A single facilitator has more flexibility in scheduling meetings and building rapport with participants. During a dialogue, however, a single facilitator may miss the exchange of important signals and information, as well as miss out on valuable debriefing and feedback opportunities with another facilitator following a session. Co-facilitators may be more appropriate if one of the facilitators does not have much experience. Co-facilitators must ensure that the participants understand the division of responsibilities, and that both facilitators will remain neutral and work on each party's behalf (Wallis and Tudor, 2008; Umbreit, 2001).

vi There are several prerequisites for a conference, and a critical one is that the offender has assumed responsibility for his or her actions.

vii As in all restorative processes, victims' participation is voluntary.

viii In some cases several types of circles may be used. For example, when a person is leaving prison, a Reintegration Circle may be used to facilitate a relationship between the individual and his or her community support. This circle, however, may be preceded by an Understanding Circle on the topic of prison life or the responsibility of the community to its members. There may also be a Healing Circle for the individual returning to the community, and perhaps a separate one for his or her victims.

ix In areas like New South Wales, Sentencing Circles began as an indigenous response to indigenous offenders, with a part of the goal being to lessen the barriers between Aboriginal communities and the state (Cunneen, 2007).

x Kathleen Daly and others warn that indigenous practices are not a monolith and can be easily glamorized (Daly, 2002; Cunneen, 2007).

xi Truth Commissions do not carry out criminal proceedings. Although some Truth Commissions have suggested prosecutions and sent their findings to a court of law, many Truth Commissions have a mandate that ensures that they will not assume a direct role in prosecuting or determining amnesty following the publication of their report. Only a few commissions explicitly forbade criminal proceedings and guaranteed amnesty following their investigations; most others only have implicitly determined not to seek prosecutions. Some countries, including Bolivia and Argentina, did allow legal, criminal proceedings to occur that were connected to and followed the publication of the commission's findings (Hayner, 1994).

xii

xiii Truth commissions are often established during periods of government transition and are often sponsored by governments. While this government sponsorship lends the truth commission authority and official status, it can also cast a shadow over the commission's credibility and objectivity.

xiv Although the Greensboro Truth and Reconciliation Commission was the first body in the United States to call itself a "truth and reconciliation commission," previous bodies have formed in the United States to investigate human rights abuses in states including Oklahoma, North Carolina, and Florida.

xv The Commission encountered reluctance on the part of several individuals to offer testimony due to fear of retaliation or a lack of trust the process (GTRC Final Report, 2006). Without any official authority, the GRTC did not have the power to subpoena witnesses. Additionally, they had no protections or safety nets to offer potentially culpable individuals. Twelve of the 145 individuals who offered formal oral statements only agreed to speak if their names were not publicly released (Magarrell & Wesley, 2008).

REFERENCES

Abramson, L., & Moore, D. (2001). Transforming conflict in the inner city: Community conferencing in Baltimore. *Contemporary Justice Review, 4*, 321–340.

Abramson, L., Moore, D., & Allan, M. M. (2000). The South African truth and reconciliation commission as a therapeutic tool. *Behavioral Sciences & the Law, 18*, 459–477.

Adams, P., & Chandler, S. (2002). Building partnerships to protect children: A blended model of family group conferencing. *Family Court Review, 40*(4), 503–516.

Allan, A., & Allan, M. (2000). The South African Truth and Reconciliation Commission as a therapeutic tool. *Behavioral Sciences & the Law, 18*, 459–477.

Baffour, T. (2006). Ethnic and gender differences in offending patterns: Examining family group conferencing interventions among at-risk adolescents. *Child and Social Work Journal, 23*(5–6), 557–578.

Baldwin, C. (1994). *Calling the circle: The first and future culture.* New York: Bantam Books.

Bazemore, G. (2000). Community justice and a vision for collective efficacy: The case of restorative conferencing. In National Institute of Justice (Ed.), *Policies, processes, and decisions of the criminal justice system: Vol. 3. Criminal Justice* (pp. XX–XX). Washington, DC: U. S. Department of Justice.

Bazemore, G., & Schiff, M. (2001). *Restorative community justice: Repairing harm and transforming communities.* Cincinnati, OH: Anderson Publishing Company.

Bazemore, G. & Schiff, M. (2005). *Juvenile justice reform and restorative justice: Building theory and policy from practice.* Cullompton, Devon, UK: Willan Publishing.

Bazemore, G. & Umbreit, M. (1999). *Conferences, circles, boards and mediations: Restorative justice and citizen involvement in the response to youth crime.* Washington, DC: US Department of Justice, Office of Juvenile Justice and Delinquency Prevention.

Beck, E., Blackwell, B., Leonard, P., & Mears, M. (2003). Seeking sanctuary: Interviews with family members of capital defendants. *Cornell Law Review, 88*(2), 382–418.

Beck, E., & Britto, S. (2006). Using feminist methods and restorative justice to interview capital offenders' family members. *AFFILIA, 21*, 59–70.

Bradt, L., & Bouverne-De Bie, M. (2009). Victim offender mediation as a social work practice. *International Social Work, 52*(2), 181–193.

Chandler, S., & Giovannucci, M. (2004). Family group conferences: Transforming traditional child welfare policy and practice. *Family Court Review, 42*(2), 216–231.

Christie, K. (2000). *The South African Truth Commission.* New York, NY: St. Martin's Press.

Connolly, M. (2006). Fifteen years of family group conferencing: Coordinators talk about their experiences in Aotearoa, New Zealand. *British Journal of Social Work, 36*(4), 523–540.

Cunneen, C. (2007). Reviving restorative traditions? In G. Johnstone and D. Van Ness (Eds.), *Handbook of restorative justice.* Portland, OR: Willan Publishing.

Daly, K. (2002). Restorative justice: The real story. *Punishment and Society, 4*(1), 55–79.

Doerfler, D. (2003). Victim offender dialogue: Healing on a deeper level. *Kaleidoscope of Justice: Highlighting Restorative Juvenile Justice, 4*(3), 4–6.

Dzur, A. W. (2003). Civic implications of restorative justice theory: Citizen participation and criminal justice policy. *Policy Sciences, 36*, 279–306.

Graybill, L. S. (2002). *Truth and reconciliation in South Africa: Miracle or model?* Boulder, CO: Lynne Rienner Publishers, Inc.

Greensboro Truth and Reconciliation Commission. (2006). Greensboro Truth and Reconciliation Commission Report Executive Summary. Retrieved October, 5, 2009, from http://www.greensborotrc.org/exec_summary.pdf

Hayner, P. B. (1994). Fifteen truth commissions—1974 to 1994: A comparative study. *Human Rights Quarterly, 16*(4), 597–655.

Hayner, P. B. (1996). Commissioning the truth: Further research questions. *Third World Quarterly, 17*(1), 19–29.

Holland, S., & O'Neill, S. (2006). "We had to be there to make sure it was what we wanted": Enabling children's participation in family decision-making through the family group conference. *Childhood, 19*, 91–111.

Hudson, J., & Burford, G. (2000). General Introduction: Family group conference programming. In G. Burford & J. Hudson (Eds.), *Family group conferencing: New directions in community-centered child and family practice: Vol. xix.* New Brunswick: Aldine Transaction.

International Center for Transitional Justice. (YEAR). Retrieved October, 5, 2009, from http://www.ictj.org/en/where/region2/517.html

Johnstone, G. (2002). *Restorative justice: Ideas, values, debates.* Cullompton, Devon, UK: Willan Publishing.

Leverton, W. R. (2007–2008). The case for best practice standards in restorative justice processes. *American Journal of Trial Advocacy, 31*, 501–530.

Llewellyn, J. (2006). Truth Commissions and restorative justice. In G. Johnstone & D. Van Ness (Eds.), *Handbook of Restorative Justice* (pp. 351–371). Portland OR: Willan Publishing.

Love, C. (2000). Family group conferencing: Cultural origins, sharing, and appropriation— A Maori reflection. In G. Burford & J. Hudson (Eds.), *Family group conferencing: New directions in community-centered child and family practice* (pp. 31–39). Piscataway, NJ: Transaction Publishers.

Lubin, J. (2009). Are we really looking out for the best interests of the child? Applying the New Zealand model of family group conferences to cases of child neglect in the United States. *Family Court Review, 1*, 129–147.

MacRae, A., & Zehr, H. (2004). *The little book of family group conferences New Zealand style: A hopeful approach when youth cause harm.* Intercourse, PA: Good Books.

Magarrell, L., & Wesley, J. (2008). *Learning from Greensboro: Truth & reconciliation in the United States.* Philadelphia, PA: University of Pennsylvania Press.

Merkel-Holguin, L. (2000). Sharing power with the people: Family group conferencing as a democratic experiment. *Journal of Sociology & Social Welfare, 1*, 155–173.

Merkel-Holguin, L., Nixon, P., & Burford, G. (2003). Learning with families: A synopsis of FGDM research and evaluation in child welfare. *Protecting Children, 18*(1/2), 2–11.

Moore, D., & McDonald, J. (2000). Guiding principles of the conferencing process. In G. Burford & J. Hudson (Eds.), *Family group conferencing: New directions in community-centered child and family practice* (pp. 49–64). New Brunswick: Aldine Transaction.

Ntsebeza, D. (2000). The struggle for human rights: from the UN Declaration of human rights to the present. In C. Villa-Vicencio & W. Verwoerd (Eds.), *Looking back reaching forward: Reflections on the truth and reconciliation commission of South Africa* (pp. 2–13). Cape Town: University of Cape Town Press.

O'Connell, T., Wachtel, B., & Wachtel, T. (1999). *Conferencing handbook: The real justice training manual.* Pipersville, PA: The Piper's Press.

O'Connor, L., Morgenstern, J., Gibson, F., & Nakashian, M. (2005). "Nothing about me without me": Leading the way to collaborative relationships with families. *Child Welfare League of America,* 153–170.

Olson, K. (2009). Family group conferencing and child protection mediation: Essential tools for prioritizing family engagement in child welfare cases. *Family Court Review,* 47(1), 53–68.

Pennell, J. (2006). Restorative practices and child welfare: Toward an inclusive civil society. *Journal of Social Issues,* 62(2), 259–279.

Pennell, J., & Burford, G. (1994). Widening the circle: The family group decision making project. *Journal of child and youth care,* 9(1), 1–12.

Pennell, J., & Burford, G. (2000). Family group decision making: Protecting children and women. *Child Welfare, LXXIX*(2), 131–158.

Pranis, K. (2005). *The little book of circle processes: A new/old approach to peacemaking.* Intercourse, PA: Good Books.

Pranis, K., Stuart, B., & Wedge, M. (2003). *Peacemaking circles: From crime to community.* St. Paul, MN: Living Justice Press.

Shea, D. C. (2000). *The South African truth commission: The politics of reconciliation.* Washington, DC: United States Institute of Peace Press.

Stuart, B. (2001). Guiding principles for designing peacemaking circles. In G. Bazemore and M. Schiff (Eds.), *Restorative and community justice: Repairing harm and transforming communities* (pp. 219–242). Cincinnati, OH: Anderson Publishing.

Szmania, S. J. (2006). Mediators' communication in victim offender mediation/dialogue involving crimes of severe violence: An analysis of opening statements. *Conflict Resolution Quarterly,* 24(1), 111–127.

Thalhuber, P., & Thompson, S. (2007). *Building a home for the heart: Using metaphors in value-centered circles.* St. Paul, MN: Living Justice Press.

Truth Commissions Project. Strategic Choices in the Design of Truth Commissions. Retrieved October 3, 2009, from http://www.truthcommission.org/about.php?lang=en

Tutu, D. (1999). *No future without forgiveness.* New York: Doubleday.

Umbreit, M. S. (2001). *The handbook of victim offender mediation: An essential guide to practice and research.* San Francisco, CA: Jossey-Bass, Inc.

Umbreit, M. S., Coates, R. B., & Vos, B. (2007). Restorative justice dialogue: A multidimensional, evidence-based practice theory. *Contemporary Justice Review,* 10(1), 23–41.

Umbreit, M. S., & Greenwood, J. (2000). *Guidelines for victim-sensitive victim–offender mediation: Restorative justice through dialogue.* Washington, D.C.: U.S. Department of Justice.

Van Ness, D. W., & Strong, K. H. (1997). *Restoring justice* (2nd ed.). Cincinnati, OH: Anderson Publishing Company.

Victim Offender Mediation Association. (2006). *VOMA Recommended Ethical Guidelines.* Retrieved February 1, 2009, from http://voma.org/docs/ethics.pdf

Waites, C., Macgowan, M. J., Pennell, J., Carlton-LaNey, I., & Weil, M. (2004). Increasing the cultural responsiveness of family group conferencing. *Social Work, 49*(2), 291–300.

Wallis, P., & Tudor, B. (2008). *The pocket guide to restorative justice.* London and Philadelphia: Jessica Kingsley Publishers.

Winfree, L. T. (2002). Peacemaking and community harmony: Lessons (and admonitions) from the Navajo peacemaking courts. In G. Weitekamp & H-J Kerner (Eds.), *Restorative justice theoretical foundations.* Portland, OR: Willan Publishing.

Yoder, C. (2005). *The little book of trauma healing: When violence strikes and community security is threatened.* Intercourse, PA: Good Books.

Zehr, H. (1990). *A new focus for crime and justice: Canging lenses.* Scottdale, PA: Herald Press.

Zehr, H. (2002). *The little book of restorative justice.* Intercourse, PA: Good Books.

Zion, J., & Yazzie, R. (2006). Navajo peacemaking original dispute resolution and a life away. In D. Sullian & L. Tifft (Eds.), *Handbook of restorative justice* (pp. 151–160). New York: Routledge.

Chapter Five

Social Work and Restorative Justice: Implications for School System Practice

MICHELE V. HAMILTON AND LESA NITCY HOPE

The classroom with all its limitations remains a location of possibility. In that field of possibility we have the opportunity to labor for freedom, to demand of ourselves and our comrades, an openness of mind and heart that allows us to face reality even as we collectively imagine ways to move beyond boundaries, to transgress. This is education as the practice of freedom.
— *bell hooks,* Teaching to Transgress: Education as the Practice of Freedom

Schools have become a microcosm for how communities at large respond to youth. For youth who are perceived as challenging, defiant, or engaged in a complicated situation, the school community often employs an array of responses to address these perceived difficulties. Unfortunately, these responses have included avoidance, labeling, punishment, and exclusion.

Zero tolerance policies are another recent change in the school environment, and a result of the rash of high-profile violence incidents of the 1990s (Jennings, Gover, & Hitchcock, 2008). Zero tolerance policies have been enacted to remove the student who threatens the safety of others by bringing a weapon on the school campus. Although zero tolerance policies vary among school systems, a common goal is to quickly carry out punishment for violating these rules. As Varnham (2005) states, "Many schools . . . focus on 'getting rid of troublemakers,' or on dealing with 'bad' behavior by standing-down, suspending or expelling students" (p. 88).

The effects of these responses have created unfortunate outcomes for many students. One is enrollment in psychoeducational centers or alternative school settings that house a myriad of young people who have been perceived as deviant, labeled as noncompliant or combative, or require more complex forms of treatment, support, and supervision. Psychoeducational centers are typically established as separate schools that serve children with mental health and behavioral challenges. Students are sent to these centers, often after suspension or expulsion, as an alternative learning setting. In theory, the psychoeducational centers are used when it has been determined by school personnel that a student needs specialized support, which the traditional school setting is not able to provide. In some cases, these centers become dumping grounds for students that the system has decided are deviant or for whom they have diminished expectations. A second outcome of punitive school-based policies is the high dropout or withdrawal rate, with disproportionately high representation in students of color (Bruns, Moore, Stephan, Pruitt, & Weist, 2005; Civil Rights Project, 2000; Dupper, Theriot, & Craun, 2009; Garcia-Reid, 2008; U.S Department of Education, 2000). In 2002, for example, tenth-graders dropped out of school across the nation for a variety of reasons:

- 37% left because they did not like school
- 38% left because they were failing
- 22% said they could not get along with their teachers
- 22% were unable to manage both school and work simultaneously.

(California Dropout Research Project, 2008)

Likewise, school-related policies can have the impact of pushing more vulnerable students out of the educational system. For example, some students become disconnected or disengaged from the school community when faced with exclusion in response to minor infractions (McNeely, Nonnemaker, & Blum, 2002). Additionally, the use of zero tolerance policies has increased the number of criminal charges filed against children (Advancement Project and Civil Rights Project, 2000). Punitive disciplinary practices can result in more activity on the school-to-prison pipeline, which is named for the predictable trajectory that at-risk students experience as they encounter difficulties in school settings which result in their marginalization and disconnection from the school community. As schools escalate their disciplinary actions, this often leads to suspensions, expulsions, and even schools filing criminal charges, with the students experiencing engagement with the juvenile courts, and later, adult courts and prison. Students who are suspended, and who subsequently spend less time in school, are more likely to smoke, abuse alcohol and drugs, get into fights, carry weapons, do poorly academically, and be incarcerated (American Academy of Pediatrics, 2003; Wald & Losen, 2003).

As a result, these students become a source of conflict or misunderstanding for the adults working in the school community, mainly because the structure of the school day rarely provides adequate time for school personnel to diagnosis, analyze, or address those students who are less responsive to intervention approaches. Moreover, student interventions are configured to focus on the individual by assigning blame, locating and attaching a label, and developing an individualized treatment plan to "fix" or eliminate the problem. This deficit-based approach does not provide adults or youth an opportunity to examine the broader context of the behavior, build relationships, or establish meaningful connections within the school community.

The connection of students to the school and larger community is important, because it provides the context for transformation and acceptance of new scripts and stories that underscore interdependence, which is framed on relationships, gifts, and our connections to one another (Condeluci, 1995; 2008). Too often, youth are either seen as disposable or unable to function within the parameters of traditional schooling. The degree to which youth are considered educationally viable may be directly related to how well they respond to school interventions and adhere to established norms. As a result, there is usually little room for deviant or atypical behavior. Students who are viewed as problematic, and have corresponding social circumstances and behavior that are at odds with the school culture, are conceptualized in terms of defiance and abnormality (Bruns et al., 2005; Dupper et al., 2009).

This act of labeling students has implications related to funding, and ultimately to what services and supports are offered to students. Trends affecting school social work include "the dominance of managed behavioral health care, privatization of mental health and social services, school-linked services, integrative services and provider networks, merging of practices and agencies, capitation as a method of financing services, and changes in the Medicaid program for children from low-income families, from federal programs to block grant programs administered by the states" (Franklin, 2000). It is imperative that social workers ensure that students who have been defined as defiant, noncompliant, or different in some way continue to receive appropriate supports to maintain their presence and engagement in school.

Restorative justice provides a framework to support the convergence of healing and personal growth based on relationships, as well as community understanding and acceptance. Restorative justice practices challenge members of the school community to capitalize on and celebrate those qualities that make young people unique and valuable, while allowing those young people to solve problems relative to their own experiences (Hamilton, 2008). By actively engaging students in the process of dialoguing, building relationships, making decisions, and resolving conflict, restorative practices position youth as active participants in the school community. This chapter will explore the ways in which restorative justice practices are currently used within the school setting, and their implications for social work practice.

CURRENT SOCIAL WORK PRACTICE IN SCHOOLS: AN OVERVIEW

Practice Methods

The National Association of Social Workers (NASW) identifies four core practice activities for school social workers. These activities include: (1) Early intervention to reduce or eliminate stress within or between individuals or groups; (2) Problem-solving services to students, parents, school personnel, or community agencies; (3) Early identification of students at risk; and (4) Work with various groups in school to develop coping, social, and decision-making skills (National Association of Social Workers, 2002). School social workers typically focus on gathering information on bio-psycho-social functioning in order to write up social histories for students identified as "at risk," or for whom challenges or problem behaviors have been identified, such as truancy or addiction issues. The bio-psycho-social report provides a context for assessing the student's situation and provides a historical and multisystem perspective on the present challenges of the student. In this assessment, connections can be established between a student's school-related problems and his or her functioning in other roles and environments. The bio-psycho-social report is built on interviews with the individual, family members, and other relevant persons, as well as a review of available documents and records, such as psychological evaluations, school reports, court reports, and medical evaluations. The report covers the person's history, current living arrangements, family situation, physical and medical needs, results from psychological evaluations, relationships, neighborhood, cultural considerations, as well as abilities and support needs. A comprehensive bio-psycho-social summary acknowledges the strengths of the individual, family, and extended support network, and makes recommendations for ways to positively support a preferred present and future for the individual. Conversely, poorly constructed reports simply become a checklist of deficits that offer little hope for a positive future and are sometimes used as justification for suspension, expulsion, or transfer to an alternative learning environment.

Another school social work responsibility is that of connecting students to resources and supports within the community. When there is suspicion that students are being mistreated or harmed, social workers are required to make reports to protective services agencies. Social workers are also asked to be a referral and intervention resource when family issues such as alcoholism, domestic violence, poverty, and other stressors on the family system are identified, connecting individuals and families to resources outside the school context to deal with these issues. Many become experts on issues specific to particular schools and communities, such as teen pregnancy, poverty, or gang activity (Bazemore & Umbreit, 1997). They may also assess students and utilize individual and group counseling skills. Depending on the school setting, they also have a role in leading or participating in Student Support Teams or IEP (Individual Educational Plan) meetings.

In terms of primary areas of intervention, school social workers work with individuals, families, groups, and the community (Staudt, Cherry, & Watson, 2005). Social work *practice with individuals* includes interventions to deal with trauma, victimization, self-esteem, bullying, pregnancy, specific behavioral concerns, and many other issues. Social workers are afforded the opportunity to address a wide range of student-specific concerns. There are likely many instances when the high incidence of particular concerns presented by individuals moves from simply needing interventions at the individual level to a more comprehensive, systemic approach. Examples include schools with high rates of drug abuse, gang activity, pregnancy, or poverty-related issues, or high numbers of students from single-parent families, or in foster care (Anderson-Butcher & Ashton, 2004; Anderson-Butcher, Stelter, & Midle, 2006; Jozefowicz-Simbeni, 2008).

School social workers also interact with the families of students. Social workers are often called upon to help families understand their children's developmental needs and milestones. Through education and discussion, school social workers help parents clarify appropriate expectations and address concerns by normalizing children's abilities and behaviors at different ages or making referrals when developmental, mental health, or behavioral concerns are recognized. Garrett (2006) cited a long list of issues on which social workers engage with families, including:

> grief and loss, family changes (including divorce, separation, and blending families), attendance, parent deployment . . . child abuse and neglect, parents who were arrested or jailed, sibling or parent addiction, family crises, emergency dental care, lack of eye glasses, eviction, poor hygiene, parent illness, and lack of resources for food, clothing, transportation, and utilities. (p 117)

Group work is a common form of intervention with school systems. A study on group work within schools indicates that the most common types of issues addressed are development of social skills, dealing with peer difficulties, and behavior management issues (Garrett, 2004). The role of the practitioner varies in group settings, depending on the participants and the nature of the content. In some, the social worker takes a more authoritarian role to control the content of the group sessions. In others, however, the participants help set the agenda, ground rules, and goals, such as the Empowerment Groups for Academic Success (EGAS) (Bemark, 2005). This groupwork approach was specifically created for students who experience multiple disadvantages within the school setting such as being a member of a racial minority, living in low socio-economic communities, and having academic challenges. Despite the variation in approaches, Bemark (2005) advocates for group work approaches with students that afford true empowerment. He explained:

> when the school counselor accepts and at times follows the group as members assume control over their experience, with in many instances, is for the first time in their lives. It means that the school's counselor honors the group members' collective and individual will as long as it is consistent with the group goals, without maintaining control of the agenda. (p. 402)

He contrasts this with a disempowering model of group work, where the school counselor or other school staff, such as social workers, are in control, and the locus of control is external to the group members. As Bemark (2005) notes, groups that have an external locus of control have limited generalization from the process that takes place inside the group to the larger environment such as the classrooms or playgrounds. However, those groups that have an internal locus of control by being part of group agenda setting and being accountability to other group members generalize these new behaviors and skills into other contexts.

The school system is a venue that offers a unique opportunity for social workers to engage in *community practice activities*. In Bell's (2001) work on building and strengthening resiliency in youth, he outlined the importance of developing emotional resilience through macro practice, or what he terms "rebuilding the village." By enhancing a community's capacity, there is increased likelihood that youth will have the ability to attract and use needed supports. He relates a powerful story of the importance of community level assessment and intervention, contending that discerning and addressing issues in the community is imperative and ethical:

> *When I was in medical school I was told that, if a child came into my office with a rat bite, and I sat in my office, examined the child, and then gave the child a tetanus shot, some antibiotics, and carefully dressed the wound, I would be a good doctor. If however, 100 children from the surrounding community came into my office, each with rat bites, and I sat in my office, examined the child, and then gave the child antibiotics, and carefully dressed the wound and that was all—then I should have my medical license revoked. The reason being that I did not go out into those children's community and get rid of the rats. (p. 381)*

This premise holds true for social workers, teachers, or other professionals working on behalf of children. If trauma, isolation, or disenfranchisement represent the school experiences of a vulnerable group of students, then social workers and others have a responsibility to address the systems and community issues that contribute to the problem.

Traditional Disciplinary Practice

Unlike restorative justice practices, where students are part of the resolution, current disciplinary practices often frame students as the "problem" instead of as a resource for healing and cohesion-building within the community. Traditional school disciplinary procedures focus on punishment versus rehabilitation and involve the use of school exclusion (suspension and expulsion) and school security measures (e.g. security guards, metal detectors, video surveillance, locker searches) resulting from zero tolerance policies (Skiba & Peterson, 1999; 2000). Punishment in the school setting is used to send a clear message to the offender and the school community that certain behaviors will not be tolerated (Skiba & Knesting, 2001).

Expulsion, suspension, exclusion, and change of placements are increasingly utilized in an attempt to rid the school community of deviant behavior by creating a matrix for deciding who is and is not "salvageable." As a consequence, zero tolerance policies are used to deter violent and unruly students from committing similar or more egregious acts of defiance (Skiba & Knesting, 2001) and to permanently remove students from the school setting (Reyes, 2006). Unfortunately, these practices place no responsibility on the school to examine its treatment of students or its current systems for addressing student needs. Under this conceptualization, the student and parent bear the responsibility for addressing youth deviancy and dependency, outside of the educational institution. Current disciplinary approaches address student behavior by assigning guilt, but do not provide opportunities for students to repair relationships and understand the impact of their behavior on the school community. Likewise, administrators have a limited array of options to address challenging student behaviors and identify resources to meet their needs. Finally, students are frequently not given opportunities to learn from their mistakes or develop skills to thwart future behavioral infractions.

One of the most troubling areas where social workers utilize counseling and treatment interventions is to deal with the negative impact of traditional discipline methods on students. Cameron and Sheppard (2006) wrote:

> *Four decades of research, however, have shown that these conventional school disciplinary policies and practices often fail to create the intended environment and appear, in some cases to have a destructive impact on children's academic and psychosocial functioning. School discipline has been linked with posttraumatic stress disorder (PTSD), depression, anxiety, aggression behavior in and outside of school, academic failure, and school drop-out. Furthermore, children of color, boys and those receiving compensatory services at schools for disabilities are disproportionately and more severely subjected to school discipline. (p. 15)*

The researchers also called for an increased awareness of the iatrogenic effects of traditional school discipline, that they note "may be used prejudicially, and in some cases, to the detriment of the students disciplined" (p. 16). Ashworth, Van Brockern, Ailts, & Donnelly (2008) add, "The traditional 'stay silent, sit still, do nothing' school detention approach is a punitive and ineffective way to change behavior. It does little to create positive school climates. For children who have been traumatized through fear, isolation, and emotional abuse, poorly managed detention can add to that trauma" (p.22).

In various ways, social workers must register the harm being done to children and youth, and advocate to change the system causing the maltreatment. If a school social worker has to provide trauma treatment to deal with the effects of actions directed at the student by the school environment, they must work to challenge the system to use more beneficent and life-affirming practices. Practitioners who take a neutral stance on practices that cause harm tacitly support the systems of oppression. Horton and Freire (1990) noted, "neutrality is a code word for the existing system. It has nothing to do with anything but agreeing to what is and will always be—that's what neutrality is. Neutrality is just following the crowd. Neutrality is just being what the system asks us to be" (p. 102). The use of traditional disciplinary procedures and of deficit-based interventions results in adults losing the opportunity to nurture or repair the relationships of those directly involved, as well as the support gained through a meaningful connection to the community.

RESTORATIVE JUSTICE INITIATIVES

Restorative practices have been implemented in a variety of private and public schools and in several large school districts throughout the United States and abroad. The practices are found in institutions ranging from private preparatory schools to schools developed for juvenile offenders, and in most of the schools, social workers have played key roles in the initiatives (Karp & Breslin, 2001; Mirsky, 2004). When used in schools, restorative practices work to support classroom management, school discipline, bullying prevention, and the moral development of children (Amstutz & Mullett, 2005). The practices seek to hold students accountable for their behavior and create a sense of community within the school setting (Amstutz & Mullett, 2005; Chmelynski, 2005; Drewery, 2004; Morrison, Blood, & Thorsborne, 2005). Moreover, restorative justice practices provide youth with tools to transform conflict, and with opportunities to develop positive relationships (Drewery, 2004; Hamilton, 2008).

The use of restorative justice in schools is emergent. The largest efforts to widely affect the culture of a school through restorative practices are found in Minnesota and Colorado. In these states, money has been provided to support district-wide initiatives. Additionally, smaller school-based initiatives are found throughout the country.

Outcome data speak to the potential impact of restorative practices in schools. For example, restorative practices have been piloted in four school districts in Minnesota. Outcomes have been dramatic, including reductions in the number of behavioral referrals, expulsions, and suspensions (Minnesota Department of Children, Families and Learning, 2001). The Buxmont Academy is a school administered on restorative practices, for youth who have been in trouble with the law. Research from the academy showed participants with a 58% reduction in re-offending following their participation in the school (McCold, Kerner, & Weitekamp, 2002).

Restorative justice principles and practices are used in the school setting for various purposes. These include initiatives to resolve conflicts and address difficult interpersonal dynamics; influence values, encourage decision-making and support life skills; and help youth feel connected to the school community. Restorative justice practices may range from dealing with informal disputes to more serious situations, such as bullying and physical violence (Dawson & McHugh, 2006; Morrison, 2006; Varnham, 2005). As Jennings et al. (2008) stated, "The ultimate goal of school-based restorative justice is for all individuals involved in the conflict and those in the larger community to recognize and understand the wrongfulness of the behavior and to prevent its reoccurrence in the future" (p. 172).

Two typical situations where restorative justice is used in school settings, are when a student is reentering the school after some hiatus, and when truancy is occurring. *Reintegration after suspension* involves assimilating students back in the school community and their classrooms after a period of separation. In serious offenses where a student has been suspended from school, the student would be required to meet with the administrator, the victim of any transgressions committed, and other individuals such as classmates, teachers, or other school personnel before returning to school or attending classes if appropriate. By reintegrating the student back into the school community through restorative justice practices, adults can help students reflect on their behavior, develop a plan for healthy decision-making, and create a support system for the youth. Reintegration after suspension allows the school community to focus squarely on the behavior without making judgments about the individual. Administrators accomplish this by creating a community of support for the student who returns to school. Likewise, students are more likely to feel like a part of the school community when a structure is in place to help them transition back into normal educational activities.

Truancy mediation resembles a family group conference and involves the parent, student, an administrator, a counselor, and the attendance secretary. The process is designed to divert truancy cases from the juvenile justice system and create a sense of belonging for the youth. Likewise, the process allows students to be active decision-makers and take ownership in fulfilling the mediation agreements. The goal is to create a plan to help both the parent and student be successful. Because the truancy mediation process is more relaxed, it is less likely to result in punitive sanctions such as fines and court appearances for the family. This non-adversarial approach to reconciling attendance can provide opportunities for all parties to voice their concerns and contribute to resolving the problem (Amstutz & Mullet, 2005).

In addition, schools that institute restorative justice practices may transform the entire culture of the school in the way that students, faculty and staff manage their relationships (Jennings et al., 2008). Morrison et al. (2006) offer a model of restorative justice that demonstrates how various levels of interventions can become part of the overall school experience (see Figure 5.1). Restorative justice interventions offer a range of responses and form a continuum that moves from preventative to intensive practices. The model presented here uses a health care analogy to delineate universal, targeted, and intensive responses.

Each stratum of the pyramid is associated with a different outcome or goal. The bottom layer, the broad base of the diagram, includes everyone as the target of interventions to develop social and emotional skills. Similar to an "inoculation" strategy, the goal is to promote skills so conflict is dealt with constructively, which has the potential to alter the entire school culture. In the middle level, the source

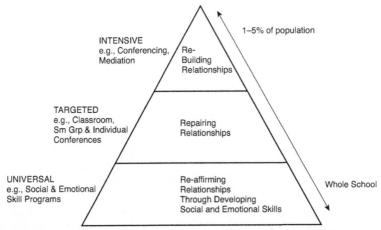

Figure 5-1. Hierarchy of Restorative Justice Responses within Schools.
Reprinted with permission from Morrison, Blood, & Thorsborne. (2005). Practicing
restorative justice in school communities: the challenge of culture change. *Public
Organization Review: A Global Journal, 5,* 335–357.

of a particular conflict situation is addressed. Typically, the consequences of the
stress have an impact on others within the school community, such as tension
between a teacher and student that affects the entire class. At this level of intervention, a third party is often involved to facilitate resolution, such as an assistant
principal who might meet with the student, teacher, and class. In repairing these
relationships, restorative justice methods provide a way to reduce the negative
impacts for a broad segment of students. Low level, consistent disruption takes a
toll on all students and can lead to more serious consequences within the school
setting.

The most intensive approaches, the highest on the pyramid, are the most
involved and serious level of intervention. Although typically used to deal with a
particularly potent situation, such as intensive bullying, there may be a broad
cross-section of individuals from the school and wider environment that participate to resolve the conflict. Taken together, this model demonstrates that restorative justice approaches can be implemented on many levels and for various
outcomes within schools.

Similar to other settings, school-based restorative justice interventions may
take different forms. Some of the most common types are Victim–Offender
Dialogue (VOD), Family and Group Conferencing, and Circles (Jennings et al.,
2008). Similar to restorative justice programs in general, these practices are used
to "encourage accountability and remorse as well as facilitating understanding and
forgiveness" (p. 172).

Victim–Offender Dialogue

In Victim–Offender Dialogue (VOD), a trained mediator facilitates conflict resolution between the victim and the offender (see Chapter 4). Unlike a punitive model, under which the offender receives punishment, he or she is expected to play a role in deciding how to handle or repair the situation. Fields (2003) provides an example of this approach with a 14-year-old girl who had been truant from school. She skipped classes with two of her friends, stayed away from home overnight without permission, and had forged her father's name on an absence note to school personnel. This behavior was part of a longer list of school-related problems that she had experienced. School personnel were distressed, her teachers were disappointed in her, and everyone was concerned that some harm might come to her without a change in her behavior.

Implementing a VOD approach, both the student and school personnel discussed her recent behavior. As part of the plan for resolution, the student was asked to describe how she would be involved in repairing the harm that she had done. She offered several ideas, including writing a letter of apology to her teachers and her parents, "grounding" herself for a week after school, "repaying" the cost of time spent looking for her with volunteer work after school, and drafting a contract with her parents and teachers which laid out her responsibilities in terms of letting them know where she is at all times.

Family and Group Conferences

Within this approach, members of the school community and family members of the youth in question participate in the process. The goal is to broaden understanding about this situation beyond the victim and the offender. Supported by their families, offenders are able to apologize, while those who have been victimized have the opportunity to describe how the offenses have affected their lives (Mutter, Shemmings, Dugmore, & Hyare, 2008).

In other situations, school personnel may be part of a conference for a student who is having difficulties within and beyond the school setting. Wearmouth, McKinney, & Glynn(2007) provide an example of a 15-year-old Maori student in New Zealand who was behaving in increasingly negative ways in various social settings, including school, where he was becoming hostile and combative with teachers. The incident that precipitated the conference was his decision to drive his mother's car without her permission, despite his being underage. He ultimately crashed into a neighbor's fence, damaging the property, garden, and several trees. Although his mother was upset, he seemed amused by the incident.

As a result of these escalating situations, one of his teachers organized a conference. Consistent with Maori culture, his extended family and friends were invited to attend. The student attended, as did his rugby coach, teachers, mother, uncle, and the neighbor. Each of these individuals stood and discussed the student's many positive qualities, such as the loyalty he demonstrated toward his rugby team, his perseverance as an athlete, and his achievements in school. In addition, the elderly neighbor told a story about the garden and how the trees were a gift from his wife, who had passed away.

When it was the student's turn, he surprised everyone by standing and starting to cry. He remembered his neighbor, now deceased, who used to give him flowers from the garden to take home to his mother. As part of his healing process, he vowed to repair the neighbor's fence and clean up the property. He also promised to quit joyriding and reengage at school. As a result of the conference, which helped him perceive that he was part of a larger community which cared about him, he was able to reconnect and act responsibly about the damage that his behavior had caused.

Circles

Probably the most typical restorative justice practice within school settings is a Circle. The Circle process within the school setting invokes an assets-based approach to engage students as active participants in the decision-making process. In this way, the talents of young people are used the process of healing, dialoguing, building relationships, and resolving conflict.

Circles are used regularly with students in response to conduct referrals and to mediate conflict between adults on campus, as well as conflicts involving adults and students (Hamilton, 2008). Circles usually result in some form of consensus decision-making or resolution that all participants accept and agree to uphold. Circles can be applied in schools at the beginning or end of the day, within the classroom, to say farewell or fulfill a ritual, to mediate school staff concerns, to provide a forum for decision-making (Amstutz & Mullett, 2005) and to celebrate accomplishments or milestones (Pranis, 2005).

Circles of Understanding, or *Reentry Circles*, have been utilized with students who wish to reenter the school community after a period of non-attendance. When students cease attending school due to academic, familial, or personal issues, they are often provided with alternative educational options, ranging from independent study to attending summer school or equivalent programs. When students request reentry into the school community to obtain their diploma, the administrator makes provisions to assist the student with this transition. Prior to the student reenrolling in the school, the administrator requests that the parent and youth participate in a Reentry Circle. The Reentry Circle will usually include the student, parent, administrator, counselor, and social or case worker if applicable, and any adult who will support the youth's transition back into the school community. The Reentry Circle serves two purposes. First, the Circle process allows the adults within the school to extend their support to the young person and demonstrate their willingness to help him or her successfully transition back into the school community. Second, the Circle provides an opportunity for the adults to express their expectations, and for the student to take responsibility for meeting those expectations. Thus, the student is welcomed back into the school community fully aware that he or she will be held accountable for his or her actions, and that he or she is not embarking on this journey alone.

A *Healing Circle* is used to help students overcome trauma, as well as to promote healing from harmful situations that result from loss or disappointment. When a streaker ran across the field during the football game at halftime, for example, the Circle process was utilized to achieve multiple goals. One was to hold the offender accountable. Additionally, the Circle was used to help the perpetrator understand the impact of his behavior on the community members, as well as the parents of the girls who were unable to perform during the halftime show because of his actions. Within the Circle process, the administrator was able to engage the youth in acknowledging the impact of his behavior, and create a true sense of reconciliation and the healing that was needed for all participants to move forward. Likewise, the youth was able to comprehend the broader context of his behavior and its affect on the greater community.

Limitations in Approaches

Although there are clearly benefits associated with the use of restorative justice strategies in schools, there are also limitations associated with utilizing these practices in general. Obstacles to successful implementation include time constraints, problems with student participation, and staff resistance. As a result, schools may choose to eschew restorative justice and continue with traditional disciplinary practices.

Overwhelmingly, restorative justice processes require more time than traditional disciplinary practices and conflict resolution strategies. Sufficient time is required to gather the appropriate participants and to ensure that each person is provided the opportunity to authentically dialogue, reach consensus, and build relationships. In order for these processes to occur, participants must feel safe and trust the process, which may require subsequent meetings to accomplish.

Restorative justice processes also require that all members willingly agree to participate. For example, parents must authorize consent for their children to participate. Voluntary participation ensures participants will agree to the guidelines set forth and authentically engage in the process.

Staff must be properly trained in restorative justice principles and practices. Without proper training, staff members are more likely to perceive the school administration as being too lenient in response to behavior infractions. Likewise, school personnel must also address issues of confidentiality between participants and instances where mandated reporting requirements prevail. In order for a restorative approach to take root in the school setting, the entire school community must embrace the practice of honoring youth and creating inclusive communities built on trust, mutual respect, and dialogue.

The following case provides an example of a successful restorative justice initiative within a high school setting. Using the Circle process, the student and staff were able to voice their conflict and hear each other's stories. The case demonstrates how restorative justice as an alternative to the more punitive disciplinary practice that might have been implemented when this conflict erupted between a student and staff member.

CASE STUDY: KEISHA MALONE

West Valley High School (WVHS, a pseudonym), started utilizing restorative justice practices, specifically Circles, to address student behavioral infractions during the 1999–2000 school year. At that time, teachers and counselors were introduced to the Circle process during a two-day training. When WVHS began using restorative measures, there were no funding sources to support the use of Circles within the school. However, the school was committed to changing their philosophy and vision in terms of restitution and student misbehavior. The school's philosophy of restorative justice is based on the belief that holding students accountable, and providing restorative measures, is in the best interest of the students. Moreover, school personnel are dedicated to helping youth understand the impact of their behavior and to providing students with opportunities to make more informed decisions. In this way, the school fulfills the goal of attending to the social and emotional needs of youth and educating the whole child.

The administrative team (the principal and three assistant principals) at WVHS has adopted a restorative approach instead of a consequence-driven approach. To the greatest extent possible, WVHS incorporates restorative measures to respond to student conduct referrals. Nonetheless, school administrators still continue to use traditional disciplinary procedures, depending upon the specific circumstances of the case and the severity of the infraction. As a general rule, the Circle process is a complement to the more formal disciplinary procedures, such as detention, suspension, expulsion, and exclusion. In this manner, Circles function as a system-wide approach to addressing conflict and promoting healing. Finally, restorative measures, including Circles, have allowed school personnel to address the root of the offense, versus simply imposing punishment in response to student misbehavior.

When employed strategically, school personnel can use restorative justice practices to create opportunities for adults and students to resolve conflict and address deeper issues or concerns. The potential is illustrated in the case between Keisha Malone, an African-American super senior (a super senior is a student who requires more than four years to graduate from high school), and Harold Burroughs, a special education paraprofessional (both names are pseudonyms). Mr. Burroughs and Keisha, along with members of the school community, participated in a *Circle of Understanding* to address an incident occurring as a result of Keisha's tardiness to class.

On the day in question, Keisha entered her classroom well before the start of the period. Recognizing a fellow student in the hallway, Keisha exited the class and begin to converse with her friend. The two young ladies were engrossed in their conversation until the tardy bell rang, at which time they ended their conversation. As a result, Keisha was late for class. When Keisha attempted to enter the classroom, Mr. Burroughs felt obligated to enforce the tardy policy and questioned Keisha. This line of questioning was not well received by Keisha, who maintained she was not late to class. Mr. Burroughs took her remarks as a sign of disrespect and felt humiliated and justified to exert his authority. As a result, he raised his voice in a loud and authoritative tone. In turn, Keisha, feeling disrespected and humiliated, attempted to defend herself by raising her voice in response to Mr. Burroughs' commands. To add to the emotion, Mr. Burroughs closed the classroom door on Keisha and demanded that she obtain a pass to return to class. Keisha had no choice but to report to the assistant principal's office.

When Keisha entered the office of the assistant principal, Mrs. Heart (pseudonym), she suggested that a Circle be used to resolve the conflict. Once Mrs. Heart had secured approval to participate from everyone involved, she arranged for the Circle to convene immediately. In an adjacent office, several individuals came together, and each had a particular role in this process. The two people involved in the conflict, Keisha and Mr. Burroughs, were present. In addition, school personnel were there to help mediate the process and provide appropriate support. These individuals included Mrs. Heart and David Gant (a pseudonym) who was a teacher familiar with Keisha.

Although Mrs. Heart typically assumed the role of facilitator, she asked Mr. Gant to assume the role of facilitator in this particular situation. She made this change for several reasons. Mr. Gant had facilitated other Circles and was highly skilled in the process. In addition, Mrs. Heart's decision is an example of how an administrator can empower staff as leaders in restorative justice practices within the school. Likewise, Mrs. Heart reinforced the principle that every adult is capable of resolving conflict and assisting students to be accountable for their behavior. Finally, Keisha was given the message that she was surrounded by a community of caring adults to assist her.

The type of Circle used for this particular situation was the Circle of Understanding, because both parties came together to gain a deeper understanding of how best to interact with each other. All parties had a chance to share their perspective and share their truth in a nonjudgmental and blameless manner. In a Circle of Understanding, there is no victim and no offender. The Circle of Understanding is similar to a Healing Circle in that is attempts to heal broken bonds or create new bonds. In this case, the parties needed a forum to heal the broken bonds and create new bonds as a means of reestablishing their relationship and moving forward.

Mr. Gant began the Circle of Understanding with a ceremonial opening to reiterate the behavioral guidelines and the purpose of the meeting. At that time, he also introduced the talking piece and passed it to Keisha, who could then explain the reason for her tardiness without being interrupted. This provided her with an opportunity to tell her side of the story. In traditional disciplinary proceedings or referrals to the office, students are usually allowed to tell their story as a means of proving their innocence. Although the student has not been found guilty, any student sent to the principal's office is assumed to have violated acceptable behavior standards and be at fault. The Circle process allows for true dialogue to occur without the presupposition of suspicion, guilt, or blame. Mr. Burroughs was also given an opportunity to explain his involvement in the situation, not as the authoritarian who maintains the power, but as a human being who accepts responsibility for his behavior. As part of the Circle process, Mr. Burroughs acknowledged how his behavior and tone of voice may have negatively affected Keisha and influenced her hostile response. Because the Circle of Understanding focused on creating a space for dialogue, Mr. Gant was able to reiterate the services available to Keisha and remind her of the importance of being on time and using positive language when misunderstandings arise with adults on campus.

Once Mr. Burroughs and Keisha felt safe within the space of the Circle, they were able to get to the root of the behavior manifested in the argument. Mr. Burroughs expressed how he struggled with his role of authority, which often resulted in his dictatorial speech toward his students. Moreover, he gained a deeper understanding of how his internal feelings were being interpreted and received by the very students with whom he wanted to create relationships. Since Mr. Burroughs understood the impact of his behavior, he was able to understand that creating relationships with students helps to minimize the use of power and coercion as a tool to direct students.

Consequently, Keisha expressed that the tone of Mr. Burroughs's voice was a trigger. Keisha's dad was not the type of father to raise his voice. Since Keisha's dad was currently in the hospital, Keisha was faced with all the emotions and concerns that youth have when a family is sick or failing in health. Keisha acknowledged that her response to Mr. Burroughs was inappropriate; moreover, she also revealed the bigger issues of feeling disconnected within the school community. Furthermore, Keisha admitted that she felt pressured to perform beyond her capability. Not only was Keisha desperately trying to acclimate herself to the school community, she was struggling with a sense of isolation, inadequacy, and inability to perform. Keisha's response to Mr. Burroughs's request was an indicator of larger issues needing attention.

Because the Circle process creates a space of authenticity, Keisha was able to express her personal issues, which were unrelated to the original incident. With this knowledge, Mrs. Heart, Mr. Burroughs, and Mr. Gant could provide Keisha with the support systems, survival skills, and resources to manage the current circumstances occurring in her life, as well as to address her feelings of isolation and alienation. The Circle process also provided Keisha with a safe environment to be her best self. The traditional process of addressing misunderstandings between adults and students usually results in the administrator assigning blame and administering an appropriate consequence to the student. However, traditional school responses to conflict do not address the root of the problem or the manifestation of the behavior.

SKILL BUILDING

In the case study presented, the gravity of the student's current experiences and her perceptions of those experiences became apparent. Within the Circle of Understanding, her frustration, worry, sense of failure, and isolation was uncovered. If the staff had simply reported the behavioral incident and assigned a detention or suspension, the student would have had an additional challenge placed on her. The Circle of Understanding allowed the staff to become aware of the student's real concerns and the supports she needed. The staff involved had a chance to recognize the impact of their actions, acknowledge their own frustrations, and understand how their interactions were perceived by the student. It appears that the group members were able to better understand one another, develop and express empathy, and engage in healing together. The Circle process allowed them to slow down and develop a richer understanding of each other's concerns and perspective. The group's work together created a new way to more forward and create a different narrative with the student.

Restorative Justice Skills

Pre-Circle

Prior to using a Circle, there are several conditions that need to be considered and put into place. At this stage, the practitioner needs to have the skills to assess whether conditions are right within the school setting to implement restorative justice. Questions about the overall philosophy about conflict and resolution, and the value of implementing restorative justice processes, are the foundation of this assessment process.

Restorative justice, especially the Circle process, provides practitioners with a different lens through which to view conflict, relationship-building, and dialoguing. In the case of Keisha Malone, a restorative justice practitioner would need to make a commitment to educating the whole child. In order for restorative justice principles and practices to be effective, practitioners must view youth from an assets-based perspective and as an integral component of the school community. Practitioners who want to build relationships with youth and co-construct optimal conditions in the schools must focus on the assets and strengths that students bring to the school community.

Likewise, this new lens challenges adults to examine their own issues of power and influence in educational institutions. If adults continue to perceive their role as authoritarian, and students as recipients of that authority, there is no room for growth or learning within the school setting. Therefore, adults must be willing to accept the reality that youth enter the school community with a variety of experiences, skills and strengths. More importantly, practitioners must be willing to acknowledge, listen to, and accept youth as functioning members of the community. In doing so, they will be able to distribute power equally among all participants and trust that students have the capacity to handle the responsibility of power. Practitioners must reconceptualize the concept that students are incapable of making informed decisions and that student interaction is deficit-based versus assets-based.

Prior to convening a Circle, practitioners must decide if the specific situation should be resolved with a Circle. The following set of questions can help assess whether the conditions are in place to implement a Circle process at the school:

1) Are participants willing to voluntarily engage in the Circle process? Or are participants feeling pressured to engage in the process? Is there adequate time and an appropriate space to conduct a Circle?

2) In cases where there is a victim and offender, has the offender taken responsibility for his or her behavior? Is the victim willing to engage in the process with the offender? Are there structures in place to allow the victim to feel empowered? Are there procedures in place to help the offender avoid feeling further penalized as a result of his or her behavior? Is the community committed to reaching a resolution that restores all parties and addresses the harm to the greatest extent possible?

3) Have parents or guardians been notified?

4) How will issues of confidentiality be addressed?

5) Who will be responsible for following up with the participants and making sure the consensus plan or agreements are kept?

During the Circle

Convening the Circle includes several processes. These include establishing guidelines by identifying shared values, encouraging storytelling as the basis for building relationships, and expressing hopes, concerns, and feelings. During the Circle process, participants probe the causes of wrongdoing to generate ideas for conflict resolution, and draw attention to the specific areas needed to reach consensus (Pranis, 2005). Practitioners must be able to provide for the safety of the members within the Circle. While safety certainly includes physical elements as part of resolving conflict between the parties, it also means creating an environment where all individuals have the opportunity to speak their truth.

In the Circle process, all participants are equal and thus are equally responsible for the outcomes. Once an adult enters the Circle, he or she becomes a part of a group, and is thus no longer responsible for individually determining the outcome. The group may consist of professionals from outside of the school setting, staff members, students, parents, or community members. Because the Circle process accommodates a variety of individuals, practitioners must broaden their perspective about who is capable and qualified to help youth (Hamilton, 2008). Practitioners must also be willing to give voice to those who are silent and listen to converging points of view, even if those views uncover hidden truths about uncomfortable events occurring at the school. In this context, practitioners must also possess excellent listening skills. Practitioners must truly listen, so as not to patronize or minimize other participants' voices or experiences. This aspect is an important one in situations where there is a power imbalance among the roles of participants, such as students and teachers. Because of the power differential, the Circle (and restorative practices in general) provides a way for everyone to have a voice in description and resolution of the situation.

Post-Circle

Once the Circle process is complete, the practitioner must agree to support the outcome. If the practitioner undermines the outcome of the Circle, the participants will not trust the process or agree to enter into that space again for fear of betrayal or deceit. Practitioners must follow up with participants after the Circle to ensure that agreements and outcomes are kept. Follow-up procedures involve assessing the degree to which obligations are fulfilled, determining the success or failure of the process, and celebrating success or making adjustments (Pranis, 2005). This may include conducting another Circle or meeting individually with participants. By doing so, practitioners send a clear message that the Circle process is valued and shared leadership is honored. Overall, time is the most important element to the success of the Circle process. Traditional school procedures provide time-efficient responses. The Circle process requires that practitioners be patient. A situation may not be resolved in one Circle setting, however, what does result is a process whereby individuals build relationships and carry forward the Circle principles into their everyday lives. Critical understanding and consciousness are achieved through the act of dialogue (Freire, 1970/2006; 1974/2007). However, true dialogue cannot exist without trust, which takes time to build and foster with youth. Moreover, the spoken word inspires action, which is required for transformation.

Social Work Skills

Like the restorative justice practitioner, there are several key roles that a social worker could play within this case study. These include helping convene and facilitate the Circle, serving as a resource informant, or being a case manager for specific areas of need identified. In Keisha's case, for example, if the group decided that in-home or home health services for the father would ease some of the stress experienced by the student, the social worker could locate and facilitate enrolment in those services. If the father's illness had created financial strains on the family, the social worker could provide information to assist with entitlements and resources to address financial needs, such as food stamps, Medicaid, energy assistance, or disability-related income supports.

The social worker could help identify bridge-builders or individuals who may enhance the social network of this student. This is done through helping uncover the student's interests, preferences and gifts (Condeluci, 1995; Mount, Beeman, & Ducharme, 1988). Condeluci (2008) contends, "All people, no matter the severity of situation, have things to add, offer, or contribute. We must always be looking for those things that might connect people" (p. 84).

Using the four primary arenas of intervention or engagement for social workers within school settings—which are individuals, families, groups, and the community (Staudt, Cherry, & Watson, 2005)—it is possible to consider a range of important interventions appropriate for Keisha's case.

At the individual level, the social worker could work with Keisha on developing a specific, individually tailored plan to cope with her concerns. The social worker could provide or connect her to counseling on managing stress and improving self-esteem. It also is important that she have an opportunity to discuss her fears related to her father's illness and its impact on her life and on her family's experiences. Identifying and connecting her with appropriate academic support to help her with academic challenges also seems to be an important consideration.

At the family level, the social worker can focus on ways to help the family reduce the overall stress that it is currently experiencing. It is clear that the family is facing significant challenges due to the poor health of Keisha's father. An approach that has shown promise is the creation of a Family Support Team, which establishes relationships with the student and family members and listens to the self-defined support needs of those family members, and makes connections to resources in the community, including tutoring, health-related services, family counseling, legal aid referrals, and referrals for entitlements and financial resources (Pritchard and Williams, 2001).

In terms of group-level work, Keisha's age cohort (that is, adolescence) is developmentally prime for group work, as peer group influences are strong. Keisha could benefit from a group focused on super seniors, for example. It is likely that these students share many of the same experiences and concerns. Group interventions are a powerful means to help diminish isolation and depression and help group members define and share possible solutions. These affinity groups also create networks of support and relationships that extend beyond the group meeting setting. Other support groups that may be relevant might include other students with parents who are ill or disabled in some way. An alternative to a group focused on challenges would be a group that is focused on some shared interest area, such as art, gardening, or music. Through connecting to and establishing relations with others with shared interests, Keisha may experience less stress and more positive interactions in her life. Her network of connection and support could expand.

At the community level, there are two communities for consideration in Keisha's case which are relevant to her situation, and would be relevant for all students when considering macro interventions. One community could be defined as her school community, while the other is her neighborhood and surrounding environment. Possible interventions in the school community would include determining participatory and leadership roles. Service projects designed by students should be considered, as these afford students the opportunity to make a contribution to the enhancement of the school community and often allow students, particularly those with academic challenges, to participate in activities where other gifts and abilities can be shared. The work carried out through student-designed service projects enhances relationships, strengthens attachment to the community, and fosters a sense of accomplishment. Macro practice interventions for the neighborhood and surrounding community include working with business leaders in the area to help students explore post-school opportunities. Job training, internships, apprenticeships, and summer and after-school employment and training opportunities are examples of connections that would be important to explore with the business community. It would also be important to look at support groups outside of the school context. In Keisha's case, are there groups that work on issues of self-esteem or grief, or are there groups that simply offer a connection to an area of interest? Siu-Ming (2007) contends "Empowerment in the school and community are perceived as political arenas that practitioners much take into account. They are highly significant for promoting outcomes associated with positive experience and performance for young people. It is therefore necessary for practitioners to treat the school and the community as both the subject of empowerment and the crucial channels for empowering services users and partners" (p. 560).

At all levels of social work intervention, it is critical that Keisha be supported as an active (versus passive) participant. This creates a sense of ownership and self-esteem, and accords her respect as an expert on her own experiences and situations. Supporting active, direct engagement will likely give her a greater sense of self-efficacy and control over her present and future.

ANALYSIS OF FIT: SOCIAL WORK AND RESTORATIVE JUSTICE APPROACHES

Restorative justice practices offer an array of opportunities for social workers to use micro and clinical practice skills as well as macro and community practice skills. Social workers need to be mindful of when and how to best use the skills of each domain. A challenge with micro or individualized social work practice in school settings is that it often comes imbued with a medical or clinically diagnostic, deficit-based framework that supports programs and interventions that are punishment based. While there has been tremendous work put forward in schools of social work to focus on identifying an individual's assets and gifts, the tendency in agency practice is toward problem identification, which often means labeling the person as the source of the problem or issue to be addressed. There are clearly times when a sound clinical intervention is important, for example, in dealing with trauma, particularly with trauma connected to traditional school disciplinary procedures (Cameron & Sheppard, 2006). However, all students may not need this level of intervention if there is the opportunity to tell their story and have their experience validated as part of the process of conflict resolution.

A youth-empowerment approach can increase the investment of adolescents in productive involvement in relationships, schools, and the community. Research conducted by the Innovation Center for Community and Youth Development and by Social Policy Research Associates reviewed the youth engagement opportunities and determined that the more youth moved from a system that viewed them as "clients" to one that afforded them opportunities for engagement and leadership, the stronger the connection to positive experiences and people in the community. Involving youth in decision making, and planning and implementation of activities, enhances their empowerment by increasing their sense of self-efficacy and their exposure to positive social roles (Funders Collaborative on Youth Organizing (2000).

This idea is echoed by Siu-Ming (2007), who noted that, although youth traditionally have not been afforded opportunities to develop and implement policies regarding education and the school arena, they should be supported to participate in that development:

> School is a microcosm of society: if students are not allowed to have a voice in matters related to their schooling, they may question their value for participating in social and political processes in the future. The findings show that youth workers can collaborate with service partners to create a climate in which adolescents can reflect critically on their needs and make recommendations for a more favorable learning environment. They can, thus, become active rather than passive learners, which in turn encourages them to take part in matters outside the school setting. In short, this approach helps prepare young people for participation in a democratic way of life. (p. 564)

Siu-Ming (2007) added that "such emancipatory politics manifest itself in personal, school, community and institutional dimensions" (p. 565).

Restorative justice practices seem clearly aligned with social work macro practice efforts, and it is critical that social workers understand what macro practice means and what macro change entails. Condeluci (2008) framed the importance of macro change:

> Macro change is about systems, communities, environments, and cultures. It is about understanding the parameters of acceptance and then influencing changes. To facilitate the macro change one must understand broader concepts that apply more to societies and collections of people, than to deficits or difference. We must understand system theory, social influence theory, cultural theories and the elements of the community. (p. 8)

Minimally, it is important that social workers understand how to assess, develop, and support functional, healthy, inclusive communities. Social work graduates need specific skills related to group facilitation, community development, and organizing. Restorative justice practices entail supporting and nurturing positive interactions and relationships in schools and in the broader community. Individuals or groups who are marginalized, isolated, or labeled in negative ways lose the opportunity to be regarded as having gifts to share with, or contributions to make to, the community. Interdependence, or the idea that all are connected to other members of the community, promotes the protective effects of nurturing relationships and supportive communities (Condeluci, 1995). Restorative justice offers an impetus for resurgence in community/macro practice skills development among social workers.

To understand the scope of the work involved, it is important for social workers to deeply understand the process and roles, particularly as it relates to the Circle process. While it is easy for the social worker or school staff member to fall into the role of expert or authority figure, it is necessary to understand the role of facilitator, which is centered on allowing the participants to embrace and drive the process of the Circle, and to support those involved in naming the issue and defining the problem. This involves supporting and honoring everyone's voice and trying to understand each person's perspective on the issue through dialogue. Horton (1990) articulated the importance of listening to gain understanding. He stated, "It is important that you understand the difference between your perceptions of their problems, and their perceptions of the problem. You shouldn't be trying to discover your perception of their perception. You must find a way to determine what their perception is" (p.125). Downey, Anyaegbunam, and Scutchfield (2009) echo the relevance of dialogue as the avenue to revealing different perspectives and creating shared understanding, a critical step in defining and addressing shared concerns: "Dialogue may help move conversations forward by presenting diverse individuals with the opportunity to present various points of view. Individuals then have the chance to internalize the views of others to enhance mutual understanding" (p. 27).

NEXT STEPS

Restorative justice presents an opportunity for youth to be perceived differently in school settings, moving from identification of deficits and pathology to narratives focused on gifts and abilities. There are a number of innovative ways for students to participate in the school setting that acknowledge their capacities and create important relationship- and community-building endeavors. These include peer support groups, cultural education projects, service learning such as recycling and conservation work, peer and cross-age tutoring, having students serve as conflict mediators, having older students mentor younger students, and having student teach or co-lead courses on anger management and addiction (Bazemore & Umbreit, 1997).

Critical steps in combining skills of restorative justice and social work need to be instituted within degree programs and continue after graduation. This process involves exposing social work students to classes on restorative justice and the Circle process in both undergraduate and graduate programs, and providing students with opportunities to engage in applying their knowledge to "real world" situations, and action/reflection in practicum placements or other experiential learning activities. For social workers currently working in school settings, it is important that they take classes or continuing education course offerings in group facilitation, with a particular emphasis on the Circle process. This will afford social workers the opportunity to offer a new process that could change the trajectory of the school experience for those students experiencing challenges, moving them from isolation and a trip through the school-to-prison pipeline, to a chance for inclusion and a more desirable future.

To be successful using the Circle process, social workers will also need to evaluate and shift their role from that of problem-solver and expert to that of good facilitator and resource informant. This requires that they examine their own stake in maintaining power relationships or the status quo. Their role moves from being prescriptive to being authentically supportive of a group's capacity to define and create change.

Social workers would be well served to move to a richer and more expansive vision of what is possible through restorative justice practices within schools. Cameron and Sheppard (2006) suggest that social workers have a responsibility to advocate for change within the school system. Social workers also should advocate for the elimination of harmful, punitive, and unfair disciplinary practices in schools, as called for in the NASW's *Standards for School Social Work Services* (National Association of Social Workers, 2002). Advocacy at the school district level, educating school district administrators and school boards about the potential harm of conventional disciplinary practices, recommending alternatives, and offering training may help prevent the discouragement, upset, and estrangement experienced by many children disciplined at school.

CONCLUSION

According to the National Association of Social Workers' Code of Ethics, the core values of social work are as follows: social justice, dignity and worth of the person, importance of human relationships, integrity, and competence (National Association of Social Workers, 1996/1999). This resonates with the premise put forward by Pranis (2005): "Circles hold at their center the importance of recognizing the impact of our behavior on others and acknowledging the interconnectedness of our fates. Harm to one is harm to all. Good for one is good for all." There is resonance between the values of the Code of Ethics and the Circle process, one framing the values and the other offering a process through which those values are implemented. van Wormer (2009) offered,

> Consider the core values of social work—service, social justice, dignity and worth of the person, important of human relationships, integrity, and competence (NASW, 2000). Each of these values is congruent with the principles of restorative justice. The service aspect of restorative justice is found through advocacy for this humanistic approach and integrity in determining for which situations these alternative forms of justice are appropriate. Social justice entails fairness or equity to provide a balance among people who have varying degrees of power in a social setting. That restorative justice is a form of social justice of special relevance to social work practice is a major argument here. The value of competence comes into play as social workers get training in restorative practices and become familiar with the emerging research literature on participant satisfaction with the process. (p. 11)

The Circle process offers a new and innovative approach to social workers and other practitioners to assist students, faculty, families, and community members in creating new stories of hope, contribution, and inclusion for students in the school system. This process can move us from giving up on children. The current system consigns some students to alternative schools, pushes others towards dropping out, or ushers them down the school-to-prison pipeline. Restorative justice practices offer a new model that moves us towards inclusive, healthy, learning environments that embrace the fundamental idea that all children have worth and that they have important gifts and contributions to make to the community.

REFERENCES

American Academy of Pediatrics. (2003). Out-of-school suspension and expulsion. *Pediatrics, 112*, 1206–1209.

Amstutz, L. S., & Mullett, J. H. (2005). *The little book of restorative discipline for schools: Teaching responsibility; creating caring climates.* Intercourse, PA: Good Books.

Anderson-Butcher, D., and Ashton, D. (2004). Innovative models of collaboration to serve children, youths, and families, and communities. *Children & Schools, 26*, 39–53.

Anderson-Butcher, D., Stelter, E., & Midle, T. (2006). A case for expanded school-community partnerships in support of positive youth development. *Children & Schools, 28*(3), 155–163.

Ashworth, J., Van Brockern, S., Ailts, J., & Donnelly, J. (2008). The restorative justice center: An alternative to school detention. *Reclaiming Children and Youth, 17*(3), 22–27.

Bazemore, G. (2001). Young people, trouble, and crime: Restorative justice as a normative theory of informal social control and social support. *Youth and Society, 33*(2), 199–226.

Bazemore, G., and Umbreit, M. (1997). *Balanced and restorative justice for juveniles: A framework juvenile justice in the 21st Century.* http://www.ncjrs.gov/pdffiles/framwork.pdf (Retrieved: May 7, 2010).

Bell, C. (2001). Cultivating resilience in youth. *Journal of Adolescent Health, 29*(5), 375–381.

Bemark, F. (2005). Reflections on multiculturalism, social justice and empowerment groups for academic success: A critical discourse for contemporary schools. *Professional School Counseling, 8*(5), 401–406.

Bruns, E., Moore, E., Stephan, S.H., Pruitt, D., & Weist, M. (2005). The impact of school mental health services on out-of-school suspension rates. *Journal of Youth and Adolescence, 34*, 23–60.

California Dropout Research Project. (2008, February). *Solving California's dropout crisis.* Retrieved April 15, 2009, from http://www.lmri.ucsb.edu/dropouts/

Cameron, M., & Sheppard, S.M. (2006). School discipline and social work practice: Application of research and theory to intervention. *Children & Schools, 28*(1), 15–23.

Chmelynski, C. (2005). Restorative justice for discipline with respect. *Education Digest, 71*(1), 17–20.

Civil Rights Project. (2000, June). *Opportunities suspended: The devastating consequences of zero tolerance and school discipline policies.* Report from a National Summit on Zero Tolerance, Washington DC. Harvard Civil Rights Project, Cambridge, MA.

Condeluci, A. (1995). *Interdependence: The route to community.* Winterpark, FL: GR Press, Inc.

Condeluci, A. (2008). *The essence of interdependence: Building community for everyone.* Wake Forest, NC: NC. Lash & Associates Publishing/Training, Inc.

Dawson, N., & McHugh, B. (2006). A systemic response to school-based violence from a UK perspective. *Journal of Family Therapy, 28*(3), 267–271.

Drewery, W. (2004). Conferencing in schools: Punishment, restorative justice, and the productive importance of the process of conversation. *Journal of Community & Applied Social Psychology, 14*(5), 332–344.

Downey, L., Anyaegbunam, C., & Scutchfield, F. (2009). Dialogue to deliberation: Expanding the empowerment education model. *American Journal of Health Behavior, 33*(1), 26–36.

Dupper, D., Theriot, M., & Craun, S. (2009). Reducing out-of-school suspensions: Practice guidelines for school social workers. *Children and Schools, 31*, 6–14.

Fields, B. A. (2003). Restitution and restorative justice. *Youth Studies Australia, 22*(4), 44–51.

Franklin, C. (2000). Predicting the future of school social work practice in the new millennium. *Social Work in Education, 22*(1), 7–12.

Freire, P. (2006). *Pedagogy of the oppressed* (30th anniversary ed.). M. B. Ramos (Trans.). New York: Continuum International. (Original work published 1970)

Freire, P. (2007). Education as the practice of freedom. In M. B. Ramos (Ed. & Trans.), *Education for critical consciousness.* London: Continuum International. (Original work published 1974)

Funders Collaborative on Youth Organizing. (2000). Youth Engagement Continuum. Retrieved April 15, 2009, http://www.fcyo.org/sitebody/about%20FCYO/index.htm

Garcia-Reid, P. (2008). Understanding the effect of structural violence on the educational identities of Hispanic adolescents: A call for social justice. *Children and Schools, 30*(4), 235–241.

Garrett, K. (2006). Making the case for school social work. *Children & Schools, 28*(2), 115–121.

Garrett, K. (2004). Use of groups in school social work: Group work and group process. *Social Work with Groups, 27,* 75–92.

Hamilton, M.V. (2008). *Restorative justice: Reconceptualizing school disciplinary theory and practice.* Unpublished doctoral dissertation. University of the Pacific. Retrieved December 11, 2008, from Dissertations & Theses: A& I database. No. AAT 3303484.

hooks, B. (1994). *Teaching to transgress: Education as the practice of freedom.* London: Routledge.

Horton, M. (1990). *The long haul.* New York: Doubleday.

Horton, M., & Freire, P. (2001). *We make the road by walking: Conversations on education and social change.* Philadelphia: Temple University Press.

Jennings, W., Gover, A., & Hitchcock, D. (2008). Localizing restorative justice: An in-depth look at a Denver public school program. *Sociology of Crime,* Law, & Deviance, *11,* 167–187.

Jozefowicz-Simbeni, D. (2008). An ecological and developmental perspective on dropout risk factors in early adolescence: Role of school social workers in dropout prevention efforts. *Children & School, 30*(1), 49–62.

Karp, D. R., & Breslin, B. (2001). Restorative justice in school communities. *Youth & Society, 33*(2), 249–272.

Lloyd, G., McCluskey, G., Riddell, S., Stead, J., Weedon, E., & Kane, J. (2007). *Restorative practices in three Scottish councils: Evaluation of pilot projects 2004-2006. A collaborative Evaluation by the Universities of Edinburgh and Glasgow funded by the Scottish Executive.* University of Edinburgh, University of Glasgow.

McClusky, G., Lloyd, G., Stead, J., & Kane, J. (2008). "I was dead restorative today": From restorative justice to restorative approaches in school. *Cambridge Journal of Education, 38*(2), 199–209.

McCold, P., Kerner, H., & Weitekamp, E. (Eds.). (2002). *Restorative justice: Theoretical foundations.* Cullompton, Devon, UK: Willan.

McNeely, C. A., Nonnemaker, J. M., & Blum, R. W. (2002). Promoting school connectedness: Evidence for the national longitudinal study of adolescent health. *Journal of School Health, 72*(4), 138–146.

Minnesota Department of Children, Families and Learning. (2001). *In-school behavior intervention grants: A three-year evaluation of alternative approaches to suspensions and expulsions.* Report to the legislature. Roseville, MN: Minnesota Department of Children, Families & Learning. 2001

Mirsky, L. (2004). Transforming school culture: An update. *Restorative Justice EForum.* Retrieved July 7, 2008, from http://www.iirp.org/article_detail.php?article_id=Mzk1

Morrison, B. (2006). School bullying and restorative justice: Toward a theoretical understanding of the role of respect, pride, and shame. *Journal of Social Issues, 62,* 371–392.

Morrison, B., Blood, P., & Thorsborne, J. (2006). Practicing restorative justice in school communities: The challenge of culture change. *Public Organization Review: A Global Journal, 5,* 335–357.

Mount, B., Beeman, P., & Ducharme, G. (1988). *What are we learning about circles of support?* New Haven, CT: Graphic Futures.

Mutter, R., Shemmings, D., Dugmore, P., & Hyare, M. (2008). Family group conferences in youth justice. *Health & Social Care in the Community, 16*(3), 262–270.

National Association of Social Workers. (2002). *NASW Standards for School Social Work Services*. Washington, DC: NASW Press.

National Association of Social Workers. (1999). *Code of Ethics of the National Association of Social Workers*. Washington, DC: NASW Press. (Original work approved 1996)

Pranis, K. (2005). *The little book of circle processes*. Intercourse, PA: Good Books.

Pritchard, C., & Williams, R. (2001). A three-year comparative longitudinal study of a school based social work family services to reduce truancy, delinquency and school exclusions. *Journal of Social Welfare and Family Law, 23*(1), 23–43.

Reyes, A. H. (2006). *Discipline, achievement, race: Is zero tolerance the answer?* Lanham, MD: Rowman & Littlefield.

Siu-Ming, T. (2007). Empowering school social work practices for positive youth development: Hong Kong experience. *Adolescence, 42*(167), 555–567.

Skiba, R., & Peterson, R. (1999). The dark side of zero tolerance. *Phi Delta Kappan, 80*(5), 372–379.

Skiba, R., & Peterson, R. (2000). School discipline at a crossroads: From zero tolerance to early response. *Exceptional Children, 66*(3), 335–346.

Skiba, R. J., & Knesting, K. (2001). Zero tolerance, zero evidence: An analysis of school disciplinary practice. In G. G. Noam (Series Ed.) & R. J. Skiba (Vol. Ed.), *New directions for youth development: Vol. 92. Zero Tolerance: Can suspension and expulsion keep schools safe?* (pp. 17–43). San Francisco: Jossey-Bass.

Staudt, M., Cherry, D., & Watson, M. (2005). Practice guidelines for school social workers: A modified replication and extension of a prototype. *Children & Schools, 27*(2), 71–81.

U.S. Department of Education. (2000). *Elementary and secondary school survey: National and state projections*. Washington, DC: Office of Civil Rights.

van Wormer, K. (2009). Restorative justice as social justice for victims of gendered violence: A standpoint feminist perspective. *Social Work, 54*(2), 107–116.

Varnham, S. (2005). Seeing things differently: Restorative justice and school discipline. *Education and the Law, 17*(3), 187–104.

Wald, J., and Losen. D. (2003). Defining and redirecting a school-to-prison pipeline. In J. Wald and D. Losen (Eds.), *New directions for youth development*. pp. 9–15, San Francisco: Jossey-Bass.

Wearmouth, J., McKinney, R., & Glynn, T. (2007). Restorative justice: Two examples from New Zealand schools. *British Journal of Special Education, 34*(4), 196–203.

Chapter Six

Restorative Justice in Prisons

BARB TOEWS AND M. KAY HARRIS

SOCIAL WORK IN PRISONS

While social work finds its roots in social institutions such as prisons (Boyer, 1992; Katz, 1996; Rothman, 2002), its practitioners increasingly have distanced themselves from corrections. Gumz (2004) cites as evidence of this shift the lack of a corrections practice area within the National Association of Social Workers (NASW), the limited number of graduate programs offering corrections special-izations, a miniscule percentage (.07%) of graduates identifying corrections/criminal justice as their specialty, and a dearth of recent publications by social work educators in this substantive area. This exodus from the field of corrections is understandable, given the correctional trend away from rehabilitation and toward punishment and social work's reported shift from work with marginalized individuals and communities to psychotherapeutic practice (Gumz, 2004).

Yet, the retreat from corrections by social workers is short sighted. It does not simply represent a turning away from an institution, but an abandonment of a vulnerable group of people—incarcerated men and women—and the personal, interpersonal, and social needs that result from their crimes, as well those that contributed to them. The effects of this limited involvement with incarcerated individuals ripple out to the victims and communities that suffer as a result of the offenses committed. Offenders typically have done little to repair the individual and social damage caused by their crimes—especially those residing in an institu-tion focused on punishment and control, not accountability. Therefore, they leave prison without having fulfilled their obligations to themselves, their victims, or the affected community, and without having received due attention to their per-sonal, interpersonal, and social needs.

The near-abandonment of corrections also represents a withdrawal from par-ticipation in the transformation of social structures and policies that contribute to the social and political context of the current trend in mass incarceration. Striking evidence is accumulating which shows that mass imprisonment is deeply entan-gled with a range of major social problems. Social workers are in a position to spotlight these troubling linkages and to play a leadership role in devising programs, policies, and practices that can both confront their problematic nature and help redress their harmful effects.

As a lens that offers a far wider perspective on the potential role of social work within corrections than one focused exclusively on a helping role, the restorative justice orientation may be especially useful in making the case for greater social work involvement in corrections. Social workers interested or involved in restorative justice practice, such as Gumz (Gumz, 2004; Gumz & Grant 2009), van Wormer (van Wormer, 2001; 2006), and Umbreit (Umbreit, Vos, Coates, & Brown, 2003), confirm that social work and restorative justice are complementary. Yet engagement within the corrections arena presents real challenges to the values, principles, and methods of both fields of practice.

This chapter looks at the potential of restorative justice in prisons to advance more immediate aims, some of which arguably are of value to prisoners, while others clearly benefit crime victims and the larger society. Discussions of restorative justice typically stress its importance in addressing the emotional and material needs of people who have been harmed by crime, placing special emphasis on the obligations of offenders to acknowledge and help repair the damage their criminal acts have caused. This chapter explores how restorative justice may encourage or support offenders in coming to terms with such accountability for their crimes from inside a prison. At the same time, it considers ways in which this orientation can help address the needs of prisoners, including the potential for restoring, or creating anew, an experience of empowerment and inclusion in an unequal world. The chapter also discusses some of the tensions inherent in employing restorative justice practices in prisons, in light of the punitive orientation of the system and the larger social and political context of imprisonment. A case study of a prison-based restorative justice practice sets the stage for considering social work skills for facilitating restorative programs, taking the benefits and risks of delivering them in a prison setting into account. Consideration of these potential rewards and dangers suggests ways in which restorative justice and social work fit together as allied fields dedicated to supporting people to be accountable for their actions, while also seeking to affirm their humanity and promote their empowerment. In addition, practitioners in both areas can explore how they together can contribute to social transformation, despite the formidable challenges that such change efforts must confront.

Accountability and Repair: Integrating Restorative Justice

Social work's renewed interest in corrections in light of restorative justice is logical, as the philosophy of restorative justice and its practices strive to promote individual, interpersonal, and social well-being in response to crime by working with those directly impacted by offenses. Central to restorative justice is a commitment to take seriously and attend to the needs of all those involved in and affected by crimes and related harms. This entails moving victims and their needs from their ancillary position in traditional criminal justice practices, to front and center in restorative ones, and also shifts the focus from simply punishing and controlling offenders to seeking to engage them in recognizing their obligations to those they have harmed and taking meaningful steps to acknowledge and repair, to the extent possible, the damage created by their actions.

Studies suggest that restorative processes, especially those that bring victims and offenders together for interaction, result in beneficial outcomes for both groups. Face-to-face encounters with the victims directly affected by their crimes, and even with the narratives of victims not related to their crimes, have been shown to enhance incarcerated offenders' understanding of victims and their needs, as well as to increase empathy and desire to talk about and make amends for their crimes (Armour, 2006; Helfgott, Lovell, Lawrence, & Parsonage, 2000; Lovell, Helfgott, & Lawrence, 2002). Sherman and Strang (2007), in their review of randomized, controlled trials of the effectiveness of victim–offender conferencing and restitution, found that restorative justice contributed to reduced recidivism rates among offenders, though the results were inconsistent across offender subgroups. There is wide variability about for whom and under what conditions restorative justice "works" to help reduce reoffending. Notably, their review found that restorative practices were more effective in reducing recidivism for those who committed violent crime than those who committed nonviolent crime. They also noted that the offending individuals involved in restorative justice programs are more likely to complete their restitution obligations to victims than if they had simply gone through the conventional court process.

Researchers speculate that there is a link between victim–offender interaction and storytelling and recidivism. Armour (2006) argues that hearing victims' stories can help to "overcome offenders' denial, self-centeredness and lack of awareness, expose offenders to the impact of their actions, and help offenders feel the pain their crimes created" (p. 5). She further suggests that "cognitive dissonance emerges between the past and the present," (p. 5) which may be alleviated by not reoffending and instead engaging in pro-social behavior. Sherman and Strang (2007) suggest that, contrary to most criminological theories, offenders commit crimes not believing that those acts are wrong. Restorative justice puts them in a position to understand the moral implications of their actions and creates the conditions in which the offending individual begins to see his or her potential for being more fully moral and law-abiding.

Victims, and society as a whole, benefit from the positive effects of restorative justice on offenders. Interaction with offenders can contribute to victims experiencing a reduction in trauma symptomology and increased ability to more forward with their lives (Umbreit et al., 2003; Sherman and Strang, 2007). Victims experience validation and vindication as they speak to their experiences, and offenders demonstrate understanding of what they have done and take steps to repair the harm (Lovell et al., 2002). Importantly, those involved in restorative processes who have experienced victimization are more likely to receive compensation for their losses

(Sherman and Strang, 2007). Society also benefits to the extent that restorative justice practices yield increased community safety and the enhanced well-being that results from lower levels of offending. In the extreme, justice expenditures could decrease in light of reduced reoffending, increased restitution completion, and heightened victim satisfaction and healing (Sherman and Strang, 2007), freeing budgets to attend to other pressing social issues, including those that contribute to crime and mass incarceration.

SOCIAL AND POLITICAL CONTEXT OF MASS INCARCERATION

The impressive potential of restorative justice to better promote justice, personal and social healing, and community harmony needs to be understood in light of the current context of mass incarceration. The scale of American incarceration is unmatched anywhere else in the world (Pew Center on the States, 2008). With 5% of the world's population, the U.S. holds almost 25% of the world's prisoners (Liptak, 2008). The 2.4 million men and women confined in American prisons and jails as of mid-2008 (Minton and Sabol, 2009; West and Sabol, 2009) represent 1 in every 100 people (Pew Center on the States, 2008). Despite the startling reach of the prison system, reasons why this phenomenon should be of concern to people besides those confined and their loved ones require some elaboration. Two major arguments are especially germane for the social work profession: the linkages between social inequality and imprisonment, and the social consequences of incarceration as experienced by the incarcerated, their loved ones, and society as a whole. Given this broader context, the social work field needs to recognize how deeply mass imprisonment is intertwined with the other social problem areas with which the discipline traditionally has been engaged.

Imprisonment and Social Inequality

As Bruce Western (2006) has documented chillingly, "state power flows along the contours of social inequality" (p. 4). The direct impact of the seven-fold increase in prison populations between 1970 and 2003 (Western, 2006) fell overwhelmingly on young, black men, both reflecting and further exacerbating the profound inequalities in American society. In 2004, over 12% of black men between 25 and 29 years of age were in prison or jail. Among black men born in the late 1960s who received no more than a high school education, 30% had served time in prison by their mid-30s. Among black male high school dropouts, 60% had prison records by that age (Ibid). Men are approximately ten times more likely to be in prison or jail than women, but women's incarceration is growing at a faster rate. For black women in their mid- to late 30s, the incarceration rate has hit the 1-in-100 level (Pew Center on the States, 2008).

Arguing that "the repudiation of rehabilitation and the embrace of retribution" (Western, 2006, p. 6) has produced a collective experience for young black men that is wholly different from the rest of American society, Western describes the results as "a profound social exclusion that significantly rolls back the gains to citizenship hard won by the civil rights movement" (Ibid). Incarceration "significantly reduces the wages, employment, and annual earnings of former prisoners, even though their economic opportunities are extremely poor to begin with" (Western, 2006, p. 7). It also disrupts the developmental trajectories through which people complete their educations, enter military service or occupations, marry and establish homes and families, and otherwise establish themselves in civil society (Laub & Sampson, 2003). We ordinarily think of prisons as unnatural environments, yet spending time behind bars is becoming increasingly likely for this segment of the population. But beyond the powerful physical, emotional, economic, and psychological effects on those confined, as well as the consequences of attendant interruptions in the normal life course, the indirect effects of incarceration have deeply troubling and far-reaching effects on the larger society.

Social Consequences

There are myriad ways in which the negative impact of incarceration reaches well beyond just those who have been incarcerated. Imprisonment also has dramatic effects on the families of those confined. It is estimated that approximately two million children have an incarcerated parent (Clear, 2007). "By 2000, over a million black children—9% of those under eighteen—had a father in prison or jail" (Western, 2006, p. 5). About half of those children had been living with their fathers before their incarceration. The impact of parental incarceration on the children left behind is profound. Children either do not see the absent parent or become regular visitors in prison visiting rooms, exposed to at least select aspects of prison life. They may enter kinship care, many living with elderly grandparents, or foster care. They struggle through periods of reentry when parents return home (Bernstein, 2005). Studies have also suggested that children of the incarcerated are at increased risk for juvenile delinquency, academic problems, substance abuse, emotional and self-esteem problems, and aggression (Clear, 2007).

Marriages and other partnerships also are fractured and strained by the incarceration of one member, and future marriage prospects are diminished as well for both men and women (Clear, 2007; Western, 2006). The latter problem is particularly important given research that suggests that men in stable marriages may end their criminal involvement (Laub & Sampson, 2003). Incarceration is one of the reasons for the increase in female-headed, single-parent households. Family and parental functioning are affected dramatically, as the incarcerated parent misses significant aspects of his or her child's development, and the at-home parent takes on extra employment to cover the loss of the imprisoned person's income and enters into new financial, housing, and relationship arrangements precipitated by the incarceration of a partner (Clear, 2007).

More broadly, recent scholarly attention has begun to shed light on the consequences of mass incarceration on a variety of important indicators of the overall well-being of our society, often with surprising and disturbing results (see Clear, 2007; Currie, 1997; Rose & Clear, 1998). Importantly, emerging studies suggest that mass imprisonment has played a major role in increasing overall poverty rates (DeFina & Hannon, 2009a). Accumulating evidence also casts serious doubt on the taken-for-granted crime reduction effects long believed to flow from increased reliance on incarceration, even suggesting that mass imprisonment may *increase* levels of violent crime (Defina & Hanon, 2009b).

Although previous research has documented the contribution to poverty of such factors as changes in family structure, minimum wage policy, globalization, and de-unionization, DeFina and Hannon (2009a) point out that the implications of mass incarceration for stubbornly high poverty rates in the U. S. have been largely ignored. Drawing on state-level panel data covering 1980 to 2004, and using a variety of poverty indexes, their estimates indicate that poverty would have fallen substantially more during the last few decades had it not been for the historic rise in incarceration. When they focused on the official headcount poverty rate, the most commonly used indicator of economic deprivation, they found that poverty would have decreased by more than 20%, or about 2.8 percentage points, in the absence of the prison boom. That would translate into several million fewer people in poverty had mass incarceration not occurred (DeFina and Hannon, 2009a).

Research on the effects of incarceration rates having increased by more than 300% over the past 30 years also suggests that the crime control benefits were far lower than usually assumed. Western's (2006) analysis concluded that growth in incarceration rates explained only about one-tenth of the decline in serious crime that occurred at the end of the 1990s. But even more recent analyses of state-level panel data (1978–2004) results suggest that the crime-reduction benefits of increased incarceration are limited to property crime and are contingent on a healthy labor market. More important, the estimates suggest that mass incarceration has actually increased violent crime (DeFina and Hannon, 2009b).

Highlighting the troubling collateral consequences of mass incarceration may appear to undermine the argument that social workers need to be engaged with the correctional system, in the sense that the forces fueling the growth and reach of the penal system can seem so overwhelming and intractable. Yet we argue that bringing restorative justice initiatives into this context offers means of quietly, but potentially effectively, challenging the values and practices that yield such harmful consequences. Restorative justice involves "empowerment of communities that are best placed to address both the causes and consequences of crime" (Willemsens, 2003, p.38). Done well, restorative justice practices can be utilized to name and examine the role played by various personal and structural harms in creation of the conditions, beliefs, and relations that set the stage for the specific offenses being addressed. Furthermore, they can direct attention to the need to transform the communities in which the conflicts and crimes arose, and where victims and those going home from prison will reside. Thus, doing restorative justice work in prisons does not involve dismantling the system directly, but it can chip away at the dehumanizing values and perspectives that support it, while searching for better responses for all involved in the aftermath of crime.

The Punitive-Restorative Dilemma

There are, nonetheless, solid reasons for hesitation and caution in deciding to undertake restorative justice practices in prisons. These institutions are set up and operated first and foremost to punish, incapacitate and control those designated as offenders. These are aims and values that are in tension with those of restorative justice as well as social work. Willingness to accommodate restorative justice activities, which must be carried out within the constraints imposed by concern for security, is likely to be inconsistent. Even more challenging are the master operating assumptions that prisoners are to be regarded as irredeemably "bad actors"— dastardly, duplicitous, and dangerous. Related concerns involve "problems inherent in the use of such notions such as 'victims' and 'offenders' and the unwavering focus on 'the crime,' and on the 'harm done'" (Lemonne, 2003, p. 58), without tempering this emphasis on individual responsibility and specific incidents in light of "the societal context of domination and structural inequality affecting victims and offenders" (Braithwaite and Parker, 1999, as cited by Lemonne, 2003, 58).

Some contend that this correctional environment and the impact of imprisonment on those confined and on concomitant programming make prison-based restorative justice difficult, if not impossible (Guidoni, 2003; Van Ness, 2007). Elliott (2007) suggests that the correctional environment places security over care, and questions the success of programs or education on such values as care when they are "hammered in from without" rather than "grown from within" the environment (p. 204). Guidoni (2003) argues that prison breeds among the incarcerated feelings of victimization and disempowerment, which contributes to minimized feelings of responsibility, a denial further exacerbated by prison social conditions. Additionally, Guidoni contends that collaborative, nonviolent responses to behavior find resistance from the coercive and punitive prison responses that grow out of inherent power imbalances.

The centrality of blame, punishment, and control within the penal and larger criminal justice systems does indeed raise serious questions about whether it is possible for practitioners to operate within them in ways consistent with social work and restorative justice ideals. This has led many of us to the view that at best, restorative justice should be offered as an alternative and competing paradigm to the traditional retributive justice model (see Zehr, 1990). Still others among us question whether restorative justice does enough to address the need for social transformation to eliminate the social inequality and injustice that permeate society and contribute to and result from mass incarceration. However, there is "no place of innocence until the revolution comes" (Kendall & Pollack, 2003, p. 89, cited in Harris, 2004, pp. 120–121). In fact, striving to operate in a manner consistent with the principles of restorative justice within a prison context can be considered a revolutionary act, in the sense of facilitating the transformation or reconstruction of social values and the nature of relationships. An abiding belief that both specific restorative practices and a general restorative justice orientation may have value for persons in prison and others whom their lives touch impels some of us to explore the ways in which this might prove true.

RESTORATIVE JUSTICE AND PRISON-BASED APPLICATIONS

Restorative justice takes many forms within the correctional environment, including practices and programs that attend to concerns for victim awareness, accountability, and making amends, build relationships between the incarcerated and the community, and create restorative spaces and milieus inside prison (Correctional Service Canada, 2006; Van Ness, 2007). This section reviews common prison applications: Victim–Offender Dialogue in crimes of violence, group dialogue processes, offender-focused initiatives, and restorative justice units or dorms. Though the form of these practices varies, they share in common the general goals of raising awareness about harm, victimization, and accountability and providing means through which offenders may act on this knowledge in meaningful ways. Such practices also provide avenues through which prisoners may receive social support, learn skills in responding to and resolving conflict, and strive for personal healing and growth. Such factors may contribute to reduced recidivism as well as otherwise aiding the offenders involved. Indeed, restorative justice practices may promote empowerment and humanity among those in prison. Assuming that prison-based practices are conducted consistently with general guiding principles for restorative approaches, they represent "collaborative problem-solving responses to misbehavior" (Wachtel & McCold, 2001, p. 121), which signal a significant departure from traditional criminal justice and penal responses. In this sense, they can be expected to support empowerment through such means as involving offenders as active participants, allowing opportunities for sharing feelings, avoiding scolding or lecturing, separating the deed from the doer, recognizing and accepting ambiguity, and viewing every instance of wrongdoing as an opportunity for learning and for grace (Braithwaite & Strang, 2001; Wachtel &McCold 2001).

The practices highlighted here do not exhaust the range of in-prison or prison-related restorative justice applications. Restorative justice, or restorative justice-consistent, practices may serve victims and their needs outside of prison while the perpetrators are incarcerated. Other like-minded practices may attend to needs of victims, offenders, and even families of offenders, during a period of parole and community reintegration. Circles of Support and Accountability (see the web sites for the Minnesota Department of Corrections and the Correctional Service of Canada) and pre-release conferencing between incarcerated individuals and their family members (see the web site for Transitional Conferencing) serve as examples of such practice. These restorative justice applications help round out the complex picture of what it means to do restorative justice in a prison context. This chapter concentrates on restorative justice applications *in* prison designed to serve offenders and related parties during the period of incarceration.

Victim–Offender dialogue in crimes of violence

Victim–Offender Dialogue (VOD) in crimes of violence offers a process specifically designed for victims and offenders in cases of homicide, rape, sexual assault, physical or sexual abuse, arson, and other forms of violence. Most dialogues occur within a correctional institution; however, others occur in the community when the victim initiates the dialogue post-release or the perpetrator earns release mid-preparation. Programs share the common goal of creating a safe place for the victim and offender to engage with each other; however, they may differ in other objectives. For instance, some programs may be more therapeutic in nature, concerned with participant healing, while others may be more focused on victim storytelling or on empowering the victim and offender to achieve their identified goals for meeting (Umbreit et al., 2003). Umbreit and colleagues (2003) found that victims, who typically initiate the process, seek dialogue to, for instance, find answers to their questions, speak to the crime's impact, move forward in their healing, and engage with the offender in a more human way. Their study further found that offenders agreed to participate for many reasons, including a desire to apologize to the victim, assist in the victim's healing, and provide the victim with personal information, while also using the dialogue for their own healing and rehabilitation.

Victims typically initiate the dialogue, after which point facilitators prepare both the victim and offender to meet each other, a preparation process that can average from four and a half to 16 months, depending on the model used and the circumstances (Umbreit et al., 2003). Because VOD is considered an advanced form of facilitation (Umbreit et al., 2003), facilitators of VOD in crimes of violence receive specialized training to ensure knowledge of and skill competency in violent victimization and offending, the prison experience, working with correctional and allied professionals, facilitating the preparation, dialogue and debriefing processes, and the associated ethics of working with victims and offenders and within correctional environments (Office of the Victim Advocate, 2003; Umbreit et al., 2003).

Victim Offender Dialogue in crimes of violence is becoming increasingly common, with 32 such programs operating in the United States and several more under development (Van Ness & Weber, 2008). Canada offers such dialogue, as well as letter and video exchanges, through the Correctional Service of Canada (Correctional Service Canada, n. d.). Recent research shows the promise of dialogue for both victims and offenders. More than half the victims in a multi-site study conducted by Umbreit and colleagues (2003) reported personal growth, a sense of healing, and improved sentiments toward the offenders as a result of the dialogue; almost half reported improved outlook in life and strengthened spirituality. The majority of offenders in the same study reported that the dialogue contributed to their own rehabilitation, growth, healing, and positive outlook, and strengthened their spirituality. Ninety-eight percent indicated that the dialogue heightened their understanding of their crimes' impacts. In an email to the author on April 21, 2009, Dr. Marilyn Armour, University of Texas at Austin School of Social Work, indicated that her current research on the Texas Victim–Offender Dialogue program collects data on attitude changes, psychological symptoms, and spirituality and health for victims and offenders at various points in the process. The results are not yet available.

Group Dialogue

Group dialogue processes bring together, over a period of weeks and under the leadership of a trained facilitator, incarcerated individuals, crime victims and, at times, other community members, for conversation about such topics as restorative justice, accountability, victimization, experiences with the justice system, and amends making. These programs often include both victims and offenders speaking to their personal experiences with crime. While these groups do not bring together victims and offenders from the same crime, these processes are consistent with restorative justice in that they are designed to bring together those who have experienced crime as victims and offenders to talk about their experiences, ask and answer questions, promote accountability and, in some cases, consider ways in which offenders can make amends or the community can better support victims and offenders (Marshall, 2005). With this restorative agenda, facilitators of these processes may face much of the same content, emotion, and questions as in a dialogue between direct victims and offenders. Several models have received considerable exposure, including Prison Fellowship's Sycamore Tree Project (Feasey, Williams, & Clarke 2005; Marshall, 2005), the Citizens, Victims and Offenders Restoring Justice Project (CVORJ) (Burns, 2001; Helfgott et al., 2000; Lovell et al., 2002) and Bridges to Life (Armour, 2006; Blackard, 2006).

Researchers who have studied each of these models find that participation contributes to a positive impact on offenders. A report on the quantitative results of a study of CVORJ at Washington State Reformatory (Helfgott et al., 2000) found that following participation, offenders had an increased understanding of the victim experience and spent more time thinking about and talking about their crimes, a process deemed important for accountability and making amends. Interestingly, incarcerated participants also believed that the seminar and its story-telling component helped them feel more comfortable talking to each other and suggested that, if offered more regularly, the seminar could have a positive effect on the prison subculture. Victim participants highlighted the importance of receiving apologies from the incarcerated participants, even though these individuals had not committed crimes against them, and of feeling reduced levels of shame for the crimes they had experienced. Both victims and offenders reported being better able to articulate their respective needs as a result of participating in the seminar, especially those related to offender accountability, and to finds ways to meet those needs.

Qualitative findings (Lovell et al., 2002) showed that CVROJ created a safe space for participants to explore issues of crime, accountability, and remorse, contributing to some degree of positive personal growth and attitudinal change for all involved—offenders, victims, and community members. Offenders reported increased empathy for their victims and an understanding of the importance of accountability, remorse, and amends making, as well as experiencing support to find ways to be responsible for their crimes. Victims reported experiencing the group as healing, and a place in which they were heard, vindicated, and supported by both offenders and community participants. Together, all participants found that their time together contributed to reduced stereotypes of each other and increased understanding of their commonalities.

Larger studies of group dialogue processes report positive effects on offenders as well. A study of the Sycamore Tree Project, using the Crime Pics II tool with a comparison group from a separate study, found that the program positively impacted participants (N=2,188). Those involved reported a significant decrease in their Crime Pics II scores, indicating that the program contributed to participants' coming to see crime as less desirable and less worthwhile than before being involved in the program. The scores also indicated the belief that recidivism was less likely after participation than before and compared to those in the separate study. Additionally, participants reported higher levels of victim empathy post-program compared to those who did not participate (Feasey et al., 2005). A Bridges to Life study explored the recidivism rates of the 1,500 program participants in the Texas program. Using data from the Texas Department of Corrections, researchers found that program graduates had a 3-year recidivism rate of 16%, compared with a 31.4% rate for those who did not participate in the program and 67.5% nationally (Armour, 2006).

Offender-Focused Initiatives

This set of restorative practices engages incarcerated men and women, individually or in groups, in a variety of forums to introduce restorative themes such as accountability and personal healing, increase awareness of the impact of crime and empathy for victims, consider material or symbolic ways in which to make amends, provide training in conflict resolution skills, and support offenders who have been crime victims themselves or simply as they serve their sentences. While these practices may involve community or family members or victim speakers at times, they are largely focused on the transformation of incarcerated people and their individual journeys toward accountability and healing, rather than mutual dialogue and benefits for victims, offenders, and community members.

Examples of this type of practice include Hawaii's Restorative Circle project (Porter, 2007), the Pennsylvania Prison Society's restorative justice workshops (Toews, 2006a), and talking circles in a Minnesota women's prison (Thalhuber & Thompson, 2007). Hawaii's Restorative Circle project brings together an incarcerated individual and others he or she designates. to discuss what that individual needs to do to make change in his or her life and to whom amends should be made, as well as to consider further needs and resources upon release (Porter, 2007). The Prison Society's Restorative Justice Program facilitated workshops that were 20 to 24 hours in length. These sessions were designed and co-facilitated with incarcerated facilitators and focused broadly on restorative justice, its common practices, and ways in which to apply the philosophy to one's daily life, including in the context of everyday life inside the prison (Toews, 2006a). Talking circles in a Minnesota women's facility provide the opportunity for incarcerated women to gather in circle to explore shared values, relationships, life experiences, and forgiveness of themselves and each other, and to experience personal and group transformation (Thalhuber & Thompson, 2007).

Hawaii's restorative justice facilitator training provides incarcerated individuals with skills in conflict handling and communication (Porter, 2007). Such training is designed to contribute to the creation of peaceful prison communities and reduce the likelihood of victimization that stems from unresolved or poorly handled conflict.

It is worth mentioning the Minnesota-based Alternatives to Violence Project (AVP) in the context of this type of restorative practice. This prison-based conflict resolution workshop, while not a restorative justice practice *per se*, reflects values and approaches consistent with restorative justice (Bischoff, 2001; Toews, 2006a). AVP "is based on the belief that there is a power in everyone that can transform hostility and destructiveness into cooperation and community" (Bischoff, 2001, p. 1). Research on this project suggests that AVP workshops assist incarcerated participants to live more peaceful lives (e.g., they are better able to resolve difficult issues, recognize others' viewpoints, trust others, take greater responsibility, and understand their feelings and actions) (Phillips, 2002) and contribute to reduced infractions during the incarceration of participants (Sloane, 2002).

Restorative Justice Units or Dorms

Restorative justice also has been adopted as a guiding framework for living units within prisons created in an attempt to establish a more healing and holistic living experience. Most of these involve housing units separate from the general population, although the original idea called for setting up entire prisons to be operated in ways consistent with a restorative justice orientation. Staff members in such units undergo training in the philosophy of restorative justice and residents commit to live by restorative values and principles in the everyday life of the unit, use restorative practices to build community and resolve conflicts, and participate in other restorative programming, often in addition to the usual prison programs. Swanson, Culliver, and Summers (2007) suggest that such units "become a model of an incarcerated community that offers its members a purpose and sense of belonging in such a way that they can potentially begin to earn back the trust of society through acting out a new way of living" (p. 63).

Recent research on two restorative justice units, Grand Cache Institution in Canada and W.C. Holman Correctional Institution in Alabama, provide insight into the potential impact of such units on their residents. Petrellis (2007) used both qualitative and quantitative methods, with comparison groups, to study the impact of the Restorative Justice Unit (RJU) at Grande Cache. Qualitative results found that RJU residents indicated that unit life and its programs contributed to an increased understanding of the impact of their crimes, greater feelings of empathy and remorse, and increased desire to make amends, as well as improved problem-solving and conflict resolution skills. Quantitative results found that RJU residents experienced increased program participation after coming to the unit and had fewer minor institutional charges than before unit residency and compared to other groups. However, those on the unit experienced an increase in major institutional charges, reported incidents, and filed grievances. Petrellis suggested that these increases may have been a result of the culture and practices in which residents and staff hold each other accountable for their behavior and are in a position to articulate their needs and find appropriate processes to deal with conflict. Additionally, the re-incarceration rate of RJU residents was comparable to that of the comparison groups, a finding that Petrellis suggested may be due to the loss of support RJU residents experience outside the unit. In their report about the faith-based restorative justice community at Holman Correctional Facility, Swanson et al. (2007) noted that there were fewer disciplinary citations among those living in the unit than in general population. They have not been able to determine at this point whether the reduction is attributable to life on the unit itself.

Caution is warranted in interpreting the above reported studies. With the exception of the Sycamore Tree (Feasey et al., 2005) and the Bridges to Life studies (Armour, 2006), most sample sizes are small. Additionally, with the exception of the Bridges to Life report (Armour, 2006) and the Grand Cache study (Petrellis, 2007), these studies did not include comparison groups. The authors of the Sycamore Tree Study (Feasey et al.,2005), however, compared its results to those of an unrelated study using the same measurement instrument. There is also the issue of selection bias, given that program participation is voluntary. Those who agree to participate when asked or who initiate program participation may be characteristically different than those who do not, which may contribute to positive results.

Restorative justice is a philosophical framework explicitly grounded in principles and values, rather than specific programs. As such, restorative justice as an applied practice takes on many forms. The key practices highlighted above suggest just some of the forms restorative justice takes in prison, particularly as it relates to offender obligations stemming from their crimes. Such initiatives also involve an expectation that correctional authorities will review and modify their processes for responding to conflict and wrongdoing, steps that should help create more positive environments for those living and working within the prisons involved (Correctional Service Canada, 2006). Such practices further hint of the revolution mentioned earlier in their ability to give voice to those who are often silenced, and to change how people relate to each other inside as well as outside of prison. The following case study exemplifies the creativity with which restorative justice can be applied and introduces additional considerations for restorative justice in prison.

CASE STUDY: *A BODY IN MOTION*

The audience of 500 men sat in silence, attentively watching the play being performed on the sparse, makeshift stage up front. This assemblage of incarcerated men had gathered in the auditorium in one of Pennsylvania's largest maximum security prisons to watch *A Body in Motion* (De Sanctis), a play about victims of violent crime. Created from transcripts of Howard Zehr's book *Transcending: Reflections of Crime Victims* (Zehr, 2001), this 70-minute production takes audience members through a series of vignettes, dramatizing victim experiences with and journeys through violent crimes and their aftermath. One narrative includes the words of a mother who no longer celebrates Christmas because that was the day her ex-husband murdered their two children, while another speaks to the experience of a woman who cleaned up the blood of her murdered sister, while yet another woman screams at God, out-yelling the thunderstorm that is beating down on her. One gentleman tells of his journey to a place where he met with the man who killed his daughter and told him "I forgive you." Another speaks of her choice to release the power that the man who raped her had over her and to resume running, her activity at the time of the rape. Incarcerated audience members would later say that the narratives went straight to their hearts, not their heads, as they witnessed the impact of crime through the actors' dialogue, emotion, and movement.

After a total of eight prison-based performances, approximately 1,500 incarcerated men and women in eight prisons had experienced *A Body in Motion*. Also in attendance at each of these performances were guests from the prisoner advocacy agency that sponsored the show, victim service providers, and correctional staff. The play tour was not limited to prison performances, however. Performances were held in community venues as well for correctional staff and volunteers, prisoner advocacy staff and volunteers, and victim advocacy staff and supporters. In total, 15 performances occurred over several months in the spring of 2004. Everyone, at each of these venues, sat in quiet, rapt attention, unable to look away from the actors or the quick, interwoven stories.

The play tour represented a collaboration among a variety of agencies. The original idea emerged from incarcerated men with whom Barb, one of the authors of this chapter, was facilitating restorative justice projects through her work at the Pennsylvania Prison Society, a prisoner advocacy and direct service organization. Within weeks of the initial idea, additional partners emerged, and the idea of one play performance in one prison was transformed into a tour organized and managed by the Prison Society. Collaborators included incarcerated individuals and their prison-based organizations, the Pennsylvania Department of Corrections, the Pennsylvania Office of the Victim Advocate, Episcopal Community Services, community-based victim service providers, and a volunteer from TOVA, a theater-of-witness organization. The Pennsylvania Commission on Crime and Delinquency/Office of Victim Services and the Inmate General Welfare Fund provided funding for the tour.

The goals of the program were many, with most centered around the theme of raising awareness about the victim experience and victims' subsequent needs, and initiating and improving the dialogue between victims, offenders, and community members. As restorative justice research suggests is possible, organizers hoped that the education and dialogue processes would instill in offenders who viewed the play a sense of remorse and accountability, and a commitment to healthy interactions with other people, both inside and outside of prison. Central to the project was raising awareness for Crime Victims Rights Week[i] in both prisons and the community. Other stated goals included: 1) initiating dialogue and interaction between members of the general community, the faith community, victims and their advocates, and prisoners and their advocates around issues of crime, victimization and justice; 2) educating people in prison and their advocates about the victim experience and facilitating dialogue with them on issues of crime, victimization, justice, and accountability; 3) providing meaningful theater in prison and in the community; and 4) exploring possibilities for dialogue and collaboration among offender, victim, community, faith group, and corrections stakeholders. As an offender advocacy agency, the Prison Society also hoped that the play would be beneficial to incarcerated individuals who also were victims of violent crime and, with the theme of transcendence, offer insight into how people in prison might be able to rise above the prison experience. This perspective, coupled with the non-threatening approach of theater, attempted to draw on the potential of restorative justice to speak to and benefit those who are marginalized from society and reduced to labels.

The play tour represented the first time *A Body in Motion* was performed in a prison setting. Everyone involved in planning for the shows—offenders and victim advocates, correctional staff and incarcerated individuals—used their combined knowledge and experience to predict the play's impact and create means through which to prepare potential audience members. Prison performances were scheduled during morning hours so that audience members had the rest of the day to process their reactions by talking about the play with other prisoners and staff, participating in debriefing sessions, or finding ways to release the emotions and energy the play churned up in them by, for instance, exercising or calling home, before being locked down for the night. Performances were scheduled on Mondays through Thursdays, not Fridays or weekends, so that staff members would be available on performance days and for several days immediately afterwards, should audience members need additional support. Correctional staff and prisoner organizations received written information about the play and its goals, so they could talk about it within the prisons in advance. Postcards and flyers were distributed throughout the institutions.

At the time of the performance, the play was introduced by an incarcerated individual and a member of the prison administration who both had been prepared to carefully review what the show would address. While the audience members were not fully informed of the play's content in advance, the organizers attempted to ensure that no one attended the performance without some advance knowledge of the play's content. Psychological staff and victim advocates attended each performance to monitor audience reactions and be immediately available for those who might need support during or just after the performances.

Post-performance debriefing sessions were offered to help incarcerated audience members to process their varied feelings and reactions to the play as it related to the crimes they had committed, as well as to their personal experiences with victimization. Initially these debriefing sessions were fairly structured, with small group and large group discussions focused on specific play characters and scenes. As the organizers learned how incarcerated audience members responded to the play, these debriefing sessions became increasingly informal, and focused on the release of emotions and discussion of what to do with those reactions from that point forward. These sessions frequently used a simple Circle process to facilitate this discussion. Due to the small number of facilitators, limited numbers of audience members were invited to attend these sessions. To address this limitation in the absence of additional facilitators, organizers included in the playbill an insert focused on individual ways to cope with emotions surfacing from the play and encouraging audience members to offer support to one other.

From the debriefing sessions and written evaluations, we learned about the powerful effect the play had on incarcerated audience members. The play and its message stirred many emotions in regards to the crimes they had committed, emotions that ranged from anger and fear to shame and remorse. Some inquired "Is it too late to say I'm sorry?" and "What have I done?!" One person said, "Before I was able to blame my actions on others. Not anymore." One man who reported being deeply moved and affected by the play said, "Everybody I shot, I had my reasons, so it never bothered me. But I never thought about the mothers of the men I shot. I never thought about the impact that my actions had on them."

As anticipated, the play also connected with those audience members who, although in prison for having committed crimes, had also themselves been victims of violent crime. During debriefing sessions, participants talked about loved ones who had been raped or murdered; one man recounted his experience of cleaning up his mother's blood after her murder. Audience members wrote such statements as "[the play] helped me with my own pain" and "I'm not crazy for wondering why I can't reach 'closure.'" This play with restorative themes assisted these victims in much the same way other restorative justice processes are beneficial to non-incarcerated victims—providing an opportunity to find validation for experiences and emotions, release emotions, and move through the violence they experienced to another place in their own journeys.

In many ways, the performance tapped into emotions and touched wounds that had lain dormant. One audience member commented that "[it was] good to see real feelings—I'm very tired of living with a bunch of people that 'are too hard to feel pain.'" Another said, "I wanted to feel defensive. I wanted to bash the play. But I just couldn't." The overwhelming message was that watching the piece allowed incarcerated individuals to connect with their own humanity and truly experience human emotions, which often can be buried in prison. Several audience members commented that they felt respected by the play and the organizers. The fact that organizers believed they could handle the intensity of the play and were capable of feeling the elicited emotions was deemed a benefit unto itself. Perhaps in the most telling statement, 95% of those who saw *A Body in Motion* said they would recommend the play to others in prison.

Community audience members were equally affected by the play and its message. One hosting victim advocate commented that even though many audience members came with some prior knowledge of victims, the play nonetheless "surprised and shook them up." Another commented that that the play allowed advocates to "let their guard down" and experience the play and its emotions, something they could not do routinely with the victims with whom they worked. Audience members also demonstrated curiosity about how people in prison reacted to the play, often showing surprise when learning of its emotional impact.

The above case study adds considerably to what it means to do restorative justice in prison. The project rested on restorative justice values and strived to address the restorative justice questions laid out by Zehr (2002), as well as the needs and obligations of those affected by crime. First and foremost, the tour intended to promote understanding of the victim experience and encourage accountability on the part of both the offender and the community in dealing with the effects of violence. Given that incarcerated individuals were recognized as offenders as well as possible victims of violence themselves, restorative justice took on a complex yet holistic tone. The play and its message served as a medium of healing and transcendence for all victims, regardless of their incarcerated or free-world status. In doing so, the play tour served a role, albeit a small one, in minimizing the distance and marginalization experienced by those in prison.

The project did not bring victims and offenders in direct contact with each other for dialogue except where victims participated in post-play debriefing sessions alongside incarcerated people. Yet, theater served as a powerful tool through which to present and exchange information between victims and offenders. The incarcerated individuals witnessed and heard the victims' narratives, and victims and victim advocates witnessed the nonverbal and verbal reactions of the incarcerated audience. Because of the power of the play to touch the heart, not just the head, many participants indicated that the play was more powerful and elicited greater impact than the more traditional cognitive-focused victim classes that examine victimization and its consequences. Debriefing sessions served to facilitate further dialogue and awareness of victim experiences and needs. In a larger sense, the project brought together victims, offenders, community members, and system stakeholders around a unified goal—a restorative achievement in and of itself.

The play also represented an invitation and an opportunity for the incarcerated people in the audience to transcend the prison and build toward a more hopeful future. Restorative justice has an orientation toward the past in its emphasis on working to repair harm done by violence and conflict, yet it has perhaps an even greater focus on the future in the aim of developing right relationships and crafting a more harmonious tomorrow. Thus, while restorative practices such as this play encourage participants to attend more seriously to the harm done by their acts, they certainly do not stop there. Building communities and right relationships requires taking into the account the needs of all, including persons who have been involved in crime and other social and personal wrongs. (see Gil, 2006; Sullivan & Tifft, 2005).

RESTORATIVE JUSTICE SKILLS

The case study, through its successes and limitations, suggests a variety of micro and macro skills necessary to apply restorative justice in prisons. The following skills represent those that the organizers felt they accomplished well and those in which they reported falling short.

Participant Preparation

Restorative justice practice that invites people to listen to stories of violence, consider their own role in similar violence, or face their own experiences with such, requires careful preparation of potential participants. Regardless of the practice, this preparation includes working to ensure that participants understand what will happen, their role in the process, and their expectations and concerns, as well as giving consideration to possible reactions and how to respond to them. This type of preparation is particularly important in prison, given that victim issues rarely are dealt with directly. The prison environment does little to promote facing one's crime and accepting responsibility or to assist incarcerated individuals who are victims of crime in working through their experiences. The emotions associated with these experiences, such as remorse, guilt, and sorrow, are squelched in prison.

To express them is to express weakness and risk victimization. Without adequate preparation, participants may find themselves in a situation with which they are ill-prepared to cope, and subsequently they may enact their distress in ways that are not constructive.

Preparation requires a collaborative effort between restorative justice practitioners, victims, correctional personnel, and incarcerated individuals themselves. Regardless of the practice, each stakeholder to a restorative justice enterprise brings legitimate concerns that inform the preparation process and expertise that can be utilized in facilitating preparation. In the case of the *Body in Motion* tour, offender advocates brought concerns for inclusion and empowerment of incarcerated individuals in determining impact and participating in preparation. Victim advocates brought their knowledge of the impact of victim narratives. Correctional staff and incarcerated individuals shared these concerns and brought knowledge about how emotional programs such as these can affect the life of the institution, in addition to their desire to support those residing in their institutions.

Collaborative preparation took many forms during the tour. The Office of the Victim Advocate sent advance information about the play to superintendents and prison staff, allowing them to make an informed decision about hosting it, taking into account facility resources, environment, and population. Superintendents and victim service providers also had the opportunity to view the play at a Department of Corrections event prior to the tour kickoff. Prison Society volunteers, who were also invited to attend the prison-based performances, witnessed the play at an agency event prior to the commencement of the tour. This performance served to not only educate them about victim issues, but also solicit their perspectives on how incarcerated individuals might respond and prepare them for supporting individuals inside who saw the play. The inmate organizations that were involved not only participated in advance planning for the overall project, but also served as resources for promoting the play inside, informing people about the play and its contents, as well as the goals of the tour.

Debriefing and Post-Intervention Support

One incarcerated audience member stated that, without post-play support, witnessing the play "was like being shot into space without an oxygen tank." This image suggests the importance of debriefing and post-intervention support in prison settings. Among those who participated in post-play debriefing sessions, each one spoke to the usefulness of the sessions for processing their emotions in a positive way. In addition, participants in the sessions were able to hear and reflect on the comments shared by other prisoners, victim service providers, and others who attended, creating an important, shared experience and providing more information about victims and victimization for those involved to consider.

Because participation in restorative justice programs may elicit strong emotions among incarcerated participants for which there are few, if any, safe outlets inside the prison, post-intervention support requires the creation of safe space and safe relationships in and through which participants can process and incorporate their emotions and experiences in healthy ways. There are many ways to do this, as illustrated by the examples given in connection with the play tour – for instance, staff availability for one-on-one support, written follow-up materials for individuals to use alone or with others, group debriefing and availability of peers for support. The play tour used a simple circle process to create the space for attendees to articulate their reactions to the narratives in the play, the meaning they took away from it and ways in which they can move forward in a healthy way with their reactions. Participants also highlighted their use of journaling, writing letters, calling home, and exercising as other ways that they worked through their experiences with the play.

The debriefing and support component requires stakeholder collaboration, including involvement of incarcerated individuals. The restorative justice practitioner, correctional staff, and incarcerated people share a common concern for the well-being of the participants and those with whom they interact. The restorative justice practitioner plays an important, though limited, role in debriefing the specific restorative practice and ensuring, to the degree possible, that participants are emotionally intact before returning to the prison community. Correctional staff and incarcerated collaborators, however, live with participants and share responsibility for the day-to-day life and health of the prison community and its members. They play an equally important, though perhaps more informal, role in providing support following restorative justice participation.

Safe and Responsive Attitudes and Approaches

Imprisonment is a dehumanizing and traumatic experience in which people struggle to maintain a sense of identity, health and well-being. Prison-based practice requires that practitioners, in their attitudes and behavior, provide for the safety (physical, emotional, and psychological) of participants and be responsive to their varied and complex needs. A key skill in this regard is remembering that incarcerated individuals have identities and experiences beyond the offenses they have committed, and therefore approaching practice with due recognition of their full humanity, including experiences with victimization.

Safe and responsive practices respect participants, regardless of where they are located in their accountability and healing journeys, and create room for participants to do the work that they need to do, regardless of what that work is, at the pace they need to follow. The play tour offers an example of what this might look like. Theater provided a nonthreatening approach to raise awareness of the victim experience and subsequent accountability, and encouraged incarcerated individuals to consider their own experiences of victimization and begin to process them. Few, if any, messages of condemnation or judgment of the audience were delivered in the opening comments or the play itself. Audience members commented later that, as a result, there was no need to be defensive while watching it. Those present could engage with the play in the manner in which they were comfortable and take away from it the messages that spoke to them. For some, this engagement pertained to the crime or crimes they had committed and feelings of accountability; for others, it pertained to violence they had experienced as victims and possibilities for healing. Organizers designed and facilitated the tour and its individual productions to communicate the intentions to meet audience members where they were in their journeys, not where they may have wished those who came would be. For instance, materials distributed in advance about the play outlined various reasons that someone might wish to see the play, reasons that included learning about the victim experience, finding healing from the narratives for those who had been victims of crime, exploring ways to transcend the prison experience, or just simply seeing a play. Facilitators of the debriefing process did not have an agenda beyond creating space for audience reactions, and thus validating all reactions. Participants put a lot of trust in the practitioner to demonstrate concern for them and to come with honest and caring intentions, intentions that communicate respect for the individual as a whole, not only as an individual obligated to a victim.

Facilitation

Prison-based restorative justice practice in its many forms relies on facilitation skills. These skills may involve helping a victim and an offender to talk with each other or leading a group of victims, offenders, and community people in a Circle process. In the case of the play tour, facilitation was the central tool for the debriefing sessions. The facilitator of these sessions used a simple Circle process to create space for audience members to speak to their reactions to the play, consider ways through those reactions, and understand that they were not alone in their experience. Small group or one-on-one conversations on topics provided by the facilitator, in addition to use of full-group circles, encouraged more in-depth sharing. This format created the space for participants to express emotions relating to guilt and remorse for the crimes they had committed, as well as sorrow and pain for crimes they had experienced. It also provided individuals with the opportunity to think about and to share, if they wished, steps they had taken or might take in seeking to repair harm done, make amends, or advance their own healing. The sessions, facilitated without judgment or specific expectations about content, served as a safe space to deal with the complexities of offending and victimization.

Practitioner Preparation and Self-Care

Restorative justice practice requires practitioners to be present in the expression of painful experiences and emotions and, as a result, requires preparation before and debriefing after providing services. Given risks of secondary traumatic stress (Bride, 2007), providing care to service providers is paramount for all forms of practice that engage people with narratives of violence and victimization.

Prison-based practice additionally requires particular attention to the experience of being in prison and being witness to the conditions, security concerns, and prison culture, and the ways in which they affect the incarcerated as well as staff and practitioner. Practitioner preparation and self-care is difficult and too easily set aside when faced with the numerous and complex tasks required to facilitate restorative justice programs in prison. The play tour was no exception.

Collaboration

The principles of restorative justice value interconnectedness and the belief that justice emerges through dialogue and collaboration among victims, offenders, and community members. This spirit of collaboration extends to those who design and facilitate programs. Prison-based restorative practices require collaboration among practitioners, prison administrators, and frontline staff, and often times, with correctional and community-based victim service providers. Prison Society staff members worked closely with personnel of the Office of the Victim Advocate, Department of Corrections, and prison administrators to facilitate the prison performances and with local victim service providers to bring the play to the community. A partnership with inmate organizations made it possible to promote the play and encourage informal post-play support systems for those needing it. The collaborative efforts of all the organizations contributed to the project's success.

The play tour demonstrates that, while each stakeholder group has different missions and constituents, one project can bring them together to achieve the goals that they share in common. This collaboration is not without its challenges. Trust must be built across organizations and institutions. The prioritization of mutual goals may require negotiation. Attending to the needs of one set of constituents may reduce, at least temporarily, attention to those of another. A project may seem too victim-focused at one time and too offender-focused at another. The meaning and practice of collaboration may also differ among the partners, contributing to some partners feeling more involved or excluded than others in the planning. Successful practice relies on committed dialogue and collaboration.

Incarcerated Individuals as Partners and Practitioners

Prison-based practice recognizes incarcerated individuals as collaborators, and possibly the driving force, in program initiation, development, and facilitation. Their roles within restorative justice extend beyond "service recipient" (as an offender or victim) to include "practitioner," program developer, and ongoing project sponsor. This involvement brings new life to the restorative justice value of participation. In the case of the play tour, incarcerated individuals initiated the project and prison-based restorative justice committees sponsored and hosted the productions. The prison-based practices described in this chapter, including the play tour, represent those that are largely designed and facilitated by outside organizations. However, it is important to recognize the tremendous resource that imprisoned people who make a commitment to restorative principles and practices represent. We authors personally work with incarcerated individuals developing and facilitating their own restorative justice, or restorative justice-consistent, programs and projects and we know colleagues who do the same. These prisoner-led approaches include restorative justice workshops, coping with victimization seminars, and even sweeping initiatives to transform the values, norms, and codes of the street crime and prison cultures in order to arrest the cycle of violence.

The *Body in Motion* tour utilized a combination of micro skills dedicated to serving incarcerated individuals in their journeys toward accountability and healing, and macro skills related to project management and implementation. Successful prison-based restorative justice necessitates both sets of skills, if not from the same provider then from a group of providers.

THE FIT BETWEEN SOCIAL WORK AND RESTORATIVE JUSTICE

Restorative justice in prison represents a unique blend of micro and macro skills and attention to individual and social needs, a blend consistent with social work practice. When coupled with shared values and ethics, there appears to be a good fit between social work and restorative justice practice. Restorative justice fits with a variety of fields, such as conflict transformation and criminal justice, and social work serves as another lens through which to understand and apply the philosophy. Restorative justice may facilitate the return of social work to corrections in a variety of ways. Social work may adopt restorative justice as a practice specialization in which social workers provide restorative justice services as their social work practice. Such practitioners, in addition to general social work education, would receive additional training in forensic and correctional social work and restorative justice theory and practice, with special attention to the experiences and needs of victims and offenders. Restorative justice also may be used to inform existing social work practice. Van Wormer (2001) proposes a "strengths-restorative approach" to correctional counseling, an approach that serves as a combination of the strengths/empowerment approach, narrative therapy, and restorative justice. Social work clinical practice, even if informed by restorative justice, should not be confused with other forms of restorative justice practice, such as facilitation of dialogues in crimes of violence. Counselors and dialogue facilitators serve different functions; the practitioner of one is not automatically prepared to do the other without specialized training.

The concern for offender accountability, and the corresponding concern for the restoration of victims and community, as well as of offenders, highlight an additional fit between restorative justice and social work. The restorative justice philosophy and its practices provide a way for social workers to serve and assist hurting and hurt individuals, creating processes to promote their health and well-being. Importantly, restorative practices focus on empowering individuals to name their own needs, and obligations, and determine how to have those needs met and fulfill those obligations, all the while receiving support from others. Given evidence that restorative justice practices have beneficial effects on offenders and victims, social workers can be comfortable engaging in this form of criminal justice practice.

The punitive-restorative dilemma deserves further consideration, however. Debate exists about whether restorative justice is or is not retributive and whether it is an alternate form of or an alternative to punishment (Johnstone, 2002; Roche, 2007). This debate becomes increasingly complex with the added concern of cooptation; restorative practices in prison may take on the punitive nature on which prison is built. Restorative approaches risk becoming something that we "do to" offenders because they have done something to someone else, rather than a process designed to bring people together to mutually address the individual and communal harms and causes of crime. Of equal concern is that restorative practices become so integral to the prison experience and programming that practitioners no longer question the role of prison and its reliance on violence, dehumanization, and punishment in response to crime. In this case, restorative justice may inadvertently justify the use of incarceration or serve as a management tool therein (Swanson et al., 2007).

Restorative justice practitioners, like social workers, must be steadfast in their commitment to the philosophical values underlying their practice in order to counter the force of the correctional environment on them as well as on those incarcerated within it. Prison-based practice requires the practitioners to constantly question and evaluate the operation and effects of restorative justice efforts in prisons and remain vigilant to assure that what is being done in the name of restorative justice actually is consistent with its tenets. The reality is that these dilemmas are not unique to prison settings. The same issues arise whenever social workers intervene in another person's life. In settings where any action that might interfere with someone's autonomy is being contemplated, we recognize the importance of such obligations as seeking consent if possible, intervening minimally and only to the extent justified by the legitimate interests being served, and striving to act to enhance the subject's future autonomy (see Gill, 2003). More generally, social workers routinely face the dilemma of whether to respond at the individual or societal level; they must make decisions about which interventions to use and in which contexts to practice based on social work values and ethics.

This dilemma begs the question of whether restorative justice is a form of practice and set of programs to offer within prisons, or is a means through which to critically question the use of prisons, their goals, and their roots in social and legal inequality. The examples provided in this chapter largely suggest it is a practice or program within prisons, separate from the larger social context that sent people there in the first place. Both restorative justice and social work recognize that individual behavior grows out of the social context, yet correctional practice has largely focused on the individual, removed from the context. Few restorative practices address contextual factors that give rise to crime such as poverty, educational disparity and racism, or policies that unfairly construct who and what is considered criminal along racial and economic lines, and rely on mass imprisonment to deal with social problems. Limiting restorative justice practice to the needs and responsibilities of offenders ignores the multiple ways in which institutions that were designed to support community members failed in their obligationsto that individual. Restorative justice in prison calls practitioners to do community work to eliminate the social conditions and structural inequalities that give rise to crime, such as poverty, inequality, racism, and violence. Restorative justice has a place in challenging crime and sentencing policies that determine who is considered an offender, what type of offender deserves or requires imprisonment, and the very use of imprisonment itself. Without this challenge, restorative justice, and social work, will serve to perpetuate the control, dehumanization, and marginalization of groups of people and do little to stop the current trend of mass imprisonment of these groups.

Some of the questions about the defensibility of engaging in restorative justice work in prisons in light of the danger of ignoring structural issues and simply shoring up the carceral state may best be answered by incarcerated men and women. The lifers' organization at the State Correctional Institution at Graterford (PA), for example, has established a Public Safety Initiative (PSI) with the goal of ending the culture of crime and violence (Harris, 2009). With strategies focused at the individual, institutional, community, justice system, and societal levels, this prisoner-initiated movement aims to build safe and just communities in ways consistent with the principles and values of restorative justice. PSI members wrestled mightily with the issues surrounding individual versus collective responsibility in crafting their overall strategy, carefully considering their personal experiences and deep knowledge of social and economic injustice along with what Wacquant (2001) describes as the "extra-penological" functions of mass imprisonment. The resultant PSI position acknowledges both the forceful push of the hardships associated with racism, poverty, urban decay, and other forms of oppression, and the powerful pull of the enticements of street-crime culture in drawing people into criminal behavior (LIFERS Public Safety Steering Committee of the State Correctional Institution at Graterford, Pennsylvania, 2004). At the same time, the PSI stance is that, while larger societal institutions and structural factors that operate as contributors to crime demand attention, the existence of such destructive forces does not excuse antisocial behavior. Arguing that participants chose to seek the psychological and economic rewards associated with street crime, despite knowing deep down that their criminal acts were wrong, PSI members hold themselves accountable for the harm they have caused. They see themselves as being obligated to seek to repair the damage that their own criminal and other antisocial behaviors helped to create, as well as the collateral damage that their very participation in the culture of street crime may have engendered. By engaging in positive peer intervention and projects designed to arrest the development of street-crime culture, involvement with PSI gives participants the impetus and opportunities to take on responsibility, promote healing and engage in a wide array of redemptive and generative endeavors (McAdams, 2006).

The perspective reflected within PSI initiatives does not resolve the tensions of doing restorative justice work in prisons, or absolve practitioners of the obligation to make their own determinations on the appropriateness of employing one or another restorative justice practice in the prison context. The PSI orientation is offered as one framework with which the practitioner may consider the tensions and make that personal determination. Incarcerated individuals, as people who experience firsthand the tension between individual and collective responsibility, carry great potential as transformative leaders. Practitioners concerned with restorative justice in prison do well to collaborate with this emerging leadership. Certainly, this collaboration is restorative justice.

NEXT STEPS

Restorative justice and social work share exciting possibilities and serious limitations in regards to restorative applications in prisons. More dialogue is required between the two fields in order to enhance restorative benefits while minimizing the limitations, if not actively transforming systems and society. At the most basic level, more dialogue between the two fields and their practitioners is warranted in order to gain a clearer understanding of where the fields converge and diverge. Such a dialogue may also include those who approach restorative justice through other lenses, such as conflict transformation, criminology, and criminal justice, as these fields are of equal concern for both social work and restorative justice.

Social work is well advised to incorporate restorative justice theories and practices into general curriculums. van Wormer (2006) outlines ways in which this can happen in classes focused on practice, policy, and research, and in field placements. Practice classes could offer sessions on restorative justice skills in process design and facilitation as well as the ethics of prison-based practice. Policy courses could explore the role of restorative justice in advocacy and systems change, including studying or joining with current efforts and imagining or creating new initiatives where there are gaps, of which there are many. Research courses could include corrections-based restorative justice studies to increase knowledge on the theory and practices and how they can best be evaluated. Field placements, in and out of prison, could provide students with forensic and restorative justice skills. While our focus here has been restorative justice processes offered in prison, the relationship between restorative justice and social work extends to practices and policies relating to victims and others within the offender's community of care during and following the offender's period of incarceration. Social work education and subsequent practice include, then, work with victims of crime and the families of incarcerated and non-incarcerated offenders, as well as with formerly incarcerated people.

The exploration of logical linkages between restorative justice and social work extends beyond education, however, and requires critical engagement regarding the tensions of social work, restorative justice, and corrections, such as those identified above. What tensions does each field identify? What practices exist that address, or attempt to address, those tensions? Which practices focus on individual accountability and transformation, and which focus on community collective accountability and transformation? What do advocacy, policy, and systems change look like through the social work and restorative justice lens, and what does that mean for practice? What is for social work and restorative justice to do separately and what can they do together? Responding to these questions sets the stage for further theoretical and practice development.

The final challenge is the careful consideration of social work and restorative justice values and the commitment to individual and collective well-being, and the meaning of each for those who are incarcerated, as well as for those whose lives they have touched in the past and will touch in the future. People in prison have complex needs, obligations, and experiences. To the human and developmental needs that they share with those outside of prison are added the problems and concerns that come from being separated from their families, having their life courses disrupted, and losing many ordinary forms of power, autonomy, and control that those not confined enjoy. Many people in prison struggle within themselves to account for past misbehavior and seek not only to make amends for past harms they have inflicted but also to show that they can live as good and honorable people. Social work and restorative justice practitioners can join hands in working to assist those in prison to make sense of their pasts, do what they can to repair damage that remains, and build better futures.

At the same time, we believe it is possible for social workers and restorative justice practitioners to help raise awareness and understanding of the fact that the problems of crime and the existence of people labeled as offenders do not arise in a vacuum. There are powerful cultural and systemic forces underlying harmful action of criminal and other kinds (Currie, 1997; Messner and Rosenfeld, 2006) and it is important to resist the tendency to cast blame and responsibility solely on individual wrongdoers. As Presser has described it, the reality is that "restorative justice encounters create space for examining social injustices as well as those injustices we call crime, and problematize victim and offender positions" (Presser, 2008, p. 154). It is up to social workers to listen well and to pass on what they learn about the problems in families, schools, peer groups, gender roles, housing, neighborhood conditions, job markets, and other contributors to harmful action and to confront the limitations of relying on imprisonment as a remedy for ongoing violence. Mass imprisonment has more to do with public policies drawn in response to crime than with crime itself (Gottschalk, 2006). Yet, as suggested earlier, there is growing evidence that the extensive reliance on incarceration now practiced in the United States has become more of a social problem than the problems it is said to serve, even contributing to poverty and violent crime while consuming resources that might otherwise go toward reducing those problems (DeFina & Hannon 2009a; 2009b). The conclusion seems inescapable: Social work and restorative justice both are needed to address forcefully the problems, both individual-level and societal, that are reflected in and grow out of America's prisons.

NOTES

i Since its inception in 1981, National Crime Victims' Rights Week is sponsored each April by the Office for Victim's of Crime, a division of the United States Department of Justice to promote crime victims' rights as well as honor victims and those who support them.

REFERENCES

Armour, M. (2006). Bridges to life: A promising in-prison restorative justice intervention. Retrieved May 10, 2009, from http://www.restorativejustice.org/editions/2006/june06/2006-05-23.6472027063/view

Bernstein, N. (2005). *All alone in the world: Children of the incarcerated*. New York: The New Press.

Bischoff, M. (2001). How restorative is AVP? Retrieved May 9, 2009, from http://www.clarityfacilitation.com/papers/rj.htm

Blackard, K. (2006). *Restoring peace: Using lessons from prison to mend broken relationships*. Bloomington, IN: Trafford Publishing.

Boyer, P. S. (1992). *Urban masses and moral order in America: 1820–1920*. Cambridge, MA: Harvard University Press.

Braithwaite, J., & Parker, C. (1999). Restorative justice is republican justice. In G. Bazemore and L. Walgrave (Eds.), *Restorative juvenile justice: Repairing the harm of youth crime* (pp. 103–126). Monsey, NY: Criminal Justice Press.

Braithwaite, J., & Strang, H. (2001). Introduction: Restorative justice and civil society. In H. Strang and J. Braithwaite (Eds.), *Restorative justice and civil society* (pp. 1–13). Cambridge, MA: Cambridge University Press.

Bride, B. E. (2007). Prevalence of secondary traumatic stress among social workers. *Social Work, 52*(1), 63–70.

Burns, H. (2001). Citizens, victims, and offenders restoring justice project: Minnesota Correctional Facility for Women at Shakopee. Retrieved April 12, 2008, from http://www.doc.state.mn.us/rj/documents/CitizensVictimsandOffendersRestoringJusticeMCFShakopee.pdf

Clear, T. R. (2007). *Imprisoning communities: How mass incarceration makes disadvantaged neighborhoods worse*. New York: Oxford University Press.

Correctional Service Canada. (n. d.). Victim offender mediation. Retrieved May 8, 2009, from http://www.csc-scc.gc.ca/text/rj/vom-eng.shtml

Correctional Service Canada. (2006). International perspectives on restorative corrections: A review of the literature. Retrieved August 4, 2007 from http://www.csc-scc.gc.ca/text/pblcsbjct-eng.shtml#restorativejustice

Currie, E. (1997). Market, crime and community. *Theoretical Criminology 1*(2): 147–72.

DeFina, R. & Hannon, L. (2009a). The Impact of Mass Incarceration on Poverty. *Crime and Delinquency*. (Crime Delinquency Online First, published on February 12, 2009 as doi:10:1177/0011128708328864).

DeFina, R. & Hannon, L. (2009b). The Impact of Mass Incarceration on Property and Violent Crime Rates. (Abstract for Seminar held at Temple University, Department of Criminal Justice, Philadelphia, PA. February 13, 2009).

De Sanctis, I. (Playwright/Director)] A Body in Motion [Play].

Elliott, L. (2007). Security, without care: Challenges for restorative values in prison. *Contemporary Justice Review, 10*(2), 193–208.

Feasey, S., Williams, P., & Clarke, R. (2005). *An evaluation of the Prison Fellowship Sycamore Tree Programme: Based on a statistical analysis of Crime Pics II data.* Research Centre for Community Justice, Sheffield Hallam University.

Gil, D. G. (2006). Toward a "radical" paradigm of restorative justice. In D. Sullivan and L. Tifft (Eds.), *Handbook of restorative justice: A global perspective* (pp. 499–511). New York: Routledge.

Gill, F. E. (2003). *The moral benefit of punishment: Self-determination as a goal of correctional counseling.* Lanham, MD: Lexington Books.

Gottschalk, M. (2006). *The prison and the gallows: The politics of mass incarceration in America.* New York: Cambridge University Press.

Guidoni, O. V. (2003). The Ambivalences of restorative justice: Some reflections on an Italian prison project. *Contemporary Justice Review, 6*(1), 55–68.

Gumz, E. (2004). American social work, corrections and restorative justice: An appraisal. *International Journal of Offender Therapy and Comparative Criminology, 48*(4), 449–460.

Gumz, E., & Grant, C. (2009). Restorative justice: A systematic review of the social work literature. *Families in Society: The Journal of Contemporary Social Services, 90*(1), 119–126.

Harris, M. K. (2004). An expansive, transformative view of restorative justice. *Contemporary Justice Review, 7*(1), 117–141.

Harris, M. K. (2009). Identity change through the transformation model of the public safety initiative of L.I.F.E.R.S., Inc. In B. Veysey, J. Christian, & D. Martinez (Eds.), *How offenders transform their lives* (pp. 143–164). Portland, OR: Willan Press.

Helfgott, J., Lovell, M., Lawrence, C., & Parsonage, W. (2000). Results from the pilot study of the Citizens, Victims, and Offenders Restoring Justice Program at Washington State Reformatory. *Journal of Contemporary Criminal Justice, 16*(1), 5–31.

Johnstone, G. (2002). *Restorative justice: Ideas, practices, debates.* Devon, UK: Willan Publishing.

Katz, M. B. (1996). *In the shadow of the poorhouse.* Basic Books: New York.

Kendall, K., & Pollack, S. (2003). Cognitive behavioralism in women's prisons: A critical analysis of therapeutic assumptions and practices. In B. Bloom (Ed.), *Gendered justice: Addressing female offenders* (pp. 69–96). Durham, NC: Carolina Academic Press.

Laub, J. H., & Sampson, R. J. (2003). *Shared beginnings, divergent lives.* Cambridge, MA: Harvard University Press.

Lemonne, A. (2003). Alternative conflict resolution and restorative justice: A discussion. In L. Walgrave (Ed.), *Repositioning restorative justice* (pp. 43–63). Portland, OR: Willan Publishing.

LIFERS Public Safety Steering Committee of the State Correctional Institution at Graterford, Pennsylvania. (2004). Ending the culture of street crime. *The Prison Journal, 84*(4), 48S–68S.

Liptak, A. (2008, April 23). Inmate count in U.S. dwarfs other nations'. *New York Times.* [national ed.]. Retrieved August 4, 2007 from http://www.nytimes.com/2008/04/23/us/23prison.html.

Lovell, M., Helfgott, J., & Lawrence, C. (2002). Narrative accounts from the Citizens, Victims, and Offenders Restorative Justice Program. *Contemporary Justice Review, 5*(3), 261–272.

Marshall, M. (2005). *A consideration of the Sycamore Tree Programme and survey results from the perspective of a restorative justice practitioner.* Prison Fellowship New Zealand.

McAdams, D. P. (2006). *The redemptive self: Stories Americans live by.* New York: Oxford University Press.

Messner, S. F., & Rosenfeld, R. (2006). *Crime and the American dream* (3rd ed.). Belmont, CA: Wadsworth.

Minton, T. D., & Sabol, W. J. (2009). *Jail inmates at midyear 2008—Statistical tables.* NCJ 225709, Bureau of Justice Statistics, Office of Justice Programs. U.S. Department of Justice: Washington, D. C.

Mumola, C. J. (2000). *Incarcerated parents and their children.* NCJ 182335, Bureau of Justice Statistics, Office of Justice Programs. U.S. Department of Justice: Washington, D. C.

Office of the Victim Advocate. (2003). *Mediation program for victims of violent crime training manual.* Harrisburg, PA: Author.

Petrellis, T. R. (2007). The restorative justice living unit at Grand Cache Institution: Exploring the application of restorative justice in a correctional environment. Restorative Justice and Dispute Resolution Division, Correctional Service Canada. Retrieved May 5, 2010 from http://www.csc-scc.gc.ca/text/rj/rj2009/kit/17-eng.shtml

Pew Center on the States. (2008). *One in 100: Behind bars in America 2008.* Washington, DC: The Pew Charitable Trusts.

Phillips, B. (2002). An evaluation of AVP workshops in Aotearoa/New Zealand. In AVPA (Ed.), Retrieved May 5, 2010 from http://www.avparoundtheworld.info/res-avp-rpteval-newzealand-2002.pdf

Porter, A. (2007). Restorative programs help Hawaii inmates reconnect with community. *Restorative Practices Eforum.* Retrieved May, 5, 2001, from http://www.iirp.org/pdf/hawaiiprisons.pdf

Presser, L. (2008). *Been a heavy life: Stories of violent men.* Urbana and Chicago: University of Illinois Press.

Roche, D. (2007). Retribution and restorative justice. In G. Johnstone and D. Van Ness (Eds.), *Handbook of restorative justice* (pp. 75–90). Devon: Willan Publishing.

Rose, D. R., & Clear, T. R. (1998). Incarceration, social capital, and crime: Implications for social disorganization theory. *Criminology, 36*(3), 441–479.

Rothman, D. (2002). *Conscience and convenience: The asylum and its alternatives in progressive America.* New York: Aldine de Gruyter.

Sherman, L. W., & Strang, H. (2007). *Restorative justice: The evidence.* London: The Smith Institute.

Sloane, S. (2002). A study of the effectiveness of Alternatives to Violence workshops in a prison system. Retrieved May 5, 2010 from http://renofriends.org/AVPreport2007.pdf

Sullivan, D., & Tifft, L. (2005). *Restorative justice: Healing the foundations of our everyday lives* (2nd ed.). Monsey, NY: Willow Tree Press.

Swanson, C., Culliver, G., & Summers, C. (2007). Creating a faith-based restorative justice community in a maximum security prison. *Corrections Today, 69*(3), 60–63.

Thalhuber, P., & Thompson, S. (2007). *Building a home for the heart: Using metaphors in value-centered circles.* St Paul, MN: Living Justice Press.

Toews, B. (2006a). *Exploring the alternatives to violence project (AVP)/restorative justice (RJ) relationship: Impressions from AVP facilitators and participants incarcerated in Pennsylvania prisons.* The Pennsylvania Prison Society.

Toews, B. (2006b). Resources for restorative justice education in prison. http://www.prisonsociety.org/pdf/rj_resources.pdf (Accessed May 15, 2009).

Umbreit, M., Vos, B., Coates, R., & Brown, K. (2003). *Facing violence: The path of restorative justice and dialogue.* Monsey, NY: Criminal Justice Press.

Van Ness, D. (2007). Prisons and restorative justice. In G. Johnstone and D. Van Ness (Eds.), *Handbook of restorative justice* (pp. 312–324). Devon, UK: Willan Publishing.

Van Ness, D., & Weber, R. (2008). In-prison victim offender dialogue in the U.S. Retrieved April 18, 2009 from http://www.restorativejustice.org/editions/2008/september08/vod

van Wormer, K. (2001). *Counseling female offenders and victims: A strengths-restorative approach.* New York: Springer Publishing Company.

van Wormer, K. (2006). The case of restorative justice: A crucial adjunct to the social work curriculum. *Journal of Teaching in Social Work, 26*(3/4), 57–69.

Wachtel, T., & McCold, P. (2001). Restorative justice in everyday life. In H. Strang and J.Braithwaite (Eds.), *Restorative justice and civil society* (pp. 114–129). Cambridge: Cambridge University Press.

Wacquant, L. (2001). Deadly symbiosis: When ghetto and prison meet and mesh. In D. Garland (Ed.), *Mass imprisonment: Social causes and consequences* (pp. 82–120). Thousand Oaks, CA: Sage Publications.

West, H. C., & Sabol, W. J. (2009). Prison inmates at midyear 2008—Statistical tables. NCJ 225619, Bureau of Justice Statistics, Office of Justice Programs. U.S. Department of Justice: Washington, D. C.

Western, B. (2006). *Punishment andiInequality in America.* New York: Russell Sage Foundation.

Willemsens, J. (2003). Restorative justice: A discussion of punishment. In L. Walgrave (Ed.), *Repositioning restorative justice* (pp. 24–42). Portland, OR: Willan Publishing.

Wright, M. (2003). Is it time to question the concept of punishment? In L. Walgrave (Ed.), *Repositioning restorative justice* (pp. 3–23). Portland, OR: Willan Publishing.

Zehr, H. (1990). *Changing lenses.* Scottdale, PA: Herald Press.

Zehr, H. (2001). *Transcending: Reflections of crime victims.* Intercourse, PA: Good Books.

Zehr, H. (2002). *The little book of restorative justice.* Intercourse, PA: Good Books.

Chapter Seven

Using Conflict to Build Community: Community Conferencing

LAUREN ABRAMSON AND ELIZABETH BECK

If it wasn't for coach Don, I'd probably be some statistic; he brought something good into the community. That is kind of helpin' everybody out in the community.
— *Young player, Patterson Park Youth League Football*

In this chapter we explore the way in which a restorative justice practice called *community conferencing* and social work's community practice worked together to create an environment in which the above member of the Patterson Park Youth Football League was able to thrive. We examine the strengths and limitations of community conferencing and community practice and show how these strategies, working in tandem, transformed a community and the individuals in it. Our examination covers both principles and practice skills, and we hope that by introducing community conferencing to the social work community practice literature, conferencing will be viewed as a tool to complement traditional community practice interventions.

COMMUNITY PRACTICE IN SOCIAL WORK

Community practice is a critical part of social work's history and mission. While community practice has been defined in a number of ways, most scholars and practitioners agree that at its core, community practice seeks to bring economic and social justice and development to neighborhoods that are low income and under-resourced, as well as exploited, including those targeted for disposal of environmentally hazardous material or unscrupulous lending practices (Beck & Eichler, 2000; Fisher, 1994; Mondros & Wilson, 1994; Pyles, 2009; Specht & Courtney, 1994; Staples, 2004). In this chapter, we explore the approaches used by community practitioners to address community issues, including a discussion of innovations in community practice and an exploration of the ways in which community and individual practice can complement each other.

In 1995, Rothman identified three approaches that social workers use to assist communities: *social action, locality development*, and *social planning*. Social action

149

is used to support low income people and communities by organizing individuals for the purpose of using their collective strength to redistribute power from its hierarchical and traditional holders to all members of communities. Its methods are adversarial, and it is closely linked to Saul Alinsky's belief that "change comes from power and power comes from organization" (Rothman, 1995 p.133). In locality development, neighbors support their community by working together to bring resources into the community. Social integration, which Rothman defines as harmonious relationships among people of various classes and ethnic groups, is critical to locality development. Social planning is often aligned with schools of public policy. Here, citizens do not control the process; rather, governmental and technocratic resources are used to address social problems (Rothman, 1995). The community practice literature is full of examples of successful interventions in each of the practice areas identified by Rothman. For example, the seventh edition of Rothman, Erlich, and Tropman's *Strategies of Community Intervention* includes exciting examples such as an advocacy campaign in Chicago that resulted in big box stores such as Walmart raising workers' pay to a living wage of $10.00 an hour, from a minimum wage of $5.15, and a review of the practices implemented by the Farm Workers Union in the 1960s.

The claim that social work had lost its community interest was broadcast in 1994 by Specht and Courtney in their book *Unfaithful Angels: How Social Work Abandoned its Mission*. The authors concluded that, with as many as 40% of the members of the National Association of Social Workers (NASW) engaged in private practice for at least a portion of their work week, social work was moving away from a practice area that focused on the poor, communities, and social justice issues and toward supporting middle-class, insurance-bearing clients. The dominance of direct practice versus community practice remains an issue in social work. However, since Specht and Courtney raised the call, exciting innovations have taken place both in community practice and in strategies that bring community and individual practice together.

One significant innovation, assets-based community development (ABCD), preceded Specht and Courtney's publication by several months. ABCD is a capacity-based approach, which is founded on the assumption that low-income communities are made up of individuals who have the gifts and skills needed to address their community's social problems. The assets of the community are identified and then become the building blocks for community development (Kretzman & McKnight, 1996). Although this approach to community development originated in the departments of social education and social policy at Northwestern University, its impact on social work community practice has been significant. By melding the strategies associated with the ABCD approach with social work's general movement, in the 1990s, toward a strengths- based approach as championed by Dennis Saleeby, social workers today are entering communities with a new perspective and tool set (Saleeby, 2006). An added dimension to the ABCD approach is found in the work of Melvin Delgado, who stated that social work could be much more effective with communities of color if social workers utilized *nontraditional settings*, which he described as ranging from a community center to a grocery store. To Delgado, nontraditional settings are culturally accessible to people of color, and an institution like a barbershop can be an ideal place for community organizing, because, for example, hairdressers have assets and professional relationships that give them a unique ability to, with training and resources, identify and address violence against women (Delgado, 1999).

Joining Delgado's efforts to support a more multicultural approach to community practice are researchers like Ann Alverez, John Erlich, Lorraine Gutierrez, and Flex Rivera[i]. In different publications, these individuals have suggested that diversity must be at the forefront of community practice—with "diversity: here meaning that people of color are not only disproportionally affected by social ills, but that inherent in their diversity are unique strengths for addressing these ills. Finally, because greater social equality underlies all of the recent trends in community practice, a movement among some in social work's community practice field embraces the human rights framework as championed by the United Nations' *Universal Declaration of Human Rights* (Reichert, 2003; van Wormer, 2004).

While social work's focus on community practice is primarily based on models of justice, fields such as public policy, public health, sociology, criminal justice, political science, business, and social work (Cnaan & Rothman, 1995; Ohmer & Beck, 2006), also contribute to our understanding of communities by exploring their relational aspects. Specifically, scholars have identified social capital and collective efficacy as concepts that represent social ties and interactions between neighbors (Putnam, 2000; Sampson, 2004). *Social capital* refers to the shared networks that neighbors have and includes two types: *bonding capital* and *bridging capital*. Bonding capital encompasses the networks and relationships that residents share within their community, and bridging capital represents networks that originate in the community but extend beyond it (Putnam, 2000). Research shows a positive relationship between social capital and community resources, and by extension, overall community health (Brisson & Usher, 2005).

Collective efficacy involves neighbors knowing one another, sharing values and norms, and being willing to act on those shared values for the good of the community. Studies have found that where collective efficacy is high, crime is low (Sampson, Raudenbush, & Earls, 1997). Given the positive effects of collective efficacy, it can be hypothesized that great value arises from creating and implementing interventions designed to enhance collective efficacy. Yet, efforts used to support collective efficacy are paltry in the literature.

COMMUNITIES AND RESTORATIVE JUSTICE

From its inception, restorative justice has identified victims, offenders, and communities as the primary stakeholders in a restorative process. While it is recognized that communities are important, the information on the role of the community following crime and examples of community-based restorative practices following crime are few in comparison to discussions of victims and offenders. Presently two major strains of discussion focus on restorative justice and communities. The first involves questions about restorative justice and its interaction with the community. The second examines restorative justice practice in communities.

Lingering Questions

Three fundamental questions about community have been central in the literature: What is the community, what is its role in a restorative justice process, and what is the relationship between communities and restorative justice?

What is Community?

Criminologist Paul McCold and Benjamin Wachtel, director of communications and technology for the International Institute of Restorative Practices, stated in 1998 that, if communities were to experience restorative effects from restorative encounters, there needed to be some type of definition of community. As evidence of the need for definition, the authors wrote that in the restorative justice literature, the term "community" is used to describe neighborhoods, society, and all levels in between. To McCold and Wachtel, commuity is a "feeling, a perception of connectedness" (1998, p. 294). Building on Braithwaite's view of reintegrative shaming, the authors then argue that this feeling of connectedness is precisely what allows restorative process to work, because people do not want to disappoint those they care about.

McCold and Wachtel's definition is clearly not based on a specific geography, and they further assert that a geographically based definition can support non-restorative responses if the community is viewed as being owed a "debt to society" by the offender. Boyes-Watson (2005) expands McCold and Wachtel's definition of community when she states that, rather than being a place, communities are a way to be; in other words, they provide the opportunity to allow people to interact, with trust and care. Perhaps Pranis (2007) comes closest to defining community, in the context of restorative justice, when she writes the community can provide the resources for reconciliation of victims and offenders, and it is where standards of behavior are monitored and enforced.

Johnstone (2005) makes an important point when he states that these views of community may be idealized, and that the descriptions of community are so rosy that they do not articulate strategies to deal with major roadblocks such as social isolation, inadequacy of resources to address the issues, and prevalence of antisocial norms or mistrust.

We also believe that the community should be defined, but that this definition ought to stem from an organic process and be based in principles of restorative justice. The definition should not be based solely on administrative data, such as census tracks or membership in an organization, but these issues should be included, and this is especially true when the issue is a place-based one, such as property crime. We further argue that the definition should not be based solely on relationships, because place does affect interaction and can influence behavior, both in positively and negatively terms. As Clear and Karp, experts in community justice, point out, community involves both place and relationships (Clear & Karp, 1999; Karp, 2004). Additionally, Karp notes that community also involves those most related to the incident in question. We also support that the definition of the community must come from the perception of those affected by an issue, the harm that was caused, the needs that resulted, and those who ought to be involved in the process of putting things right.

What is the Role of the Community?

The second significant round of questions that restorative justice practitioners and theorists ask focus on the role which the community plays following a crime, and the needs of that community after a crime has been committed. In the beginning of the restorative justice movement, communities were largely seen as "victims" that needed to regain a sense of safety (McCold, 2004; Walgrave, 2002). For example, Howard Zehr (1995) in *Changing Lenses* poses four questions regarding what a community needs to put things right after a crime. Three of these questions are close to the ones he raises for victims in the wake of crime and include issues of safety, restitution, and insuring their inclusion in the process.

Perry (2002) views the community as an entity that owes repair, rather than as an entity that has been victimized. In his view, the community owes a debt to both the victim and the offender, as the community failed the victim by not protecting him or her, and failed the offender for not providing ample opportunities that would have allowed him or her to succeed, rather than turn to crime. Beck, Britto, and Andrews (2007) expand on Perry as they argue that, in a number of cases, communities not only failed to provide opportunities, but that at times what they did offer was inadequate or destructive. In their study of men on death row, the authors explored the many ways in which most of the capital offenders in their sample had fallen through the cracks of community institutions and supports (e.g. child protective services, schools, mental health care, domestic violence supports, and substance abuse treatment), often multiple times. They suggest that in these instances, the community might best respond by developing a review panel to assess service gaps in relevant community institutions, and make policy recommendations based on those assessments.

Communities and Restorative Justice - What Is the Interaction?

The final question raised by restorative justice theorists considers the interaction between the community and restorative practice, and here a number of scholars have put forth ideas regarding the resources of the community, outcomes, and the interplay between restorative justice and democracy.

From its earliest indigenous roots, restorative justice has viewed communities as places that can resolve problems. For example, Walgrave (2002) and Karp (2004) believe that communities provide the social context for restorative practices such as reintegrative shaming. Johnstone (2005) includes an additional component stating that the community can support the offender to stay on a pro-social path.

While communities provide tools to support restorative justice, communities can also be strengthened through restorative processes. Walgrave (2002) believes that the ideal community, conceptualized as supporting harmonious living, citizen responsibility, and mutual respect, is created through the healing social relationships that develop from restorative practices. Johnstone (2005) has found that restorative practices bring together opportunities for moral development with community building. Bazemore and Umbreit (2002) identify five community-based outcomes that should occur with a restorative process: 1) creating and strengthening of relationships; 2) increasing skills, including in the area of conflict resolution; 3) increasing capacity and efficacy to address problems; 4) creating awareness of common good; and 5) increasing social supports for victims and offenders. Given that community conferencing provides a forum for neighbors to meet and articulate norms, we believe that the creation or strengthening of collective efficacy is another important benefit (Pranis, 2007; see also McCold & Wachtel, 1998).

Others believe that restorative justice strengthens democratic governance by shifting power from the state to the community (Bazemore, 2000; Pranis, 2007). Bazemore suggests that when decision-making is moved from traditional power-holding institutions, such as courts, to the community, both the community and democratic processes are supported as power is more evenly distributed (Schweigert, 2002; Wahrhaftig, 1981). Walgrave (2002) sums up the role of restorative justice and communities: "Indigenous movements demanded the right to resolve crime in their own way which was community and resolution oriented" (p. 72).

While notions of community power hold value, it is also important to note that communities can be, as McCold and Wachtel (1998) point out, punitive and stigmatizing, and the tension between community control and equality has been at times a very strong undercurrent during the history of the United States. McCold (2004) argues that, when restorative processes are to be used, work must be done with the community to insure that processes are rooted in restorative principles. Only then will restorative processes be able to repair the ruptured bond that has occurred and strengthen the community at the same time.

Restorative Practices in Communities

In this section we explore two types of community-based restorative interventions: community justice and community conferencing.

Community Justice

Community justice includes community policing, community crime prevention, the community playing an active role in supporting youth on probation, community prosecution, and reparative boards (Karp & Clear, 2002; Perry, 2002). Because each of the community justice strategies incorporates restorative justice values and ideas but is not based on its principles, some scholars have raised questions as to whether these interventions can be truly considered restorative justice (Arrigo, 2004; McCold, 2004).

The reparative board is probably most aligned with restorative justice. Karp and Walther (2001) state that the mission of the reparative board "is to enhance social control at the local level by involving citizens in the justice process" (p.199), such that community members work with the offender to repair harm and address the needs that follow his or her crime. Like other restorative processes, the reparative board promotes citizens' roles in the criminal justice system, provides an opportunity for victims and offenders to interact, and requires accountability on the part of the offender. While the data collected on reparative boards is small, it does show that they hold benefits for the victims who choose to participate, offenders, and communities (see Karp, Sprayregen, & Drakulich, 2002).

However, concerns have also been raised about reparative boards. For example, given the power imbalance between the community members and the offenders, critics recognize that community members can exert coercive control. Additionally, studies have found that the restorative boards lack consistency, varying in their relative leniency and emphasis on rehabilitation (Karp & Clear, 2002). Finally, the concern has been raised that community-based volunteer boards may not reflect the diversity of the community; instead, members can represent hegemonic views that that may not underscore equality (Arrigo, 2004). In order to address this issue, White (2003) believes that it is imperative to include the "politically and social weak" members of the community (p. 148).

Community Conferencing

When individuals or groups are in conflict, or have engaged in destructive actions, conferencing creates the potential for *constructive* engagement. This community-based process is used most commonly with groups affected by interpersonal conflict, crime, or community (neighborhood, school, workplace, etc.) conflicts. In conferencing, a group of people—including everyone who is affected by the situation, their respective supporters, and other community stakeholders such as individuals who represent community organizations –meet to address a common concern. These participants typically achieve some shared understanding about the causes and consequences of that conflict, then devise a plan of action to address the ramifications of the conflict (Abramson & Moore, 2001; Abramson & Moore, 2002). The restorative nature of a community conference is partially illustrated by the three questions asked in a conference: 1) What happened? 2) Who has been affected and how? 3) What can be done to repair the harm and make things better in the future?

The conferencing process has, perhaps, been best described by Australian David Moore. Moore and McDonald (2000) distill the literature on participatory democracy down to four principles: participation, equality, deliberation, and non-tyranny. They then shows how these principles help to guide conferencing, in that they allow the organizer to:

- Make sure everyone is invited to participate (Participation)
- Ensure that all participants have an equal voice (Equality)
- See to it that all viewpoints are fully discussed (Deliberation)
- Prevent anyone from dominating the conversation. (Non-tyranny)

The *primary* emphasis of conferencing is not on entitlements and rights, but rather on responsibilities and resolution. In this way, conferencing can be used to help restore, maintain, or create positive connections between people. Community conferencing can be viewed as a type of relationship management because it provides people with the opportunity to verbalize feelings, give voice to their experiences, listen to others, state how they would like to be treated; build or rebuild relationships, and work together as a community collaboratively, creatively, and in ways that satisfy everyone.

An example of effective conferencing is found in the Community Conferencing Center, which was established in 1998 to support low-income neighborhoods by addressing the lack of available, effective, and community-based responses to interpersonal conflict and to crime, and by using the conferencing process as a community-building tool (Community Conferencing Center, n.d.). (Today the Community Conferencing Center supports: 1) juvenile justice through court diversion; 2) schools by providing alternative to suspension and arrests; 3) neighborhoods and community organizations by addressing conflicts; 4) individuals returning to communities following such major events as incarceration and military services; and 5) treatment and aftercare planning in human service provision.

To date, 98% of the 900 conferences conducted by the Community Conferencing Center have resulted in the participants reaching their own agreement about how to resolve the matter. Many of those agreements—even in court diversion cases where an arrest has been made—end up with the "victims" coming forth with some way they can help and or work with the "offender." One of the 900 conferences conducted by the Community Conferencing Center involved the Streeper Street community in Baltimore. This conference provides a remarkable illustration of how conferencing uses conflict as a stepping-stone to building connected communities.

CASE STUDY: THE COMMUNITY CONFERENCING CENTER AND STREEPER STREET

The Problem

The consistent football games in the streets were downright infuriating to a number of the residents of Streeper Street. It was not enough that residents were forced to hear the noise late into the night, but they also had to pay for the damage done when the children's daring maneuvers hurt their trees and damaged their cars. Making matters worse, there was a very large park a mere two blocks away.

When one resident tried to confront one of the young people, he found his car fouled with animal feces. In another incident the youth poured sugar in a resident's gas tank. A long series of arguments and calls to the police ensued. The adults were angry about the damage the youth were causing and began to believe that the children were really there to deal drugs. For close to two years the tensions built on the north end of Streeper Street.

Against this backdrop Banner Neighborhoods, a community organization, began exploring ways to help the residents on Streeper Street resolve this ongoing conflict. One of the agencies that Banner Neighborhoods reached out to was the Community Conferencing Center. Each time the residents came to Banner's office to complain about the problem of kids playing ball in the street, the staff offered them the possibility of going to mediation or community conferencing. The residents understood that mediation would involve a couple of adults and a couple of young people sitting down to figure things out, and that a conference would involve the entire "community of people affected" sitting down to try to figure things out for themselves. After 18 months of the adults calling the police on the kids but not getting the results they hoped for, they finally came to Banner staff and said, "OK, we'd like to try that meeting you've been talking about where we all get together to work it out ourselves."

Conference Preparation

The Community Conferencing Center assigned one of their facilitators, Misty, the task of setting up the conference, which included making sure all of the stakeholders were invited. Over a period of two to three weeks, at different times of the day and on different days of the week, she covered the neighborhood. She knocked on doors and spoke to people wherever she found them in order to make sure that everyone affected by this situation was invited to the conference. As Misty spoke to residents, she introduced herself and inquired about each person's concerns related to the ball games in the street.

She spoke with adults and young people alike, being careful not to take sides or voice her own opinion. She listened to everyone's concerns and made sure that everyone was clear about how the conference would work. She used these conversations to build both the residents' trust in the Center and their sense of ownership of the issue. She explained that if they had been affected by the situation they now not only had a chance to voice their concerns, but also to invest their time in coming up with a solution that made sense to them. She assured people that the conference would be facilitated to help prevent it from deteriorating into a brawl. Just hours before the start of the conference she made her last visit, encouraging residents to attend and sharing with them the names of others who had agreed to join the conference.

The Conference

Forty-four people came to the conference. The crowd was diverse in terms of age, ethnicity, class, and gender, and included families, single parents, young children (the youngest of whom was a toddler), business owners, and senior citizens. Members of the Banner Neighborhoods staff also participated.

Phase One: Sharing Stories and Building Understanding

All of the participants came to the conference with stored-up emotions and anger. The conference began with a flurry of heated remarks and accusations. The young people first talked about playing in the street. This discussion drew additional comments from their parents, who felt their children were being targeted by disgruntled neighbors, and the parents became defensive and argumentative. On the other hand, many residents were dismayed at the number of children who played on the street late into the night. Nonetheless, as the neighbors talked, the conversation shifted from their anger to their fears. Several of the angry adults voiced their concern about the danger posed to the children from speeding cars. At this moment a shift occurred within the circle; a unity was created and all of the adults agreed that there was an inherent danger to playing in the street. Eventually the uniformity of purpose and emotion shifted the anger to concern and finally to interest in finding a way toward a productive resolution. Not long after, a father said that it was time now to stop pointing fingers, get together as a neighborhood, and start trying to get at the heart of the problem. Participants immediately then realized they were not there to argue and leave angry, but to find a resolution. According to the facilitator, the defining crescendo of the conference occurred with this moment of an awareness of "collective responsibility."

The young people then spoke about how they did not have a place to play. The adults heard for the first time that the park was not a place they could play—people did not clean up after their dogs at one end of the park, and they got beat up by older kids and drug dealers at the other end of the park. Residents began to offer ideas for helping ease the situation. A staff member representing Banner Neighborhoods offered information about the area's recreation center. Parents suggested finding places to set up activities for the kids. One father offered to escort the boys to the park for a game of football. Amazingly, all of the adults began to talk about the respect the children deserved, not just at the conference but every day. One mother offered, "Children are people, too. If you want to *get* respect, you have to *give* respect." Not only was it important for the children to start demonstrating more caution around other people's property, but the adult neighbors needed to respect each other as well as the children.

At this point, the conference began to fulfill one of its important functions: a community of people began to define for themselves how they want to be treated, what kinds of behaviors are acceptable and what kinds are not, and how they can promote behavior that is acceptable. Further, the conference, which had begun with the adults complaining about the young people's behavior, was now focused on the needs of the young people. The discussion had moved from damage and disruption to a plan to help the young people find safe and fun ways to play.

Phase Two: Agreement

The facilitator then led participants in a discussion of ways in which the situation could be improved. She asked participants to elaborate on their ideas, including how they might be implemented. Most of the solutions involved adults volunteering to support activities for the children and included adults offering to take young people to the neighborhood's recreation center for activities in the evening, chaperoning kids at the park so that they could play football, and shuttling kids to and from activities such as ice skating (which occurred at the park) and movies. One of the children said that the neighborhood should help Mr. Willy, an elderly resident, who cleaned up the litter on his block every morning. Mr. Willy received two standing ovations for his efforts—representing the first time he was ever publicly recognized for his daily contributions. It was agreed that when anyone saw Mr. Willy picking up they would offer help if possible. Within 20 minutes, the group had finalized their agreement.

Phase Three: After the Conference

Each of the participants confirmed that the conference was a success. Almost immediately there was significantly less ball-playing in the street. Both the adults and children kept the promises they made at the conference. These actions, however, do little to illustrate the truly remarkable outcomes associated with this community conference.

The day after the conference, Don, who the children refered to as Mr. Don, went to chaperone the kids who wanted to play in the park, as he had agreed to do. Twenty-two children showed up to play football. Within three weeks, the number of young people showing up to play reached 64, and by the summer a football league had been organized.

The coed league, now in its eighth year, is coordinated by Banner Neighborhoods and is staffed by 40 adult volunteers from the neighborhood (Sullivan, 2002). It is made up of four teams and includes a cheerleading squad, to provide an opportunity to participate for those children who do not want to play football. The league emphasizes education and family rather than winning. Each team has an agreement that must be signed, and although each team lays out the requirements for their individual agreement, they all must participate in an hour of homework before practice and maintain passing grades to play. Other items found in the agreements include not cursing and community engagement. Each team also requires its players to keep their block and the park clean.

CASE STUDY ANALYSIS

The Streeper Street conference signified not so much the end of a conflict, but rather the beginning of a cohesive and child-friendly community. In this section, we analyze the conference by examining its outcomes, the theory and principles that guide the Community Conferencing Center's work, and facilitator skills.

Community-Based Outcomes

Resource Mobilization

The conference helped to open up a new set of resources to the residents of Streeper Street. During the conference, parents learned about places and activities already in existence for their use, and made specific plans to help the children access them. The recreation center and Banner Neighborhoods had programs for kids that some of the parents just needed to hear about, as they were unaware of these programs. After seeing the enthusiasm at the conference, Banner Neighborhoods vowed to take an even more active role with the neighborhood youth and began establishing more activities for kids. Realizing the effort community associations were willing to put into the neighborhood, parents talked about asking other associations, not represented that night, to develop activities for the children.

Perhaps even more important, however, was the extent to which the neighbors saw themselves as resources. The level of community involvement dramatically increased between residents. Parents and other adults began to make great efforts to support the youth in their new activities. One man, who had, before the conference, called the police many times about the kids, began to get to know them, and within the month he had taken several young people to attend the monthly meeting of the neighborhood organization He later became a mentor for one boy and participated in a few field trips with the young people. Parents who never played outside with their kids were now going to the park to watch the football teams practice and play games. The young people also made a concerted effort to work toward community cooperation and unity. One of their activities on the football team was to clean up the yards of some of their elderly neighbors.

Embracing Diversity

Coach Don was not alone in his efforts to provide the young people with activities. Over forty other adults volunteered their time to help run the league. Prior to his involvement with the league, one of the coaches had been called horrible names with a racial overtone by the kids, but today he is greeted as "coach." The breaking down of racial, ethnic, and class barriers has continued rapidly, as the league has expanded so that children from adjacent streets are befriending one another. According to a report put out by Banner Neighborhoods, one white family was anxious to move away from the neighborhood due to difficulties their son was having in a predominantly black school. Their son joined the football league and made so many friends that the parents had a change of heart and decided to stay in the area.

The case study clearly shows how, once the residents had a chance to give voice to their frustrations and to understand their neighbors' different perspectives, a transformation occurred in how they felt about each other, allowing them to begin looking at possible solutions in a much different, more creative, and more collaborative way.

Collective Efficacy

One of the first components of collective efficacy that must be in place is that neighbors must know each other. During the conference neighbors got to know each other, and the relationships among participants have flourished following it. These relationships include those between adults and children. A second component of collective efficacy is sharing norms. The conference provided a space where all the residents could decide for themselves—*and articulate for each other*—the kinds of behavior they wanted to support in their neighborhood, as well as the kinds of behaviors they wanted to eliminate. For example, in response to the adults' complaints about the noise caused by kids playing in the street at late hours, all of the young people agreed that they would play in the street only during certain agreed-upon times. In addition, all of the neighbors agreed that they would not use curse words with each other. Thus began the neighbors' journey toward being collaborative and clear about their expectations. The final component of collective efficacy is a willingness of neighbors to act on shared norms. Warner (2003) suggests that one of the major reasons that neighbors do not enforce norms is they believe that their norms are not shared by others. Therefore, the joint establishing of norms and the signing of agreements to support them is foundational to collective efficacy. In sum, the Streeper Street conference provided a real-life example illustrating McCold's (2004) argument that restorative justice brings together individuals in such a way that informal social control is strengthened (see also Bazemore, 2000).

Theory: The Biology of Emotion

One of the unique contributions of the Community Conferencing Center's approach to conferencing is that they base their approach to the conferencing process on a theoretical understanding of the role of emotion in conflict transformation. The center grounds their work in Silvan Tomkins' (1962, 1963), theory of human motivation which states that emotions—not "drives" and not cognitions—are, biologically, the primary motivational system in human beings. Emotions are critical biological functions that help us survive. What is important about Community Conferences is that they provide people in conflict (which is made up of negative feelings) with a safe space to give voice to their negative feelings, and in doing so, to better understand each other and thus find a lasting solution. Think about the many ways we have to resolve conflicts. Most of them force us to stifle our emotions. But what good is a great solution, if people still do not see the good in each other? Conferencing, therefore, is based in our biology—understanding that participants are more likely to find ways to cooperate with each other when they can communicate within a structure that allows negative emotions associated with conflict to be *expressed* and *transformed* into positive emotions associated with cooperation.

A community conference involves a simple framework that supports participants in telling their stories, and in doing so to allow them to shift their emotional state from conflict to cooperation (for a detailed discussion of how conferences provide for a transformation of emotions, see Abramson & Moore, 2002). The grouping of the three discussion questions (What happened? How has each person been affected by situation? What can be done to repair any harm and prevent this from happening again?) supports a collective change of mood among participants by allowing people to talk about the past, the present, and then the future, sharing their genuine feelings throughout. By focusing on these questions in sequence, participants experience a shift from the initial, and most strongly negative, emotions associated with conflict (anger, disgust, fear) to less strongly negative emotions that motivate us to seek comfort and connection (distress, shame), and finally to the positive emotions that motivate us to cooperate with one another (interest, joy). In the language favored by the Harvard Negotiation project, participants first have a chance to "get to peace" (during Phases I and II), allowing them to ultimately "get to yes" (during Phase III) (Fisher & Ury, 1991).

Examining the biology of emotion and motivation helps us understand this transformation process more clearly. The Community Conferencing Center appreciates that allowing for the expression of the full range of emotions 1) is vital for healthy emotional functioning and 2) is a fundamental reason for the effectiveness of the conferencing process. Tomkins' theory drew heavily from Darwin's prescient work on the motivational function of emotions (Tomkins, 1962, 1963), detailing the importance of emotions to survival. When we are angry, our pupils constrict in order to bring a threat into sharper focus, and our heart pumps more blood to our muscles in preparation for attack, and motivating us to attack in return. In contrast, interest motivates us to "engage" in positive ways with our environment and the people in it. Table 7.1 outlines nine "basic emotions" and the specific ways that they motivate us. When facilitators understand that strong negative emotions are an important and *necessary* part of the process by which the conflict can be transformed, they are more accepting of and comfortable with the expression of negative emotion, and less likely to control the expression of emotion by participants, which in turn, helps them to be more able to maximize the likelihood that participants will voice their feeling and be able to move from the emotions that generate conflict to the emotions that generate cooperation.

Table 7.1 Motivation and the Nine Emotions

Basic Emotion	Motivation
DISSMELL	Stay away!
DISGUST	Get rid of it
ANGER	Attack
FEAR	Get away
SADNESS	Comfort
SHAME	Seek to restore
SURPRISE	Stop, look, listen
INTEREST	Engage
JOY	Affiliate

This understanding of biology and emotions further supports community conferencing's aims of supporting diversity and cultural sensitivity. All human beings are born with emotions, and they play an important role in motivating our behavior. Therefore, the conferencing process, by allowing human beings to give voice to our biologically-driven emotions, is relevant and culturally sensitive for any culture or combination of cultures and subcultures. Although different cultures may have different ways of expressing certain emotions, the structure of the conference allows for that, and creates spaces for people to better understand the differences in how feelings and cultural norms are expressed.

Principled and Effective Practice and the Role of the Facilitator

Perhaps the most important role of the facilitator is to insure that conference principles are being met. The Community Conferencing Center helps facilitators develop their skills by rooting their practice in the basic principles and process of conferencing—not in a rigid script that dictates how to facilitate a conference. At the Community Conferencing Center, the conferencing process is likened to jazz. All of the notes could never be written down, so good facilitators need to have a strong internalized sense of the principles and theory behind the "music" so that, as they improvise based on what comes up at any given moment (which is entirely unpredictable), they play off of and respond to these incidents in alignment with the principles and spirit of the process. Thus, rather than being able to provide the facilitator with a precise recipe for how to facilitate, care is taken to make explicit the underlying principles upon which the process is based. These principles are now explored.

Transparency

Conferencing is based on a belief that individuals truly do have the capacity to resolve many complex and difficult conflicts themselves, and if they are going to be empowered to make their own decisions, then there needs to be complete transparency about the process that they are using to make those decisions. Everything about how the conferencing process works is made clear to the participants during the initial contact, so that at every point they are able to make the most informed decisions possible. Therefore, in the Streeper Street conference the facilitator took special care throughout the preparation, conference, and follow-up phases of the process to make sure that participants were clear about what choices they had with regard to different interventions, how the process works, what would happen if an agreement is reached, and what would happen if not, for example.

The facilitator did this by providing participants with very clear information during the preparation phase about how the "meeting" would work, by saying: "This is a meeting for people who are interested in trying to make this situation better. Everyone will have an opportunity to speak, and everyone will have the opportunity to listen" (thus adhering to the principle of transparency). She then explained the process and outlined the three phases of the conference. She also explained that once everyone had had a chance to speak, the group then would decide how to repair any harm and how to move forward in a better way, and shared ideas would be written into an agreement that everyone would sign.

Inclusion and Participation

Another fundamental principle for conferences is that everyone who is affected and who will play a role in making decisions about the future needs of the community should be invited to participate. In this case, that meant including adult neighbors, the children of the neighborhood, and resource people (that is, someone from a relevant neighborhood organization, such as a community organizer, or a representative of an after-school program or neighborhood church).

This conference would not have been as successful if only a few adults and a few of the children had participated in the process. Everyone who attended the conference was heard, and nearly every participant decided for themselves what role they would or would not take in the plan to move forward. If a few people had attended the conference and decided what everyone in the neighborhood *should* do, instead of letting people decide for themselves what they *wanted* to do, then the exact same agreement would have had little chance of being adhered to. Or imagine if someone had simply approached Mr. Don (who later became Coach Don) and said, "You know, those kids who put dents in your car and poured sugar in your gas tank probably won't do that if you'd just go down to the park and coach them." None of us wants someone else telling us what to do. Thus, it is critical that everyone who can be part of the solution is included in the process, so they can make decisions for themselves at the same time that others are also making decisions about how to improve the situation. When people come together and do this collectively, the results can be impressive in both reach and in sustainability.

To that end, as noted earlier, the facilitator spent about three weeks conducting preparation in the neighborhood, knocking on doors at different times of the day and on different days of the week, to make sure that everyone who wanted to attend would know about the meeting. Flyers were also distributed to each door just in case face-to-face contact was not possible.

Do With, Not For, Participants
One of the key principles of conducting a conference is to always allow the participants to decide for themselves how they will agree to treat each other. For example, if someone bursts out with a flurry of profanity during the conference, clearly upsetting several participants in the circle, this outburst may evoke a great deal of anxiety and distress in a facilitator who has not yet internalized that principle. In an attempt to quell his or her own anxiety, as well as to bring some calm and control to the group, the facilitator then might be inclined to react and say, "Please don't use that kind of language during this meeting." However, a facilitator who is firmly grounded in the principles of the process would most likely be inclined to ask the group, "I want to just cut in for a second and ask how participants feel about the language that was just used." If people express discomfort with it, then the facilitator might follow up with, "Some people expressed discomfort with the use of profanity. Can everyone agree to not use profanity during this meeting?"

The Structure of the Conferencing Process Itself Provides the Ground Rules
The Community Conference Center views a conference as a structured conversation among a community of people who have been affected by a conflict. The structure of that conversation is deceptively simple, and yet vitally important to the success of the conference. Simply put, a conference is a conversation about the past, the present, and the future, in that order, which is conducted by asking the group three questions: What happened? How have people been affected? What can be done to repair any harm and prevent it from happening again?

Though it is not immediately apparent, these three "conditions" of the structure of the conversation become the ground rules for the conversation. Every participant has, during preparation, agreed to this structure for the conversation. So, for example, the young people started off the conversation by talking about playing ball in the street, and the events that transpired in the aftermath of doing so. When an adult participant began to repeatedly interrupt the young people (as is often the case), the facilitator reminded the adult that he had agreed to "first hear what happened," and that "everyone will, indeed, get a chance to speak, but first we are going to hear from the young people about what they have been doing."

Similarly, early in this conference one of the adults became impatient with the arguing and just wanted the group to talk about solutions. However, to do so before everyone had a chance to speak would undermine the entire process, because participants need to be given the chance to give voice to their own story; when they are allowed to do so, the other participants learn new pieces of information.

Together, then, the group collectively paints a fuller picture of what happened and comes to understand why people are behaving the way they are. For example, before this particular conference, the adults never knew why the kids didn't play football in the huge park nearby. As the conference unfolded, they learned from the young people that they did not play in the park "because there's dog poo at one end of the park, and we get beat up by the older kids and drug dealers who hang out at the other end."

Rushing to a solution would bypass the important emotional aspects of the conversation in favor of a speedy, more cognitively-derived resolution. Yet if the group quickly came up with an ideal solution, but they still hated and feared each other, then it would never work. The process allows for the group collectively to come to a meaningful resolution by taking the time for each person to have a voice and speak their piece. And it is the facilitator's responsibility to ensure that this happens.

FACILITATOR TOOLS AND SKILLS

The Script as Guide

Conferencing facilitators have a script that lays out the general order of the conversation and includes the kinds of questions to be asked. The order is important as it helps guide the participants through an understanding of both the past and the future. The conversation always begins with those directly involved in the incident talking about what happened and what they did. Then everyone further fleshes out the picture by telling how they have been affected by the situation. Once everyone has had a chance to speak, the group is asked to discussed what can be done to improve the situation.

Within the conferencing field, there is a fair amount of debate about the conference script. Some programs and practitioners eschew the idea of using one, while others request that facilitators never stray from the conference script. The Community Conferencing Center falls somewhere in the middle, asking facilitators to follow the script exactly as it is written for the first three times they facilitate. From then on, the facilitators are encouraged to use the script as a general guide only, while keeping in mind the reasons why the script is worded and structured the way it is.

Early on in this particular conference, a lot of heated back-and-forth discussion occurred among the participants, both young and old. The facilitator took care not to intervene, too early because a lot of important information was being shared. At the same time, the facilitator made sure that no one was directly attacking anyone else and that all of the comments remained focused on how that person was affected, as opposed to what that person thought about someone else.

It takes restraint on the part of the facilitator to let what seems like chaos unfold and run its course. We have found that if people are able to converse as they normally do, without imposing rigid guidelines, then they are provided with an important gift—an opportunity to learn for themselves how to talk to each other and to decide collectively how they want and expect to be treated. The community, then, is creating their *own* norms for behavior and thus will be far more likely to follow them, than if some authority figure who neither knows them nor lives in their neighborhood told them how they should be behaving.

Facilitator Qualities

The Community Conferencing Center has gleaned a significant amount of knowledge about how to make the process successful, based on 11 years of experience in training and working with a variety of facilitators. However, unfortunately, the conclusion reached is that there is neither a foolproof way to predict who will be a good facilitator, nor is there one field or area of training that produces the best facilitators. Facilitators need to draw on *who they are* as a person far more than their educational background or professional credentials. In fact, each staff facilitator at the Community Conferencing Center is highly skilled, yet their backgrounds range from community organizing, to real estate, to teaching, to psychology, to public relations. Each person brings a variety of qualities that contribute to their success as facilitators.

Some qualities that Community Conferencing Center staff agree contribute to being a successful facilitator include:

- A willingness to *unlearn*
- Good judgment and common sense
- Sincerity
- Not being attached to the *outcomes* of the process
- Belief in people's capacity to learn from their own and each other's behavior
- Belief in every person's dignity and worth
- Ability to remain emotionally separate from participants
- Not "put off" easily (by other peoples' strong emotions, logistical challenges, unresponsive families or agencies, etc.)
- Ability to follow several conversational threads
- Ability to move a group through a script appropriately
- Makes appropriate comments
- Ability to give and receive constructive feedback

COMMUNITY CONFERENCING AND SOCIAL WORK COMMUNITY PRACTICE

In this section, we analyze the linkages and synergy between community conferencing and social work's community practice. Because Banner Neighborhoods's values, goals, and practice skills are aligned within social work's community practice, we will use it as a representative institution for community practice as we explore areas of shared elements and divergence within the organizations and the interventions they represent.

Shared Elements

Values

Supporting a seamless interaction between Banner Neighborhoods and the community conference process was a set of shared values. First, both Banner Neighborhoods and the Community Conferencing Center believed in empowerment for low-income and marginalized individuals, and articulated this belief with the notion that they each sought to do *with*, not *for*, a community. Second, each organization was committed to engaging with the community. Third, each believed in providing opportunities for transformation; for community conferencing, the emphasis is often on individual or relationship transformation, while in traditional community organizing, transformation tends to focus on power relationships, or a problematic area or issue.

Ethics

The overlap between the National Association of Social Workers (NASW) code of ethics and the practice of community conferencing is strong. Mirroring community conferencing goals is NASW's ethical principle that "Social workers understand that relationships between and among people are an important vehicle for change. . . . Social workers seek to strengthen relationships among people in a purposeful effort to promote, restore, maintain, and enhance the wellbeing of individuals, families, social groups, organizations, and communities."

NASWs ethical principles, as well as some specific aspects of social work practice, also relate well to guidelines for community conferencing. For example, social workers respect the inherent dignity and worth of each person. This code speaks to treating people with care and respect, being aware of cultural diversity, and promoting among clients socially responsible self-determination.

An important ethic found in community conferencing is self determination, such that participation is voluntary and therefore coercion is, from the outset, significantly reduced.

Areas of Divergence

One of the important differences between traditional community organizing practices, in particular as related to the area of social action, and community conferencing is the view of anger. Taking a page from Saul Alinsky, community organizers tend to view anger as a motivator for social change. In conferencing, the role of anger is also a motivator for change, but in a very different way. Alinsky believed that anger needed to be harnessed to promote social action, and once it was harnessed, the systems of oppression could be attacked and power redistributed.

Community conferencing allows for the expressions of that anger with the understanding that, if it can give way to moments of shared vulnerability, then it can be transformed ultimately, into strong motivation for cooperation.

A second difference between organizing and conferencing is the type of participants. One of the problems identified with community organizing is the issue of broad participation. For example, it is not uncommon for some neighborhood organizations to be run by a small group of residents. While these individuals spend a lot of time volunteering and tend to have an understanding of internal politics, they also sometimes develop a sense of being an elite group. This division can often create alienation between those who "run" the neighborhood organization and the rest of the residents of the neighborhood. The organization leadership may feel they are acting on behalf of the other residents, but this is not necessarily the case. In community conferencing, everyone engages as equals, and no one can speak on behalf of anyone else.

Finally, while both practices hold that residents need to identify the problems and lead the efforts toward solution, the issue of resident control occurs on a continuum. Organizers tend to have an idea about how an issue might be addressed, and then the specifics of it are determined with residents. With conferencing, the facilitator does not participate in offering solutions or strategies for implementation. Instead, a conference truly is based on "the people's agenda." This viewpoint is best articulated by Cindy, who worked both as an organizer for Banner Neighborhoods and as a facilitator with the Community Conferencing Center. Cindy explained that when she was knocking on doors as an organizer she was looking to help the neighborhood develop and implement a plan. As a conference facilitator, she invites people to a process in which she holds no bias or particular perspective.

NEXT STEPS

Community Conferencing, Social Work, and Economic and Social Justice

To social workers, perhaps the most significant problem associated with restorative justice is also the most neglected: the role of economic and social inequality offending. Thus not only is a just and responsive justice system needed following crime, but a just social and economic system is also essential to prevent crime and the harms that come from inequality. White (2003) therefore argues that repairing harm must carry a social component. Perhaps without fully recognizing it, White has created an important nexus for social work and restorative justice: "If we are successfully to change the lives of offenders in a positive direction then we must begin the hard task of changing their wider social environments" (2003, p. 157). By working with a traditional community-based organization, Banner Neighborhoods, that is precisely what occurred in the Streeper Street case study.

Banner Neighborhoods was founded in 1982 with the mission "to promote resident-based leadership, neighborhood pride and stability, and provide direct services that contribute to the overall viability throughout 10 communities in southeast Baltimore." As indicated, Banner Neighborhoods approached the Community Conferencing Center to help the residents resolve the Streeper Street conflict. Since that time, Banner has formed an enduring relationship with Streeper Street residents. During the conference, one of the issues identified was the fact that the neighborhood center had shortened its hours. A Banner staffer who was present at the conference immediately addressed the issue and began bringing local young people to the community center to take part in youth activities and programs.

Additionally, Banner played a key role in helping to organize and sustain the football league. Banner worked with the community to organize the football effort into four leagues and raise grant money, with the help of the youth, so that each team member had his or her own individualized jerseys. Banner also helps to recruit volunteer coaches to the league. Banner worked with each of the leagues as they undertake their community projects, so that together Banner community organizers and the football league members addressed issues such as litter, while supporting beatification efforts by planting trees. One of the Banner organizers said that after the conference her job totally changed, as her work moved from community organizing to youth development. In this capacity she supported the football league, which included finding a place to hold an hour of homework time before practice. Additionally, she began to organize a number of activities for non-football-playing youth, such as a sleepover in the park for 250 children with movies, popcorn, pizza, and homemade baked goods donated by neighbors.

It is difficult to say what would have happened to the football effort had it not been for the continued support of Banner. It may not have had an 8-year history, nor would it necessarily have included community organizing and development projects. It is probably fair to say that the resultant onslaught of activities for youth organized by Banner would not have occurred. On the other hand, it is also difficult to say what Banner's contribution to the community would have been without the conference. The positive relationships that grew between youth and adults, and residents of color and white residents, as well as the young people's increased commitment to their community might very likely have not occurred had it not been for the conference. Working in tandem, the Community Conferencing Center and Banner Neighborhoods were able to affect individual relationships and create collective efficacy, a result that neither organization could have achieved on its own.

From Justice to Interaction

We believe, however, that what is needed in order to both strengthen the fit between social work and restorative justice, and to make restorative justice more accessible to a broader range of disciplines and communities, is to reframe the description of this being a movement about "justice"—which binds this to a criminal justice application and which implies that we are *reacting* in a better way once a wrong has been committed—to being a movement about positive relationships and healthy, empowered communities. Restorative "methods" provide *proactive* ways to build healthy communication, relationships, and communities, so that people have skills that serve to both prevent conflicts and allow them to respond to conflict in healthy ways when they do occur.

Thus, if our language and our interventions could shift away from problem-solving, harm reduction, and harm prevention and toward the promotion of positive traits and outcomes (such as behavior, connected communities, and social and economic justice), we believe that these effective principles would be more likely to be embraced by fields and disciplines that can benefit from them, but which have not yet taken advantage of the (documented) efficacy of these theories and methods. Social work is certainly one of these fields.

Restorative justice practitioners seek a significant culture shift, from one that values punishment and blame to one that values communication, relationships, and accountability. Social workers also seek a cultural shift from inequality, poverty, and the marginalization of groups and individuals to one of economic and social justice. Perhaps by working together and utilizing the strengths of each other's approach, we can make significant inroads so that the opportunities and lives of individuals in all communities will be transformed. However, our effort certainly needs to remain evidence-based and our work guided by empirical data derived from our interventions.

ACKNOWLEDGMENTS

The authors would like to thank Cynthia Lemons and Misty Fae for her assistance with and contributions to this chapter.

NOTE

i These authors can be considered some of the pioneering as well as leading researchers in the area of social work and multicultural practice with communities.

REFERENCES

Abramson, L., & Moore, D. B. (2002). The psychology of community conferencing. In J. Perry (Ed.), *Restorative justice: Repairing communities through restorative justice* (pp. 123–140). Lanham, MD: American Correctional Association.

Abramson, L., & Moore, D. B. (2001). Transforming conflict in the inner city community conferencing in Baltimore. *Contemporary Justice Review, 4*(3–4), 321–340.

Alinsky, S. (1972). *Rules for radicals.* New York: Vintage Books.

Arrigo, B.A. (2004). Rethinking restorative and community justice: A postmodern inquiry. *Contemporary Justice R*

Bazemore, G. and Umbreit, M.S. (2002). *A comparison of four conferencing models.* Washington, DC: Office of Juvenile Justice and Delinquency Prevention, U.S. Department of Justice.

Bazemore, G. (2000). Community justice and a vision for collective efficacy: The case of restorative conferencing. In National Institute of Justice (Ed.), *Policies, Processes, and Decisions of the Criminal Justice System: Vol. 3 Criminal Justice.* Washington, DC: U.S. Department of Justice.

Beck, E., Britto, S., & Andrews, A. (2007). *In the shadow of death.* Oxford: Oxford University Press.

Beck, E., & Eichler, M. (2000). Consensus organizing: A practice model for community building. *Journal of Community Practice: Organizing, planning, development & change, 8,* 87–102.

Boyes-Watson, C. (2005). Community is not a place but a relationship: Lessons for organizational development. *Public Organization Review: A Global Journal, 5,* 359–374.

Brisson, D. S., & Usher, C.L. (2005). Bonding social capital in low income neighborhoods. *Family Relations, 54*(5), 644–654.

Canaan, R., & Rothman, J. (1995). Locality development and the building of community. In J. Rothman, J. Erlich, & J. Tropman (Eds.), *Strategies of Community Intervention* (5th ed.). (241–257). Itasca, IL: F.E. Peacock Publishers.

Clear, T. R., & Karp, D. R. (1999). *The community justice ideal.* New York: Westview.

Community Conferencing Center (n.d.) retrieved April 2, 2009 from http://www.communityconferencing.org/

Delagado, M. (1999). *Social work practice in non-traditional urban settings.* Oxford: Oxford University Press.

Fisher, R. (1994). *Let the people decide: Neighborhood organizing in America.* Boston: G. K. Hall & Company.

Fisher, R., & Ury, W. (1991). *Getting to yes: Negotiating agreement without giving in* (2nd ed.). New York: Penguin Books.

Johnstone, G. (2005). *Restorative justice: Ideas, values, debates.* Portland, OR: William Publishing.

Karp, D. R., & Clear, T. R. (2002). The community justice frontier: An introduction. In D. R. Karp & T. R. Clear (Eds.), *What is community justice? Case studies of restorative justice and community supervision.* (p. ix). Thousand Oaks, CA.: Sage Publications.

Karp, D. R., & Walther, L. (2001). Community reparative boards in Vermont. In G. Bazemore & M. Shiff (Eds.), *Restorative community justice: Repairing harm and transforming communities* (pp. 199–218). Cincinnati, OH: Anderson Publisher Co.

Karp, D. R., Sprayregen, M., & Drakulich, K. M. (2002). *Vermont Reparative Probation: Year 2000 Outcome Evaluation. Final Report.* Retrieved September 30, 2009, from http://www.doc.state.vt.us/about/reports/reparative-v-probation/view

Kretzmann, J., & McKnight, J. P. (1996). Assets-based community development. *National Civic Review, 85*(4), 23–29.

McCold, P. (2004). Paradigm muddle: The threat to restorative justice posed by the merger with community justice. *Contemporary Justice Review, 7,* 13–35.

McCold, P., & Watchel, B. (1998). *Restorative policing experiment: The Bethlehem Pennsylvania police family group conferencing project.* Washington, DC: U.S. printing office.

Mondros, J. B., & Wilson, S. (1994). *Organizing for power & empowerment.* New York: Columbia University Press.

Moore, D. B. and McDonald, J. M. (2000). *Transforming conflict in workplace and other communities.* Sydney: TJA.

National Association of Social Workers. (2008b). *Code of Ethics.* Retrieved May 4, 2009, from http://www.socialworkers.org/pubs/code/code.asp

Ohmer, M., & Beck, E. (2006). Citizen participation in neighborhood organizations in poor communities and its relationship to neighborhood and organizational collective efficacy. *Journal of Sociology and Social Welfare, 23,* 179–202.

Perry, J. (2002). Challenging the assumptions. In J. Perry (Ed.), *Restorative justice: Repairing communities through restorative justice* (pp. 1–18). Lanham, MD: American Correctional Association.

Pranis, K. (2005). *The little book of circle processes: A new/old approach to peacemaking.* Intercourse, PA.: Good Books.

Pranis, K. (2007). Restorative values. In G. Johnstone & D. W. Van Ness (Eds.), *Handbook of Restorative Justice* (pp. 59–74). Portland, OR: Willan Publishing.

Putnam, R. (2000). *Bowling alone: The collapse and revival of American community.* New York: Simon and Schuster.

Pyles, L. (2009). *Progressive community organizing: A critical approach for a globalization World.* New York: Routledge.

Reichert, E. (2003). *Social work and human rights: A foundation for policy and practice.* New York: Columbia University Press.

Rothman, J. (1995). Approaches to community intervention. In J. Rothman, J. Erlich, & J. Tropman (Eds.), *Reflections in community organizing. Enduring themes and critical issues* (3rd ed., pp. 22–63). Itasca, Il: F. E. Peacock Publishers.

Saleebey, D. (2006). *Strengths perspective in social work practice.* Boston: Pearson Publishing.

Sampson, R. (2004, December). A conversation with Robert Sampson. A meeting sponsored by the United Way of Metropolitan Atlanta. Atlanta, GA.

Sampson, R., Raudenbush, S., & Earls, F. (1997). Neighborhoods and violent crime: A multilevel study of collective efficacy. *Science, 277,* 918–924.

Schweigert, F. J. (2002). Moral and philosophical foundations of restorative justice. In J. Perry (Ed.), *Repairing communities through restorative justice* (pp. 19–37). Lanham, MD: American Correctional Association.

Specht, H., & Courtney, M. (1994). *Unfaithful Angels: How social work has abandoned its mission.* New York: The Free Press.

Staples, L. (2004). *Roots to Power: A manual for grassroots organizing.* Westport, CT: Praeger.

Sullivan, E. (2002, November 13). *A league of their own.* Retrieved September 30, 2009, from www.citypaper.com/news/story.asp?id=3385

Tomkins, S. S. (1962). *Affect imagery consciousness: Vol. 1. The positive affects.* New York: Springer Publishing.

Tomkins, S.S. (1963). *Affect imagery consciousness: Vol. 2. The negative affects.* New York: Springer Publishing.

van Wormer, K. (2004). *Confronting oppression, restoring justice: From policy analysis to social action*. Alexandria, VA: Council on Social Education.

Wahrhaftig, P. (1981). Dispute resolution retrospective. *Crime & Delinquency, 27*(1), 99–105.

Walgrave, L. (2002). From community to dominion: In search of social values for restorative justice. In E. G. Weitekamp & H. J. Kerner (Eds.), *Restorative justice: Theoretical foundations*. Portland, OR: William Publishing.

Warner, B. O. (2003). The role of attenuated culture in social disorganization theory. *Criminology, 41*(1), 73–94.

White, R. (2003). Communities, conferences and restorative social justice. *Criminal Justice, 3*, 139–157.

Zehr, H. (1995). *Changing lenses: A new focus for crime and justice*. Scottdale, PA: Herald Press.

Chapter Eight

Restorative Justice and Child Welfare: Engaging Families and Communities in the Care and Protection of Children

DAVID S. CRAMPTON AND PATRICIA L. RIDEOUT

SOCIAL WORK AND CHILD WELFARE: OVERVIEW AND HISTORY

From the earliest days of child welfare, social workers created a wide variety of practices to engage families and communities in the care and protection of children. As described in Chapter 2, friendly visitors developed into caseworkers who went to the homes of new parents and provided information about child rearing. Settlement houses helped new immigrant families adjust to living in urban environments in America. Settlement house workers also became community organizers, who collected data about the plight of poor families and used this evidence to lobby for public policies that improved child and maternal health, while also addressing other important social issues. Social workers played a central role in the creation of the juvenile court, a body charged with determining what should be done with abused and neglected children and juvenile delinquents.

Following this rapid development of policies and practices to promote child welfare, there was a period from 1929 to 1962 in which child welfare, like a number of efforts designed to support individuals, became one of many responsibilities of government social workers. However, there was little discussion in the social work field or in public discourse about child abuse and neglect (Myers, 2006).

Then, suddenly, there was an explosion of interest in child abuse and neglect, triggered by physicians who discovered how to use radiology to identify physical child abuse (Myers, 2006). Medical journals published articles that documented cases of physical child abuse, which showed that such abuse occurred more often than physicians and the general public realized. Media attention to these discoveries contributed to the enactment of laws that made it mandatory to report child abuse. In 1963 the American Humane Association shared their research on physical child abuse with the U.S. Children's Bureau and then the Children's Bureau proposed a model statute for states to adopt to encourage reporting of child abuse (Nelson, 1984). States rapidly adopted these laws and this interest culminated in the passage of the federal Child Abuse and Prevention and Treatment Act in 1974, which included regulations that strengthened child abuse reporting laws nation-wide (Myers, 2006).

Mandatory child abuse reporting laws resulted in a rapid increase in reports of child abuse, from about 10,000 in 1962 to 836,000 in 1978 (Lindsey, 2004). During the federal fiscal year 2007, state child welfare agencies received an esti-mated 3.2 million referrals, involving the alleged maltreatment of approximately 5.8 million children (U.S. Department of Health and Human Services, Adminis-tration on Children, Youth and Families, 2009). Lindsey (2004) argued that the mandatory reporting laws and the increase in reporting transformed the field of child welfare into the more narrowly focused area of child protective services:

> *In earlier times the public child welfare system would have assisted (poor families) with supportive services, but that system no longer exists, replaced by a child protection system whose sole concern is finding and removing a relatively few children from situations of severe child abuse. The child who is simply poor and disadvantaged is not the client of the child protection system. (Lindsey, 2004, p. vii)*

While there is broad agreement that poverty and other forms of social inequal-ity are major contributors to child abuse and neglect, policy and practice today are largely directed at individual factors such as assessing and trying to change the behavior of individual parents (Pennell & Crampton, in press). While helping parents learn to parent is a critical part of reducing child abuse, without concur-rent efforts to reduce environmental stressors, parenting interventions are unlikely to have long-term benefits.

Public child welfare systems most often become involved in a family's life when a call comes into a child abuse hotline. In part due to social workers' high numbers of cases and limited resources, an assessment of that hotline call is less about whether the family needs help and more about whether the concerns meet the statutory definitions of child maltreatment. An initial hotline report of suspected child abuse or neglect is called a referral. Approximately one-third of referrals are screened out each year, because a hotline worker determines that the allegations do not meet the legal definitions of child maltreatment; these referrals do not typically receive further attention from child welfare agencies. The remaining referrals are "screened in" and an investigation or assessment is conducted by the child welfare agency to determine the likelihood that maltreatment has occurred or that the child is at risk of maltreatment (U.S. Department of Health and Human Services, Administration on Children, Youth and Families, 2009).

Families whose problems are assessed as lower risk are sometimes provided with assistance through "alternative response" procedures, which can include referrals to community programs or assistance on a voluntary basis (Waldfogel, 2009). However, the stigma associated with any involvement in the public child welfare system may prevent families from accepting services voluntarily. Typically, it is only when threats to the safety of their children are deemed immediate and significant that parents are brought to the attention of family courts for nonvoluntary intervention. In the most serious cases, the court may decide to remove the children from the home and place them in a foster home or with a relative. These decisions about out-of-home placement are the most contested in child welfare practice and policy, and there is a range of opinion about how to prevent placing children in temporary foster care. For example, some advocates promote "family preservation," which includes providing intensive services to the family while the children remain at home (Nelson, Blythe, Walters, Pecora, & Schweitzer, 2009)[i].

At the other end of the spectrum, some child advocates believe many troubled families cannot adequately care for their children, and so the children should quickly be placed for adoption with parents who have more resources and who live in better neighborhoods. Elizabeth Bartholet (1999) argues that social workers should be "willing to take action immediately upon removal to terminate parental rights and place children in adoptive homes, in cases when there is no real chance children will or should grow up with their original parents" (p. 204).

The Annie E. Casey Foundation's Family to Family Initiative is one of several broad efforts to move the debate away from a false choice about whether foster care is always the best option or worst option for children, and instead develop strategies for engaging families and communities in the care and protection of children. While these practices do not explicitly use the language of restorative justice, they are consistent with the values and skills associated with restorative justice practice.

In this chapter, we briefly review some of these efforts to promote family-centered and community-based child welfare practices and their fit with restorative justice, present a case study that illustrates one example of this practice, describe the skills social workers need to use these methods in child welfare, and speculate about future directions in restorative justice and child welfare.

Thus far, there are some promising examples of methods that can engage families in the care and protection of children, but consistent success in promoting child safety and well-being requires an ability to engage the broader community as well as the family in supporting children and their families. Successful strategies for engaging families and communities draw on the early experiences of social work and settlement houses and combine these efforts with systems reform. This system reform seeks to shift child welfare services from a child-protection focus to a broader effort to promote child and family welfare. After decades of the narrower child protection mandate, which often alienated members of the communities from which most children were removed, one major challenge for child welfare system administrators and staff is convincing community members that the public agency now wants to partner with the community in promoting child welfare. In order to address this challenge, child welfare agencies must change both how they work with individual families and how they partner with community-based organizations. Furthermore, these family-centered and community-based practices must work together in order to be effective.

In this chapter, we use the Family to Family Initiative as one example of a combined effort to change how child welfare agencies work with families and communities. Family to Family includes Team Decisionmaking, a strategy that engages family and community members in making placement decision about children. The initiative also includes specific strategies for partnering with community-based organizations to support Team Decisionmaking and other key child welfare activities. Restorative justice provides a useful lens for seeing how this integration and extension of family and community practice can be implemented. More specifically, restorative justice highlights the need to simultaneously reform practice and policy as well as educate the broader society about what children and families, need and how we can all help support them.

CHILD WELFARE SERVICE DATA AND IMPLICATIONS

Until approximately the mid-1990s, the United States did not have reliable national statistics on the number of children investigated for maltreatment or placed in foster care. The federal government made limited efforts to collect national data, and many states did not report their statistics to Washington. More recently, systems for collecting statistics have improved and all the states are participating in reporting—in part, because they are required to report their data in order to receive federal funds.

The reach of child welfare services in the United States is becoming clearer as we develop better systems for tracking data and analyzing trends. For example, studies by the Urban Institute are beginning to estimate the cost of child welfare services. In state fiscal year 2004, states spent at least $23.3 billion from federal, state, and local sources on child welfare activities (Scarcella, Bess, Zielewski, & Geen, 2006). In 2007, 3.2 million child abuse and neglect referrals (including 5.8 million children) were made to Children's Protective Service agencies (U.S. Department of Health and Human Services, Administration for Children and Families, 2009). Approximately two-thirds of these referrals were accepted for investigation. Of the 3.6 million children investigated, an estimated 794,000 were found to be victims of maltreatment, which translates into a national rate of 10.6 per 1000 children. However, the rate for African-American children was significantly higher, at 16.7 per 1000 children.

These statistics give a sense of the scope of child welfare, yet recent analyses using life table methods show that an even larger number of children are involved in child welfare services (Crampton & Coulton, 2008)[ii]. Life tables are frequently used to describe fertility, marriage, and mortality and can illustrate the greater occurrence of these events over a lifetime or life stage compared with cross-sectional analysis such as annual occurrence rates. Using life table analysis, rather than cross-sectional data based on annual service use, shows that child welfare services reach a large number of children, especially African-American children.

These data suggest that African-American families may be especially disadvantaged by child welfare services that focus on individual behavior, rather than environmental stressors such as poverty and racism. Conversely, they also suggest that developing child welfare services with a restorative justice perspective may be especially beneficial for African-American families.

Until fairly recently, child welfare research was severely limited because of the paucity of reliable data on child welfare services. Wulczyn, Barth, Yuan, Jones Harden, and Landsverk (2005) synthesized findings from recent national child abuse data, foster care data, and the National Survey of Child and Adolescent Well-Being (NSCAW), which is the first nationally representative longitudinal survey of children served by the child welfare system. Their analysis demonstrates that the types of maltreatment and the system's response to that maltreatment are distinct for infants, children entering school, and adolescents. Because these three developmental groups each have unique needs, responding to child maltreatment requires age-specific attention to both child development and the family environment.

Children are most likely to enter the child welfare system as infants and most often for reasons of neglect. When infants enter foster care, they are 60% more likely to be adopted, rather than reunified with their parents (Wulczyn et al., 2005). They are also at high risk of developmental delay. The child welfare system's response to maltreatment for infants must include helping families learn to parent children with high needs, and providing support to allow families to do so as soon as possible, so these delays can be resolved. Given the extensive history of home visiting in social work, social workers are ideally suited for promoting greater parent involvement in early intervention services that can address developmental delay. For this reason, social work education now combines traditional family work with the latest research on evidence-based early intervention (Mahoney & Wiggers, 2007).

Children entering school are at lower risk of child welfare involvement, but when they do come to the attention of the system, it is often for reasons of physical abuse (although, like other groups, the most frequent concern is neglect). For this age group, the child welfare system must learn how to support parents, families, and communities in coordination with schools. There is growing evidence that school-based mental health services can be especially effective in reaching disadvantaged children who otherwise might not be able to access these services (Armbruster & Lichtman, 1999). Combining social work's tradition of community engagement with human services and education integration and reform could be a better means of meeting the needs of school-aged children and their families.

Maltreatment of adolescents has another distinct dynamic. Nearly half of these youths who enter care are placed in some sort of group-home setting, rather than a family setting, and they have elevated levels of child behavioral problems, delinquency, and suicidality (Wulczyn et al., 2005). This finding suggests that child welfare services for this group must address the behavior and mental health needs of the adolesents, while also providing services for their parents. This is especially true because so many adolescents involved in the child welfare system enter it via the juvenile justice system, or are involved simultaneously with both systems, increasing the complexity of service planning for both children and parents. Successful exit from the child welfare system for these older children requires helping families parent a child with behavioral issues of their own, and providing community support that allows both parents and adolescents to thrive. New research is examining how natural mentors and parent advocates can assist older youth with the transition from foster care into adulthood (Munson, Hussey, Stormann, & King, 2009; Munson & McMillen, 2009). While these forms of community support seem to be beneficial at the family level, extensive system reform is needed in order to ensure that all young people and their families who want this type of support are able to benefit from advocates, mentors, or other engaged community members.

What is apparent across all three stages of child development is that effective caregiving should include the involvement of both familial and community supports. This understanding guides how we can move forward in addressing child maltreatment and increasing our knowledge of successful strategies.

RESTORATIVE JUSTICE AND CHILD WELFARE APPLICATIONS

Since the 1980s, a variety of family meeting approaches have emerged that are designed to engage family and community members in making key decisions and developing plans for the care and protection of children who are at risk of child abuse and neglect. The inclusion of family members is necessary so they can share information about themselves and contribute to making decisions that will change their lives. Engaging community members helps bring more assets to potential solutions for child maltreatment concerns.

These family meeting practices have become widely used throughout the world. They include Family Group Conferencing (FGC) which originated in New Zealand, Family Unity Meetings (FUM) from Oregon, Team Decisionmaking (TDM) from Ohio, Family Team Conferences (FTC) from Alabama, and many other variations. The FGC approach is used in Australia, Canada, Finland, New Zealand, Norway, Sweden, the United Kingdom and many other countries, while there are a variety of different approaches used in the United States (including FGC, FUM and TDM). None of these models specifically grew out of restorative justice ideas, nor were the origins of all of these family meeting practices related to each other. However, as will be discussed later in this chapter, there are many common themes across these practices which resonate with restorative justice. Thus far, there is limited research on the outcomes of these practices, but more evidence is developing as the field reaches agreement on the outcomes these meetings should encourage (Crampton, 2007). Restorative justice research may help these family meeting practices develop more outcome studies that are consistent with the values of restorative justice.

New Zealand was the first nation to legislate family group conferencing and specify its principles and practices. In New Zealand, the extended family must be invited to a FGC when a child is considered to be in need of care or protection, and must be involved in decision-making in situations of involuntary child placement (Crampton & Pennell, 2009). Many other countries have been inspired by New Zealand to develop FGC in child welfare and other fields of practice, yet FGCs are still not as extensively used in other countries as they are in New Zealand.

The growth in the use of Family Meetings in child welfare decision-making is due to dissatisfaction with conventional child welfare approaches and the positive results gained from these Family Meetings, which children, youth, and families in service planning. Practitioners have discovered that Family Meetings improved the child welfare agency's decision-making by giving caseworkers access to more information and giving families the opportunity to "buy into" the process by involving them in developing a plan for the child (DeMuro and Rideout, 2002). Practitioners also see the benefits of family members gaining an opportunity to add their own cultural identity and strengths to plans for children (Pennell & Anderson, 2005).

As detailed in a report issued by the Center for the Study of Social Policy (2002), all Family Meeting practices should include:

1. shared values that emphasize the need for child welfare agencies to interact with children, families, and communities with mutual respect;
2. common expectations that power will shift from being exclusively held by the child welfare system and the courts to being shared with families and communities;
3. a broad and inclusive definition of who is included in the "family team" that is making these decisions;
4. a meeting place that provides an environment that is supportive of families in the decision-making process;
5. a commitment to providing sufficient preparation, coordination and facilitation of the family meetings in order to balance the needs of all parties while remaining focused on the child's safety and well-being.

Since the 1980s, Family Meetings in child welfare practice have spread to more than 150 communities in sixteen countries (Crampton, 2007). The extent of the use of Family Meetings in the United States and the rest of the world is not easily determined, but there is evidence that the potential of these practices is strong and growing. For example, the Campbell Collaboration Social Welfare Group, which conducts international systematic reviews of the effectiveness of significant social welfare programs, recently published a protocol for their review of Family Group Decision Making, which will evaluate the effectiveness of this practice in terms of child safety, permanence, child and family well-being, and client satisfaction with the decision-making process (Shlonsky et al., 2009). In the United States, the federal government's evaluation of each state's child welfare programs includes an assessment of whether parents and children are consistently included in case planning. A recent review of the federal government's evaluations of each state's performance found that 45 states are using specific family-centered child welfare practices, such as FGDM or TDM, to meet this federal requirement (Munson & Freundlich, 2008). A study of Family Group Decision Making (FGDM) in the National Survey of Child and Adolescent Well-Being (NSCAW) found that 11% of children in the child welfare system experienced a FGDM meeting as part of their initial assessment of child maltreatment, which suggests that the families of over 100,000 children participated in a FGDM meeting in 2000 (Weigensberg, Barth, & Guo, 2009).

A growing body of international research shows that Family Meetings keep children and youth connected with their siblings, families, relatives, and cultural groups without further endangering their safety. So far, few of these outcome studies of Family Meeting practices have appeared in peer-reviewed journals (see Crampton, 2007; Crampton & Jackson, 2007; Pennell & Burford, 2000; Sundell & Vinnerljung, 2004). The studies that have been published indicate that the Family Meeting shows "promising outcomes" (Pennell & Anderson, 2005, p. 4) for families with a wide range of characteristics (Crampton, 2006) and from diverse cultures (Burford & Hudson, 2000).

Among the various Family Meeting practices, restorative justice is typically associated with Family Group Conferences in New Zealand, as described in Chapter 4. However, the terminology of restorative justice was not part of the 1989 New Zealand legislation that created FGCs; the language of restorative justice in New Zealand evolved over time (MacRae & Zehr, 2004). As these practices have spread throughout the world, FGCs have become a key decision-making process in child welfare, school discipline, and juvenile and adult criminal justice, and FGCs are regarded as one of the most promising models of restorative justice (MacRae & Zehr, 2004).

One of the key principles of restorative justice is that community participation and community caring is not undermined by establishing government responses to social problems like child maltreatment. Kay Pranis (2000) a leading restorative justice advocate, suggests that conferencing can strengthen or weaken a community's cohesiveness and sense of efficacy. She believes that the Family Meeting can be part of a broader effort to reinforce mutual accountability and responsibility, or it can become another way for professionals to undermine community, by creating dependence on formal services to solve community problems. Pranis (2000) is concerned that, "community members have increasingly removed themselves from taking responsibility for the behavior of children and youth in public places" (p. 46) and that we need to ensure that Family Meetings reinforce rather than undermine a restoration of this sort of community accountability for children and families. Similarly, Braithwaite and Strang (2002) suggest that families, communities, non-governmental organizations, and the state should work together to prevent family violence. This can be a daunting task when families become deeply involved in the child welfare system, yet a restorative justice framework highlights the need to set a goal for a time when every family can care for their children, free of government involvement.

Community Engagement and Family Meeting Practices

This discussion of child welfare and restorative justice suggests several possibilities and limitations when using restorative justice principles in child welfare practice. Particularly in the United States, child welfare practice often fails to engage families and communities in the care and protection of children. The Family Meeting can help change this dynamic by including families themselves in the decision-making process.

Yet Family Meetings alone are not likely to change the broader service delivery context, so restorative justice principles must also be used to change child welfare systems to support family meeting practice. The needs of families and children depend on the ages of the children. While Family Meetings by themselves cannot address all service needs they should help link families to early intervention services when infants are involved, collaborate with schools when school-age children are of concern, and engage adolescents themselves in meetings and case planning when they are the subject of the maltreatment report.

Family Meetings in child welfare can help promote values of inclusion, respect, and responsibility, but simply having a meeting does not mean these values will be put into practice. Reform efforts must position family meeting practice within a broader systemic effort to align all child welfare activities with core values around family and community engagement. Authentic implementation of these values in the context of family meetings requires skills in facilitating the meeting and the establishment of mechanisms for engaging the broader community.

While the public child welfare system partners with the community to promote the care and protection of children, the goal is for families and communities to become independent of child welfare services, and be able to take responsibility for children without government interference.

The Family to Family Initiative is an example of a reform effort that combines family and community engagement through several different strategies that reinforce and encourage family-centered and community-based child welfare practices and policy.

Team Decisionmaking (TDM) is one of the four core strategies of the Family to Family Initiative, a child welfare reform program sponsored by the Annie E. Casey Foundation. It has been implemented at approximately 60 sites across 17 states. The theory of change central to Family to Family is that certain core strategies are mutually reinforcing and, if effectively implemented, will identify and draw community resources into decision-making and family support. This is consistent with other restorative justice practices, which emphasize the need to have both macro and micro efforts to address social problems. In addition to TDM, the other core strategies include *Building Community Partnerships* (BCP) with community-based organizations in neighborhoods with the highest child welfare caseloads, in order to broaden the scope of safety and support available to families; innovative strategies to *Recruit, Develop and Support* (RDS) foster and kinship care providers in those same neighborhoods; and efforts to monitor and improve all these activities with *Self Evaluation* (SE), in which agencies and communities engage in a collaborative effort to identify needed changes in agency policy and practice and, once changes are made, determine if outcomes are improving.

The linked strategies of Building Community Partnerships and Team Decisonmaking provide an illustration of the Family to Family Initiative's focus on combined family and community engagement. In the Building Community Partnerships strategy, public child welfare agencies strive to develop relationships with neighborhood organizations, which are invited to form coalitions that agree to partner with the public child welfare agency in child protection work. The public system provides financial support to these collaborative groups, which offer a range of services and supports to families who are involved in the child welfare system, and which they can provide in the families' own communities. Another key aspect of this effort is the geographic assignment of child welfare cases, so that the same child welfare staff consistently serve the families from the same neighborhoods. There are many potential benefits to this approach; most notably, caseworkers can become more knowledgeable about the neighborhoods where they work and the supports available to families in those neighborhoods. Caseworkers learn to work in collaboration with local service providers, and neighborhood residents benefit from getting to know the child welfare staff who serve their community, which nurtures relationships built on respect and trust. Social workers can advocate for and recruit neighborhood foster parents to care for local children needing out-of-home care, which the community partners are in a unique position to identify. Because caseworkers travel less when they serve families in a smaller geographic area, they can visit more families; their community partners may even provide space for meetings in the community they serve (DeMuro & Rideout, 2002). Community coalitions are invited to send a representative to Team Decisionmaking meetings for families residing in their neighborhoods, so that they can provide direct input and support on these critical decisions affecting their community.

This kind of partnership between child welfare agencies and community-based organizations again illustrates the importance of strengthening family and community connections. Through this partnership, the child welfare agency provides financial support to the neighborhood organizations, which allows them to hire staff to help coordinate services between all the service organizations and the families in the neighborhood. The partnership strengthens the resources of both the child welfare agency and their partners, and creates significant ties between the agency and neighborhood residents. Lastly, the partnership promotes community ownership by allowing the local community organizations to help determine how child welfare services are delivered in their neighborhood.

The Team Decisionmaking strategy incorporates the values and key elements of BCP, as it provides a vehicle for tapping into the power of family meetings to increase family and community engagement, while tackling some of the most challenging work of child welfare: placement-related decision making.

Team Decisionmaking includes six specific key elements:

1. A TDM meeting, including birth parents and youth, is held for *all* decisions involving child removal, change of placement, and reunification, or another permanency plan.
2. The TDM meeting is held *before* the child's move occurs, or, in cases of imminent risk, by the next working day—and always before the initial court hearing in cases of removal.
3. Neighborhood-based community representatives are invited by the public agency to participate in all TDM meetings, especially those regarding possible child removal.
4. The meeting is led by a skilled, immediately accessible internal facilitator, who is not a case-carrying social worker or line supervisor.
5. Information about each meeting—including participants, location, and recommendations—is collected and ultimately linked to data on child and family outcomes. This ensures continuing self-evaluation of the TDM process and its effectiveness.
6. Each TDM meeting resulting in a child's removal serves as a springboard for planning an 'icebreaker' family team meeting, which is ideally held in conjunction with the first family visit so that the birth parent–foster parent relationship can be initiated (DeMuro & Rideout, 2002, p. 11).

TDM differs from many other Family Meeting practices most significantly in the focus on placement decision-making, and the volume of meetings required to hold a TDM for every placement decision. By requiring a TDM as part of every placement decision (i.e., child removals, transfer from one placement to another, and family reunification or other forms of permanency), the agency ensures that all families are heard, but this volume of meetings means that the resources devoted to each meeting are necessarily less than in jurisdictions which use Family Group Conferences or other family meeting practices in highly selective circumstances. In many FGC practices, the time between a referral and a meeting is generally two weeks to one month (Pennell & Anderson, 2005). In contrast, many TDM meetings are held when an immediate decision is needed regarding a removal or there is a high risk that a placement will disrupt (DeMuro & Rideout, 2002).

The purpose of the meetings also differ. TDM meetings are designed to make a "live" decision regarding a child's placement, while FGCs are often designed to develop a comprehensive plan for the care and protection of the child. The frequency and purpose of the meetings determine many of their other differences. TDM meetings, especially those addressing child removals, typically have limited time for preparation and meeting as compared with FGC. These differences can result in a smaller number of participants in TDM and may require more active facilitation of the meeting by a trained facilitator in a TDM, compared to a FGC. Both practices encourage the participation of the family group—that is, the immediate family of concern, their relatives, friends, and other close supports. The following composite example illustrates how TDM and the other Family to Family strategies worked together in a specific child welfare case.

CASE STUDY: THE MARSHALL FAMILY

A call came into the child abuse hotline in Smith County, alleging physical abuse and neglect of the Marshall children[iii]. After investigative/assessment social worker Lynn Lopez responded to the referral and conducted initial interviews with the children, parents, extended family members, and other collateral contacts, she assessed the level of safety threat to the children. Using a structured tool designed both to evaluate immediate threats to children's safety and to predict the likelihood of future harm, Lopez came to the conclusion that these children were experiencing moderate to high safety concerns. Critical data influencing the assessment included the children's ages and ability to self-protect, the parents' life experiences (including child welfare and criminal history, patterns of substance use, and willingness to access support services in the past), and the insights of several extended family members and the confidential referral source (one of the children's teachers). With this information in hand, Lopez called the Team Decisionmaking unit at her agency to request a TDM meeting. Because the children's paternal grandmother had agreed to stay with the family that night, Lopez scheduled the meeting for the following morning.

Lopez invited the birth parents to the TDM meeting, explaining that its purpose was to have an extended conversation with them and any other persons they chose to invite, along with herself, other members of the child welfare agency, and a member of the Family to Family community collaborative in the Marshall family's neighborhood. The collaborative is a coalition of community-based organizations developed using the Family to Family community partnership strategy. The meeting would focus on the safety concerns Lopez had identified in her preliminary assessment, which she outlined for the Marshalls in their discussion, being careful to specifically link issues of concern with their impact on the children's safety. Lopez explained that it was her hope that the family team which would assemble for the meeting might be able to develop safety plans which would address her concerns and support the family in keeping their children safely at home. But she was also clear that if the family team was unable to put together a strong plan which addressed the safety issues, and which the Marshalls could support, that there was a possibility the agency would ask the court to remove the children from their parents' care and place them in a relative's or foster home. Lopez helped the Marshalls identify which friends and family members they would like to invite to the meeting, and assisted them in contacting several of these people.

The next morning, Mr. and Mrs. Marshall arrived for the meeting, which was held at the Midtown Neighborhood Center. This agency is part of the collaborative that is near their home. Mrs. Marshall's sister, Maya Davis, came with them, as did Mr. Marshall's 90-year-old mother. Other attendees included Lopez and her supervisor, Ann Anderson, from the agency's home-finding office, and the TDM Facilitator, Karen Johnson. Also present was David Hart, a community specialist. In this role, Hart routinely works with neighborhood families involved with the child welfare system, introducing them to supportive services such as child care, parent education, and housing resources.

Johnson facilitated a 90-minute meeting in a structured format, which was designed to create a respectful and comfortable tone for the difficult discussion that the team needed to have. She supported Lopez, who provided facts regarding the family's current situation and historical information regarding their past involvement with child welfare. Johnson also elicited active participation from the Marshalls as well as Maya Davis. Hart, the community specialist, sat next to the Marshalls and often helped by asking clarifying questions and suggesting possible resources which the family might access in their home community. Anderson, the homefinder, whose responsibility is to help match children needing placement with appropriate foster homes, listened and offered information about foster care to the family. When it became apparent that there was a viable kinship care option in this family, she excused herself from the meeting.

In facilitating the meeting, Johnson worked through a multistage process. The steps involved clarifying the issues of concern, seeking each person's ideas for resolution, leading a discussion designed to reality-test possible solutions for their ability to actually address safety concerns, and seeking the group's consensus around a final plan. Ultimately the team came to the difficult conclusion that Mrs. Marshall needed to enter an inpatient drug treatment program immediately. Based upon past history and current preferences, Mr. Marshall was not deemed a safe full-time caregiver for the children. The maternal aunt, Davis, offered to provide temporary care for the children. Based on agency policy and state law, the team decided that a court petition seeking temporary custody was appropriate in this case.

Immediately following the meeting, Lopez and her supervisor completed several tasks to move the plan forward. They took steps to initiate the court process by providing the meeting summary to the legal department, along with other pertinent information. They also accomplished a preliminary assessment of Maya Davis's ability to be a kinship caregiver. Unfortunately, they learned that she had an open case regarding her own child in a neighboring county, and was therefore ineligible to serve as caregiver for the Marshall children. After unsuccessfully seeking other relative care options with the Marshalls and Davis, Lopez visited the homefinding unit to assist in the identification of an appropriate foster home. The homefinders focused their search on a home in the family's own neighborhood, in hopes that the children could remain in their current school and child care settings and see their father, grandmother, aunt, and friends often.

Lopez was successful in finding an available family who lived seven blocks from the children's home. On the third day after the children's placement, Lopez and the family's new ongoing foster care worker co-facilitated an "icebreaker" meeting at the Midtown Neighborhood Center. Other attendees included Mr. Marshall and his mother, the new foster mother, Ellen Robinson, and Hart, the community specialist. Mrs. Marshall was unable to attend, as she had begun her treatment program at an inpatient facility.

At this informal meeting, the foster mother and birth family met and talked primarily about the children's habits, schedules, and personalities. The foster mother asked many questions to help her determine the best way to parent the children and make them comfortable, seeking the Marshalls' advice and input. She even asked Mr. Marshall for his preference regarding what the children should call her (they agreed on "Ellen") At the end of the meeting, the Marshalls had a visit with the children and made plans to speak regularly with Robinson.

In the months ahead, the benefits of using the TDM process to guide the difficult decision about child placement became apparent. The Marshalls often visited with their children and developed a cooperative relationship with the foster family. Staff at the Midtown Center coordinated or provided supportive services, as outlined in the family's case plan, both to Mr. and Mrs. Marshall and the foster family, in locations close to their homes. The older children remained in the same school, and their mother developed a closer relationship to teachers there with the assistance of the social worker and Midtown staff. Five months after placement, reunification planning began after thorough discussion and reevaluation of safety and risk at a "permanency TDM" meeting.

SKILLS BUILDING

This case study illustrates the critical role played by many individuals in the case and the different skills required to make Team Decisionmaking and community partnership strategies work well. One of the critical elements that is less apparent in a discussion of a single case is the significant effort required to implement practices like Team Decisionmaking. Because Family Meeting practices can be very different from the ways child welfare agencies typically operate, the agency leadership must strongly communicate their intention to consistently require these practices and ensure that sufficient resources are allocated to make the process work (Crampton, Crea, Abramson-Madden, & Usher, 2008). Beyond clear messaging and strong resource commitments, agency leadership must also ensure that Team Decisionmaking is nested within overarching agency practices that promote high quality, values-based activities that engage families and communities in all the casework practices which occur between and outside of family meetings.

The case example above illustrates a number of the tangible resources which child welfare administrators and their community partners must supply to ensure successful Team Decisionmaking practice. There must be a Team Decisionmaking unit in place so facilitators are ready to facilitate a meeting for every placement decision, even on short notice. The unit must have someone tasked with maintaining schedules, to make sure meetings occur promptly and efficiently. The agency needs to have agreements with community-based organizations, so those organizations can host meetings and send community representatives to TDM meetings, as occurred in this case. The agency needs to recruit foster homes from the neighborhoods where they serve the most families, and have staff and community partners who can help them identify foster families and support them. These resources help keep children in their neighborhoods so they can stay in their home school, as they were able to do in this case example. The agency also needs to have collaborative relationships with other key community organizations. For example, in this case a recommendation made in a TDM meeting was then brought to legal personnel, who were able to present the agency's petition strongly and gain the support of the court for the plan developed in the meeting. Finally, the child welfare agency must provide training in TDM practice to their staff and community partners so everyone involved has the knowledge and skills needed to allow them to work as a team in a TDM meeting.

In addition to these macro-level resources and skills, many of the individuals in the case needed to be well-trained in order to fulfill their role. The caseworker, Lynn Lopez, knew when to request a TDM meeting and how to explain the process to the family in an honest and unthreatening manner. The homefinder and community specialist needed to attend the meeting and be ready to support the process as needed. Because all of these staff and community members have participated in TDM training (often together in specific neighborhoods), they understand their roles and how to help encourage a productive process.

Perhaps most importantly, the facilitator needed to make sure that everyone was heard, while still staying focused and on task. These skills are frequently taught as part of task group work in social work education (Crampton & Natarajan, 2005). In some Family Meeting models in child welfare, group facilitation techniques are not emphasized and are sometimes even discouraged. For example, some Family Group Conferencing advocates have suggested that FGC coordinators should intervene as little as possible in the family's deliberations. In fact, in some models of FGC, key decisions are made during "private family time," when the coordinator and the other professional staff leave the room and family members develop their plan on their own.

Team Decisionmaking, on the other hand, places a greater emphasis on facilitation skills. These skills are described as the ability to: focus on family strengths, develop collaborative service interventions, find common ground among diverse participants, help present risks without making the family feel defensive, and keep family meeting participants focused on the tasks at hand (DeMuro and Rideout, 2002). Facilitators' modeling of these skills in meetings regularly attended by less experienced child welfare staff provides "teachable moments" and is considered another positive benefit of TDM. TDM facilitators are even expected to participate in substantive discussions around safety and risk during meetings, should the team discussion require their input. In the case example, the facilitator and other professionals helped the group consider allowing the children to remain in the home, and when that was not viable, helped them consider a relative placement. When that was not possible either, the process then moved on to a foster family placement and a meeting between the foster parents and other family members. The whole process emphasized inclusion of all family members, respect for their ideas and strengths, and the development of a plan that everyone supported.

ANALYSIS OF FIT BETWEEN CHILD WELFARE AND RESTORATIVE JUSTICE

This discussion of family meetings and the specific case example involving Team Decisionmaking illustrates the potential fit between child welfare and restorative justice practices. Typical child welfare practice in the United States does not follow restorative justice ideals. For example, the federal government reviews every state's compliance with a variety of performance indicators as part of the Child and Family Service Reviews, and has so far found that almost all the states are failing to adequately include family members in case planning. Family Meetings can potentially help improve family involvement in case planning, but simply having family meetings in some instances is not enough.

System reform is also needed to reorient services from a narrow child protection focus to a broader commitment to child welfare and community engagement. Child welfare agencies must make a commitment to involving all families in decision-making and to providing sufficient resources to make that happen. Thus far, we have some research which suggests that Family Meetings can include family and community members in child protection, but we do not yet have evidence that these practices can be implemented consistently and with sufficient quality to make sure all families are benefiting from the practice. Communities participating in the Family to Family Initiative are using databases to track key TDM meeting characteristics and then link those characteristics to the outcomes of the children they serve. The databases record who attends TDM meetings, meeting time and location, service needs identified at TDM meetings, and custody and placement recommendations (Usher, Needell, Wildfire, & Webster, 2007). When TDM and out-of-home placement data are combined, they can be used to test for correlations between relative attendance at TDMs and increased kin placements, birth parent attendance and increased reunification, and foster parent attendance and fewer foster placement disruptions. Although the data that demonstrate positive correlations between TDM attendance and positive child outcomes do not prove causation, these data can be used by communities to examine the potential benefits of TDM (Crampton, 2004).

NEXT STEPS

A consistent research finding is that family meetings can promote child and youth residential permanency without jeopardizing child or youth safety. This benefit appears particularly pronounced for children and youths from cultural backgrounds typically overrepresented in the child welfare system and, thus, family meetings hold the promise of reducing such disproportionate representation in state care. Nevertheless, more research on the outcomes of Family Meeting practices is needed to help the field justify the allocation of scarce resources to Family Meetings, and to evaluate more thoroughly how family meetings can better promote child and youth safety, permanency, and well-being. In child welfare systems with high caseloads, is it practical to create positions for facilitators who carry no cases so that they can devote their energy to facilitating TDM meetings? A decision to do so can be complicated, given that other staff members realize that creating a non-case-carrying position may increase their own caseloads in systems that rely on rigid caseload-based staffing formulas.

A recent evaluation of the Family to Family Initiative noted that TDM can be much more effective when the Family to Family theory of change is followed, and there are parallel strategies to recruit resource families and other community partners from the neighborhoods where families served by the child welfare system live (Batterson et al., 2007). These additional strategies help improve TDM attendance and community support for TDM plans, but these community-wide reforms make it impossible to randomly assign some families to family meeting practices and other families to conventional practices if they all live in a community that is under reform. Therefore, future research will likely include developing some enhancements to family meeting practices, and then randomly providing this enhancement to some cases and not others while all cases still participate in family meetings. The design of these enhancements could draw upon the work of restorative justice in other fields.

Despite the significant challenges of reforming child welfare systems so they support family meeting practice and the challenges of evaluating these efforts, there is a growing body of research that suggests that family meetings can improve the lives of children and their families served by the child welfare system. With additional information about the effectiveness of Family Meetings and how to deepen their impact, it may be possible to increase available resources and begin to address the challenges of engaging family and community support for all children and their families. These resources could include providing training to all child welfare professionals and social work students, so they understand why and how they should participate in family meetings. With a significant commitment to these practices, the promise of restorative justice in child welfare may be finally realized.

ACKNOWLEDGMENTS

We would like to thank the dedicated community partners, family members, and Team Decisionmaking practitioners who have helped us understand the value of including all voices in child welfare decision making. The writing of this chapter was supported by the Annie E. Casey Foundation. We thank them for their support. The views presented in the chapter are those of the authors alone and do not necessarily reflect the opinions of the foundation.

NOTES

  i A recent review of the research on family preservation services noted that there are some promising results from evaluation studies, but there is a need for more evidence that these services can prevent foster care placement and more data about which families benefit from which types of services (Nelson, Blythe, Walters, Pecora, & Schweitzer, 2009).
 ii A study of Cuyahoga County (Cleveland), Ohio noted that in 2001, 10. 1% of African-American children and 4.0% of Caucasian children in the county under the age of 10 were investigated for child abuse and neglect. Using life table methods to analyze child welfare records from 1990–2001, however, the researchers found that an estimated 49% of African-American children and 21.1% of Caucasian children in the county were investigated for child maltreatment at least once before their 10th birthday (Crampton & Coulton, 2008).
iii All names in this section are pseudonyms.

REFERENCES

Armbruster, P., & Lichtman, J. (1999). Are school based mental health services effective? Evidence from 36 inner city Schools. *Community Mental Health Journal, 35*(6), 493.

Bartholet, E. (1999). Nobody's children: Abuse and neglect, foster drift, and the adoption alternative. Boston: Beacon Press.

Batterson, M., Crampton, D., Crea, T., Harris, F., Madden, A. A., Usher, L., & Williams, J. (2007). Implementing Family to Family. Chapel Hill, NC: The University of North Carolina at Chapel Hill.

Braithwaite, J. (2002). *Restorative justice and responsive regulation*. New York: Oxford University Press.

Braithwaite, J., and Strang, H. (2002). Restorative justice and family violence. In H. Strang and J. Braithwaite (Eds.), *Restorative justice and family violence*. New York: Cambridge University Press.

Burford, G., & Hudson, J. (Eds.). (2000). *Family group conferences: New directions in community-centered child and family practice*. Hawthorne, NY: Aldine de Gruyter.

Center for the Study of Social Policy (2002, March). *Bringing families to the table: A comparative guide to family meetings in child welfare*. Washington, DC.

Crampton, D. (2004). Family involvement interventions in child protection: Learning from contextual integrated strategies. *Journal of Sociology and Social Welfare, 31*(1), 175–198.

Crampton, D. (2006). When do social workers and family members try family group decision making? A process evaluation. *International Journal of Child & Family Welfare, 9*(3), 131–143.

Crampton, D. (2007). Family group decision making: A promising practice in need of more program theory and research. *Child and Family Social Work, 12,* 202–209.

Crampton, D., & Coulton, C. (2008). The benefits of life table analysis for describing disproportionality. *Child Welfare, 87*(2), 189–202.

Crampton, D., Crea, T. M., Abramson-Madden, A., & Usher, C. L. (2008). Challenges of street-level child welfare reform and technology transfer: The case of team decision-making. *Families in Society, 89*(4), 512–520.

Crampton, D., & Jackson, W. (2007). Family group decision making and the over-representation of children of color in foster care: A case study. *Child Welfare, 86*(3), 51–70.

Crampton, D., & Natarajan, A. (2005). Connections between group work and family meetings in child welfare practice: What can we learn from each other? *Social Work with Groups, 28*(1), 65–79.

Crampton, D., & Pennell, J. (2009). Family-involvement meetings with older children in foster care: Intuitive appeal, promising practices, and the challenge of child welfare reform. In B. Kerman, M. Freundlich, & A.N. Maluccio (Eds.), *Achieving permanence for older children and youth in foster care* (pp. 266–290). New York: Columbia University Press.

DeMuro, P., & Rideout, P. (2002). *Team decisionmaking: Involving the family and community in child welfare decisions*. Baltimore, MD: The Annie E. Casey Foundation.

Lindsey, D. (2004). *The welfare of children*. New York: Oxford University Press.

MacRae, A., and Zehr, H. (2004). *The little book of family group conferences, New Zealand style*. Intercourse, PA: Good Books.

Mahoney, G., & Wiggers, B. (2007). The role of parents in early intervention: Implications for social work. *Children & Schools, 29*(1), 7–15.

Munson, M., Hussey, D., Stormann, C., & King, T. (2009). Voices of parent advocates within the systems of care model of service delivery. *Children & Youth Services Review, 31*(8), 879–884.

Munson, M., & McMillen, J. (2009). Natural mentoring and psychosocial outcomes among older youth transitioning from foster care. *Children & Youth Services Review, 31*(1), 104–111.

Munson, S., & Freundlich, M. (2008). *Families gaining their seat at the table: Family engagement strategies in the first round of child and family services reviews and program improvement plans.* Denver, CO: American Humane Association.

Myers, J. E. B. (2006). *Child protection in America: Past, present and future.* New York: Oxford University Press.

Nelson, K., Blythe, B. J., Walters, B., Pecora, P. J., & Schweitzer, D. (2009). *A ten-year review of family preservation research: Building the evidence base.* Seattle, WA: Casey Family Programs.

Nelson, B. (1984). *Making an Issue of Child Abuse.* Chicago, IL: University of Chicago Press.

Pennell, J., & Anderson, G. (2005). *Widening the circle: The practice and evaluation of family group conferencing with children, youths and their families.* Washington, DC: NASW Press.

Pennell, J., & Burford, G. (2000). Family group decision making: Protecting children and women. *Child Welfare, 79*(2), 131–158.

Pennell, J., & Crampton, D. S. (in press). Parents and child maltreatment: Integrating strategies. In J. W. White, M. P. Koss, & A. E. Kazdin (Eds.), *Violence against women and children: Consensus, critical analyses, and emergent priorities: Vol. II. Navigating solutions.* Washington, DC: American Psychological Association.

Pranis, K. (2000). Conferencing and the community. In G. Burford and J. Hudson (Eds.), *Family group conferencing: New directions in community-centered child and family practice.* Hawthorne, NY: Aldine de Gruyter.

Scarcella, C. A., Bess, R., Zielewski, E. H., & Geen, R. (2006). *The cost of protecting vulnerable children V: Understanding state variation in child welfare financing.* Washington, DC: Urban Institute.

Shlonsky, A., Schumaker, K., Cook, C., Crampton, D., Saini, M., Backe-Hansen, E., & Kowalski, K. (2009). Family group decision making for children at risk of abuse and neglect (Protocol). *Cochrane Database of Systematic Reviews.* Issue 3. Art. No. CD007984. DOI: 10.1002/14651858.CD007984.

Sundell, K., & Vinnerljung, B. (2004). Outcomes of family group conferencing in Sweden: A 3-year follow-up. *Child Abuse & Neglect, 28*(3), 267–287.

U.S. Department of Health and Human Services, Administration on Children, Youth and Families (2009). *Child Maltreatment 2007.* Washington, DC: U.S. Government Printing Office.

Usher, L., Needell, B., Wildfire, J., & Webster, D. (2007). *Evaluation plan for family to family.* Chapel Hill, NC: The University of North Carolina at Chapel Hill.

Waldfogel, J. (2009). Prevention and the child protection system. *The Future of Children, 19*(2), 195–210.

Weigensberg, E. C., Barth, R. R., & Guo, S. (2009). Family group decision making: A propensity score analysis to evaluate child and family services at baseline and after 36-months. *Children and Youth Services Review, 31,* 383–390.

Wulczyn, F., Barth, R. P., Yuan, Y-Y. T., Jones Harden, B., & Landsverk, J. (2005). *Beyond common sense: Child welfare, child well-being, and the evidence of policy reform.* New Brunswick, NJ: Aldine Transaction.

Chapter Nine

Feminist Perspectives on Family Rights: Social Work and Restorative Practices for Stopping Abuse of Women

JOAN PENNELL AND MARY P. KOSS

"Now he is just a humble man."
—*Ruth Johnson, mother of Alex*

"Family was worth more than what we were putting before them."
—*Jennifer Johnson, wife of Alex*

Whether family is defined by custom, law, or choice, our connections teach us who we are and how we should act. On the positive side, these familial lessons provide a sense of cultural identity over the long term and traditions to guide our lives. On the negative side, family practices may well lead to violations of human rights.

Feminists have repeatedly identified that prevalent family traditions undermine not only the rights of women and children but also the responsibilities of men. To oppose these norms, feminists have appealed to universal human rights, and their claims have been supported by the United Nations declarations (1979, 1993) that governments should work to change cultural patterns that oppress women and should not use culture to excuse violence against women. Yet at the same time, the United Nations (1948, 1989, 2007) recognizes the family as the fundamental societal group for all people, and the rights of children and indigenous peoples to their cultural heritage.

Combining "family" and "rights" into the single term "family rights" invokes respecting diverse familial cultures and upholding universal human rights. These are both worthy aims and ones advanced by the social work profession and the restorative justice movement. The concept of family rights, however, is a paradox that juxtaposes claims of diversity and universality. The former urges maintaining group differences, and the latter urges exerting controls over these very differences. When all members in a family are respected and their rights safeguarded, the paradox of family rights is muted.

Engaging fathers and extended family members may appear antithetical to the well-being of victimized women and children, as has been argued in terms of impoverished families of color (e.g., Bartholet, 2009). Nevertheless, family norms,

195

whatever people's cultural backgrounds, are not monolithic and inflexible and are expressed differentially depending on the context and incentives (Bandura, 2002). Family norms have sustained family members over time and can respond to interventions that advance the goals of family members within the parameters of human rights. Here is a place for social workers and restorative justice practitioners to work together. The restorative justice movement can inspire the profession of social work to stay on track with its longstanding traditions of individual and collective empowerment (see Simon, 1994). Social work offers well-honed person–environment practices (Kemp, Whittaker, & Tracy, 1997) that enrich restorative processes. Within a feminist framework of family rights, their synthesis is a vehicle for countering abuse of women.

In this chapter, we examine how integrating social work approaches and restorative justice practices is a means of creatively fashioning feminist solutions based in family traditions that protect women and children and hold men accountable for their abuse. We illustrate this process through examining the series of Family Group Meetings held for the Johnson family to address abuse within the family. These meetings served as a reminder of the value of family, or as Jennifer Johnson later said, her "family was worth more than what we were putting before them." The shortfalls of their family, however, were all too apparent when the neighbors, overhearing fighting between Jennifer's husband, Alex, and her father, Ricky, dialed 911. On arriving, the police found a terrified Jennifer and, after subduing a belligerent Alex still grasping one of their four young children, arrested him for disorderly conduct. Worried for the children's safety, the police called in child protection, who arranged for the children to stay with relatives that night. Two years later, Alex's mother Ruth, reflecting on her son's progress, observed, "Now he is just a humble man."

Given their family's history of abuse, what does it mean for Alex to be "humble," and what does it mean for a Jennifer to recognize the "worth" of family? This chapter explores these questions within a feminist framework of family rights. It begins by explicating the paradox of family rights in situations of women abuse, examines different American colonial cultural practices controlling gendered relations, and reviews, from a feminist perspective, the contributions of social work and restorative justice in stopping women abuse. Using the Johnson family example, the chapter sets forth how integrating social work and restorative processes advances feminist perspectives on family rights, and prevents the coercive control exerted by men over their partners that restricts their liberty (see Stark, 2007).

In working with this paradox, the two authors bring feminist views on restorative justice. Joan, a social worker, has practiced and researched family-engagement strategies to stop abuse within the family; Mary, a psychologist, has studied and tested restorative practices to address sexual assault and intimate partner violence. Our work has convinced us that restorative processes can be applied to violence against women, but only under certain conditions and only with adequate safeguards in place (Koss, 2000; Pennell, 2005b). We both emphasize that delivery of these interventions should be locally planned in order to attune them to the community's strengths and cultures (Hopkins & Koss, 2005; Pennell & Burford, 2002; Pennell & Weil, 2000).

THE PARADOX OF FAMILY RIGHTS

The concept of family rights is a paradox, and all the more starkly so against the backdrop of women abuse. In the social world, the most compelling paradoxes encompass sets of principles that are each morally valid and logically irreconcilable, and these paradoxes require divergent thinking rather than fastening onto one solution (Rappaport, 1981). As presented in Figure 9.1, and explained above, the term "family rights" combines two mutually negating principles. The first principle is respecting the diverse cultural practices of families and their sense of identity stretching out of the past and into the future. Such respect is important for all families in fostering a sense of continuity and belonging, especially necessary in societies racializing certain groups and privileging others, but contentious when family norms oppress members along lines of gender and generation. Responding to the limitations of engrained practices, the second principle upholds the human rights of every family member regardless of individual characteristics such as gender, age, or sexual orientation, encompasses both just processes that are fair, and creates a sense of efficacy or control over one's affairs and just and safe outcomes in the home and community.

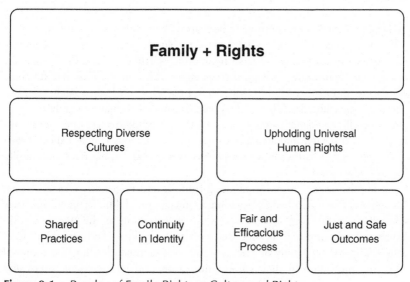

Figure 9-1. Paradox of Family Rights as Culture and Rights.

Both in general and specifically in the context of women abuse, principles based on the customs of particular families' cultures and on claims of universal human rights can run headlong into each other and provoke repression and resistance. Optimistically, such strongly held and contrary principles create a dialectic that enriches understandings, multiplies solutions, and strengthens collaborations for social change.

With leadership by women of color (e.g., Collins, 2000; hooks, 1981; Lorde, 1984), feminist scholars have increasingly recognized the importance of analyzing the intersection of sexism with racism, classism, heterosexism, ageism, and other forms of oppression (Zinn & Dill, 1996). Indigenous and Black women brought attention to the necessity of reclaiming their cultural identities. In the aftermath of colonization, they spoke against human rights violations and spoke for family ties and community healing (e.g., Combahee River Collective, 1979/2001; McCaslin, 2005; Strega & Esquao, 2009). With good reason, White feminists in the United States approached their own colonial heritage with caution, acknowledging its history of oppressing women and children whatever their color or background. At the same time, they increasingly identified that cultural identity and practices are sources of support and constraint and as such are viable means of stopping women abuse. Understanding this historical background and its ongoing influence, therefore, helps in figuring out how to apply interventions in a manner that respects families and safeguards all their members.

AMERICAN COLONIALISM AND HISTORICAL GENDERED CULTURAL PRACTICES

Today, familial relations continue to be shaped by the folkways transplanted from different regions of Britain to the American colonies (Fischer, 1989). These settlers arrived in four relatively large migrations, starting in the early seventeenth century and continuing through the late eighteenth century. They had much in common—most spoke English, adhered to British law, held Christian beliefs, and cherished their liberties. They all had mechanisms for regulating family relations and controlling violence in the home, but these methods were by no means uniform. This diversity, interacting with those of indigenous people (Allen, 1986) and other settlers, cultivated varied perspectives on gender, marriage, and family in the "New World."

In the first wave, Puritans, migrating from eastern England to Massachusetts, brought humanitarian beliefs regarding women's and children's rights, and they enacted the 1641 *Body of Liberties*, the first legislation in the Western world expressly outlawing wife beating and cruelty to children and servants (Pleck, 1987). They viewed family violence as sinful and potentially leading to withdrawal of divine protection of their communities from Indian attacks, disasters, and disease. Their primary goal for the family was preserving harmony under the father's rule and tempering, rather than stopping, abuse. The community monitored family safety and intervened to stop abuse, and murders within the family were rare.

The second large group of emigrants was Royalist elites and their indentured servants, who relocated from southern England to Virginia. They brought their Anglican faith, enforced its orthodoxy and ritual, and banished nonconformists. The heads of households referred to themselves as the "patriarch," with the authority to protect and chastise their family, broadly defined to encompass not only nuclear family but anyone under their roof (or roofs), including staff, visitors, and slaves (Fischer, 1989). Rural elites instructed husbands to physically discipline their wives but sought to moderate the violence. Wife-beating was viewed as dishonorable, and was punished by public shaming.

The third wave of migration involved the Quakers (Society of Friends), from Wales and the North Midlands area of England. They settled in the Delaware Valley. Having suffered intense persecution for their belief in the equality of all people, they held strong commitments to building families and communities based on love and simplicity rather than fear, promoting tender care of children and their education, and encouraging pacifist approaches to resolving disputes, including those with American Indians (Brinton, 1952; Woolman, 1774/1961). Although not an egalitarian society, among the early colonists the Friends came the closest to effecting gender equality, referring to husbands and wives as "helpmeets for each other" (Fischer, 1989, p. 490).

The fourth and largest migratory group came from the borderlands between England and Scotland and from northern Ireland and settled in the Appalachian backcountry. They arrived with a strong aversion to the established church and militantly insisted on their own reformed religion (Fischer, 1989). Struggling to survive in their wilderness settlements, men and women labored side by side. Nevertheless, marital and parent-child relationships were extremely patriarchal and repressive, and not infrequently prospective grooms kidnapped their brides or were forced at gunpoint to marry young women whom they had impregnated. As commemorated in traditional mountain songs, love and violence were closely entwined.

Although the Puritans made family violence a public issue, it did not gain national prominence until the mid-1800s, with the initiation of the temperance movement. Women activists in large numbers crusaded against male drunkenness, which they saw as the cause of domestic violence and incest and grounds for divorce (Valverde, 1991). After the Civil War (as the case with wars in general), violent crimes and family homicide rapidly rose; in reaction, Americans became more accepting of state intervention into family life, and anti-cruelty societies were established to protect children (Pleck, 1987). By the end of the nineteenth century, the profession of social work had emerged, and child welfare workers were not only trying to protect children but more covertly, as revealed in case records, their abused mothers (Gordon, 1988).

FEMINIST AND SOCIAL WORK APPROACHES TO WOMEN ABUSE

Early Initiatives

Lagging behind practice and reflecting publications generally in the social sciences, the social work literature did not explicitly reference family violence until the late 1960s (Elbow, 1980). Nevertheless, in keeping with the profession's traditions of empowerment, many advocates of battered women were social workers. A prime example is movement activist and social worker Susan Schechter (1982), author of a widely acclaimed history of the battered women's movement. Social workers (including Joan) were among those founding early shelters for abused women and their children (Pennell, 1987). During this period, feminist social workers, both female and male, struggled to integrate their professional role with their political aspirations and personal experiences (Pennell & Allen, 1984). For example, social workers were taught to avoid taking sides and passing judgments on clients and to mediate between a husband and wife, all of which contradicted their feelings about perpetrators in their own families and their activism on behalf of abused women. Male social workers identified that their gender prohibited them from applying their professional skills to programs for abused women and floundered in finding alternatives, such as facilitating groups for perpetrators, which they viewed as diverting much-needed resources from women's services.

These struggles point to the nascency of programs for abused women at the time, but also to the emphasis on what is now termed "women-defined" advocacy, which focused on survivors setting their own goals, as opposed to "service-defined" advocacy, which narrowed survivors' goals to those available from a particular provider (Goodman & Epstein, 2008, p. 42). The initial drift toward service-defined advocacy accelerated with increased dependency on public funding for shelters, community services, and legal interventions. Social workers, psychologists, lawyers, and other professionals were part of this turn toward a service orientation, one that was rejected by the Battered and Formerly Battered Women's Caucus of the National Coalition Against Domestic Violence. In its 2004 statement, the caucus urged battered women's organizations "to stop using clinical language, and mental health/social work models in their work with Battered Women and Children," which "inadvertently aided batterers using institutional systems to persecute Battered Women, in areas such as child custody proceedings" and diverted efforts away from promoting an abused woman's "safety, support and justice and her inherent autonomy to direct her life and define her identity" (http://www.ncadv.org/resources/BatteredandFormerlyBatteredWomensStatement.php).

Legalization of Interventions

As women and their children left the shelters, they required ongoing support and assistance in the community. Despite their suspicions of the law, battered women's programs increasingly turned to legal recourse, with no-contact orders and mandatory arrests frequently applied by the 1980s (Pleck, 1987). This served to formally acknowledge that domestic violence was a crime, but its outcomes for women were mixed. Law enforcement provided some immediate protection for abused women and helped to shift the power dynamics between perpetrators and survivors (Ptacek, 1999). If they fought back, though, victims were also cited, and women of color were at particular risk for dual arrests (McGillivray & Comaskey, 1999). Abused women were compelled to testify against their abusers, seek protective orders, or leave their home. This crime-centered approach too often jeopardized not only the safety of women and their children, but also their material resources, and in the case of undocumented immigrant women, residency in the United States, all of which increased their future vulnerability to abuse (Coker, 2004). If an abused mother did not comply, child protective services were increasingly likely to remove her children because of her failure to protect her children from witnessing her own victimization (Edleson, 2004). This rise in child removals was a function of the extensive overlap in women abuse and child maltreatment, combined with the decision of some states to redefine children's exposure to domestic violence as an injurious environment for which parents (usually mothers) were held accountable (Pennell, 2006b).

Limitations of Approaches

Overall, legal interventions led to sharp reductions in homicide against partners, but far more to the advantage of men than women; the prevalence of violence against women remained unchanged, and even if the physical violence stopped, male batterers continued to exert coercive control over their partners, exploiting them emotionally, sexually, and economically (Stark, 2007). A case in point is the ongoing effort to change the men through batterer-intervention programs. These appeared to reduce violent assaults over time for men completing the group sessions, an important development in itself (Gondolf, 2004); however, other forms of abuse may have increased, possibly because the men reinforced each other's justifications for male dominance in partnerships (see summary in Stark, 2007). This abuse produced in the women a chronic sense of psychological vulnerability, and of being powerless in an unjust world, associated with marital dissatisfaction, low self-esteem, depression, anxiety, poor health, and injury (Smith, Earp, & DeVellis, 1995).

Such psychological vulnerability, coupled with diminished social and economic resources and ongoing abusive tactics by the father of their children, eroded women's ability to mother (Bancroft & Silverman, 2002), yet at the same time these women were blamed for the impact on their children (Radford & Hester, 2006). These impacts varied depending on the child's resilience and context; nevertheless, children and adolescents exposed to domestic violence were more likely to act aggressively and attempt to resolve disputes through violence or to become anxious and depressed. In addition, as they enter adulthood, women were more likely to suffer from depression and low self-esteem (Edleson, 2004). After separating from abusive partners, women struggled to find ways to keep their children and themselves safe while meeting their children's need for access to their fathers (Tubbs & Williams, 2007). The ongoing struggles of abused women point to the limitations of the current strategies of the battered women's movement and to its becoming sidetracked away from its original social change aspirations (Goodman & Epstein, 2008; Stark, 2007).

RESTORATIVE PRACTICES: CAUTIONS AND STRATEGIES

The term *restorative justice* applies to programs that view crime as a violation of people and relationships, causing harm which offenders and communities are accountable for, and have an obligation to repair (Umbreit, Vos, Coates, & Lightfoot, 2006). Although this framework would appear congruent with efforts to stop domestic violence, restorative programs for the most part paid little attention to abuse of women or child maltreatment. Some restorative justice proponents spoke out or stressed that great care needed to be taken in applying conferencing in situations of domestic violence, because of its potential to revictimize abused women (e.g., Zehr, 2002).

Expanding upon this danger, feminist scholars have enumerated very legitimate reservations about restorative practices, including concerns that victims/survivors would not be at liberty to state their views with decisions reached through coercion rather than consensus (Busch, 2002); senior members of the family or community elders would lecture women to comply with traditional practices (or what are presumed to be traditional) to their detriment (Cameron, 2006; Coker, 2006); the family group might push gendered expectations (Cook, 2006), pressure women to forgive and reconcile with their abusers (Stubbs, 2002), and especially among immigrant groups, sacrifice their safety to keep their families together and in their new country (Goel, 2005); and domestic violence would once again be treated as a private matter rather than a crime, thus invalidating the experience of abused women (Curtis-Fawley & Daly, 2005; Daly & Stubbs, 2006).

Anti-domestic violence workers further cautioned that where child protection was involved, restorative processes could exacerbate the victimization of the mothers. In particular, they feared that social workers might approve plans that were unsafe to women, or would blame women if their partners failed to carry out the steps in the plans. At the same time, abused women and shelter staff saw Family Group Conferencing as a means of increasing safety and supports and overcoming painful isolation (Pennell & Francis, 2005). Likewise, Cherokee, African-American, and Latino communities have identified Family Group Conferencing as holding out the promise of advancing both their goals of safe homes and cultural affirmation (Waites, Macgowan, Pennell, Carlton-LaNey, & Weil, 2004).

Indigenous groups warned that when governments and professionals impose restorative practices without community planning, they recolonize native communities (McCaslin, 2005). At the same time, Aboriginal women recognized that the criminal justice system oppresses their communities, and some view restorative justice as a viable alternative toward self-determination (Nancarrow, 2006). To further self-determination within their cultural settings, indigenous women have emphasized the necessity of local control over the design of the intervention and screening of referrals (Bushie, 1997).

Sharing these concerns, feminist program developers treaded carefully into the arena of gendered violence, but with hopes that restorative processes could be a vehicle for stopping violence against women and children. In Australia, restorative justice proponents Braithwaite and Daly (1998) offered an early proposal to apply restorative processes to addressing gendered violence. They observed that police or courts revictimize women who are treated as suspect sources of evidence, rather than as people whose stories of suffering should be validated and acted upon. They advised against turning to mediation because the two "parties" are not equals in power. And they urged consideration of Family Group Conferencing as a means of constructing culturally-based "communities of care and concern" to challenge masculinist views that reinforce exploiting women and to reconstruct ones that support egalitarian relationships (Braithwaite & Daly, 1998, p. 156).

Agreeing with Braithwaite and Daly, Koss and other colleagues (2000) in the United States utilized restorative theory and practice in developing an intervention to address violence against women. They deliberately selected for their trial demonstration first-time sexual assaults where there was not an ongoing relationship between the perpetrator and victim; they reasoned that this mitigated the risk that the victim would be intimidated during the conference and susceptible to further victimization in the home (Hopkins & Koss, 2005). The program was developed in consultation with community and professional groups and carried out with extensive preparation of participants and careful follow-up after the conferences (Koss, Bachar, Hopkins, & Carlson, 2004). The results are promising. Victims made informed decisions about whether to participate or not, all conferences to date were carried out without additional abuse taking place during the meeting, and observers were impressed by the extent to which moral justice and victim validation were realized (Bletzer & Koss, under review).

In Canada, social workers Burford and Pennell were influenced by developments in New Zealand, and did not initially connect their work with the restorative justice movement. They quickly, though, found Braithwaite's (1989) theory of reintegrative shaming helpful in analyzing the family group dynamics in situations of family violence (Pennell & Burford, 1996). From the outset they were (and continue to be) wary of applying restorative processes to abuse of women in cases where children are not involved. Their reasoning was that the children maintain ties between partners, whether or not they stay together; the presence of children is particularly effective at galvanizing extended family involvement to stop the abuse; and the involvement of child protection, along with law enforcement, exerts controls over the proceedings to safeguard participants. Their study found that Family Group Decision-making (a form of Family Group Conferencing) reduced indicators of child maltreatment and women abuse (Pennell & Burford, 2000b).

The following family example, of the Johnson family in North Carolina, illustrates how social work group interventions and restorative processes can be combined to stop women abuse and child maltreatment. The scenario also points to the influence of the family's background. All family members were White (as were all the involved service providers), and of British heritage. They lived in what has been referred to as the "Bible Belt" area of the country because of its adherence to conservative Christian beliefs, and their family relations were influenced by Appalachian traditions (see the above description of the fourth colonial wave of American settlers). As their story testifies, these cultural norms reinforced the husband's sense of inadequacy when he became unemployed, and more positively, became the source for change and moving toward responsible partnership and fatherhood. The steadfast caring and courage of the family group in tackling family violence is evident throughout. They were rightfully proud of their accomplishments. The case example is based on interviews with family and staff. In order to respect the privacy of the family, their names have been altered and their identities have been masked.

Their family meetings were called "child and family team meetings," a term originating in child mental health to refer to a team planning process that wraps a "system of care," that is, a comprehensive and unified array of services and supports, around children and their families (Stroul & Friedman, 1986). In North Carolina, various child-and-family-serving agencies—including child welfare organizations, juvenile justice, schools, and mental health, and public health agencies—use the term Child and Family Teams (CFTs) to designate forums that involve the family group and service providers in planning. In 2001, the state legislature appropriated funds for a major child welfare reform to institute a system of care with CFTs as one of its major strategies. The policy of the North Carolina Division of Social Services (2008) stipulates time frames for convening CFTs on a regular basis for in-home and foster care services. CFT training, technical assistance, and evaluation (provided by Joan's center across the state), are grounded in practices developed by social workers, and global developments in family group conferencing and restorative justice.

CASE STUDY: THE JOHNSON FAMILY

"The Night of the Big Fight"

Called by a panic-stricken Jennifer, Alex's parents rushed over to find two police holding their son down on the floor. Flat on his back, an explosive, intoxicated

Alex was still holding his little daughter Kim; her twin Lynn was crouching down next to baby Renee, and their older brother Tommy was standing in the corner. His parents were quickly followed by Jennifer's mother and eldest sister and then by the after-hours child protection worker. They learned that Alex had gotten into a fight with Jennifer's father, Ricky, who had been pushing his daughter and her husband to smoke marijuana. Before the police arrived, Ricky had taken off out the back door.

Alex was jailed for disorderly conduct, and to avoid emergency placements, the four children were split up, with the twins and the baby going to the home of Jennifer's mother (long divorced from her "no-good" husband) and Tommy going with Alex's parents. Under pressure from the on-call worker and her mother, Jennifer took out a protective order stipulating that Alex had to stay away from her and the children. To the consternation of the social workers, two days later his mother Ruth and Jennifer bailed Alex out of jail.

Child protection categorized this case as "domestic violence," assessed Alex as "domineering," and with tensions mounting, anticipated that he would become increasingly abusive and controlling if no intervention took place. They informed the family that they would be filing a "compliance petition" with the court to ensure that the parents followed the treatment plan or, if the judge so ruled, that they would place the children in the care of Social Services. At the same time, the agency allowed a 2-month window before moving to court adjudication (a judicial decision on the case). As the child protection supervisor explained, "DSS [Department of Social Services] used a strong hand" but also left room for the family to demonstrate that they could make "significant changes" to provide for the children's safety.

This was the second time that child protection had investigated the family. Two months earlier, the family doctor had contacted Social Services because Renee, the baby, was failing to thrive; she was losing weight and appeared lethargic. At that time the social worker also had received reports that 9-year-old Tommy, who previously had been a good student, was talking back to his teacher and getting into fights on the playground. At home, Tommy, identifying with his father, was refusing to listen to his mother and teasing the twins more than ever.

With cutbacks at his plant, Alex had recently been laid off and was refusing to take just any "sorry job." This meant that Jennifer was working longer hours, with Alex refusing to take up any domestic duties. Initially Alex brushed off Jennifer's complaints; as she became more strident, he began shoving her. Jennifer, petite but no pushover, hit back at her tall, lanky husband. He became all the more overbearing and drank heavily.

Unable to pay their bills, the couple borrowed repeatedly from their parents. The two sides of the family were fed up with the couple—Alex for his demands, drinking, and explosive temper, and Jennifer for neglecting her children, from whom she had become more and more emotionally distant. Her sister, a nurse, was particularly troubled by the baby's failure to thrive and blamed Jennifer.

Both sides of the family had lived in the community for many generations, and trouble like this shamed the whole family. All this led to more and more isolation of Jennifer, Alex, and their children.

The night of Alex's arrest was just one more of many incidents. Reflecting later, though, Ruth acknowledged, "The family was a mess, all the signs were there, but I had just missed it until the night of the big fight." The child protection worker had previously raised the idea of convening a Child and Family Team (CFT) meeting; after the fight, the relatives were ready to be involved in planning for the safety and care of the children. Given the need to stabilize the children's arrangements and the escalating domestic violence, the first of five CFT meetings was rapidly organized by the social worker and held within two days.

"It Wasn't to Badger Us"

Jennifer realized she needed help and accepted the referral to the CFT. She appreciated that the worker suggested the meeting but did not "badger" her to go along with the referral. Not sure how Alex would react in the meeting, she was relieved to learn that he would not be invited. With the no-contact order in place, the agency's policy was to hold separate meetings for the husband and wife. In addition, Alex did not want a CFT at all, which he perceived as outsiders interfering in his business, and was decidedly opposed to Jennifer having her own meeting. On his mother's urging, he reluctantly agreed to his CFT being held. Both sides of the family hoped that the meeting would get them on the "right path." They also did not want Alex and Jennifer in the same meeting as they knew how Jennifer could get "hot-tempered" and worried about how Alex would react if confronted by his wife.

The facilitator at each meeting was the same seasoned social worker, who was solely responsible for conducting the meeting, and did not work with the family outside of the CFTs. He was a long-term member of the community and held strong convictions about stopping domestic violence. Demonstrating their steadfast support for their relatives, Jennifer's mother and Alex's sister and mother attended each meeting. The social worker and her supervisor were also present. All the meetings were held at the Social Services building and in the evening, when it was convenient for the adult family members to attend (although the children did not attend). Much of the planning work, though, transpired outside of the formal meetings, when this closely knit family group conferred among themselves.

"We Are Through with This"

At the first meeting, the family vented their anger at both Jennifer and Alex (in his absence). They insisted that they had done everything they could to support the couple and were "through" with paying their bills and always bailing them out. For her part, Jennifer saw herself as the "victim" and felt blamed for what was happening in her family. As iterated by the supervisor, child protection "left the family with the issues for them to develop the plan on how they wanted to address . . . safety for the children" and how they would "assure the agency" that their plan was working. Given this charge, the family members agreed to continue providing care for the children, to avert the need to place them outside the family. They were also mobilized to monitor the couple rather than leaving this role to child protection alone.

"Why Are You in My Life?"

Two days later the separate meeting with Alex was held. Upon entering the room, he immediately took over a whole side of the board table, lounging in his chair and draping his long arms over the two neighboring chairs. Everyone else, family and staff, seated themselves across the table from him. During the session, he complained about the family interfering in his life and would not acknowledge that he needed any support. Nevertheless, he agreed to go along with the plan developed by his female relatives. Ruth had decided that her son was entering an alcohol treatment program and offered to pay the fee. The family built into the plan a schedule of monthly CFT meetings to "catch things before they headed south."

"A Turning Point"

A month later, Alex started his treatment program, and Jennifer, no longer fearful of Alex's rage, had the protective order rescinded. This meant that both Jennifer and Alex attended the third meeting. No longer stubbornly defiant, Alex sat between the facilitator and Jennifer, who had her mother on her other side; Alex's sister and mother, the social worker, and the supervisor were also present. Still upset with the couple, the other family members demanded reports of progress from Alex and Jennifer.

During the meeting, the family group gained a better understanding of Jennifer's struggles with depression and how this reduced her capacity to mother her four children. Jennifer acknowledged her need for counseling and asked to be enrolled in an anger-management course. Ruth volunteered to drive her daughter-in-law to her sessions. The social worker said that she would arrange for an assessment for Jennifer. In addition, counseling was planned for Tommy. Child protection had been skeptical of Alex and Jennifer's "motivation to change" but now saw the strong impact that the relatives were having on the couple. The agency felt that they did not have to "push" the couple because the family had taken over this role.

At the fourth meeting, Alex was well into his alcohol treatment, and as Ruth noted, the meetings had a "big impact" on her son. Alex reported that he was actively looking for work. At Jennifer's request, her counselor attended and shared a very positive assessment of Jennifer's progress. By this time, Jennifer was regularly visiting with her children, and Alex was doing so under supervision.

"I'm Glad that You Made Me Do This"

By the fifth and last meeting, the children had all returned home to their parents, who were sharing parenting duties. At the meeting, Alex, in a quivering voice and almost in tears, thanked his family:, "I didn't like having to do this [the meetings], but I'm glad that you made me do this." For her part, Jennifer was relieved that "everything was out in the open" and they had the "support" of their families. Both Alex and Jennifer were ashamed of the hard time that they had put their families through and proud of the progress that they had made.

The court appointed guardian ad litem whose job it is to advocate for the children was present to hear the medical report that baby Renee had gained weight and was making good progress, and the child development assessment which stated that Tommy had settled back into school. The family group was now confident that Alex and Jennifer would maintain this progress and were comfortable with child protection removing its services. For its part, the agency concluded that their expectations for validation of progress had been met, dismissed the agency's petition before the court, and closed the case. A while later, the Johnson family relocated to another county where Alex had found a good job, and Jennifer likewise found work.

"Just a Humble Man"

Interviewed two years after the case was closed, the child protection supervisor noted that the agency had received no further reports of child abuse or neglect regarding the Johnson family. Alex's mother and Jennifer's sister continued to stay in close contact with them. Ruth commented, "I talk with them a couple times a week, and they are doing great." Jennifer agreed: "Alex and I are stronger than ever. We still have to work on marriage every day but everybody has to do that. We both have realized that family was worth more than what we were putting before them. I'm glad that we went through it [the meetings]; if not, we would still be in the mess we were in." Ruth summed up her son's progress in the simple comment, "Now he is just a humble man—they [Alex and Jennifer] work together." In the context of the Johnson family group, "a humble man" had a particular import. Ruth, a regular church attendee, was expressing the view that her son had become a responsible husband and father who quietly and faithfully went about his business of providing for his family and staying out of trouble.

Alex was now realizing his family's expectations of the type of man he should be, and redirected himself to meeting the expectations of child protection, backed by the police and courts. He wanted to ensure the safety and well-being of his family. These desired ends are identified in Figure 9.1 above as "continuity in identity" and "just and safe outcomes." We next examine how the meeting integrated the family group's "shared practices" with a "fair and efficacious process" that together built the family's sense of efficacy, and pride in reaching these ends.

THE MEETING PROCESS: PRACTICE AND SKILLS

The series of five CFT meetings was a memorable experience, and two years later, the participants freely sharing what had happened and how they felt about it. They rated very favorably the manner in which the meetings were conducted and the plans were reached. Jennifer described the meetings as "a wonderful process" and wished that everyone's meetings could be as "successful." Similarly, Ruth characterized the process as making it possible for the family to "work out their problems," would "highly recommend this process," but stressed that "someone has got to stay on top of it to be sure it happens."

Leadership within the Family Group

Ruth, the natural leader of the group, was especially instrumental in making sure that "someone"—that is, herself—stayed "on top" of developments inside and outside the meetings. As is the case in other close-knit extended families (e.g., the Inuit community described in Pennell & Burford, 1995), much of the planning took place between meetings, when the family group members informally conferred among themselves. The men in the family participated in these discussions and avoided the official meetings at the Social Services office building. The one exception was Alex, who at first was very resistant to attending the official meetings.

In particular, the women in the family demonstrated leadership roles. The CFTs at Social Services were the forum in which the more senior women on both sides of the family group negotiated with the service providers. Their responsibility for family matters was consistent with their cultural background, and women exerting leadership appears to be a pattern in conferences addressing family violence in diverse cultures (see Pennell & Burford, 2002). As is often the case in other families, the deliberations facilitated bonding among the women across generations and sides of the family (Pennell, 2005b; Pennell & Burford, 2000a). This lessened the blaming of the mother (in this case, Jennifer), which often happens when abused women become depressed, angry, and withdrawn from their children. It also lessened the risk that the extended family will pressure the couple to reconcile. And it increased the confidence of Social Services in the plan, because both sides of the family were in agreement (see Pennell, 2006b).

Issues Related to the Meeting

Notably, the family's main area of complaint about the CFT meetings was that they were held at Social Services. This "embarrassed" some family members, who would have preferred convening the meetings in one of their homes and felt thwarted by the social worker's ruling out of such a possibility. Holding a meeting in a family member's home may be appropriate within the family's culture and community (see Waites et al., 2004), or conversely, pose challenges. It may elevate the status of the side of the family at whose home the meeting is held, reducing the say of others, or thrust hostess duties on the woman of the house, disadvantaging her as a full participant in the deliberations. Specifically in situations of women abuse and child maltreatment, another major concern is that the home may be experienced as unsafe by some family members. Preferably the location is selected in consultation with the family, and when asked, North Carolinian families have opted for a church or community center over Social Services to provide a sense of neutrality, safety, and comfort (Pennell, 2006a; Pennell & Kim, in press).

Prior to holding the meetings, preparations are necessary. The rapid convening of the first meeting precluded careful preparations in which family members were consulted on the arrangements; the family did not complain about the location over the course of the five meetings; and the arrangements were not revisited in advance of subsequent meetings (see Burford, Pennell, & MacLeod, 1995; North Carolina Division of Social Services, 2008). In most counties in North Carolinia, including the one where the Johnsons live, typically the family's case worker is responsible for organizing the meeting. This differs from the practice in some other countries or jurisdictions where the facilitator (also referred to as the coordinator) carries out this function. When the case workers hold the dual responsibilities of child protection and meeting organizer, their attention and that of the family members are often diverted away from planning for the meeting to negotiating terms for the care of the children, and this may inhibit families from voicing their discomfort with meeting logistics. In the case of the Johnson family, the limited preparations may well have lessened the direct involvement of family members.

Where preparations have been more extensive, family members in North Carolina have participated in greater numbers, with men, youth, and children far more present (Pennell, 2006a). Preferably, preparations include the following steps, carried out in consultation with family members and service providers: clarifying the purpose for holding the meeting; explaining its process and figuring out guidelines for respectful and effective deliberations; developing an invitation list that taps into the family's informal and formal supports; making arrangements for inclusion of family members of all ages; planning how to open and close the meeting in a manner congruent with the family's traditions; and carefully assessing whether it is safe to proceed (Pennell, 2005a).

Facilitation

One detail which led to success in the case of the Johnsons was the independent facilitation that characterized the process. Despite the limited preparations, the family members, including Alex eventually, were highly satisfied with the meetings. Like so many other families, when given the opportunity to make plans for their relatives, the Johnson family group figured out how to make the process work. Moreover, they had great confidence in the CFT facilitator, whose sole role was supporting them through the planning process. Unlike the social worker, he did not have case-carrying responsibilities, and his independence from child protection functions helped to keep his role clear in the eyes of the family and in compliance with the North Carolina Division of Social Services (2008) CFT policy. The Division stipulated that in high risk situations such as that of the Johnson family, a "facilitator, who is neither the social worker for the family nor the supervisor of that social worker, shall be used in all cases" (Section IV.A.). Research has found that having an independent coordinator adds to the family group's leadership during the deliberations (Pennell, 2004).

Another key aspect of the facilitation process was having a male lead the process. Significantly, after his first meeting, Alex chose to sit between Jennifer and the facilitator, a male who was more senior than him, and someone on whom he could count on to both support him and keep him in check. In other words, Alex's model on how to act as a man in the meeting became the male facilitator rather than other men such as Jennifer's father, Ricky. Research has found that abusive men know how to select other men whom they respect and know will exert controls over them during the deliberations (Pennell & Burford, 1995). In describing her experience of the meetings, Jennifer commented, "It was good to have a facilitator to control the process." Elaborating on the role of the facilitator, Ruth observed: "The facilitator assisted the meeting process. He sat at the head of the table and showed that a free–for-all was not to be tolerated. I don't think you can have a meeting like this without a facilitator who keeps everybody on track and has all points of view included."

Family Private Time

Family private time refers to a stage of the meeting when family groups are left on their own to make a plan, with the facilitator and workers outside the room but available as needed. In North Carolina, family private time is applied on a limited basis, in large measure because of the high volume of referrals, limited staffing for organizing meetings, and worker and agency uncertainty about leaving families alone to deliberate (for similar concerns in other countries, see Lupton & Nixon, 1999; Sundell, Vinnerljung, & Ryburn, 2002; Trotter, 1999). The particular facilitator for the Johnson family had used private time with other families. Given the abbreviated preparations and high tensions at the first and second meetings for the Johnson family, however, the facilitator would have been ill-advised to have included family private time. The state policy manual reads, "Sometimes private family time is used so that the family and their natural supports can develop a plan in privacy without the facilitator and service providers present. Private time would be planned ahead of time with clear expectations and assurances for participant safety" (North Carolina Division of Social Services, 2008, Section V. A.).

Research supports this caution: When family members are not adequately prepared for conferencing, the likelihood of manipulation occurring during the family private time significantly rises (Pennell, 2006a). Such manipulation is of particular concern when there is a history of family violence. Nevertheless, with adequate preparation, family groups, including in situations of women abuse, use well their private time to confront issues and reach decisions through consensual processes (Pennell, 2006a; Pennell & Burford, 1995).

The later monthly meetings were a means of monitoring the family's progress and revising plans as needed. Typically, such meetings are convened by the case worker in many jurisdictions and do not include family private time. Wisely, in the case of the Johnson family, the CFTs continued to be facilitated by the same experienced social worker, who provided a consistent structure over the course of the meetings.

Structured Process

At the beginning of every meeting, the facilitator reviewed the purpose of the meeting (to ensure the safety and well-being of the children), the agreement on confidentiality (to respect the family's privacy), and the guidelines (to make for a safe and productive meeting). The meeting guidelines emphasized: "This is about the children," "your input is the key to success," "honest, open discussion is essential for all attending," "everyone will have the chance to share his/her point of view and offer solutions," "everyone is to feel safe to participate in the discussion," and "the meeting's focus is on the future of this children and family." Although initially the facilitator had reservations about Alex's capacity to change, he trusted opening the decision-making to the family. He conveyed his support for the process through his even-toned voice, reassuring eye contact, and clarifications when he detected quizzical looks on their faces. At the end of each meeting, he distributed a brief form so that the participants could give him feedback on how to improve future sessions for them and other families.

What the facilitator was doing was applying good social work practice to a restorative process. He was doing so in an agency and state setting that promoted the use of CFT meetings. Both his competence and the context helped to make the deliberations fair ones that worked with, rather than against, the cultural norms of the Johnson family. In effect, he helped the group to balance the two sides of the paradox of family rights on cultural practices and just processes.

INTEGRATING SOCIAL WORK PRACTICE AND RESTORATIVE PROCESSES

Good social work practice, informed by feminist perspectives, makes restorative processes work well in complex family situations such as child maltreatment, abuse of women, and other types of gendered maltreatment. Particularly helpful are social work approaches to group work that cultivate a sense of social responsibility. In these approaches, a firm commitment exists to advance both individual and communal empowerment.

Nurturing social responsibility is central to the earliest model of social work with groups and resonates with feminist aspirations. This model, referred to as "social goals" in the schema developed by Papell and Rothman (1980), is founded upon the work of settlement houses and recreational, educational, and socialization groups and intersects with community development (Breton, 2004). Its seeks to educate group members so that they can collectively set their own goals and formulate their social action steps and, thus, diverges from the aims of therapy groups to rehabilitate individuals, and mutual-aid groups to encourage reciprocal support among the membership (Toseland & Rivas, 2008).

Although components of all these group work models can be found in Family Group Meetings, their overall intent aligns most closely with that of the social goals model (Macgowan & Pennell, 2001). Among the early group workers, Grace Coyle (1937/1939) proposed a theory of democratic participation to foster responsible citizenship. Emphasizing that democratic group processes in themselves inculcate social consciousness and promote social action, she iterated, "Where autocracy can be banished, where each is freed from fear or sense of inferiority to make his contribution creatively to the group, there may spring up a wide expanding of experience for us all" (pp. 563–564). While her male-oriented language reflects her era, her message remains profoundly relevant today for family groups addressing women abuse.

Coyle further urged that social workers enrich their practice by utilizing both casework's understanding of family relationships and group work's understanding of group dynamics. This integration is what happens in family group conferencing and was evident in the CFTs for the Johnson family. Present at the CFTs was both a natural group (the Johnson family and their relatives) and a formed group (the family group and service providers). This can make for a clash of family and professional cultures, and the facilitator for the Johnson family CFTs was there to ease these interactions and orient the group to making decisions together. He was "neutral" in the sense that he did not take sides and did not push for a particular action plan. But he was decidedly biased in pushing all participants to act in a socially responsible manner on behalf of the Johnson children and their parents. Their work paid off in stopping abuse and child maltreatment, and advancing the well-being of all the family members.

Battered women advocates and restorative justice proponents are right to be cautious about bringing together family groups to address women abuse. Gendered abuse is so widely prevalent because norms in families and society at large perpetuate human rights violations. Respecting family culture and upholding human rights is a paradox, but not one that keeps us stuck. Gender norms are not uniform and inflexible; rather, they reflect diverse histories, interactions among belief systems, and changing social and economic conditions. Through the CFT process, the Johnson family remained rooted in their Appalachian culture while developing women's leadership to advance human rights. To move forward, feminist perspectives offer empowerment goals for all people. Social work practices can inform restorative processes about how to put these goals into action.

ACKNOWLEDGMENTS

We wish to acknowledge the contributions of William Poindexter and Ryan Reikowsky in preparing this chapter. William brought experience about how to translate social work approaches into restorative processes, and Ryan brought an understanding of how masculinities shape gender-based relationships. Our deep appreciation goes to the family and staff interviewed for the case example.

REFERENCES

Allen, P. G. (1986). *The sacred hoop: Recovering the feminine in American Indian traditions.* Boston: Beacon Press.

Bancroft, L., & Silverman, J. G. (2002). *The batterer as parent: Addressing the impact of domestic violence on family dynamics.* Thousand Oaks, CA: Sage.

Bandura, A. (2002). Social cognitive theory in cultural context. *Applied Psychology: An International Review, 51*(2), 269–290.

Bartholet, E. (2009). The racial disproportionality movement in child welfare: False facts and dangerous directions. *Harvard Law School Public Law & Legal Theory Working Paper Series.* Paper No. 09-21. Retrieved August 1, 2009, from http://papers.ssrn.com/sol3/papers.cfm?abstract_id=1373892#

Battered and Formerly Battered Women's Caucus, National Coalition Against Domestic Violence. (2004). Statement. Retrieved August 1, 2009, from http://www.ncadv.org/resources/BatteredandFormerlyBatteredWomensStatement.php

Bletzer, K., & Koss, M. P. (under review). Restorative justice in criminal cases of sexual assault: A textual analysis.

Braithwaite, J. (1989). *Crime, shame and reintegration.* Cambridge: Cambridge University Press.

Braithwaite, J., & Daly, K. (1998). Masculinities, violence, and communitarian control. In S. L. Miller (Ed.), *Crime control and women: Feminist implications of criminal justice policy* (pp. 151–172). Newbury Park, CA: Sage.

Breton, M. (2004). An empowerment perspective. In C. D. Garvin, M. J. Galinsky, & L. M. Gutiérrez (Eds.), *Handbook of social work with groups* (pp. 58–75). New York: Guilford Press.

Brinton, H. H. (1952). *Friends for 300 years: The history and belief of the Society of Friends since George Fox started the Quaker movement.* Wallingford, PA: Pendle Hill and Philadelphia Yearly Meeting of the Religious Society of Friends.

Burford, G., Pennell, J., & MacLeod, S. (1995). *Manual for coordinators and communities: The organization and practice of family group decision making* (revised ed.). St. John's, NF: Memorial University of Newfoundland, School of Social Work. Retrieved April 14, 2010, from http://faculty.chass.ncsu.edu/pennell//fgdm/manual

Busch, R. (2002). Domestic violence and restorative justice initiatives: Who pays if we get it wrong? In H. Strang & J. Braithwaite (Eds.), *Restorative justice and family violence* (pp. 223–248). Cambridge: Cambridge University Press.

Bushie, B. (1997). A personal journey. In Sivell-Ferri, C. (Ed.), *The Four Circles of Hollow Water*. Hull, Quebec: Aboriginal Peoples Collection, Aboriginal Corrections Policy Unit, Supply and Services Canada, JS5-1/15-1997E.

Cameron, A. (2006). Stopping the violence: Canadian feminist debates on restorative justice and intimate violence. *Theoretical Criminology, 10,* 49–66.

Coker, D. (2004). Race, poverty, and the crime-centered response to domestic violence: A comment on Linda Mill's Insult to Injury: Rethinking our responses to intimate abuse. *Violence Against Women, 10,* 1331–1353.

Coker, D. (2006). Restorative justice, Navajo peacemaking and domestic violence. *Theoretical Criminology, 10,* 67–85.

Collins, P. H. (2000). *Black feminist thought: Knowledge, consciousness, and the politics of empowerment* (2nd ed.). New York: Routledge.

Combahee River Collective. (2001). A Black feminist statement. In B. Ryan (Ed.), *Identity politics in the women's movement* (pp. 59–66). New York: New York University Press. (Original work published 1979)

Cook, K. J. (2006). Doing difference and accountability in restorative justice conferences. *Theoretical Criminology, 10,* 107–124.

Coyle, G. (1939). Case work and group work. In F. Lowry (Ed.), *Readings in social case work 1920–1938: Selected reprints for the case work practitioner* (pp. 558–564). New York: Columbia University Press. (Original work published 1937)

Curtis-Fawley, S., & Daly, K. (2005). Gendered violence and restorative justice: The views of victim advocates. *Violence Against Women, 11,* 603–638.

Daly, K., & Stubbs, J. (2006). Feminist engagement with restorative justice. *Theoretical Criminology, 10,* 9–28.

Edleson, J. L. (2004). Should childhood exposure to adult domestic violence be defined as child maltreatment under the law? In P. G. Jaffe, L. L. Baker, & A. Cunningham (Eds.), *Protecting children from domestic violence: Strategies for community intervention* (pp. 8–29). New York: Guilford Press.

Edleson, J. L., & Williams, O. J. (2007). Introduction: Involving men who batter in their children's lives. In J. L. Edleson & O. J. Williams (Eds.), *Parenting by men who batter: New directions for assessment and intervention* (pp. 3–18). New York: Oxford University Press.

Elbow, M. (Ed.). (1980). *Patterns in family violence.* New York: Family Service Association of America.

Family Rights Group. (2007). *Annual report and review.* London: Author. Retrieved July 26, 2009, from http://www.frg.org.uk/pdfs/FRG%20Annual%20Report%2007.pdf

Fischer, D. H. (1989). *Albion's seed: Four British folkways in America.* New York: Oxford University Press.

Goel, R. (2005). Sita's trousseau: Restorative justice, domestic violence, and South Asian culture. *Violence Against Women, 11,* 639–665.

Gondolf, E. W. (2004). Evaluating batterer counseling programs: A difficult task showing some effects. *Aggression and Violence Behavior, 9,* 605–631.

Goodman, L. A., & Epstein, D. (2008). *Listening to battered women: A survivor-centered approach to advocacy, mental health, and justice.* Washington, DC: American Psychological Association.

Gordon, L. (1988). *Heroes of their own lives: The politics and history of family violence.* New York: Viking.

Hopkins, C. Q., & Koss, M. P. (2005). Incorporating feminist theory and insights into a restorative justice response to sex offenses. *Violence Against Women, 11,* 693–723.

hooks, b. (1981). *Ain't I a woman: Black women and feminism.* Boston: South End Press.

Kemp, S. P., Whittaker, J. K., & Tracy, E. M. (1997). *Person-environment practice: The social ecology of interpersonal helping.* Hawthorne, NY: Aldine de Gruyter.

Koss, M. P. (2000). Blame, shame, and community justice responses to violence against women. *American Psychologist, Nov.,* 1332–1343.

Koss, M. P., Bachar, K. J., Hopkins, C. Q., & Carlson, C. (2004). Justice responses to sexual assault: Lessons learned and new directions. In M. Eliasson (Ed.), *Undoing harm: International perspectives on interventions for men who use violence against women* (pp. 37–60). Uppsala, Sweden: Uppsala Universitet.

Lorde, A. (1984). *Sister outsider.* Freedom, CA: Crossing Press.

Lupton, C., and Nixon, P. (1999). *Empowering Practice? A critical appraisal of the family group conference approach.* Bristol, UK: Policy Press.

Macgowan, M. J., & Pennell, J. (2001). Building social responsibility through family group conferencing. *Social Work with Groups, 24*(3/4), 67–87.

McCaslin, W. D. (Ed.). (2005). *Justice as healing: Indigenous ways.* St. Paul, MN: Living Justice Press.

McGillivray, A., & Comaskey, B. (1999). *Black eyes all of the time: Intimate violence, aboriginal women, and the justice system.* Toronto: University of Toronto Press.

Nancarrow, H. (2006). In search of justice for domestic and family violence: Indigenous and non-Indigenous Australian women's perspectives. *Theoretical Criminology, 10,* 87–106.

North Carolina Division of Social Services. (2008, July). *Family Services manual: Vol. 1. Chapter VII—Child and family team meetings.* Raleigh, NC: Author. Retrieved June 30, 2009, from http://info.dhhs.state.nc.us/olm/manuals/manuals.aspx?dc=dss

Papell, C. P., & Rothman, B. (1980). Social group work models: Possession and heritage. In A. S. Alissi (Ed.), *Perspectives on social group work practice* (pp. 116–132). New York: The Free Press.

Pennell, J. (1987). Ideology at a Canadian shelter for battered women: A reconstruction. *Women's Studies International Forum, 10*(2), 113–123.

Pennell, J. (2004). Family group conferencing in child welfare: Responsive and regulatory interfaces. *Journal of Sociology and Social Welfare, 31*(1), 117–135.

Pennell, J. (2005a). Before the conference—Promoting family leadership. In J. Pennell & G. Anderson (Eds.), *Widening the circle: The practice and evaluation of family group conferencing with children, youths, and their families* (pp. 13–32). Washington, DC: NASW Press.

Pennell, J. (2005b). Safety for mothers and their children. In J. Pennell & G. Anderson (Eds.), *Widening the circle: The practice and evaluation of family group conferencing with children, youths, and their families* (pp. 163–181). Washington, DC: NASW Press.

Pennell, J. (2006a). Restorative practices and child welfare: Toward an inclusive civil society. In B. Morrison & E. Ahmed (Eds.), Restorative justice and civil society [Special issue]. *Journal of Social Issues, 62*(2), 257–277.

Pennell, J. (2006b). Stopping domestic violence or protecting children? Contributions from restorative justice. In D. Sullivan & L. Tifft (Eds.), *Handbook of restorative justice: A global perspective* (pp. 286–298). New York: Routledge.

Pennell, J., & Allen, D. (1984). Personal self, professional self and the women's movement. *Atlantis, 9*, 50–58.

Pennell, J., & Burford, G. (1995). *Family group decision making: New roles for "old" partners in resolving family violence: Implementation Report: Vols. I–II.* St. John's, NF: Memorial University of Newfoundland, School of Social Work. Retrieved April 14, 2010, from http://faculty.chass.ncsu.edu/pennell/fgdm/ImpReport/index.htm

Pennell, J., & Burford, G. (1996). Attending to context: Family group decision making in Canada. In J. Hudson, A. Morris, G. Maxwell, & B. Galaway (Eds.), *Family group conferences: Perspectives on policy & practice* (pp. 206–220). The Federation Press: Annandale, Australia; and New York: Criminal Justice Press.

Pennell, J., & Burford, G. (2000a). Family group decision making and family violence. In G. Burford & J. Hudson (Eds.), *Family group conferencing: New directions in community-centered child and family practice* (pp. 171–185). Hawthorne, NY: Aldine de Gruyter.

Pennell, J., & Burford, G. (2000b). Family group decision making: Protecting children and women. *Child Welfare, 79*(2), 131–158.

Pennell, J., & Burford, G. (2002). Feminist praxis, Making family group conferencing work. In H. Strang & J. Braithwaite (Eds.), *Restorative justice and family violence* (pp. 108–127). Cambridge: Cambridge University Press.

Pennell, J., & Francis, S. (2005). Safety conferencing: Toward a coordinated and inclusive response to safeguard women and children. In J. Ptacek (Ed.), *Violence Against Women, 11*(5), 666–692 [special issue].

Pennell, J., & Kim, M. (2010). Opening conversations across cultural, gender, and generational divides: Family and community engagement to stop violence against women and children. In J. Ptacek (Ed.), *Restorative justice and violence against women* (pp. 177–192). New York: Oxford University Press.

Pennell, J., & Weil, M. (2000). Initiating conferencing: Community practice issues. In G. Burford & J. Hudson (Eds.), *Family group conferencing: New directions in community-centered child and family practice* (pp. 253–261). Hawthorne, NY: Aldine de Gruyter.

Pleck, E. (1987). *Domestic tyranny: The making of social policy against family violence from colonial times to the present.* New York: Oxford University Press.

Ptacek, J. (1999). *Battered women in the courtroom: The power of judicial responses.* Boston: Northeastern University Press.

Radford, L., & Hester, M. (2006). *Mothering through domestic violence.* London: Jessica Kingsley.

Rappaport, J. (1991). In praise of paradox: A social policy of empowerment over prevention. *American Journal of Community Psychology, 9*(1), 1–25.

Schechter, S. (1982). *Women and male violence: The visions and struggles of the battered women's movement.* Boston: South End Press.

Simon, B. L. (1994). *The empowerment tradition in American social work: A history.* New York: Columbia University Press.

Smith, P. H., Earp, J. A., & DeVellis, R. (1995). Measuring battering: Development of the women's experience with battering (WEB) scale. *Women's Health: Research on Gender, Behavior, and Policy, 1,* 273–288.

Stark, E. (2007). *Coercive control: How men entrap women in personal life.* New York: Oxford University Press.

Strega, S., & Esquao, S. A. (2009). *Walking this path together: Anti-racist and anti-oppressive child welfare Practice.* Halifax, & Winnipeg, Canada: Fernwood.

Stroul, B. A., & Friedman, R. M. (1986). *A system of care for severely emotionally disturbed children and youth.* Washington, D.C.: Georgetown University Child Development Center, CASSP Technical Assistance Center.

Stubbs, J. (2002). Domestic violence and women's safety: Feminist challenges to restorative justice. In H. Strang & J. Braithwaite (Eds.), *Restorative justice and family violence* (pp. 42–61). Cambridge: Cambridge University Press.

Sundell, K., Vinnerljung, B., & Ryburn, M. (2002). Social workers' attitudes towards family group conferences in Sweden and the United Kingdom. *International Journal of Child & Family Welfare, 5*(1–2), 28–39.

Toseland, R. W., & Rivas, R. F. (2008). *An introduction to group work practice* (6th ed.). Boston: Allyn and Bacon.

Trotter, C. (1999). *Working with involuntary clients: A guide to practice.* London: Sage.

Tubbs, C. Y., & Williams, O. J. (2007). Shared parenting after abuse: Battered mothers' perspectives on parenting after dissolution of a relationship. In J. L. Edleson & O. J. Williams (Eds.), *Parenting by men who batter: New directions for assessment and intervention* (pp. 19–44). New York: Oxford University Press.

Umbreit, M. S., Vos, B., Coates, R. B., & Lightfoot, E. (2006). Restorative justice in the twenty-first century: A social movement full of opportunities and pitfalls. *Marquette Law Review,* 253–304. Retrieved August 6, 2009, from http://law.marquette.edu/s3/site/images/restorative/lawreviews/Umbreit.pdf

United Nations, General Assembly. (1948, December 10). *Universal declaration on human rights.* Retrieved June 30, 2009, from http://www.un.org/en/documents/udhr/

United Nations, General Assembly. (1979, December 18). *Convention on the elimination of all forms of discrimination against women.* Geneva, Switzerland: 85th Plenary Meeting. Retrieved June 30, 2009, from http://www.un.org/womenwatch/daw/cedaw/text/econvention.htm

United Nations, General Assembly. (1993, December 20). *Declaration on the elimination of violence against women.* Geneva, Switzerland: 85th Plenary Meeting. Retrieved June 30, 2009, from http://www.un.org/documents/ga/res/48/a48r104.htm

United Nations, General Assembly. (2007, September 13). *Declaration on the rights of indigenous peoples.* Geneva, Switzerland: 107th Plenary Meeting. Retrieved June 30, 2009, from http://www.un.org/esa/socdev/unpfii/documents/DRIPS_en.pdf

United Nations, Office of the High Commissioner for Human Rights. (1989). *Convention on the rights of the child.* Retrieved December 9, 2008, from http://www2.ohchr.org/english/law/crc.htm

Valverde, M. (1991). *The age of light, soap, and water: Moral reform in English Canada 1885–1925.* Toronto: McClelland and Stewart.

Waites, C., Macgowan, M. J., Pennell, J., Carlton-LaNey, I., & Weil, M. (2004). Increasing the cultural responsiveness of family group conferencing. *Social Work, 49*(2), 291–300.

Woolman, J. (1961). *The journal of John Woolman and A plea for the poor* [John Greenleaf Whittier Edition Text]. Secaucus, NJ: Citadel Press. (Original work published 1774)

Zehr, H. (2002). *The little book of restorative justice.* Intercourse, PA: Good Books.

Zinn, M. B., & Dill, B. T. (1996). Theorizing difference from multiracial feminism. *Feminist Studies, 22,* 321–331.

Chapter Ten

Coming Together After Violence: Social Work and Restorative Practices

NANCY J. GOOD AND DAVID L. GUSTAFSON

"The ultimate weakness of violence is that it is a descending spiral begetting the very thing it seeks to destroy. Instead of diminishing evil, it multiplies it. You may murder the liar, but you cannot murder the lie, nor establish the truth. You may murder the hater, but you do not murder hate, nor establish love. Returning violence for violence multiplies the violence, adding deeper darkness to a night already devoid of stars. Darkness cannot drive out darkness. Only light can do that. Hate cannot drive out hate; only love can do that."
—Martin Luther King, Jr., WHERE DO WE GO FROM HERE? CHAOS OR COMMUNITY

Social work and restorative justice are professions that grew out of an organized impulse to help those in need. This chapter deals with responding to the needs of victims, offenders, and communities in the wake of severe violence. We will consider the worst and best of human conduct. The worst is understood as people treating each other in hateful, destructive ways that impact individuals, families, and communities for a lifetime, perhaps for generations. The best includes people who have suffered great harm, yet strive to find ways to transcend and transform their pain and harm by taking emotional risks to heal and restore their capacity to trust, find safety and autonomy, build or rebuild relationships, and find a degree of well-being. Our shared goal is to support healing responses to violence.

In this chapter, we consider a question we have confronted as practitioners: What does healing justice require when a community member commits intra-family murder? We draw wisdom from a case study involving such a murder, and offer practical tools and strategies for best practices for social work and restorative justice responses in the aftermath of severe violence. The events took place in British Columbia, Canada; Fraser Region Community Justice Initiatives Association (FRCJIA) guided the restorative justice response, with Dave Gustafson and Sandi Bergen as co-facilitators.

Chapters 3 and 4 of this book include an overview of applications of restorative justice in criminal justice, with an emphasis on the United States. Since our case study is located in British Columbia we provide a brief introduction to the influence of First Nations on restorative justice in Canada, and we place the practice model of FRCJIA in the context of victim–offender models in other countries. We also look at current scholarship on trauma, trauma healing, and cultural considerations—areas of knowledge we view as essential to competent practice in the arena of violence.

RESTORATIVE JUSTICE IN CANADA: AN OVERVIEW

Just as ideas now thought of as "restorative" were taking hold in Canada, a number of thinkers insisted that the new (and some would say newly rediscovered) alternative justice approaches needed to be guided by premises quite different from the prevailing and limited suppositions in Western contemporary justice systems. The seasoned Canadian prosecutor, author, and educator, Rupert Ross, spoke of being taught patiently by his First Nations guides to view crimes as a disruption of relations (Ross, 1996). He acknowledged puzzling over much of what he was witnessing en route to his own redefinition of crime as something beyond an act that constituted a violation of a criminal code. His new and more adequate definition encompasses an understanding of crime as harms suffered, harms that affect people's relationships not only to one another but also to their surroundings and all of the in-between relationships *within* those surroundings (Ross, 1996). Seeing through a relational lens challenges us to examine how we see our clients and their presenting problems and, equally important, *ourselves* as the professionals working with them. Relational themes suggest that in many communities (and certainly in Canadian First Nations ones) a humble, respectful, teachable spirit is more likely to be welcomed and better equipped to practice than a professional without these understandings, no matter how impressive his or her credentials might be.

Victim–Offender Mediation Program (VOMP) at FRCJIA

FRCJIA is a community-based nonprofit organization located in Langley, British Columbia. From the agency's opening in 1982, staff members have embraced a vocation that focuses on harms done to persons and relationships, beyond the more common definitions of crime and justice based in violations of law codes. The Victim–Offender Mediation Program (VOMP) began in 1990, following the findings of a study conducted in the late 1980s, which found that a number of victims and convicted offenders wanted to engage in therapeutic dialogue in a safe setting with a skilled facilitator (Gustafson, 2005). Initially VOMP covered British Columbia and the Yukon Territory; in 2004, the program was implemented throughout Canada. Beyond the healing of individuals, VOMP attempts to address systemic structures in need of challenge by demonstrating better and more healing ways of responding to violent crime.

VOMP stretches understandings of many existing restorative justice models for a number of reasons. It is a post-incarceration victim–offender mediation model dealing with the most serious crimes in the Canadian Criminal Code at a national level. It is a program designed to be a therapeutic intervention and it deals with a plethora of trauma and treatment issues not normally encountered within the purview of either social work or restorative justice program interventions. The supportive relationships formed with program participants (both victims and offenders) extend, in many cases, over a long duration and in a number of directions that participants experience and describe as "deeply healing." It is a program requirement that at least one member of each co-facilitator team be professionally credentialed and experienced in working with highly traumatized victims or offenders with known mental and personality disorders. Dialogue facilitators and practitioner teams at VOMP are encouraged to continue relationships with participants beyond the time required for monitoring of restitution and reporting to the referring authorities, as part of the on-going "healing" and support processes. Finally, this model accepts cases in which all offender participants have been sentenced to prison terms ranging from two years to Life-25 (i.e., the individual must serve 25 years in prison before reaching eligibility for parole).

In a paper comparing Canadian, American, and South African programs, Sharpe and Lai Thom (2007) found fewer than a score of jurisdictions, internationally, where similar models have been used. They underscore (as do a number of others, below), two things: 1) the imperative of modeling programs on best practices; and 2) how difficult it is, given how little substantive literature exists, to discover just what practices actually qualify as "best."

The question of best practice in restorative justice is particularly important in cases of violent or otherwise serious crime. Yet there is relatively little experience to draw on in assessing what constitutes best practice for people in those circumstances.

In North America, restorative justice has been used in relation to serious crime for many years, although very cautiously and far less often than in other kinds of cases. While there are programs doing such work in Canada and in at least thirteen U.S. states, many of those programs have dealt with only a handful of cases per year. The situation is different in South Africa, where the use of restorative justice is much newer in cases of serious crime, but has been embraced more quickly (which may offer practitioners more opportunities to learn by observing what works under a variety of circumstances). In all three countries, evaluations of this application of restorative justice have found high rates of success, an indicator of sound practice (Sharpe & Lai Thom, 2007).

VIOLENCE, TRAUMA, AND TRAUMA HEALING

Traumatization after violence produces devastating changes, so that a person's life can never just go back to the way things used to be (Frankl, 1986; Good Sider, 2006;

Hart, 2006; Van der Kolk & McFarlane, 1996). This shift highlights the necessity for practitioners in social work and restorative justice to be knowledgeable about the effects and process of trauma and trauma healing before participating in restorative practices. Further, practitioners need to take steps to offset vicarious trauma, develop resilience, and model effective self-care.

What Is Trauma?

Trauma is commonly defined as an intense feeling of helplessness and powerlessness in the face of an overwhelming threat to one's life, security, or sense of self (Herman, 1997; van der Kolk, 1987; Yoder, 2005). One's coping skills and normal response to threatening situations are interrupted when trauma occurs. Trauma alters people's perceptions and beliefs, challenging previously held notions of safety, fairness, and moral meaning (Beck, Britto, & Andrews, 2007). Traumatized individuals often feel isolated, stigmatized, and unable to connect with others (Beck, Blackwell, Leonard, & Mears, 2003; Herman, 1997; van der Kolk, 1987; Yoder, 2005).

While ordinary stress is commonly defined as the strain we experience when our coping abilities are challenged, *traumatic stress* is a surprising occurrence of piercing intensity that is outside the range of usual human experience and frightening to almost anyone (Bartsch & Bartsch, 1997). Table 10.1 illustrates the difference between ordinary stress and traumatic stress.

Traumatic stress is a psychological injury, and trauma wounds live on many levels: the social, physical, spiritual, mental, behavioral, and economic (Rothschild, 2000; van der Kolk & McFarlane, 1996; Yoder, 2005). According to Herman (1997), "Traumatic events produce profound and lasting changes in physiological arousal, emotion, cognition, and memory" (p. 34). When an individual experiences a traumatic event, the brain's limbic system, which controls emotion, and the brain stem, which governs instinct, override the cerebral cortex, the rational part of the brain. Stress hormones are released and the fight-or-flight response is triggered (Yoder, 2005). Severe trauma can disrupt the link between cognition

Table 10.1 Comparison of Stress

Ordinary Stress	Traumatic Stress
Gradual	Sudden
Wears one down, like a cloth rubbed for a long time	Piercing intensity, like a thin cloth sliced by a knife
Accumulates over time	Sudden events that have long-term effects
People are affected differently	Frightens almost everyone

and emotion, leading to a continued state of hyperarousal (Chefetz, 2006). Rational thinking and self-reflection are impaired, causing the trauma to be reexperienced whenever a sight, sound, or smell reminds the individual of the traumatic situation (van der Kolk, 1987; Yoder, 2005). Phases of physiological hyperarousal and traumatic reexperiencing are followed by phases of psychic numbing and avoidance (van der Kolk, 1994). In an effort to prevent the vivid flashbacks or memories of the trauma, the individual may withdraw from social interactions, avoiding emotional attachments at a time when social support is most needed (Chefetz, 2006; van der Kolk, 1987; Yoder, 2005). This response helps explain the dilemma that Judith Herman (1997) describes: "The conflict between the will to deny horrible events and the will to proclaim them aloud is the central dialectic of psychological trauma" (p. 1).

Trauma Caused by Murder

Homicide in particular has certain elements that place survivors at a higher risk of experiencing trauma (Bucholz, 2002; Rando, 1993). Murder is viewed as the result of malicious intent and deviance from social and moral norms, whereas accidental sudden death is seen as an uncontrollable misfortune (Michalowski, 1978 as cited in Rando, 1993). Knowing that the last moments of the victim's life likely involved unimaginable terror, pain, and powerlessness brings additional distress to the survivors of homicide victims (Rynearson, Correa, Favell, Saindon, & Prigerson, 2006). The violence, unpredictability, and malicious intent of the homicide, which survivors must confront in addition to their grief, can lead to overwhelming feelings of fear, anger, injustice, and helplessness, culminating in traumatization (Bucholz, 2002; Rando, 1993). Offenders and their families are traumatized by the murder, as well, but their suffering is rarely acknowledged and little support is offered (Beck et al., 2003; Beck et al., 2007; Maruna, 2004). Finally, the community is impacted by the shock, outrage, and loss of security following a homicide (Herman, 1997; Toews, 2006).

Impact of Trauma on Homicide Survivors

Homicide survivors must cope with nightmares, vivid reimagining of their loved one's death, and intense rage, fear, and grief brought on by the sudden shock of their loss (Bucholz, 2002; Herman, 1997; Yoder, 2005). Survivors' belief systems are often shattered by the senselessness and violence of murder (Bucholz, 2002; Dignan, 2005). Throughout the initial period of shock and grief following a homicide, survivors must also deal with police investigators, the medical examiner, and often, the media, adding stress to an already overwhelming situation (Rynearson et al., 2006).

Three important judicial needs of homicide survivors are the needs for information surrounding the homicide, for justice, and for validation of their loss (Bucholz, 2002; Yoder, 2005). When those needs are not sufficiently met, as is often the case, feelings of powerlessness and victimization result, compounding the trauma (Bucholz, 2002; Herman, 1997). All of these stressors can lead to post-traumatic stress disorder (PTSD), a diagnosis commonly given when trauma symptoms (hyperarousal, emotional constriction, anxiety) continue for more than a month (van der Kolk, 1997; Yoder, 2005). Whether or not a survivor is diagnosed with PTSD, symptoms ranging from panic attacks to insomnia are common following the murder of a loved one. Victims report feeling like they are "going crazy" as their minds and bodies try to absorb and process the trauma (Dignan, 2005; van der Kolk, 1997; Yoder, 2005).

Impact of Trauma on Offenders
The impact of trauma on offenders is often overlooked. The trauma experienced by offenders can be both a cause and an effect of their perpetration of a murder. Many offenders have also been victims, experiencing trauma throughout their lives (MacNair, 2002). However, trauma can also result from participating in homicide. This type of trauma is known as perpetration or participation-induced traumatic stress, and it can be just as severe as the trauma experienced by victims (MacNair, 2002; Yoder, 2005). Lieutenant colonel and psychologist David Grossman found that humans are psychologically wired to resist killing, and to do so leads to psychiatric casualties (Grossman, 1995). The trauma of taking a life, whether the act was accidental or intentional, can lead to the development of PTSD in offenders (MacNair, 2002). Damaged family and community relationships, the stresses of prison life, and, for some offenders, the stress and fear of the death penalty, can prolong the effects of trauma for offenders (Beck et al., 2007; MacNair, 2002; Yoder, 2005).

Offenders' families also experience significant trauma as they attempt to come to terms with the crime committed by their family member, the grief another family is experiencing as a result, and their own grief at the incarceration, or potential execution of their loved one (Beck et al., 2007).

Impact of Trauma on Communities
When a homicide occurs within a community, or is perpetrated by a community member, the community as a whole is affected and its sense of security is threatened (Toews, 2006; Yoder, 2005; Zehr, 2002). Individuals become hypervigilant, ensuring doors are locked and alarms are set. Community members might also become suspicious of others in the community (Toews, 2006). Secondary, or vicarious, trauma can occur when community members hear stories or see media reports depicting the homicide (Yoder, 2005). Community members who are deeply affected by the violence, particularly those who may have witnessed the homicide firsthand, might experience numbness, anger, memory loss, sadness, and shame. It is not unusual for communities traumatized by violence to experience increased violent crime and aggression.

Healing Trauma

Herman (1997) outlines three stages of trauma recovery: establishing safety, mourning and remembering, and reconnecting with ordinary life. For victims to begin healing from the trauma, they must first reestablish a sense of safety (Herman, 1997; Yoder, 2005). Retelling the story of a loved one's death, and the life and memories shared prior to the death, can assist victims in the process of reclaiming safety, and help them redefine themselves in the aftermath of the trauma (Rynearson, 2001; Yoder, 2005). This restorative re-telling builds resilience by reconnecting the bereaved with memories of the deceased, and eliminating the sense of separateness that can prolong traumatic grief (Rynearson, 2001). Reconstructing the narrative of the traumatic incident allows victims to own the story, to testify to the truth of what happened, and to reclaim control over their lives (Herman, 1997). As Good Sider (2001) puts it, "In order to forget, we [trauma survivors] need to remember," (p. 11) and the survivor who wants to recover needs to engage with the trauma story in order to develop a transformative narrative (Good Sider, 2001; 2004).

In a study of victims who survived violence, all the participants spoke about the difficult step of separating the traumatic violence from their own identity. It is a step toward moving from victim to victim–survivor when a victim is able to accept the fact that they were victimized, but refuse to remain a victim. The next step is to claim a survivor identity that transcends the trauma. Yolanda Blacklock, a participant in the FRCJIA Victim–Offender Mediation Program, described her movement from victim to survivor in her poem, "Transforming Trauma:"

I long to dance again
to stretch out twirling,
flying on
the wings of inspiration
to be
connecting with my heart song
overflowing with joy
entrenched in laughter
bubbling up from the deepest place
of pain transformed to peace!

I did not die!
What was meant
to destroy
has shaped, rocked, moved me
into a deeper sense of why
life is dancing
juggling demons and delights
into a whirling worth living for!

Armour (2006) identifies a process of meaning-making as another way to help survivors heal the trauma of violent death. Meaning making consists of three actions: "(1) declarations of truth; (2) fighting for what is right; (3) and living in ways that give purpose to the loved one's death" (p. 101). This process honors the life of the deceased and gives new meaning to the life of the bereaved, helping them cope with their grief.

Healing Processes

For some victim–survivors of homicide, therapeutic support groups may provide a forum for remembering and mourning the deceased (Herman, 1997). Groups offer social support and can help survivors normalize their emotions and other symptoms of trauma (Rynearson et al., 2006). As victims are able to validate their experiences and make meaning of their loss, they regain a sense of empowerment, which can open the door to forgiveness (Gustafson, 2005; Toews, 2006). While not necessary for trauma recovery, forgiveness is reported to have a powerful impact on both victims' and offenders' healing (Gustafson, 2005; Toews, 2006). Victim–Offender Mediation (VOM) is one path to forgiveness, affording the victims and offenders an opportunity to share stories, express emotions, and ask questions (Dignan, 2005; Gustafson, 2005; Umbreit, 2001). The dialogue between victims and offenders can occur face-to-face or through videotapes, letters, or a mediator. VOM is a common restorative justice practice in the U.S., but it takes time, and all parties involved must voluntarily choose to participate (Gustafson, 2005; Toews, 2006). The act of choosing whether, when, and how to participate in VOM is empowering for victims, offering them a degree of control generally not afforded by the criminal justice system (Dignan, 2005; Toews, 2006).

Offenders begin to heal their trauma through acceptance of their actions. Offenders need safety and relationships with others to take accountability for harms they have caused, and to acknowledge harms they have suffered (Maruna, 2005; Toews, 2006). In telling their stories and sharing their feelings, offenders develop a greater understanding of the effect of the crime on themselves. An important step in healing their trauma comes when offenders play a role in deciding how they should repair the harms they caused (Toews, 2006). Support and guidance from restorative justice practitioners and community members are needed to help create a sense of safety in a prison setting and to connect offenders with their community (Toews, 2006).

Communities also must reestablish safety in order to heal trauma (Toews, 2006; Yoder, 2005). In the wake of trauma and the insecurity it brings, communities risk dehumanizing offenders, which can increase feelings of anger, aggression, and a desire for vengeance, by creating negative, "good-vs.-evil" narratives that strip offenders of any redeeming qualities (Weingarten, 2003; Yoder, 2005). In this way, communities perpetuate trauma, rather than promote healing. When communities engage in compassionate witnessing, acknowledging the trauma while seeing both victim and offender as whole human beings who deserve to be cared for and treated with dignity, transformation and healing can take place (Weingarten, 2003).

Unhealed Trauma

Psychiatrist James Gilligan, who has studied the origins of violence, sees a link between unhealed trauma and violence. He asserts that "[m]uch of the violence that plagues humanity is a direct or indirect result of unresolved trauma that is acted out in repeated unsuccessful attempts to re-establish a sense of empowerment" (Gilligan, 2001). Trauma that is not healed may be transferred, perhaps outwardly as violence to others, or inwardly as destructive acts toward oneself. Summerfield, van Wormer, and Zehr join Gilligan in calling for a radical paradigm shift, where it is asserted that responding to violence with violence creates additional layers of harm. These leaders have urged professionals in criminal justice, restorative justice, and the helping professions to incorporate trauma healing as part of their efforts to support human rights and global social justice (Summerfield, 1995; van Wormer, 2001; van Wormer, 2004a; van Wormer, 2004b; Zehr, 2005).

CASE STUDY: HEALING AFTER LOSS[i]

Wisdom, as our First Nations friends insist, is often best conveyed in stories. This story took place over four years, with 15 months lapsing between the first referral and the face-to-face dialogue in June 2006 in a British Columbia city near the survivor's First Nations reserve (Gustafson, 2007).

> I've taken part in many Talking Circles, been a part of many Healing Circles in my life. I've never seen anything as powerful as this. There are so many wounded people in our communities, maybe this process could help heal some of those wounds, restore bruised and badly broken relationships in our communities. Maybe this type of "Healing Circle" is one of the ways Creator has in mind to help heal our families.

These words (as close to verbatim as I, Dave, can recall them) were spoken by an Aboriginal Elder present at the close of a Healing Circle that Sandi Bergen and I conducted in 2006 between the family survivors of a homicide and Colleen (not her real name), a woman serving a life sentence for the murder of her common-law partner, Aaron. Common factors that contribute to violence were involved at the time of the crime, including personal histories of trauma and drugs, alcohol, and other intoxicants. The triggering incident might have ended differently, without violence, except for the volatility of the mix.

Lorraine, who represented the family survivors, was Aaron's sister. Because of earlier conflicts in their family of origin, Lorraine and Aaron had been estranged for many years and had only recently reconnected. Lorraine had just begun to get to know him as her brother and to value their relationship when he was murdered. Lorraine's therapist, a credentialed professional woman and gentle Métis healer, supported Lorraine's contacting us to explore the possibility of our convening a Healing Circle.

From the beginning, Colleen felt a need to reach out to Lorraine and her family but was concerned that contact might revictimize them. After a number of years in prison and hard work in programs and on her own personal trauma, Colleen was fighting a cancer that could potentially end her life, and while she was incarcerated her father and two children had died in a house fire. Even so, she continued to hope and pray for an opportunity to provide some solace to Lorraine and her family, to apologize for the pain she caused, to attempt to establish peace between them by making herself vulnerable and accountable to them. Colleen prayed and sought the counsel of her Elder about a process she had heard about, facilitated by staff at a nonprofit agency that worked with prisoners and trauma survivors to enable healing conversations. The Elder advised Colleen to seek to be referred and to leave the process and outcomes in the hands of the Creator.

Lorraine also longed for such a meeting. No one else could answer the questions that continued to plague her and impede her progress in almost all aspects of her life. When the referral came to Sandi and me, supported by Colleen's Elder and the prison psychologist, we began to assess whether an adaptation of our Victim–Offender Mediation Program (VOMP) might prove helpful. In a number of meetings over a number of months, Sandi and I worked with Colleen, her Institutional Elder, Lorraine, and Lorraine's therapist to tailor a process informed by First Nations teachings. Colleen was to prepare a letter of apology that would be taken to Lorraine by Sandi and me, along with ceremonial tobacco over which Colleen had prayed for her victim and for acceptance of her initiative. Sandi and I consulted with the elders involved, to ensure that we understood how to offer the tobacco, how to discern whether Lorraine's response was to accept it or not, and how to convey Lorraine's message to Colleen.

We arranged to meet Lorraine and her therapist in an interior community in British Columbia, which was a four-hour drive over a high mountain highway from our own. The tobacco was offered and accepted. The ceremony needed no explanation. (Sandi and I, after all, were the only newcomers to this sacred rite.)

When Lorraine began to read Colleen's letter the dam burst: pent-up emotion, hurt, and pain poured forth. We sat with her, caring, but mute. Almost spent, Lorraine made it clear that among her emotions were gratitude and relief. She had long prayed that she would have an opportunity to meet face-to-face with Colleen, invite relatives to sit in Circle with them, and discuss Colleen's attitudes about her crime and the harms she had caused. Most importantly, Lorraine hoped to gather information from Colleen about her brother and learn things she'd not had the opportunity to discover because his life was cut short.

At our first meeting, Lorraine told us that out of compassion for Colleen she had attended the funeral of Colleen's father and two children and that she had worked up the courage to approach Colleen, who had been granted a compassionate temporary release under prison escort to attend the funeral. Without a word about her own loss, Lorraine, a young mother herself, approached Colleen and gave her three personalized sympathy cards, one for her father, and one for each of the children she had lost in the fire. As she passed her each card, Lorraine embraced Colleen as her sister, as another woman devastated by loss. Deeply touched, Colleen returned to prison that night resolved to turn her life around, to heal herself from all past trauma, and to seek to make amends. Almost a year from the time we met Colleen and her Elder, three correctional staff and the Institutional Elder accompanied Colleen to the appointed meeting place in the community. Lorraine's husband, two relatives, and Elders from her home community accompanied her. Following traditional prayers in separate places outdoors, we brought the two women into the room and seated them with us and Colleen's Elder on five chairs in the inner of two concentric circles. The others in attendance were seated in the outer circle. I opened the Circle, welcoming the participants and asking them to briefly introduce themselves, which they did. Beyond naming themselves, the people in the Circle described their lineage, establishing where they fit in the wider circle of relations. Following that circle, I asked Colleen and Lorraine to briefly share their hopes: what, if all went well, would we have accomplished by day's end? They spoke from the heart about their hopes and aspirations for each other and for themselves.

Our task was to facilitate dialogue about the past (their respective stories and the need for information about Aaron and each other), the present (their thoughts and feelings about the encounter as it unfolded), and the future (the possibility of further process, hopes, expectations, and intents).

The dialogue was powerful, the emotions deep, the interchanges many and punctuated by needed silences, befitting sacred space. As they spoke of their brief meeting at the funeral, we were deeply moved. Some quietly wept. Colleen took full responsibility for what she had done and the hurt she had caused all those in the circle and beyond. She asked for nothing. Lorraine rose from her chair, took Colleen's hands, and gently helped her to her feet. Then Lorraine moved to the outer circle and picked up a blanket spread on a chair that held a framed portrait of Aaron and the plate of food that would later be burned at his ceremonial sacred fire, together with all the tear-dampened tissues used that morning[ii].

Lorraine returned to the center of the circle, ceremonial blanket in hand. She gently wrapped it around both her shoulders and Colleen's, saying "I forgive you . . . we are sisters; I forgive you, we are members of one family." We prayed, quietly marveling at what we had witnessed. We next enjoyed a feast of traditional foods (salmon, bannock, greens, and local vegetables) that had been prepared for us before we reconvened for the circles of the afternoon. Breaking bread together ended a decade of division.

When we convened again after the meal, we opened the circle to the others present. As the talking piece went around, participants spoke to what they had seen. Profound things were shared. Lorraine's auntie and uncle spoke, addressing Colleen and telling her they had not judged her. "To judge you would be to judge ourselves," they said, and added, "Our grandsons are now in prison, also for murder, and the victims of their crime are still in terrible pain. . . . Maybe this Healing Circle is one way to help us heal our families."

Just then, Lorraine's niece arrived. "Auntie Lorraine phoned me," she said, "and asked me to come to sing a song for Colleen." Then she sang the Women's Warrior Song to honor the courage that brought them together.

In preparing this case study, I contacted Colleen, Lorraine, and Lorraine's therapist to ask their permission to use their stories. Lorraine's therapist wrote, "What stands out in my mind is, first, the profound welcoming and inclusion of love; the acceptance that 'this has happened and we've got to work with it.' . . . For 'Lorraine' [the outcome] was a lifting of hurt and heaviness and anguish about questions that were never answered—not through the trial process, and not since—until the women met (Derrick 2007)."

A few days later, Lorraine sent us her thoughts, eleven months after the meeting:

> Forgiving the woman who murdered my brother and having the gift of speaking to her in person was a form of healing. The sacred day was meant to happen exactly the way it did take place with honesty, truth, and respect from each of us. I knew . . . where my brother was murdered, and had heard a lot of stories. I had a lot of "what ifs and if onlys" and wished I could turn time back; then I got to the point in my life that what was important for me was to hear Colleen's side of the story. I wanted to know if she remembered and what she remembered of the incident. I needed closure. . . . I wanted Colleen to know what this murder had done to me and how much I hurt for my brother to have been stabbed 35 times. This all happened on that special day and I give thanks again to all of the people who shared with me. . . . This day provided me with serenity and more strength to live a healthy life. This day allowed me to let go of my brother Aaron and to send him home to heaven to be with our mom. I believed I had to give my brother permission to carry on his journey to the spirit world and this day provided me with that opportunity.
>
> The Circle . . . was beneficial and healing for all involved. I will continue to pray and someday offer the tobacco I received from Colleen as an offering to strengthen our healing journeys. I dream of another Circle to give thanks to all those who cared to come and support me.

I mailed a draft to Colleen, for her approval. She called from the First Nations treatment center where she was working on further healing and growth, to say:

> You not only have my permission to print this, I'd like you to add that I completely agree with the Elder: so much could be done for so many of our people using this approach.

If possible, as soon as possible, let's convene further circles to share what Lorraine and I experienced. Perhaps the grandsons and their victims would meet with us, in time, to hear of our experience. Perhaps we can open a door to others, so they can walk through it toward part of their own healing journey.

Over the years, staff members of our agency have sought to increase our involvements in First Nations Communities, with Aboriginal and Métis prisoners, and with their elders and chiefs. Like many, we are concerned about the disproportionate representation of people of First Nations ancestry in Canadian prisons. Credibility as White service providers in these communities can be difficult to achieve. We are deeply grateful for the increased trust and collaboration we have experienced with First Nations participants, elders, and community members.

EPILOGUE

This case culminated in a parole hearing conducted on Colleen's reserve, prefaced by a washing and claiming ceremony that many were invited to witness. Invitations were extended to us and to Lorraine and others of her family, including the Elders who participated in the Healing Circle we conducted a few months earlier. National Parole Board Members and staff members, along with staff members of the Correctional Service of Canada were invited. During the ceremony, Colleen was claimed by the Nation as one of their own. The Elder leading the ceremony asked Colleen to choose whom she wanted to receive the two ceremonial blankets she had to give away. She offered one to the Elder, and he accepted.

"And the other?" he asked.

"Lorraine," she said, "I want to give the other blanket to Lorraine." Hearing her name, Lorraine made her way across the dirt floor of the longhouse, to the center of the gathering. Colleen, who hadn't known Lorraine was present, gently offered the blanket to her. Lorraine accepted it, smiled, and mouthed "Thank you" as she turned and went back to her seat.

Later, as part of Colleen's parole hearing, Lorraine's victim impact statement included her testimony concerning the power of the Healing Circle process. She described changes she had witnessed in Colleen over the duration of their involvements, making it clear that she was there to support and argue for Colleen's release. The parole board members thanked Lorraine for her submission, but reminded the gathering that their primary concern was public safety; that is, whether Colleen could be safely managed in the community. They adjourned to deliberate. They decided Colleen had gone far beyond what was required of her by her correctional treatment plan (demonstrating victim empathy and genuine remorse). She had made what amends she could from within the confines of prison and had, through the Healing Circle and its processes, made herself accountable to the victim and the victim's community. The Parole Board was prepared to believe she could be safely managed in the community. "Parole Granted."

Over a year later, I was asked to help resource a Provincial Aboriginal Justice Conference in Vancouver. Since I don't consider myself an expert on First Nations Issues, I asked if I might invite Lorraine, Colleen, and Colleen's Elder to tell their stories of the Healing Circle and its outcomes. The organizers decide to end the conference with the women's stories, a time for responses, and a Closing Circle as the capstone. The conference attendees at the banquet the night before would not have guessed Lorraine and Colleen's history, as they watched them share dessert, eating from one plate and laughing together. The enmity is ended, and new possibilities emerge. The healing one achieves helps the healing of the other. They continue to communicate through our office and to support one another as members of one race, of one family, as sisters.

Additional Healing Circles are in process.

BUILDING SKILLS FOR VICTIM–OFFENDER DIALOGUE IN CASES OF SEVERE VIOLENCE

More than 500 cases to date have been referred to the Fraser Region Community Justice Initiatives Association's (FRCJIA) serious crime program since its 1990 genesis. The number of cases corresponds with the number of offenders referred; the number of individuals served is significantly greater and includes victims, family survivors of homicides, and other extended family victims. (In one murder case, for example, we provided "significant service" to an extended family of 23; and, in another, we helped over 30 community members who were traumatized by the murder of a student in their normally peaceful rural high school.) The fear in these communities at the prospect of the offenders' release from prison and possible return to the community cannot be overestimated. Yet, as this case study demonstrates, meaningful redress, the rebuilding of relationships, and outcomes participants describe as "deeply healing" can occur even in contexts as grave as these.

Preparation Phase

The healing work of restorative justice is designed and refined over time, according to the needs of participants, the resources of the community, and the skills and knowledge of the facilitators.

Establishing a Community Network and Referral Base

The case study makes it clear that before a client ever reaches out for assistance, it is necessary to establish a network and referral base in the community. The Victim–Offender Mediation Program (VOMP) receives referrals from victims, victim–survivors, therapists, victim service agencies, and prison staff persons who refer offenders, sometimes doing so because of their awareness of victim needs that could potentially be addressed through the process (Gustafson, 2005). Through efforts that support their reputation as respectful, compassionate, competent, and effective facilitators, VOMP continues to build a community-wide referral system. This, in turn, aids facilitators in earning the trust of the participants and their communities. We have learned that in building networks and earning referrals, a good reputation is more important than a flashy brochure, a fancy website, or an impressive fee structure.

Building a Trusting Relationship with Participants

Every contact with participants in restorative justice processes is critical, whether it is a phone call or a face-to-face meeting. VOMP strongly agrees with Judith Herman's (1997) assertion that "[n]o intervention that takes power away from the survivor can possibly foster her recovery" (p. 133) and in every case and at every stage, the emphasis is on providing safety, respect, and empowerment.

Facilitators hold a series of separate sessions over time with the victim and offender. VOMP staff use written correspondence or phone calls to set up preliminary meetings, inviting the potential participant to meet with us to explore whether VOMP is a resource that might address some of their ongoing needs. At that initial meeting, VOMP staff list and discuss a number of process options, including correspondence, videotaped interviews, provision of information (usually by the prisoner, and always with informed consent and signed releases), videotaped responses to lists of questions, and video or DVD exchanges. They make clear to victims that they will honor their choices at every point—whether to proceed at all, their choice of process options, the pacing of the process, the time required between each of the steps, and whether to proceed to a dialogue when the time seems right. Whatever their decisions might be, VOMP staff will support them.

For facilitators to create a space where trust can grow, they must provide safety, structure, honesty, and respect for all participants. In the aftermath of violence, victims often experience considerable cognitive confusion. Facilitators should expect to repeat the explanation of their role and anticipate that participants may test the guidelines to learn if their wishes and needs will, indeed, be followed.

It is important for facilitators to share the conviction that the harmful acts of the offender were destructive, wrong, against the law, and that they caused irreconcilable pain and must never happen again. The great skill of a restorative justice facilitator is the capacity to face the violence the offender committed and the harm it caused the victim and others, while remaining concerned about the physical, emotional, and spiritual well-being of all the participants in the restorative process.

How Do We Know When Clients are Ready for a Facilitated Dialogue?

A series of separate preparatory meetings with the victim, offender, and their supporters may lead to a joint restorative dialogue, with all participants present or (as happened with Lorraine and Colleen) several joint meetings. Each meeting can be prefaced by an exchange of letters or videotapes. We, the authors, would not suggest to trauma survivors that restorative dialogue is a necessity or a prerequisite to healing, but many participants have asserted that without their face-to-face facilitated dialogues, the degree of healing and recovery they experienced would never have occurred.

If and when the joint meeting happens, it must happen when victim and offender are ready; there is no proscribed timetable. Drawing from their experiences over decades, VOMP staff have developed a series of questions to help plan for a restorative dialogue, if that is the choice of both victim and offender. The list of questions, called "Criteria for Assessing Participant Readiness to Proceed to a Facilitated Dialogue in Serious & Violent Crime" (Gustafson & Bergen, 2009) is presented in Table 10.2. As with any checklist, these points are merely a tool to help facilitators and participants prepare adequately and choose whether to go forward with a face-to-face facilitated dialogue. Further, it is important to remember that VOMP is a therapeutic model that differs from the other models of Victim–Offender Dialogue used around the world in less serious crimes.

Table 10.2 Criteria for Assessing Participant Readiness for a Facilitated Dialogue in Serious and Violent Crime

For Both (or all) Participants:

What are the specific issues for each that must be addressed?

Is there relative certainty that a face-to-face meeting and dialogue will, at the very least, do no further harm?

Is positive benefit for both parties a likelihood?

What are the psychological/emotional strengths of each of the participants?

Is there sufficient self-awareness, or has self-awareness increased through the steps of the preparation for the process?

Do avoidance tendencies continue unabated or have these decreased?

Are support systems in place for each participant?

Is there a sense of openness or receptivity to each other and to what the other might have to say?

Is there a realistic sense of common ground between the participants that might prove helpful in facilitating beneficial dialogue?

Is there clear and reliable evidence of participant's trust in the facilitator? In the process? In themselves as capable of participating meaningfully and respectfully?

(Continued)

Table 10.2 Criteria for Assessing Participant Readiness for a Facilitated Dialogue in Serious and Violent Crime (cont'd)

For the "Offender"

Is there evidence of authentic victim empathy?

Is there evidence of social awareness/responsibility?

Is there evidence of authentic remorse?

What evidence exists (from files, practitioner interviews, and consultation with others) that this particular offender can participate in ways that the victim seeks and are likely to be mutually beneficial?

For the "Victim"

Is the victim sufficiently prepared to lay down any need to be avenged? Does it appear that they will be able to participate according to at least basic restorative values and principles?

Is there evidence that the victim has given up any need to 'demonize' the offender and is willing to at least accept that they, too, troubled as they might be, are human?

Is the victim prepared to be somewhat flexible and creative in terms of what symbolic and practical suggestions might be made or negotiated as attempts at amends or "making things right" to the greatest possible degree?

Process Guidelines

In Victim–Offender Dialogues, facilitators collaborate creatively with victims, offenders, and their supporters to reach a healing outcome that supports the well-being of all participants. During the preparation process, issues pertaining to honest communication, listening skills, and respectful interaction are addressed, and the concept of "do no harm" is agreed upon by all participants. This process allows participants to practice new ways of being with themselves and with other people.

In meetings or other forms of communication between victims and offenders, the facilitator is guided by questions that address the victim's need to move toward healing, and how the offender can respond to those needs. Part of the preparation process involves discussion of participants' wishes concerning who should speak first. Often, the victim chooses to speak first and tells his or her story. However, especially in prison-initiated referrals, the victim often wants the offender to speak first, in answer to the question, "What motivated you to participate in this process with me?" In either case, the offender has an opportunity to respond, take responsibility for the harm he or she caused, make apology, and offer to make amends to the extent possible for an incarcerated person. In some cases, the making of amends meaningful to the victim(s) continues well after the offender's release.

There is no script for Victim–Offender Dialogue, which is guided by values of respect, humility, honesty, compassion, and transformation. The role of the facilitator is to support both the victim's efforts to regain safety, autonomy, and relatedness (Gustafson, 2005) and the offender's capacity to respond to those needs.

Trauma survivors participating in VOMP frequently express the need for the offender to take responsibility for the injuries they have inflicted and offer a meaningful apology. Conversely, offender participants express the need to convey their remorse and offer apology. They usually do not ask for forgiveness, recognizing that to do so puts unreasonable onus on their victims. However, often (and often to their astonishment) forgiveness flows, sometimes in almost immediate response to what is perceived as sincere apology, and sometimes, after a period of consideration, or following the offender's keeping commitments made, or in a subsequent meeting. It is difficult to find the words, the tone, and a forum to convey such deep feelings, feelings which are in some ways beyond words. But when the elements of genuine remorse and apology are present, the words have power. As in the case study, VOMP facilitators, with the help of tribal elders, simply built the bridge that enabled Colleen prepare to speak authentically to Lorraine, which gave Lorraine the opportunity to hear Colleen's heartfelt remorse and sincere apology, expressed in writing and person, and to decide how to respond.

Facilitator Skills

Facilitators of restorative dialogue must be thoroughly trained in restorative justice theory and practices, with advanced training in Victim–Offender Dialogue. Decades of experience and data coming from VOMP indicate that facilitators of restorative practices, especially when working in the arena of violent crime, must be versed in trauma and its impacts (Gustafson, 2005).

VOMP facilitators work in pairs (usually one male, one female), and at least one of the pair possesses a thorough grounding in trauma and the post-traumatic syndromes. Safety is paramount in trauma healing, and VOMP participants are clear that they find comfort in knowing that at least one member of the facilitator team has these credentials. Further, participants value the ethic of care that both facilitators provide and their willingness to form strong relational bonds, as well as the knowledge and experience facilitators have in working with trauma survivors and offenders (Gustafson, 2005).

Facilitators need skills and knowledge regarding the rules, regulations, and customs that affect their work. For example, facilitators at VOMP are familiar with the laws that control victim–offender contact, prison regulations, and cultural traditions. Further, they have a thorough understanding of the processes of restitution, victim impact statements, parole, and reentry. The ability of facilitators to navigate the criminal justice and prison systems can be particularly reassuring and empowering to survivors of homicide, who likely experienced criminal justice proceedings as passive onlookers.

THE FIT BETWEEN SOCIAL WORK AND RESTORATIVE JUSTICE

Is there a fit between social work and restorative justice initiatives and interventions when working with crimes involving severe violence? Where does congruence between these disciplines appear clear or likely when responding to violent crime, and where, if at all, are they at odds?

Definitions and Goals

Among the many definitions of social work, this one is particularly useful in assessing congruence between it and restorative justice processes:

> *Social Work is the professional activity of helping individuals, groups, or communities enhance or restore their capacity for social functioning and creating societal conditions favorable to this goal. Social Work practice consists of the professional application of Social Work values, principles, and techniques to one or more of the following ends: helping people obtain tangible services; counseling and psychotherapy with individuals, families, and groups; helping communities or groups provide or improve processes. The practice of Social Work requires knowledge of human development and behavior; of social, economic, and cultural institutions; and of the interactions of all these factors. (Wright University School of Social Work, http://www.cola.wright.edu/Dept/social_ work/sw_definition.htm).*

The same website identifies three major goals of social work:

- to enhance the problem-solving, coping and developmental capacities of people;
- to promote the effective and humane operation of the systems that provide people with resources and services;
- to link people with systems that provide them with resources, services, and opportunities. (Wright State University School of Social Work, http://www.cola.wright.edu/Dept/social_work/sw_definition.htm)

These descriptions of social work highlight areas where the goals of restorative justice and social work intersect. The mission statement below articulates the shared goals of restorative justice and social work as we authors see them:

> *We seek to alleviate distress in the aftermath of trauma, especially shame, humiliation, and degradation;*
> *We accompany those who choose to journey with us, assisting them to build upon their own strengths additional pathways toward the recovery (or achievement) of healing, well-being, dignity, hope and healthy pride by linking them with resources, opportunities and institutions;*

> *Beyond our commitment to each individual, we endeavor to encourage systemic change that contributes to the prevention of new harms and supports healing interventions where harms have occurred.*
> —Good and Gustafson

Shared Perspectives

Over the last decade, the fields of social work and psychology slowly have expanded their focus on pathology to include strength-based approaches that support resilience, health, and growth. Dennis Saleebey (2008) noted that social workers might learn a great deal from looking more closely at those clients who not only survive trauma, but in many cases learn to flourish in the aftermath of illness, violence, and abuse. Empowerment, Saleebey argued, is not something that caregivers provide to people, and attempts to empower others are based on the fallacy that they are not powerful. Therefore, empowerment approaches must support people discovering and developing their own strengths and power.

Attention to Strengths

Violence and its effects impose a spiral of terrible suffering—a problem—on victims (and offenders) and their communities of support. Social workers and restorative justice practitioners recognize that this problem, though great, does not constitute the entirety of the client's life, and every person is more than his or her problem(s). Especially when working with victims of severe violence, the helping professions need to provide a both/and approach that understands the problem *and* focuses on strengths to support the trauma healing process. We believe that training in social work and restorative justice must reflect the both/and approach. This is especially true for those who intend to work with survivors of violent crime.

Work Toward Transformation

Working from strength-based healing and empowerment approaches, rather than pathologizing ones, is our common approach. In our work we employ a wide spectrum of interventions in hopes of accomplishing those goals, including interventions drawn from psychology, victimology, criminology, social work, and restorative justice modalities. Dialogues, conferencing, or Healing Circles (like the one in our case study) are only part of a spectrum of interventions.

Theodore Zeldin (2000), the Oxford scholar and thinker, advocates that participants in dialogue take risks and be active and willing to recognize and incorporate useful new ideas: "[C]onversation is a meeting of minds with different memories and habits. When minds meet, they do not just exchange facts, they transform them, reshape them. . . . Conversation doesn't just reshuffle the cards, it creates new cards" (p. 14).

Zeldin may not have envisioned facilitated dialogues in prisons or between trauma survivors and those responsible for harming them. But in those settings, meaningful dialogues can shape and transform participants' realities, create new cards, quiet hypervigilant traumatic chaos, and often usher in post-traumatic growth (Gustafson, 2005). Over the last two decades, we have observed that when properly prepared and facilitated, encounters and dialogues do create shifts for participants—shifts that enable the persistent and fragmented traumatic images and memories to begin to be replaced by more human, and where warranted, less fearsome, moving images.

The Value of Apology

Apology involves a ritual exchange. In offering apology, I make myself vulnerable before you, accepting that you have power to reject my initiative, even to shame me. If you accept my apology, you exercise power to free me from my guilt and shame. This ritual exchange of shame and power gives power to both of us and reduces shame for both of us.

Martha Minow (1998) wrote, "An apology is inevitably inadequate" (p. 114). But, as Tavuchis (1991) points out, "[A]n apology, no matter how sincere or effective, does not and cannot *undo* what has been done. And yet, in a mysterious way and according to its own logic, this is precisely what it manages to do" (p. 33). In our case study, that happened. Making and receiving a truly meaningful apology may play a greater role than is commonly understood in enabling healing, reconciliation, and transformation.

INCONGRUENCE DUE TO GAPS BETWEEN SOCIAL WORK AND RESTORATIVE JUSTICE

Several significant gaps in both social work and restorative justice practices exist where bridges need to be constructed:

- gaps between practitioners who work at the micro (individual) level and those working for macro (system) level social change;
- gaps between restorative justice workers and social workers; and
- gaps between those who analyze the source of the violence (past), those who deal with the immediate crisis (present), and those who address how to live together or apart after relationships have been shattered (future).

These and other gaps show up within and between the fields of social work and restorative justice when professionals become isolated and miss opportunities to engage in dialogue. Cases of severe violence call our attention to these gaps and remind us of our responsibility to bridge them. After violence occurs, the skills and collaboration of social workers and restorative justice practitioners are needed. Minimally, this chapter (and book) exhorts us to bridge these gaps through interdisciplinary dialogue and initiatives.

NEXT STEPS

Strengthening the Fit

When VOMP began to research and develop restorative justice models for use in serious crime, staff members were confronted with the immensity of the trauma healing process. Healing is needed in all four human domains: physical, mental, spiritual, and emotional (as our First Nations sisters and brothers might name them). We based our models on the best available psychological trauma recovery theory and prison treatment programs. Today, as we cautiously move toward greater integration of social work and restorative justice in cases involving extreme violence, much will be needed.

Restorative justice and social work practitioners need to clarify and commit to a united theory of change. According to some theorists, both fields are engaged in a struggle to redefine their work as a focus on strengths rather than pathology, a focus "that will benefit the community at all levels, a shift from reliance on auto-cratic power-based structures to more democratic forms of righting the wrongs that have been done; wrongs that have hurt individuals, family members, and the community" (van Wormer, 2001, p. 49). van Wormer (2001) proposes joining the strengths perspective from social work with the restorative model from crimi-nal justice to suggest a new, improved iteration: a "strengths-restorative paradigm" (p. 29). The idea is compelling.

Carefully conceived research, informed and overseen by those who understand that trauma survivors heal most fully in the context of their own cultures, is needed. We need to learn what works and why in a number of diverse contexts, and then be prepared to revise and refine our understandings.

We need to identify basic skills sets for practitioners who hope to enter this field as vocation and avocation, and provide them with opportunities to train and to practice under supervision by those who are more skilled and seasoned.

We need to encourage discourse among practitioners, theorists, researchers, and program participants far beyond the levels we currently experience. We must recognize that those who have experienced something profound may well under-stand it at a level we have not (and perhaps cannot), no matter how competent or empathetic we are as practitioners and clinicians.

How to Change Systems?

How do we change systems to be more responsive to innovative approaches? Systemic change can occur at a glacial pace. Here are a few thoughts on encourag-ing systemic change.

Public monies tend to follow effective research. Monies rarely flow without good research having been done, simply because expenditures of public funds must be rationalized to taxpayers. Ultimately, that requires political processes and persuasive argument, unless private monies are sought. Even then, funders and philanthropists invest in things that pay demonstrable dividends.

Developing courses in our schools and training institutions that study the most successful community models would be an excellent start. Perhaps we could invent a new form of social capital barter enabling exchanges that would provide credit courses for community program staff, in return for providing university students practicum placement spaces and supervision.

We also need to cultivate relationships. VOMP, for example, could not function for long without inside-outside connections: that is, relationships between our agency staff and the leadership (including inmate leadership) in the prisons who believe in what VOMP is doing. If "location, location, location" is the mantra for success in the business world, "relationship, relationship, relationship" is the mantra for success in this one. Therefore, VOMP staff take advantage of virtually every invitation to present at relevant conferences, inviting past program participants to testify about their experiences in university and college classes, law schools, correctional training centers, victim services conferences, and in-service staff training days in prisons.

It is imperative that we emphasize the strength-based approach, which is beginning to inform fields beyond direct practice such as community organization, social administration, and policy analysis. Training materials and curricula have been developed for practitioners, and scholars have moved toward the development of a theory of strengths (Saleebey, 2000).

Envisioning How We Might Prepare Future Restorative Justice and Social Work Practitioners to be More Effective

How did Desmond Tutu, Martin Luther King, Jr., and Jane Addams bring about social change? Most of us practitioners, educators, and mentors do not have their eloquence, but we can follow their examples of envisioning how individuals, institutions, and research can serve as change agents.

Nurture Values, Knowledge, and Skills of Individual Practitioners

What if it were possible to move quickly to establish requisite criteria for competencies, develop training programs, and assess for readiness to deliver services? This would require identifying individuals with—and training them in—a combination of elements described in some of the early victim–offender mediation/ restorative justice literature as "knowledges, skills, abilities and other factors (KSAOs)" (Gustafson & Gilman, 1994). That article argues for a combination of factors, including character and personality attributes, and stature in the community (based on respect and trustworthiness), as vital to the discussion of qualifications when determining who is considered competent to be a practitioner or intervener. While education and professional credentials are important, we argue here for a standard based on demonstrated competence, rather than on arbitrary minimums for academic and professional credentialing.

Build a Visionary Institution

What if it were possible to place responsibility for implementing an interdisciplinary Healing Justice Project Initiative (call it what you will) based on best-practice restorative justice and social work foundations in the hands of senior staff persons at local, state, and national levels? Responsibilities would include:

- *Briefly* researching efficacious models already proving supportive of healing in cases involving severe violence. (Borrowing from the "Conceptualize it, Build it, Try it, Refine it" praxis implementation strategy, rather than the "Tinker with It Endlessly in Hopes of Making it Perfect Before Ever Attempting to Try it" type of implementation strategy). Trauma survivors are languishing now and, in far too many cases, are either doing themselves enormous harm—to the point of taking their own lives—or perpetrating further violence against others. In the short term, we must act our way into a new way of thinking for the long term.
- Rapidly creating leadership partnerships with First Nations, faith, and ethnic community leaders to ensure that growth, development, and refinement of these approaches are not top-down impositions of what could be perceived as a further exercise of colonial treatment, but rather grassroots, from-the-ground-up developments that honor community wisdom and autonomy.
- Ensuring necessary levels of funding (beyond the usual 2-or 3-year pilot project funding, which often seems to dispatch to the scrap yard even the best of ideas).
- Continuing to convene meetings of the requisite government branch leaders in departments of health, Aboriginal affairs, criminal justice, and others as necessary, to ensure that the initiative has strong support and that the likelihood of its gains being undermined, eclipsed, or scuttled altogether by other priorities or political partisanship are minimized.

Support Best Practices Through Restorative Research

Since governments must be accountable to citizens, and public funding for projects can only be sustained where there is demonstrated benefit, it is important to establish research components early on, with parameters and terms of reference defined (and refined, as necessary) in consultation—at the very least—with those individuals in the communities. It is necessary to ask, Who is delivering the services? Who are (or who are likely to be) the participants in the programs and processes being tested? Who are members of the participants' Healing and Support Circles?

It is essential that any such research be properly funded (with a sharp eye directed toward the proportion being spent on research, as opposed to service delivery), well-conceived, and responsibly conducted, recognizing two humbling research axioms: It is impossible to observe a thing without changing the nature of the thing observed; and we tend to get what we measure.

In conclusion, our hope and conviction is that moving alongside participants in our processes, supporting them in finding their own resiliencies and strengths, helping to normalize their post-trauma reactions and adaptations, engaging in trauma recovery treatment if they invite that, enabling them to discern whether or not they will choose to engage with the other, and facilitating dialogue between them if they do will prove to be transformative for them. We hope our efforts will help them realize they have power and agency to fashion new possibilities that can enable them to live their lives more fully, perhaps even shaping new options, new vocations, and new transcendent futures from the wreckage of devastating experience.

ACKNOWLEDGMENTS

Dave Gustafson wishes to acknowledge and honor the contributions of the women whose stories appear in this chapter as the case study. Their courage, faithfulness to their own First Nations teachings, and willingness to share their stories are harbingers of hope to people everywhere.

NOTES

Authors' Note: *The case study in this chapter is about a direct meeting between one who offended and one who was victimized. However, it is imperative to state clearly that interventions for trauma healing and restorative justice after acts of severe violence do NOT necessarily require face-to-face meetings. In fact, numerous initiatives that are both restorative and healing have no requirement for a victim–offender meeting. In cases of violence, it is necessary to consider the full array of restorative tools, skills, and interventions.*

  i Originally published as Gustafson, D. L. (2007). In search of healing justice: A healing circle case study. *Les Cahiers de PV: Antenne sur la victimologie, 3,* 35–38. Les Cahiers de PV is the Journal for Plaidoyer Victimes, a Quebec-based victims organization. It is used here with permission of the original publisher.

 ii To Western perceptions, practices such as these may seem foreign. But that is precisely the point. To these participants, the tissues, as symbols of their pain, deserved respect. But, beyond that, they believe tears shed in a circumstance such as this contain residue related to the grief and pain, and therefore the tissues that contained them, together with selected medicines, would be burned in a sacred fire and offered up to Creator.

REFERENCES

Armour, M. P. (2006). Meaning making for survivors of violent death. In E. K. Rynearson (Ed.), *Violent death: Resilience and intervention beyond the crisis* (pp. 101–122). New York: Routledge.

Bartsch, K., & Bartsch, E. (1997). *Stress and trauma healing: A manual for caregivers.* Botha's Hill, South Africa: Mennonite Central Committee.

Beck, E., Blackwell, B. S., Leonard, P.B., & Mears, M. (2003). Seeking sanctuary: Interviews with family members of capital defendants. *Cornell Law Review, 2*(88), (382–418).

Beck, E., Britto, S., & Andrews, A. (2007). *In the shadow of death.* Oxford: Oxford University Press.

Bucholz, J. A. (2002). *Homicide survivors: Misunderstood grievers.* Amityville, NY: Baywood Publishing Company, Inc.

Chefetz, R. A. (2006). Considering medication use in the wake of traumatic experience: Neurobiology, affect dysregulation, and the psychiatrist as a witness who may also prescribe. In E. K. Rynearson (Ed.), *Violent death: Resilience and intervention beyond the crisis* (pp. 123–144). New York: Routledge.

Derrick, J. (2007). Personal correspondence with Dave Gustafson.

Dignan, J. (2005). *Understanding victims and restorative justice: Crime and justice.* New York: Open University Press.

Gilligan, J. (2001). *Preventing violence: An agenda for the common century.* London: Thames and Hudson.

Good Sider, N. (2001). At the fork in the road: Trauma healing. *Conciliation Quarterly, 2*(20), 7–11.

Good Sider, N. (2004). *Trauma writing as haiku.* Harrisonburg, VA.

Good Sider, N. (2006). Peacebuilders healing trauma: The journey from victim to survivor to provider. *Dissertation Abstracts International, 67,* 1208.

Grossman, D. (1995). *On killing: The psychological cost of learning to kill in war and society.* Boston: Little, Brown, & Company.

Gustafson, D. & Gilman, E. (1994). Of VORPs, VOMPs, CDRPs and KSOAs: A case for competency based qualifications in victim offender mediation. In Morris, C. & Pirie, A. (Eds.). *Qualifications for dispute resolution – perspectives on the debate.* University of Victoria Institute for Dispute Resolution.

Gustafson, D. L. (2005). Exploring treatment and trauma recovery implications of facilitating victim-offender encounters in crimes of severe violence: Lessons from the Canadian experience. In E. Elliott and R. M. Gordon (Eds.), *New directions in restorative justice: Issues, practice, evaluation* (pp. 193–227). Portland, OR: Willan Publishing.

Gustafson, D.L. (2007). In search of healing justice: A healing circle case study. *Les Cahiers de PV: Antenne sur la victimologie, 3,* 35–38.

Gustafson, D.L., & Bergen, S. (2009, July 12–20). Training curriculum for victim offender mediation dialogue facilitators in Canadian prisons. Presented at Algonquin College, Ottawa, Ontario, Canada.

Hart, J. (2006). Trauma: Get over it—When to let go, how to heal. *Utne Reader.* Retrieved October 1, 2009, from http://www.utne.com/2006-07-01/TraumaGetOverIt.aspx

Herman, J. (1997). *Trauma and recovery: The aftermath of violence—from domestic abuse to political terror.* New York: Basic Books.

King, M. L. K., Jr. (1967). *Where do we go from here? Chaos or community.* Boston: Beacon Press.

MacNair, R. M. (2002). *Perpetration-induced traumatic stress: The psychological consequences of killing.* Westport, CT: Praeger.

Maruna, S. (2004). *Making good.* Washington, D.C.: American Psychological Association.

Minow, M. (1998). *Between vengeance and forgiveness: Facing history after genocide and mass violence.* Boston: Beacon Press.

Rando, T. A. (1993). *Treatment of complicated mourning.* Champaign, IL: Research Press.

Ross, R. (1996). *Return to the teachings: Exploring aboriginal justice.* Toronto: Penguin Canada.

Rothschild, B. (2000). *The body remembers: The psychophysiology of trauma and trauma treatment.* New York: W. W. Norton & Co.

Rynearson, E. K. (2001). *Retelling violent death.* New York: Routledge.

Rynearson, E. K., Correa, F., Favell, J., Saindon, C., & Prigerson, H. (2006). Restorative retelling after violent dying. In E. K. Rynearson (Ed.), *Violent death: Resilience and intervention beyond the crisis* (pp. 195–216). New York: Routledge.

Saleebey, D. (2008). *The strengths perspective in social work practice* (5th ed.). Boston: Allyn & Bacon.

Sharpe, S., & Lai Thom, G. (2007). Making sense of North American and South African differences in the practice of restorative justice. *Justice Connections, 1*(4), 14–16.

Summerfield, D. (1995). Addressing human response to war and atrocity: Major challenges in research and practices and the limitations of Western psychiatric models. In R. J. Kleber, C. R. Figley, & B. P. R. Gersons (Eds.), *Beyond trauma: Cultural and societal dynamics* (pp. 17–29). New York: Plenum Press.

Tavuchis, N. (1991). *Mea culpa: A sociology of apology and reconciliation.* Stanford, CA: Stanford University Press.

Toews, B. (2006). *The little book of restorative justice for people in prison: Rebuilding the web of relationships.* Intercourse, PA: Good Books.

Umbreit, M. (2001). *The handbook of victim offender mediation: An essential guide to practice and research.* San Francisco: Jossey-Bass.

Umbreit, M. S., & Coates, R. B. (1999). Multicultural implications of restorative juvenile justice. *Federal Probation, 63*(2), 44–52.

van der Kolk, B. A. (1987). *Psychological trauma.* Washington, D.C.: American Psychological Association.

van der Kolk, B. A. (1994). The body keeps score. *Harvard Review of Psychiatry, 1,* 253–265.

van der Kolk, B. A., & McFarlane, A. C. (1996). The black hole of trauma. In B. A. van der Kolk, A. C. McFarlane, and L. Weisaeth (Eds.), *Traumatic stress: The effects of overwhelming experience on mind, body, and society* (pp. 3–23). New York: The Guilford Press.

van Wormer, K. (2001). *Counseling female offenders and victims: A strengths-restorative approach.* New York: Springer Publishing Company, Inc.

van Wormer, K. (2004a). *Confronting oppression, restoring justice: From policy analysis to social action.* Alexandria, VA: Council of Social Work Education.

van Wormer, K. (2004b). Restorative justice: A model for personal and societal empowerment. *Journal of Religion and Spirituality in Social Work, 23*(4), 103–120.

Weingarten, K. (2003). *Common shock: Witnessing violence every day.* New York: New American Library.

Wright State University School of Social Work. (2009). Retrieved October 05, 2009, from http://www.cola.wright.edu/Dept/social_work/sw_definition.htm

Yoder, C. (2005). *The little book of trauma healing: When violence strikes and community security is threatened.* Intercourse, PA: Good Books.

Zehr, H. (2002). *The little book of restorative justice.* Intercourse, PA: Good Books.

Zehr, H. (2005). *Changing lenses: A new focus for crime and justice.* Scottdale, PA: Herald Press.

Zeldin, T. (2000). *Conversation: How talk can change our lives.* Mahwah, NJ: Paulist Press.

Chapter Eleven

Social Work and Restorative Justice in an International Context: The Case of Liberia

NANCY ROTHENBERG WILLIAMS AND THOMAS K. CRICK

Regardless of cultural context, international social work practice addresses universal concerns that are associated with the health and well-being of populations impacted by oppression, poverty, war, and disease. Conversely, related principles, such as valuing human relationships within a framework of community responsibility, and respecting justice and accountability, also serve as the foundation for the practice and principles of restorative justice. While both social work and restorative justice hope to repair and restore relationships within communities, there are also significant differences between these two approaches. Direct social work practice in the West traditionally provides supportive and direct services to individuals and families who are vulnerable and may be members of socially oppressed groups. In addition, practice is guided by a strong code of ethics undergirded by human rights and social justice values. In contrast, restorative justice programs focus on establishing structures to enforce accountability through addressing specific injustices and abuses of human rights.

It is the purpose of this chapter to focus on both restorative justice and social work as practiced in a post-conflict, developing country, using Liberia as a representative example. In addition, the chapter will examine challenges, opportunities, and the overlap in values, ideas, and practices that can inform and potentially strengthen both of these approaches. An in-depth description of modern Liberia and the types and levels of problems it is facing will be detailed later in the chapter to highlight the unique challenges that social workers and peace workers face in working toward rebuilding that country and promoting social justice policies. Additionally, the state of the profession of social work, as described by a practicing Liberian social worker, is also included, to present the realities facing the profession currently in that country. While local social work practices will be addressed, general themes that affect social work practices in other developing countries will also be discussed. Finally, restorative justice processes currently in progress will be presented and examined in terms of current impact, potential for change, and barriers that are being confronted.

INTERNATIONAL SOCIAL WORK

Overview and History

Although there is an increased interest in international social work as a context for practice, there does not appear to be a universally accepted definition of it. According to Healy & Thomas (2007), the ensuing debate appears, historically, to be a reflection of the times, rather than of the specificity of the tasks. They also suggest that "international social work is a concept (that is) still evolving" (p. 584).

Over the years, different scholars have tackled the task of developing a definition. As far back as the 1930s, definitions have been specific and task-driven, and have included such ideas as "practice across borders, international assistance, and work through international bodies such as the League of Nations" (Healy & Thomas, 2007 p. 584). Healy (2001) describes international social work in terms of practices and links it to specific actions: "internationally related domestic practice and advocacy, professional exchange, international practice, and international policy development and advocacy" (p. 7). Building on Healy's definition, Cox and Pawar (2006) emphasized the development of social work as a global profession in order to respond competently and appropriately to local challenges that impact the well-being of large sectors of the world's population. They spoke to the importance of making social work education available in developing countries and as a way to spread the profession globally, and argued that "The global and local promotion of social work education and practice is based on an integrated-perspectives approach that synthesizes global, human rights, ecological and social development perspectives of international situations and responses to them" (p.21). This definition stresses the importance of active promotion at various levels of global challenges. However, the authors are also strong advocates for the importance of linking education and practice at the local as well as global levels. In addition, they stress the importance of redefining the limits and extent of practice based on level of need and cultural considerations.

From an historical perspective, international social work has its roots in the earliest days of the social work profession, under the leadership of Jane Addams. Commonly acknowledged as one of the founders of the profession, Addams was also known to be a passionate proponent of human rights both on the domestic and international fronts (Schugurensky, 2005). She was a founding member of several national and international human rights organizations that continue their work today, including the American Civil Liberties Union (ACLU) and the Women's International League for Peace and Freedom (Healy, 2008). Addams's significant work in human rights was recognized in the awarding of the Nobel Peace Prize to her in 1931. Her legacy continues on in the field of international social work, as practitioners continue to follow closely in Addams's philosophic footsteps, with an emphasis on human rights and social justice issues.

A Focus on Human Rights

Two of the formal representatives of international social work, the International Federation of Social Workers (IFSW) and the International Association of Schools of Social Work (IASSW), took on the task of elaborating on the fundamental significance of human rights in relation to social work practice in their manual, *Human Rights and Social Work* (Center for Human Rights, 1994), a collaborative effort between the two organizations and the Office of the United Nations High Commissioner for Human Rights (OHCHR):

> While . . . social work has, from its conception, been a human rights profession, having as its basic tenet the intrinsic value of every human being and as one of its main aims the promotion of equitable social structures, which can offer people security and development while upholding their dignity, IFSW and IASSW believe that greater knowledge and understanding of human rights will improve the actions and interventions of social work professionals for the benefit of those who require their services. (p.3)

The social work profession appears to be broadly represented on the local level around the globe, and linked by a similarity of structures and values. In their book *International Social Work: Issues, Strategies, and Programs,* Cox and Pawar (2006) suggest that the social work profession as it is practiced internationally (particularly in developing countries) suffers from similar constraints regarding public perception—specifically, concerns about the profession's autonomy from government and its ties to bureaucratic functions. They suggest that while there are similarities in practices, there are significant differences between countries and cultures that are dictated by issues such as socioeconomic factors, history, available resources, and local professional education and practice. Particularly, the profession's responsiveness on the local, regional, and national levels to changing needs varies in different locations.

Additionally, international social work involves philosophic differences that are shaped by culture, social issues, and circumstances. For example, Latin America has strong ties with the Catholic Church, which has been influenced by the unique social justice approach of Paulo Freire, who addressed principles of empowerment in his seminal work, *Pedagogy of the Oppressed* (1972). In contrast, "capacity-building" is the buzzword linked to social development strategies of the non-governmental organizations (NGOs) in developing countries in Africa. Across the globe, the various influences within the particular country and region shape the roles and activities that are assumed by social workers.

Trauma, Recovery, and the Legacies of War

Among the realities facing social workers practicing in developing nations is the devastating impact of war on combatants and civilians alike. as well as its ultimate destruction of communities. Cox & Pawar (2006) describe four areas of war-related trauma that create opportunities for social work intervention: exposure to physical violence and accompanying torture associated with fighting and conflict; experience of abusive violence, such as the rape of women and the exploitation of children; lack of access to basic needs such as food, clothing, and shelter; and the psychological stresses associated with a loss of meaning and control that lingers long after the immediate trauma ends. Of particular note is the inevitable displacement and suffering of children, who are often separated from family and support systems. As a result from being torn from their primary relationships, these children are vulnerable targets of those who might recruit them to continue the legacy of war into the future. Child welfare practices and concerns in relation to displaced and disenfranchised children are often a particular focus of social workers worldwide.

Social work interventions involve a variety of approaches and responses for victims of trauma. While therapeutic interventions may be effective in the Western world, these approaches are unrealistic in war-torn areas due to the massive level of need, the woeful lack of resources, and oftentimes unreceptive cultural attitudes. Social workers are in a greater position to effect change at a community level by becoming involved in reconstruction efforts that mobilize and empower communities to reclaim control and balance (Goodwin-Gill & Cohn, 1994; Lewis, 1999). In keeping with this strategy, Cox & Pawar (2006) distinguish between focusing on a "relief" approach as opposed to a "development" approach. *Relief* is crisis-focused and primarily attends to short-term issues and needs. A *developmental* approach, the one which they advocate, is a slow and participatory process that engages the community in healing by focusing on human rights. Like social work, international restorative justice models (described later in this chapter) address the processes necessary to bring about recovery on a community level, which include partnering with traditional, indigenous healers and incorporating the cultural mores of the locale.

RESTORATIVE JUSTICE APPROACHES

Truth and Reconciliation Commissions

Within the developing world, restorative justice has most commonly been associated with truth commissions at the macro or state level (see Chapter 4). However, these similar principles are also seen at work in many traditional justice structures and in community mediation initiatives in a range of developing countries. Most commonly, such processes are in place in states recovering from conflict where formal justice mechanisms are weak or lack popular confidence. Truth commissions can take a variety of forms, but commonly they are temporary bodies which work to discover and reveal the truth about past abuses, in the hope of managing prior conflicts and bringing societal healing and reconciliation (Hayner, 1994).

Within the literature, the source of much discussion has been the relationship between justice and reconciliation, and amnesty and prosecution. Some truth commissions have been formally linked to amnesty agreements, some have aimed at reconciliation, while some have aimed to protect the guilty. Most notably, the South African Truth and Reconciliation Commission granted amnesty to perpetrators who were judged to have made a full confession to the Commission of their acts. In other cases, such as El Salvador (1993) and Uruguay (1985), unfavorable truth commission reports led governments to issue broad amnesties protecting themselves from prosecution (Robertson, 2000). Also, in Sierra Leone, the perpetrators of the war created a process with a mandate to grant amnesty.

With recent developments in international criminal justice, including the formation of the International Criminal Court, it has become increasingly difficult for commissions to be given powers of amnesty where grievous crimes against international law have been committed. The South African model of offering amnesty in exchange for truth to all perpetrators is no longer a realistic option that the international community would find satisfactory. At the time of writing, the Kenyan government has created an independent Truth, Reconciliation and Justice Commission to look at the violence surrounding the 2007 elections. (For an update, see the International Center for Transitional Justice website at http://www.ictj.org/en/where/region1/648.html). This new and specific emphasis on justice highlights the current human rights orthodoxy that there cannot be lasting peace when perpetrators are not punished. The prevailing international human rights position strongly holds that impunity can only be ended by direct judicial action against, at minimum, those most responsible for human rights abuses. At the international level, therefore, ideas of restorative or traditional justice seem at odds with the need for prosecution.

Even as the prosecutorial approach has gained ascendancy, proponents for truth commissions have identified at least three ways in which they complement judicial approaches. First, truth commissioners typically go beyond the investigation of specific abuses, to document the wider causes, nature, and extent of wrongdoings. Second, they provide a forum for victims to describe their abuse that goes far beyond that of trial testimony. And finally, in their outcomes they are able to give recommendations on reform that have broader impact than merely the sentencing of individuals (International Center, 2002).

Traditional Dispute Resolution Structures

In many developing countries, formal justice mechanisms are weak or distrusted by the population. In such situations, individuals either have no formal recourse to resolve disputes or prefer to resolve them through traditional mechanisms. Many of these practices are actually compatible with restorative principles that aim to bring back wholeness to the victim and reintegrate the perpetrator into society (see discussion below). Efforts to promote the rule of law in developing nations cannot ignore these important community resources. It is heartening that, in some instances, community-level traditional justice is being seen as a strength on which to build rather than an archaic relic. In Sierra Leone, for example, a paralegal group called Timap for Justice consciously works to apply both formal and traditional solutions, and has traditional leaders on its oversight board. In Liberia, the Carter Center is working to strengthen the capacity of Liberia's traditional leadership by providing training in mediation and dispute resolution, along with explanation of and dialogue on the national laws. Similar initiatives increasingly are being conducted throughout Africa.

Community Mediation Initiatives

A final restorative justice initiative used in the developing world has been the creation of community mediators. A good example is the Community Peace Program in South Africa. Supported in part by government funding and also by overseas aid, the program has imported alternative-dispute-resolution best practices to complement indigenous ones, in order to help local communities establish peace committees, which work to resolve community conflicts and address the social problems faced by the community (Roche, 2006). Community mediation initiatives are also linked to a number of paralegal and community legal advisor programs, which train individuals within communities to guide local people through the different formal, informal, and traditional means of settling disputes. Examples include TIMAP for Justice in Sierra Leone, the Catholic Justice and Peace Commission in Liberia, Black Sash in South Africa, and the Law and Human Rights Center in Gujarat, India. These programs provide avenues for legal advice and redress from within the community, and are particularly effective where the formal system is either not trusted or does not reach down to community levels.

CASE STUDY: LIBERIA

Liberia is a small country on the coast of West Africa that is struggling to rebuild and reinvent itself following a history of oppressive rule and a brutal 14-year civil war. In the aftermath of the war that ended in 2003, Liberia elected Africa's first female head of state in 2005. While President Ellen Johnson Sirleaf's government is receiving high marks from the international community, a history of poor governance and the devastating civil war have resulted in massive social problems and a crippled infrastructure. These are daunting obstacles that must be overcome.

Liberia's history reflects its population mix. Approximately 95% of the population are indigenous Africans, including 16 different ethnic groups, who have been dominated politically and economically since the creation of the modern state in the early nineteenth century. The members of this small (approximately 5% of the population) but historically powerful minority are known as Americo-Liberian or Congo. They are descendants of immigrants who were former slaves from the U. S., or slaves released en route to the US.

In 1980, an indigenous-led coup marked the start of a political collapse leading to two civil wars between 1989 and 2003. From a pre-war population of roughly 3,000,000 these events left approximately 250,000 dead—a staggering proportion of the total population. As a consequence, the problems that face modern Liberia are unusually extreme, even for a developing nation recovering from conflict. Despite progress, the country remains divided along class, ethnic, religious, gender, and generational lines, and efforts at reconciliation between the various groups are as yet incomplete.

Internal Colonialism

Liberia's system has been described as one of internal colonialism, in which the settler elites extracted wealth from the country while giving little, if anything, back to the country's indigenous population. Although the country never formally colonized by an outside power, the Americo-Liberian and Congo settlers that came to Liberia in the early nineteenth century acted in many ways like European colonists. For indigenous Liberians, the settlements marked a significant change in power dynamics.

Over the centuries, broad migrations of certain linguistic and cultural groups took place across West and Central Africa. Tribes from the groups of the Mende, Mel, and Mandingo had settled into what is today known as Liberia. These groups coexisted in an agrarian society led by a hierarchical chieftain-based structure and a deep belief in indigenous spirituality. Gradually, after the new settlers took root, their central remit began to impact local political institutions, as local chieftaincy structures were transformed by the growing reach of the settler government (Levitt, 2005). The government, based in the capital of Monrovia, worked through cooperative local chiefs, which allowed the government to acquire power. Prior to these events, governance in Liberia had been local, and relations between the various ethnic groups were fairly stable—although occasionally violent—from generation to generation.

The early settlers used resources provided by supporters in the U.S. and built relationships with local tribal leaders to allow them to establish settlements. Where these agreements were not enough to guarantee their security and resources, the settlers used force, either by combining forces with other local leaders, or through their own superior weapons. Gradually, a number of coastal settlements began to take root and in 1847, the Americo-Liberian and Congo settlers declared Liberia to be Africa's first republic, in part responding to threats of territorial expansion from British and French interests nearby.

From 1847 until the coup of 1980, the True Whig Party (TWP) politically dominated the country, ruling continuously. Although the newly formed Republic of Liberia adopted a constitution similar in most major ways to that of the US, it never put the idea of separation of powers into practice. Political power was concentrated almost wholly in the presidency, and from that position government was conducted through personal patronage (Liebenow, 1987). Vast tracts of land were expropriated for rubber farming, and indigenous labor was provided by local chiefs to work on these plantations. In many ways, the social and economic structure of Liberia mirrored that of the American South prior to the American Civil War, with the settlers bringing with them the political and social attitudes and expectations of the Southern ruling classes.

Indigenous Conflict Resolution Practices

Historically, indigenous practices dictated conduct and provided the structure for relationships within the community, including the process of conflict resolution. Prior to the development of a centralized government, this ruling structure gave the chief of each community governance powers, in consultation with elders and spiritual leaders. Order was maintained through complex processes and rituals that allowed communities to resolve conflicts. While each ethnic group and sub-group had slightly different ways of doing things, there were, and are today, significant commonalities in conflict resolution practices between Liberian tribes. These practices are based on a community-based approach to problem solving, very much akin to contemporary notions of restorative justice. Resolving a dispute was based on restoring and reconciling relationships that had been damaged within the community, with an emphasis on relationships between families and within the community as a whole. A common understanding in Liberia is that, reconciliation processes involve confession, apologies and acts of supplication and reparation by the wrong doer (Resource Center for Community Empowerment and Integrated Development, 2005). Although the process varies between ethnic groups, common elements of the conflict resolution process tend to be "begging, holding of feet, offering of apology, acceptance of apology and stating of forgiveness, presentation of white chicken, exchange of handshakes, sharing of kola nuts and eating and drinking to appease the ancestors and divine power" (Resource Center for Community Empowerment and Integrated Development 2005 p. 17).

Today, all Liberian citizens have access to the same rights guaranteed to them under the constitution, and are subject to the same penalties under the law, regardless of whether they live in rural or urban areas. In practice, however, traditional forms of dispute resolution continue to predominate especially in remote areas, where formal systems do not extend much influence, and where people have little trust in government. Insights can be gained by understanding how the social milieu is impacted by the tensions between the will of the state and the customary practices that hold so much local influence. In the following sections, examples are offered in which contradictory processes are described that shape the work and challenges facing social workers and peace workers in Liberia.

RESTORATIVE JUSTICE IN LIBERIA

During the past 25 years, there have been more than 20 truth commissions held around the world, with the best-known example of restorative justice on the national level being South Africa's Truth and Reconciliation Commission (TRC). In Liberia, the TRC was established as an integral part of the 2003 Accra Comprehensive Peace Agreement (CPA), a document that was basically negotiated between the three main warring factions. Because of this unavoidable reality, there was little incentive among the agreement's principle architects to propose a TRC with strong judicial powers, as these would likely be used against these same leaders. The final agreement, therefore, included the creation of a TRC that would attempt to address the challenges associated with impunity, a weak formulation that appeared to pay no more than lip service to the human rights community's belief that peace cannot be sustained if impunity is not addressed through prosecuting those guilty of human rights violations (Jalloh & Marong, 2005).

As noted, the most commonly referenced model of a TRC occurred in South Africa; in essence, this commission was predicated on a simple bargain that, if people told the truth about what they had done, they would not be prosecuted. The Liberian model was more complex and, consequently, harder for the ordinary person to understand. It was intended by supporters to employ a "people-centered" approach that did not only focus on the most serious perpetrators. The original intent was that victims be allowed to directly confront perpetrators and make a recommendation to the commission as to whether the perpetrator should be referred for prosecution or not, based on whether the victim accepted any apology that might be given. In this way, the Liberian TRC's method was intended to both allow the opportunity for redress and healing to all affected Liberians, but also, perhaps, to mirror elements of the Liberian traditional culture of dispute resolution.

Unfortunately, the effort at allowing ordinary victims to confront the perpetrators was unsuccessful. One reason was that the process was based on whether the victims accepted the guilt of the accused and often this determination was complex and multifaceted. Also, the accused quickly started accusing others of being responsible for the alleged crimes. These factors rendered the hoped for restorative elements of the hearing virtually moot.

As described, in Liberia there already exists a clear understanding of how crimes committed within the community should be dealt with, even as these same indigenous values have been fractured by the war and other factors. However, this approach does not satisfy the TRC's need for punitive measures to be taken against the most serious perpetrators of human rights violations. The TRC in Liberia has interpreted its mandate on impunity broadly and, at the time of writing, has recommended roughly 200 people for prosecution.[i] The commission believes that punitive measures will prove to be a deterrent for further crimes, and that war will be a recurring problem, unless the perpetrators of the worst crimes are prosecuted.

This view is in direct contrast to the alternative perspective expressed in Liberia—namely, that there should be no prosecutions, because these will raise old enmities and fuel new conflict. This alternate view is strengthened by the sheer number of atrocities in Liberia, as noted above, with people arguing both that it is impossible to prosecute all those who committed crimes and, also, that to some degree all Liberians played a role in allowing the national tragedy to occur. This basic dichotomy has divided the Commission and continues to divide the country. However, the TRC reports that 22,500 people gave statements to the Commission, which suggests that a lot of people (overwhelmingly victims) wanted to have their experiences be part of the historic record, and were willing to participate in the formal TRC process.[ii]

Notwithstanding the activities of the TRC, since the end of the fighting in 2003, communities have largely been left to address the past in their own ways. In some places, perpetrators have made their peace with their victims and with their communities through traditional means. Elsewhere, there are reports that victims have decided not to tell their stories, as they do not see any value in stirring up memories that they have come to terms with, or because they are afraid to confront the perpetrators because they occupy positions of power.

A fundamental question is whether restorative justice can work in Liberia. At the national level, there has been an open debate between Liberians and members of the international community about the efficacy of restorative justice approaches when dealing with serious human rights violations committed during the war. The debate is part of a wider effort by large sections of the international community to make universal human rights standards enforceable. In practical terms, finding ways to sustain peace and achieve justice and reconciliation are multilayered and intertwined challenges where a local community's understanding of how such processes should work and the international community's principles and priorities come into direct contact. The task of balancing and reconciling what can be differing ideas of the enforcement and priorities of punitive justice and community healing often falls to truth and reconciliation commissions, as in Liberia.

SOCIAL WORK IN LIBERIA

Paralleling the peace workers and the challenges they are facing in Liberia are the social workers who are working in a country without resources or structures that address human needs and who are surrounded by social justice and human rights issues. Social work is a fledgling profession in Liberia and is working toward legitimacy and respected status. The National Association of Liberian Social Workers, an affiliate of the International Federation of Social Workers, was founded in 2007. The organization has fewer than 300 members across the country, and it recognizes two levels of academic credentials in social work: the Bachelor of Arts degree, attained after 4 years of study, and an associate degree that can be obtained in 2.5 years. There is reportedly an overwhelming need for services, and yet Liberian social workers function with almost no investment in social welfare services and resources on the part of a cash-strapped government.

In preparation for this chapter, an American-trained social worker on assignment[iii] agreed to interview a Liberian social worker, Ms. Agnes Duncan, called "Ma" Agnes[iv]. She was asked about the focus of her work, the conditions that affect Liberian social work practice, the status of social workers in Liberia, and the cultural challenges and customs that inform practice perspectives. Ma Agnes is a coordinator for women's health and development at a Liberian College of Health Sciences, a position she has held for over 14 years. She holds an associate degree in social work, with more than 28 years of experience in the human services field in Liberia. As a native Liberian practicing social work during a very tumultuous time in Liberian history, she has a unique grasp of the sociocultural issues facing Liberia today.

Ma Agnes's description of the professional role of social work highlights several issues described in this chapter. She offers an interesting perspective on the evolution and progression of social work, a nascent profession in Liberia, and the evolution of social work in general (discussed in Chapter 2). Additionally, her summary highlights the ways that social work and restorative justice are both integrated and disparate in a war-ravaged nation. The following are some key points from the interview that shed light on the state of social work through her unique cultural lens.

Status of the Profession

Ma was deeply involved in establishing a unifying organization in 2007, the Association for Liberian Social Workers, to promote the professionalization of social work. She acknowledges that social work does not get the professional recognition that it deserves and is often misunderstood and devalued:

> Social work is actually a new program, and a lot of people who do not work in the field of providing services for people don't understand what social work is. For we need a lot of awareness. A lot of students are now coming to the program, but we still need more awareness. Because a lot of Liberians don't know, a lot of institutions don't know what social work is. But I do think there is a potential for social work developing here. Our social needs are beyond numbers.

Ma Agnes stated that she was involved in developing an educational program to professionalize and train human services workers in basic social work skills, which has evolved into a 4-month certificate program. She described the typical functions of social workers in direct practice roles (micro) as follows:

> What we have been doing in Liberia was providing services, especially when we started, providing services to the needy (the handicapped, the disabled). . . . Neglected and abandoned street children who, during civil crisis were found in the streets because they

either lost their parents, or their parents got killed, and some of them just followed friends, some of them were recruited into the civil war, when they were much younger, and after maybe they grew a little bigger, their families were not taking them on, and the commanders didn't continue with them.

Because of the extent of unrest, war, and trauma in Liberia, there are multiple and complex social needs. As described earlier in the chapter, social work roles span practice with individuals to work with the entire community. Ma Agnes described the needs at various levels of practice:

We have a lot of social issues that we can talk about. We have all these boys that are still in the street, we have a lot of handicapped in the street, we have the home of the blind, we have people that have been abandoned, we have the issue of homelessness that is now coming because the government is in reconstruction. A lot of people (have been left) homeless. People are sleeping by the market. Family members are sleeping outside the market. All these issues are coming as the government continues to reconstruct.

She continued to expound on the multiple roles of social workers:

To a large extent, [social workers] are doing community work, and advocacy, awareness, and that sort of thing . . . they do general community activities, organizing community members to take action to bring about development in the community and change, awareness on some issues. Like getting the community members to get out and participant in community projects, like building a bridge or building a school. Those are the general community activities that most social workers are engaged.

Essential Skills

Given the dearth of resources, the interpersonal and professional communication skills of a social worker take on keen significance. Often, these are the only tools available to them. Ma Agnes described the skills necessary to be effective as a community developer that included leadership skills as a group facilitator and educator in order to be a change agent:

One specific skill you need as a social worker is (that) you need facilitation skills. Facilitation skills means that in your work, in your community development activities, there will be times that you will pull participants together, and in that process, either you are creating awareness, or you are explaining a process, what method will you use to get a message across so that they can actually get that message. You need that skill to create awareness so that the message can get across, so that change can take place.

Ma Agnes emphasized the importance of training social workers to be interpersonally and culturally adept as the most important skill in their work. She suggested that being able to communicate with a broad spectrum of the community was an essential piece of a social worker's effectiveness and took precedence over availability of resources: "As a social worker, you need interpersonal skills. How do you relate well with people. How do you relate to your police, and how do you relate to the community member with respect to the culture, in context of culture, so that you have not violated the culture."

Conflict and Trauma Recovery

Violence and trauma have been pervasive constants in the recent past in Liberia, and have affected most citizens. Wearing the dual hats of being a Liberian and a social worker, Ma Agnes described the way trauma is processed from both a family and community perspective, particularly as it relates to violence toward women. She refers to a process of community responsibility, and ultimately normalization, which provides an interesting cultural alternative to the way in which trauma is viewed and handled in other parts of the world.

> For us, every Liberian that lives in this country may not have experienced the same kind of trauma the same way. But let me be frank with you. Liberians have very strong feelings about those things. Some of the trauma that women went through, and you see them today, moving around like (nothing has happened). And so, that is a plus for us. So, it is not that we don't need it, but people are solving their problems and are getting along. . . . You have a lot of people saying, we do not want to open the old wounds again. We have forgotten and want to move on with our lives.

As described by Ma Agnes, the family plays a strong role in handling crises, particularly as it relates to domestic violence. In fact she indicates that the family has its own specific protocol for violations:

> So what they do, the family member takes care of most of the problems. So if I have a problem, my husband is battering me, we go to my family and we talk about it. We go to his family and we talk about it. We go to the elders in the town and talk about it. They have their own way of solving their problems. . . . Maybe in the long run, when things are much settled . . . services are being provided, people might start seeing the need, I need to work on this, I need to do this, but now, they are not there.

She goes on to describe the influence of culture on the way people experience and process grief and loss:

> It is part of the culture. It is part of the culture that people will always use their own families and support system, people will always get over their problems. They don't need to go to any professional to solve their problems. The only time people go to a professional is for a medical problem and they go to a medical doctor for medicine. If someone lost their father during the war, as a matter of one or two years, with support from family and friends, that grief will go. That grief will not remain as before. The grief goes away.

Understanding how social workers face their jobs and the culture in which they try to impart social justice and practice healing provides us with valuable insights into an environment in which other forms of social reconciliation and healing are also being implemented. The issue of how well the principles attributed to the culture fit with the approaches taken to wider-scale healing make for interesting reflection.

CONSEQUENCES OF WAR IN LIBERIA: RAPE AND SEXUAL VIOLENCE

In order to further explore the consequences of the war and violence experienced by Liberians, one of the challenges is presented from both a social work and restorative justice perspective. Sadly, rape and sexual violence are ubiquitous, and affect many women and girls in Liberia. As a community challenge, these issues will be described and community responses from both social work and restorative justice will be highlighted.

A Community Challenge

As a tragic consequence of the violence and war, rape and sexual assaults are pervasive challenges for both social workers and restorative justice workers alike. Prior to the war, rape by a stranger was rare, although it is suspected that intimate partner sexual violence was common and culturally accepted. During the war years, however, the number of rapes exploded and the practice became commonplace. The army and militia soldiers were poorly disciplined, and encouraged looting and general destruction of rival ethnic groups. These practices included the brutal rape of women and girls by young fighters, who were often high on drugs. In other instances, women and girls were forcibly taken by fighters as "wives," or forced into sex in order to protect or feed themselves or their families. While rape was endemic, less recognized is how women successfully used their bodies as a means of survival (Utas, 2005). The Truth and Reconciliation Commission's final report describes this in terrible detail (Republic of Liberia Truth and Reconciliation Commission, 2008).

Even after the war, the rates have remained extremely high (see below). When she came into office, one of President Johnson Sirleaf's top priorities was to reduce rape, and she signed the Rape Law of 2005 as one of her first acts in office. The new law increased penalties, raised the age for statutory rape to 18, made gang rape a crime, and generally addressed gaps in the previous laws pertaining to rape. Since its passage, the government has made concerted efforts to educate the public on the seriousness of rape as a criminal offence, and one that must be prosecuted by the state rather than negotiated between families. Beyond awareness-raising, steps are being taken to strengthen the legal processes, including the establishment of a new sexual and gender-based violence (SGBV) Crimes Unit in the Ministry of Justice, and a Women and Children's Protection Unit in the police force, as well the addition of more services victims of SGBV, such as health clinics, safe houses, and counseling.[v]

Despite the state's efforts at encouraging women to come forward and make use of the formal legal system, the reality is that the post-conflict legal system is ill-equipped to respond effectively or fairly to the task of prosecuting or even deterring SGBV crimes. A scarcity of human and financial resources challenge the system at every turn, and the police and the criminal justice system remain particularly weak. Victims who are willing to bring their cases to the police rarely see them reach court. Instead, victims who come forth are more likely to experience stigma and retraumatization, as their cases languish in the legal system and they are forced to push their own cases through, often paying fees at every step of the process. Judges are often skeptical of victims, and there is no forensic evidence capacity in the Liberian criminal justice system. In rural areas, the problems are more acute, exacerbated further by the small number of police and judicial resources, the lack of public trust in representatives of the state, the long travel distances involved, and the social pressures put on victims, stemming from patriarchal cultural traditions, not to take cases to court.

While SGBV is an extremely serious issue for women and girls in post-conflict Liberia, it is difficult to determine the full extent of the problem. Several issues account for this situation such as surveying difficulties (both inherent in the subject and particular to Liberia), including the fact that many of the statistics commonly cited do not differentiate between violence perpetrated during the conflict and violence perpetrated post-conflict, or sexual violence within marriage and rape by strangers, or between violence against women and sexual violence. Perhaps the most methodologically rigorous survey produced recently was a women's reproductive health survey conducted by the Centers for Disease Control and Prevention (CDC) in Lofa County in 2006 (Centers for Disease Control, 2007). Lofa County has a population of 276,347 and was selected as a site of this research because of the almost complete destruction of its infrastructure during the conflict with concomitant high population displacement. This study found that more than half of the women interviewed (58.9%) reported at least one sexually violent incident during the most recent conflict, and almost 90% reported at least one physical violation, although violent incidents have reportedly decreased since the end of the war.

However, SGBV continues to be a serious issue for women and girls. Unlike during the war, the survey found that violence against women is now much more likely to be committed by a family member or someone known to the victim. An additional category of violence for which there is strong anecdotal evidence is a high number of sexual violations being committed against school-age girls. One possible indicator of this phenomenon of "sex for grades" is the high number of teen pregnancies reported among young women attending school.

The pervasiveness of rape and sexual violence presents significant challenges for both social workers, who are working from a preventative, community-education perspective while attempting to provide post-trauma care, and restorative justice peace workers. For the latter, the challenges are a consequence of pursuing an approach of criminal prosecution and deterrents when the state's ability to implement such measures is limited. For social workers, there are substantial cultural constraints regarding community attitudes towards rape, as well as a lack of resources for providing safe haven as an alternative for women at risk. Ma Agnes described the lack of receptivity of the victim to such services as a shelter for women who are the victims of sexual violence:

> *You may not find a lot of people coming, especially after we resolved our civil crisis, people say I was raped and I didn't die, and so what happened is I got on with my life.*

She continues to pragmatically explain that due to lack of resources, energy is not invested in promoting an alternative for women at this point, such as a specific center to provide a safe place outside of the community for victims. Given the sheer number of women, she also implies that there is some community normalization of this experience:

> *And another thing is that the service is not there. . . . There are no rooms for battered women. So why start a program when you know that when you start, you don't have anywhere to put them. You don't have the resources to retain those places. The U.N., I think they are starting with one NGO. But the safe home is nothing compared to the level of battered women that we have in our community.*

Community Solutions

Traditionally, communities have set procedures for dealing with rape when it occurred, as with to other categories of crime. The Resource Center for Community Empowerment and Integrated Development Report of Traditional Justice (n.d.) contains the following description of how rape cases are dealt with in different areas:

> *Among the Kru, Grebo, Belleh and Krahn, when a rape occurred, the families of the raped victim and the rapist secretly handled the issue to avoid the victim being stigmatized. The rapist was not allowed to take part in the deliberations. At the meeting, the head of the rapist's family walked to the family of the raped victim with the youngest palm branch in his hand and knelt down bare footedly holding the raped victim's father's feet. The man remains bowing and held the raped victim's father's feet until the palm branch was taken away. The man making the appeal also had to begin to ask for forgiveness and to apologize to the raped victim's family. To express an acceptance of forgiveness, the raped victim's father took the palm branch and placed his right hand on the back of the one asking for forgiveness. (p. 32)*

The resolution of the conflict further involved the payment of fines by the rapist.

> In River Gee, the story was told of a girl who was raped. The fines paid by the rapist included one billy goat, one black rooster, half bag of rice and three gallons of red oil. If the raped victim was married or not, the rapist shouldered the responsibility for the health care of the raped victim. However, the trend and weight of a rape case depended on what stance the victim's family pursued; and how the community perceived the issue. In the three counties of River Gee, Maryland and Grand Kru, after the resolution the doer was still not considered free until the unmarried raped victim is able to give birth. If over a protracted period the unmarried raped lady was unable to give birth to a child, the rapist is made to marry the girl (p. 33)

While forcing the rapist to marry the victim may appear abhorrent and counter-intuitive to the Western mindset, this approach has strong logic in a society that values women socially and economically for their ability to bear children. Equally, a man's status is measured by the number of wives and children he has. Therefore, if a woman is unable to have a child as a result of rape, she will be unable to keep a husband, and so it will be the rapist's responsibility, in the eyes of the community, to look after the woman as his wife.

Skill-Building

In her interview for this chapter, Ma Agnes described social work as a fledgling, yet determined profession. In Liberia, social workers have less to do with counseling or service delivery, and much more to do with community organization and mobilization. For these roles, social workers need to be adept in facilitation, communication, and community-building skills.

At this point in Liberia's recovery, social workers often function as important supporters and implementers for international NGO humanitarian and development projects. While the positions may not specifically call for social workers, many NGO's hire social workers to facilitate and implement their mission. The Carter Center, for example (where one of this chapter's authors is employed), works on sexual violence issues as part of its access to justice work in Liberia, and has recently hired a social worker to facilitate the Center's work in rural areas of Liberia.

According to Ma Agnes, social work does not receive respect as a profession from the larger community (see also Cox & Pawar, 2006; Healy, 2005). Mohan (2008) lays out a challenge to consider international social work as a unique discipline of academic significance in which the profession's vocabulary of change and social well-being is crucial to the process of social transformation. Although there is no formalized link between restorative justice and social work in Liberia, they operate in a parallel process as they address family and community needs, as demonstrated in the description provided by Ma Agnes.

Given the dearth of resources, coupled with strong community traditions based on values that embrace peaceful solutions in spite of the violence that has so marred the country, both restorative justice practitioners and social workers must logically partner with the strengths that lie within the community to solve the problems that lie within. Some scholars suggest that the notion of PTSD and trauma-related disorders is a Western construct, and that trauma is culturally determined (Maynard, 1997). Maynard described a 5-phase process of psychosocial recovery that is critical to healing from the trauma of war and conflict. This model seems quite relevant to the issues addressed in this chapter, and also speaks to the underlying goals of restorative justice processes and the human rights and relational healing work of social workers both globally and in Liberia. The phases are as follows:

1. Establishing safety
2. Communalization and bereavement
3. Rebuilding trust and the capacity to trust
4. Reestablishing personal and social morality
5. Reintegration and establishing democratic discourse

Safety, as in Maslow's hierarchy of needs, is a crucial first step in a recovery process. Here, safety refers to being physically safe so that a sense of security can be established. Communalization and bereavement occur in the mutual sharing of stories of traumatic experiences, and the comfort derived from sharing with other people who understand and are able to listen. This stage validates the grief process and allows it to occur freely, paving the way for healing emotional wounds while laying the groundwork for the rebuilding of trust, which is critical in the repair and regeneration of interpersonal and intimate relationships. Next come the reestablishment of the agreed-upon codes of behavior and morality that communities require to function successfully and which are so broken in times of war and extreme conflict. This step is particularly relevant to the work of peacekeepers and the restorative justice process. The final step, of reintegration and valuing diverse voices within the community, leads to the development of openness, openmindedness, and growth from new information. This last phase is essential to the future growth and development within the community and lays the groundwork for a democratic process. These phases speak to the work that restorative justice and social work share in creating a society where, ideally, civil discourse and social justice are able to evolve.

NEXT STEPS AND CONCLUSIONS

In this chapter, the authors have explored some of the challenges facing Liberia, a country very recently torn apart by a prolonged and vicious war, as well as the issues that human service workers are confronting in their healing work to help in overcoming those challenges. The war pitted communities against each other, as many in the population could be considered perpetrators and many more as victims. Liberia, like many developing countries, is struggling to integrate diverse and polarized groups within an accepted moral and civil code of behavior and ethics.

Social work, a new and emerging profession in Liberia, is slowly working to establish its professional presence in a country where problem-solving and healing traditionally took place within the community, guided by indigenous practices and cultural mores. Faced with an abysmal lack of resources as well as a staggering level of need, social workers must shoulder the task of integrating professional values with the realities of the current state of the culture. Similarly, restorative justice processes are making slow but steady progress in rebuilding the fabric of a just society where there is a rule of actual and unwritten rules to guide the moral conduct and interpersonal behaviors of Liberians.

Many in the human services arena have written about the human impact of wars in African countries, particularly as related to trauma. Liberia's recent history has been particularly violent and yet, even with its massive problems, progress is occurring, as social workers and peace workers partner with the communities and often discover the solutions that have seemed so elusive. As Ma Agnes stated:

> So, because of the training, a lot of changes are taking place. Most of the orphanages are being closed down because we have social workers assigned to them, and the social workers saw how the children were being treated, and they reported cases. Reported the cases, before then, you wouldn't do that because they didn't know, they didn't know what they were supposed to do there. All they knew was they were supposed to take care of the children. Some of the orphanages you went to, you couldn't get the history of the children. There were no records that were being kept. But now you can walk into the orphanages that are left open now, and they have trained social workers, and you can pull a child's file, and get the child's history, you can locate a chart, you can read about a child. . . . So it is actually changing from what it used to be.

When considering the connection between social work and restorative justice in international contexts, various areas emerge as points for collaboration and intersection. As the example of Liberia suggests, national issues that involve widespread violence and trauma call for responses that involve redress and promotion of human rights. In addition to war, poverty, and abuses, those in Liberia require a way to integrate the experiences of their past while making a way to forge forward into new eras. While social work often focuses on interpersonal and community wounds, restorative justice practice provides methods to enable those involved in these incidents to address each other. In places where there have been grave offenses such as Liberia, involvement from both sets of professionals is warranted.

In spite of the potential intersection and collaboration between restorative justice and social work practitioners, there may be a different "fit" between the two areas in different global contexts. In this chapter, there were several areas of practice detailed that required involvement by both approaches, as the focus was on empowerment and reconciliation at the community level. In other countries and cultures, different orientations to practice may exist that place restorative justice and social work at different philosophical places. Just as the practice of social work in the U.S. developed from divergent perspectives and orientations (see Chapter 2), so different cultural perspectives will dominate the forms of practice in different parts of the world. As such, restorative justice and social work may have different involvements across cultural contexts. In spite of potential differences, international social work and restorative justice initiatives have great potential. Places across the globe where strife, civil unrest, and violence have occurred would benefit from both practices.

ACKNOWLEDGMENTS

The authors would like to sincerely thank Ms. Laurie Reyman, MSW, Project Officer, Access to Justice Project, the Carter Center/Liberia for her insightful interview; Ma Agnes, (not her real name), a Liberian social worker, for generously agreeing to be interviewed; and Meredith Tetloff, MSW, University of Georgia, doctoral student in social work and Pamela Owenta, University of Georgia, graduate student in social work for providing research assistance with this project.

NOTES

i A copy of the final report, THE TRUTH AND RECONCILIATION COMMISSION OF LIBERIA (TRC) can be accessed at: https://www.trcofliberia.org/news-1/press-releases/the-truth-and-reconciliation-commission-of-liberia-trc-have-release-the-publication-of-its-final-reports-after-several-weeks-of-editing-and-technical-work-leading-to-its-publication-the-report-which-is-an-edited-version-of-the-201ctrc-final-report

ii As a proportion of the population, this number is significantly higher that the equivalent for the South African TRC.

iii The authors would like to acknowledge both Ms. Laurie Reyman, MSW coordinator for the Community Legal Advisors program of the Carter Center in Liberia for conducting this interview with Ma Agnes, and Meredith Tetloff, MSW, University of Georgia doctoral student assistant, for transcribing it.

iv Both "Agnes Duncan" and "Ma Agnes" are pseudonyms.

v For a critical description of the international community's unsuccessful approach to service delivery on sexual and gender-based violence in Liberia see: "Nobody Gets

Justice Here: Addressing Sexual and Gender Based Violence and the Rule of Law in Liberia," Niels Nagelhus Schia and Benjamin de Carvalho, Norwegian Institute of International Affairs, Department of Security and Conflict Management, Security in Practice 5, 2009 [NUPI Working Paper 761].

REFERENCES

Center for Human Rights. (1994). *Human Rights and Social Work: A Manual for Schools of Social Work and the Social Work Profession.* Centre for Human Rights. A Report from the United Nations, New York & Geneva.

Centers for Disease Control and Prevention. (2007).Women's reproductive health in Liberia: The Lofa reproductive health survey. Retrieved September 14, 2009, from http://www.aidsandemergencies.org/cms/documents/20080901_Liberia_RH_survey_report.pdf

Cox, D., & Pawar, M. (2006). *International social work: Issues, strategies, and programs.* Thousand Oaks, CA: Sage Publications.

Freire, P. (1972). *Pedagogy of the oppressed.* London: Penguin.

Goodwin-Gill, G. S., & Cohn, I. (1994). *Child soldiers: The role of children in armed conflicts.* Oxford: Clarendon Press.

Hayner, P. B. (1994). Fifteen truth commissions—1974 to 1994: A comparative study. *Human Rights Quarterly, 16*(4), 597–655.

Healy, L. M. (2008). Exploring the history of social work as a human rights profession. *International Social Work, 51*(6), 735–748.

Healy, L.M. (2001). International social work: Professional action in an interdependent world. NY: Oxford University Press.

Healy, L. M., & Thomas, R. L. (2007). International social work: A retrospective in the 50th year. *International Social Work, 50,* 581–596.

International Center for Transitional Justice. (2002). Exploring the relationship between the special court and the truth and reconciliation commission of Sierra Leone. Retrieved May 7, 2010 from http://www.ictj.org/images/content/0/8/084.pdf.

Jalloh, C., & Marong, A. (2005). Ending impunity: The case for war crimes trials in Liberia. *African Journal of Legal Studies, 11,* 53–74.

Lewis, N. (1999). Social recovery from armed conflict. In G. Harris (Ed.), *Recovery from armed conflict in developing countries* (pp. 95–110). London: Routledge.

Levitt, J. (2005). *The evolution of deadly conflict in Liberia, from paternaltarianism to state collapse.* Durham, NC: Carolina Academic Press.

Liebenow, J. G. (1987). *Liberia: The quest for democracy.* Bloomington, IN: Indiana University Press.

Maynard, K. A. (1997). Rebuilding community: Psychosocial healing, reintegration, and reconciliation at the grassroots level. In K. Kumar (Ed.), *Rebuilding societies after civil war* (pp. 203–226). Boulder, CO: Lynne Rienner Publishers.

Mohan, B. (2008). Rethinking international social work. *International Social Work, 51,* 11–24.

Republic of Liberia Truth and Reconciliation Commission. Final report. Retrieved October 3, 2009, from https://www.trcofliberia.org/reports/final/final-report/trc-of-liberia-final-report-volume-ii.pdf

Resource Center for Community Empowerment and Integrated Development. (2005). Exploring the relationship between the special court and the truth and reconciliation commission of Sierra Leone. Retrieved October 4, 2009, from http://www.ictj.org/images/content/0/8/084.pdf

Resource Center for Community Empowerment and Integrated Development. (n.d.). *Traditional forms of reconciliation in Liberia.* Archived at the The Carter Center Resource Room, The Carter Center, Atlanta, GA.

Robertson, G. (2000). *Crimes against humanity: The struggle for global justice.* London: Penguin Books.

Roche, D. (2006). Dimensions of restorative justice. *Journal of Social Issues, 62*(2), 217–238.

Schia, N., & De Carvalho, B. (2009). *Nobody gets justice here: Addressing sexual and gender based violence and the rule of law in Liberia.* Norwegian Institute of International Affairs, Department of Security and Conflict Management, Security in Practice 5, [NUPI Working Paper 761].

Schugurensky, D. (2005) History of education: Selected moments of the 20th century. Retrieved April 15, 2009, from http://www.oise.utoronto.ca/research/edu20/home.html

Utas, M. (2005). Victimcy, girlfriending, soldiering: Tactic agency in a young women's social navigation of the Liberian war zone. *Anthropological Quarterly, 78,* 403–430.

Chapter Twelve

Restorative Justice and Aging: Promise for Integrated Practice

ALEXANDRA LEE CRAMPTON AND NANCY P. KROPF

This century will bring significant demographic changes within the population, especially among the oldest cohorts. Currently, 13% of the population is 65 years of age or older; however, this percentage is expected to double as the baby boomer generation reaches later life. By 2050, 25% of the population is expected to be over 65, with the greatest increase expected in the population over age 85 (National Center for Health Statistics, 2009).

The expected changes have important implications for family and community life. First, there will be greater numbers of older adults who will need increased supports into their later years. This is in part due to longevity trends, in which average life expectancy has increased by 10 years over the past generation, to just under age 80 (United Nations, Department of Economic and Social Affairs, Population Division, 2009). In addition, family composition has changed as family structures have shifted. Family trees are becoming more like beanpoles, in which each generation is smaller (e.g., fewer children are born) and the older members live longer lives. In addition, most adults have other responsibilities such as jobs and careers, caring for children, and other affiliations (e.g., PTA, religious memberships). Although a myth of aging is that significant numbers of older adults are placed into long-term care facilities, the reality is that 80% of care is provided by informal supports, such as family members and friends (Hooyman, 2008). For many midlife adults, eldercare requirements are superimposed on full lives that have limited room to assume the time-consuming and intimate demands of some later life situations.

One shared concern in geriatric[i] social work and restorative justice is helping older adults who become frail, dependent, and vulnerable. Given shrinking family size and geographic separation, care provision often falls on a spouse or one adult child. Those who do provide care often go to extraordinary lengths to provide assistance to older family members, sometimes to the detriment of their own physical and emotional functioning (Greenberg, Seltzer, & Brewer, 2006; Schulz & Beach, 1999). However, elder maltreatment does exist and includes physical, emotional, financial, and sexual abuse by both formal and informal care providers.

Abuse cases are hard to estimate, given the reluctance of many older adults to report cases or accept help (Nerenberg, 2008). However, estimates based on surveys of older adults and reported cases have found a range of 1.6% to 7.5% of older adults are victims of abuse (Brandl et. al., 2007).

Social workers are mandated to report cases of abuse to Adult Protective Services (APS). As APS has become more integrated with formal legal processes, elder advocates have sought alternatives to a retributive justice system. They have adapted restorative justice practice as used in child abuse and neglect cases (Nerenberg, Baldridge, & Benson, 2004). They have also developed mediation for adult guardianship and caregiving cases (Butterwick & Hommel, 2001). These interventions provide the greatest area of overlap between geriatric social work and restorative justice practices. In both approaches, severe cases of maltreatment or power imbalances may require referral to the criminal or civil justice system.

In this chapter, the benefits and limitations of social work and restorative practice approaches are explored in working with older adults. A basic contrast between the two disciplines is that geriatric social work focuses on care of individual older adults, while restorative justice focuses on harm caused to individuals, families, and community. Social work outcomes focus on preserving or enhancing the older adult's autonomy and dignity, while restorative outcomes focus on healing injury and repairing relationships. In addition, there is a social justice perspective in restorative justice that promotes accountability for the entire community when an offense has occurred. In the introduction to their book on restorative justice practices, Sullivan and Tifft (2006) state that, "as members of [the] community, we must rally to support those harmed by providing the short- and long-term care they require even in cases when no one has been identified as the offending person" (p. 2). Unfortunately, there continues to be inadequate responses in situations where older adults are at risk or have been harmed. This level of accountability is needed to create a greater array of social and health services when older adults have been maltreated by their family, others in the community, or service providers.

Another difference between social work and restorative justice is the wider range of roles that older adults may have within restorative justice practice. In particular, the role of older adults as mature advisors and spiritual healers as historically practiced among the Maori, Australian Aboriginal peoples, First Nation people, Native Hawaiians, and Native Americans, as well as in African-American communities. In this way, restorative justice has been able to harness the talents, experiences, and wisdom of the older population in ways that other fields (including social work) have not.

This chapter concludes with ways to integrate geriatric social work and restorative justice practices. The focus is on shared interest in cases of elder abuse and neglect. In these cases, social work interventions hinge on capacity assessment and preserving or promoting autonomy. Restorative justice interventions hinge on assessment of harm and reducing risk. While the assessment tools and intervention processes can differ, there are shared interests in elder empowerment, strengthening family systems, and identifying community resources.

GERIATRIC SOCIAL WORK

Current intervention approaches in geriatric social work promote functioning of the older individual, support families of older adults, and work to create elder-friendly communities. With advanced age, there is the probability that older adults will require additional supports from both formal and informal sources of support. In addition, decreased independence may also make the older population vulnerable to abusive situations from care providers and others with malicious intent.

As the aging population continues to grow, geriatric social work will need to expand interventions to both provide greater opportunities for older adults to stay as engaged and involved as possible, and to deal with situations where older adults have been mistreated. Within communities, opportunities for engaged and productive social outlets (e.g., meaningful volunteer work, leadership roles in communities) are needed to provide older adults with avenues to use their talents and feel worthwhile. The following section provides an overview of social work interventions in aging, and outlines approaches that have specific relevance to elder maltreatment, which is the focus of the case study.

Practice with Individuals

As the body ages, there are numerous normative and nonnormative physical changes that take place. Normal age-related changes include decreased visual acuity, hearing loss, reduced stamina, and changes in appetite and sleep-wake cycle. Although these changes create transitions for older adults, most people adjust to these changes and adapt without major problems or disruption to their lives.

However, the magnitude or cumulative impact of physical changes may overwhelm the coping ability of some individuals (Greene, 2008; Putnam & Stark, 2006). This situation might lead to increased isolation and social disengagement. Interventions with older adults involve helping them cope with new levels of functioning. In addition, psychoeducational approaches help older adults learn how to manage late life conditions such as living with cardiac problems or diabetes. The goal is to help individuals remain as independent and functional as possible, even when an older adult experiences changes in physical functioning.

In later life, the older adult experiences multiple areas of grief and loss. As people age, they may have to relinquish some activities or roles that have great meaning for them. When older adults need to stop driving, for example, this event may be very traumatic and affect their sense of independence (Ragland, Satariano, & MacLeod, 2005). In addition, social losses occur, such as retirement from a meaningful career and widowhood or widowerhood. Although losses are experienced at all life stages, the magnitude and cumulative impact of late life losses is a factor in geriatric depression, which is the primary mental health problem of late life. Social work interventions focus on helping the older adult remain engaged and socially connected. For example, widow-to-widow groups have demonstrated efficacy and help normalize the grief that comes from losing a partner in late life (Steward, Craig, MacPherson & Alexander, 2001). Other interventions can assist older adults in remaining actively engaged in meaningful social roles, such as offering activities and programs at senior centers that are convenient and accessible.

Geriatric depression is a particular risk situation of later life. Although depression is not a normative part of aging, significant numbers of older adults struggle with this mental health condition. Because various definitions are used, prevalence estimates for depression in community-based older adults are estimated between to be 8–20% of the population (Adamek & Slater, 2009). The highest rates—over 50%—are found in older adults who reside in long-term care facilities, such as nursing homes (Adamek, 2003). Particular risk situations for geriatric depression are health problems, significant losses without opportunities for new roles or life experiences (e.g. part-time employment or volunteering after retirement), and social isolation. In addition, geriatric depression can result from a perception of being burdensome to others, such as caregivers, or feeling helpless in overall functioning. Several intervention approaches have demonstrated efficacy with older adults (Adamek & Slater, 2009). These include cognitive behavioral therapy, reminiscence and life review, and pharmacological interventions.

Practice with Families

The aging process impacts not only older individuals, but the entire family. Those who care for aging relatives can experience stresses related to the balance of caregiving tasks, other family responsibilities such as their own children and marriage, and work demands. Caregivers are at increased risk for depression, anxiety, and other mental and physical health conditions that result from the challenges of care. A number of interventions are effective in helping caregivers with care provision, such as in-home supports and respite, psychoeducational approaches to teach new skills and coping, and support groups to connect with others in the caregiving role (Cassie & Sanders, 2009). These may be provided through both federal and state funding and service agencies; they are generally provided by the Aging Network as funded through the Older American's Act. These intervention approaches can assist the caregiver with the tasks associated with caregiver stress, to preserve their own health and well-being. In addition, the older adult is often able to remain in their home and community and prevent or forestall long term-care placement, due to the care and support of family members.

Significant numbers of older adults provide care to younger generations as well. When older adults are in this type of caregiving role, there typically are complex issues associated with care provision. Examples of older adult caregiving situations are grandparents who are raising their grandchildren, and parents of adults with physical, psychiatric, or developmental disabilities. Several social work interventions are helpful with these families. Case management helps the family become connected to resources in the community to receive appropriate health, mental health, and other needed resources (McCallion & Nickles, 2009; Myers, Kropf, & Robinson, 2002). In addition, older adults may need assistance with managing their own late-life issues, in conjunction with care. Permanency planning is a method used extensively with older parents of adult children with developmental disabilities. This intervention helps families construct plans for care if or when the older parent can no longer assume the caregiving role (Botsford & Rule, 2004).

Community and Policy Practice

Although a common myth of aging is that the majority of older adults live in residential settings, most live within their homes and communities (Federal Interagency Forum on Aging, 2008). Older adults who live in areas that lack resources, such as transportation or amenities (grocery stores, banks, pharmacies, etc.), often do not have the personal means to compensate. In these situations, older adults may go without vital necessities, or be vulnerable to risks associated with relying on others to take care of these needs (e.g., hiring someone unknown).

Community organizing and development activities can help address resource and access issues. These efforts can increase social capital within communities and enhance interpersonal relationships to better the environment overall. Although these practice methods have a long history in social work, there is limited application in working with older adults. One reason is the ageist view that older adults are not able or willing to participate in community activities, or that they are solely focused on recreational or leisure pursuits (Austin, Des Camp, Flux, McClelland, & Siepert, 2005). However, the aging of the population affords a significant challenge to recreate vital communities that include caring, compassion, and neighborhood connections (Siebert, Mutran & Reitzes, 1999).

Besides geographic communities, social work practitioners also work with non-place-based communities of older adults. Although these individuals may not live in the same geographical area, they may share similar life situations or sources of oppression. For example, the community of older adults who are gay and lesbian experiences issues as a community of individuals that affect their later life functioning. Examples include lack of trust in traditional service delivery models, which tend to be based upon a heterosexual model of relationships; lack of validation of and sensitivity to their primary relationships by many service providers; and lack of access to shared decision-making and resource-sharing for couples, due to their status as unmarried persons. Social work interventions can help establish bonds and relationships among these older adults by bringing these individuals together to foster a sense of community and efficacy (Zodikoff, 2006). Other non-place communities are individuals with physical challenges such as older adults who are deaf, blind, or have limited mobility; people who share a faith community such as older Jews or Muslims; and older adults who are non-English speakers.

At the more macro level of practice, debates have been waged about the inter-generational relationships between older adults and members of younger genera-tions. This intergenerational conflict perspective, often visible in a political context, sets up the false premise that supporting older adults takes away resources from children. From an advocacy perspective, social workers need to redefine the political debate and highlight these false dichotomies. The intergenerational sup-port provided by older adults as taxpayers and workers throughout their adult lives needs to be acknowledged. From an advocacy perspective, social workers need to be involved in the policy arena to have a voice in the way that policy debates, and subsequently resource allocation decisions, are made.

In summary, current intervention approaches in geriatric social work primarily focus on preserving functioning of the older adult. As the aging population con-tinues to grow, geriatric social work will need to expand interventions to both provide greater opportunities for older adults to stay as engaged and involved as possible, and to deal with situations where older adults have been mistreated. As the following section indicates, restorative justice practices have the promise of helping practitioners promote principles of social justice in geriatric social work.

RESTORATIVE JUSTICE AND OLDER ADULTS

Unlike social work, restorative justice does not center specifically on questions of aging and the challenges of growing older. Those who meet bureaucratic defini-tions of "old" as a chronological age (such as 60 or 65) may simply participate as adults. However, older age can be important in two ways. The first is found in restorative justice as developed from historic practices of indigenous groups. For example, Hawaiian elders in Kahuna have worked with mental health profession-als to restore use of a process called *Ho'oponopono* (Hurdle, 2002). These types of programs recognize elder leadership in convening meetings, facilitating dialogue, and determining outcomes that help heal injured parties, families, and communi-ties. In a focus group study asking Latino, African-American, and Cherokee par-ticipants about the cultural relevance of a restorative justice intervention model, each group commented on the value of including this role for family elders (Waites, Macgowan, Pennell, Carlton-LaNey, & Weil, 2004). This role has also been recognized in culturally sensitive practice with African-American families and kinship care (Wilhelmus, 1998). In child welfare cases, grandparents may not only play an important role as interested parties, but also provide temporary child care so that the child is not removed from the family. In a study with African-American grandmothers, for example, great pride was expressed by women in their ability to take responsibility for raising all children in the extended family (Murphy, Hunter, & Johnson, 2008).

A more recent development is the second way in which aging is important in restorative justice practice. This approach recognizes that older adults may be abused or neglected as they grow older and become more frail and dependent. These cases, like child welfare cases, must deal with the complication of victims who are dependent upon abusers for care. Taking initial direction from retributive justice alternatives developed in child welfare, restorative justice, when applied to cases of elder abuse or neglect, focuses on addressing harm and repairing relationships. This approach can be more appealing to older adults themselves, who may be afraid or simply reluctant to accuse family and caregivers (Groh, 2003).

Unlike children, however, older adults can refuse intervention. In fact, the more common challenges in Adult Protective Service (APS) cases are older adults who "self-neglect" and refuse help (Dubble, 2006). These situations create ethical dilemmas about harm and safety, and the competency of older adults to continue to make decisions in their own lives (Linzer, 2004; Wolf, 2000). In other cases, there is no criminal activity or overt harm as much as there is family conflict or avoidance of difficult decision making. Restorative justice can help focus discussion on meeting the needs of older adults in a more informal way than a court-based solution. In addition, family- and community-based interventions have been developed as a more culturally sensitive approach to working with Native American and other indigenous communities (Holkup, Salois, Tripp-Reimer, & Weinert, 2007).

Practice with Individuals

The romantic image of respected elders in traditional societies is often more complex in reality. While physical age may signal lifelong experience, elder status may require more than reaching a particular chronological milestone (Crampton, 2009). Additional factors include demonstrated maturity through decision-making, behavior, and roles played in the family and community. Life-cycle experiences, such as getting married, raising children, and mourning the death of one's parents, can be important (Oppong, 2004). As people turn to older adults for advice and conflict resolution, elder status is affirmed and strengthened (Bradford, 2002–2003).

Restorative justice is a way to build from the strength of these cultural practices. In working with indigenous communities across North America, Australia, and New Zealand, as well as African-American and Latino communities, respect for elder status can be an important way for professionals to build rapport. Invitation to elders as interested parties in cases can bring greater legitimacy and demonstrate cultural sensitivity. It may also lead to better outcomes, given the greater knowledge that lifelong community members will have about those directly involved in legal cases, as well as their greater insight into how suggested outcomes can repair relationships. This approach recognizes that formal education is not the only source of expertise, and that solutions should strengthen, rather than replace, family and community decision making.

To help resist romanticization of elder status, cases in which older adults are abused and neglected must be recognized. Restorative justice practices help empower abused and neglected elders to safely acknowledge this harm and decide how to better meet their needs. They are also used to encourage older adults to report cases and seek help. Using a restorative justice lens, harm has not only been caused to the older adult but to the family system, and all family members are encouraged to include their concerns in family meetings.

Whether to use a retributive or restorative justice approach depends upon an evaluation of the power dynamics between victim and abuser. Assessment skills are in part drawn from domestic violence scholarship and the study of victimology (Nerenberg, 2008). The psychological, emotional, and physical dynamic between victim and abuser can raise questions about the autonomy of victims in these cases. A severe power imbalance does not realistically allow the victim to fully participate without risk (or fear) of harm. In many programs, participation must be voluntary. Special attention is given to how intervention may risk escalating violence, such as when the abuser retaliates against the victim for bringing a case to the attention of private entities. In these circumstances, the case may be referred to criminal or civil court systems.

Practice with Families

Family dynamics, history, and capacity to care for each other are often key issues in elder abuse and neglect. They can also help explain why older adults withdraw and risk self-neglect. Thus, while some cases include abusive or neglectful family members, they may also include members who were unaware of problems until a crisis arose. Gaining the trust and voluntary participation of family and informal caregivers is important for successful intervention. Examples of programs include a Family Care Conference (FCC) program developed with a Northwestern Native American community (Holkup et al., 2007).

Mediation and family conferences are related interventions developed to address the shortcomings of the court system when it comes to addressing elder care cases. One Native American caregiver program, for example, uses family conferences to "help families that are in conflict or having difficulties related to caregiving, including burnout and sibling rivalry, the need to address end-of-life issues, and confronting anger and guilt" (Nerenberg, 2008). While elder mediation does not typically include a social justice component, this intervention similarly focuses on identifying the needs of older adults and how to strengthen family systems to provide care. Mediation with older adults was pioneered by the Center for Social Gerontology for use as part of, and as an alternative to, guardianship (Nerenberg, 2008). In recognition that guardianship petitions can be filed out of frustration in the face of family conflict, adult guardianship mediation can be used to help families work through difficult decisions and perhaps identify less restrictive alternatives to full guardianship (Butterwick & Hommel, 2001).

Community Practice and Policy

In restorative justice, the larger context in which individual incidents cause harm is a key focus. Crimes and crises of care are viewed not only as individual events, but also as an issue of social justice, where wounding extends beyond the traditional perpetrator–victim model. From a strengths perspective, older adults have much to contribute to this process from their life experiences. In repairing relationships and healing community, older adults can act as leaders, caregivers, and care recipients. In historic practice, Native Americans who facilitated peacemaking processes had "lived a long and exemplary life in spiritual and temporal terms" (Bradford, 2002–2003, p. 166). This peacemaker provides

> *"guidance" that encourages people to live up to their communal responsibilities, requests apologies, suggests means and amounts of restitution, and ensures that all parties depart with "their tails up [rather than one] with tail up, one with tail down." (Bradford, 2002–2003, p. 166)*

The previously mentioned elder abuse intervention program called the Family Circle Conference draws from such tradition (Holkup et al., 2007). A community-based approach not only creates a larger scope of responsibility, but can also be a more comfortable way for older adults to receive help. For example, the refusal of elders to prosecute through a retributive system prompted Arlene Groh (2003) to develop a restorative justice program in collaboration with community agencies representing, "health, justice, social services, ethno-cultural, faith, and First Nations" in Ontario, Canada (p.1). Additionally, Bazemore (1999) describes examples of juvenile court reform programs across the United States in which youth may be assigned to help older adults as part of community service.

The following case study provides an example of an older man who became a widower after 51 years of marriage. As a result, one of his adult children assumed a primary caregiving role with him, and there was suspicion that she was taking advantage of her father. This case situation is not atypical, as it requires practitioners to determine whether the older adult is being maltreated, assess the safety risk of the older person, and determine level of ability the older adult has to make independent decisions about this situation. However, it also brings up other issues about care provision in later life. Overall, the case provides a good example of interventions from both a social work and restorative justice perspective.

CASE STUDY: THE SCHNEIDER FAMILY

John and Martha Schneider (all names have been changed to protect the privacy of individuals) moved to Littleton, a medium-sized Western city, almost 50 years ago. They raised four children, all of whom attended the local public schools. John, now age 74, retired at the age of 65. His health has been generally good, although he was a smoker up until his first grandson was born 15 years ago. Martha, however, became sick with cancer four years ago and died about one year ago. The four children and their families attended the funeral. The youngest, Sarah, was 42 years old, recently divorced, and had one 7-year-old daughter, Chloe. She and Chloe stayed after the funeral to help John. She was able to do this in part because she had recently lost her job.

John and Martha had been active in a local church—or, rather, Martha was active and John attended services with her. As she became more ill, members of the church helped out with errands and often dropped by to visit. One of them, Kathy, remembers being relieved to learn that Sarah was going to be able to stay while John grieved and adjusted to life without Martha.

In the first couple months after the funeral, Sarah, John, and Chloe were seen around town running errands and attending some local events. Over time, however, John seemed to prefer to stay at home. Sarah would then leave Chloe with John while she was out. John also stopped attending church as regularly, which in some ways made sense given that his wife had been more directly involved. When asked about her father, Sarah politely thanked Kathy and other church members for their concern and told them that John was starting to get along just fine and so they did not need to worry.

Over time, however, Kathy did become more concerned. She wondered why John seemed to be withdrawing, rather than reintegrating into the community after his loss. She dropped by one day when Sarah was out and Chloe was in school. She was appalled by the messy state of the house. John had not shaved and seemed extremely withdrawn. He had previously been an active person, with a clear disdain for television. Yet, the television was on as a sort of background noise throughout her entire visit. Something just didn't seem right. She waited for Sarah to come home and then confronted her. At first, Sarah seemed sympathetic to Kathy's concerns and explained that John was keeping to himself a bit more as he lost more of his hearing and short-term memory. He was also feeling less able to move around easily. But Sarah then became defensive when Kathy asked whether Sarah had been taking him to a doctor—Sarah retorted, "It's just old age. Leave him alone."

John was embarrassed as the women argued over his health and well-being, but he did not say anything. Sarah told Kathy that she had no right to judge how Sarah kept house and eventually asked Kathy to leave. Kathy did leave and called APS. The APS worker arrived, interviewed both Sarah and John, and conducted a capacity assessment. John politely refused her help, repeatedly mentioned how grateful he was to his daughter for her help, explained how delighted he was to be with his granddaughter, and was evasive in answering questions about his health and mental health. Because the APS worker determined that John had the capacity to decide whether he wanted help, she could not do much more than refer father and daughter to available services.

A few weeks later, Kathy was expressing her concerns about John with church members. One of them happened to work at the local bank and mentioned that

John had recently added Sarah to his bank account. This prompted the comment that Sarah had been seen out shopping quite a bit, and was often seen withdrawing cash from ATMs. When the bank employee then checked on recent activity and discovered increasing numbers of checks written by Sarah for what were clearly her own expenses, Kathy felt she had to find another way to intervene. Clearly, this relationship had become one of dependency and exploitation. She considered contacting the police and reporting elder abuse, trying APS again, or filing a guardianship petition. She called the police, who opened a case file for alleged financial abuse and also referred her to an elder justice program to better address ongoing family caregiver issues.

When Kathy called the program, a case coordinator listened to her concerns and opened a case file. She took notes based on Kathy's concerns and a need to screen for domestic violence. She also noted prior APS involvement and the police investigation. She then called John, explained how she had been contacted by Kathy, explained the restorative justice process briefly, and asked for permission to visit John. As with the APS worker, John was polite and accepted the request. (The case coordinator ideally visits the older adult in order to better assess the home situation as well as the capacity of the older adult to communicate his wishes and to understand information. This capacity is important for determining if his participation in a restorative justice meeting would be helpful.)

At the end of the visit, the coordinator asked for John's permission to interview Sarah, and also asked whether there were others whom he thought should be involved in the conversation. She suggested that Kathy or perhaps another church member might attend, or that he might like to invite another support person. John explained that he felt other family members should not be involved, but allowed for the pastor to participate, given the important role he had played over the years in that family.

The next step for the coordinator was to repeat the communication process that started with John. She called Sarah and the pastor, explained background information as permitted by John, explained the restorative justice process, answered questions, took notes from Sarah and the pastor, and invited them to the meeting. Each agreed to attend and a meeting was scheduled. In this case, John was more comfortable meeting at home while Chloe was playing at a friend's house, so the meeting took place at his house.

During the meeting, each person shared their perspective and concerns. John was given the opportunity to speak first. Discussion included the pain of losing a wife and mother, Sarah's loss of her marriage and job, and the ways in which Sarah had become overwhelmed. She realized that she had started spending John's money out of resentment of her situation and a need to feel she was doing something for herself. She apologized to John. In addition, John mentioned briefly how lonely he had become and yet how much he wanted to be more of a part of his daughter's and granddaughter's lives. The meeting next addressed how to help John and Sarah to better manage finances and the household, as well as how

John might become better connected to the church and become involved in the local senior center. The facilitator also explained support services available to Sarah. The meeting facilitator encouraged them to contact her again if any party was interested and that she would check in with them in six months to see how things were going. If this meeting had been scheduled through the courts as part of an elder abuse case, then a written statement as agreed upon by all parties could be used to explain resolution on the financial issues and how Sarah could better meet John's needs in the future.

Key Points

Abuse/Neglect

The case example demonstrates how the allegation of maltreatment is typically uncovered—by a person outside of the immediate situation. In the Schneider example, Kathy, an acquaintance from church, sensed that something was wrong, and she focused on Sarah as abusive and neglectful. Kathy was particularly concerned about financial exploitation.

This allegation may have been true, but there were additional issues that complicated the case. Investigation of elder abuse and neglect usually involves asking how the older adult has changed, and what life transitions (biological, social, financial, etc.), may have prompted the change. This case began as one focused on John's grief over the death of Martha. John's continual withdrawal, coupled with changes in self-care and habits, raised questions of self neglect as well as adequacy of care provision. Isolation can indicate depression and also embarrassment over changes in health that bring some level of disability, such as when older adults avoid social occasions due to hearing or short-term memory loss. Health and mental health issues are easily intertwined. At the same time, the dynamic between Sarah and John may have become difficult, possibly indicated by Sarah's dismissive response that John was just "getting old." The financial exploitation issue raised questions of why Sarah felt entitled to withdraw John's money, whether she was spending for the household or just herself, and how John handled finances before her arrival.

Caregiving

This case is typical in that one family member was providing care, and that person was a daughter (the other common caregiver is a spouse). The case also brings up another typical care provision role, that of the so-called "sandwich generation," which describes a caregiver who has responsibilities for both older parents and younger children.

In this example, Sarah was providing care to both her father and her daughter. Abuse or neglect can emerge over time, as the caregiver becomes overwhelmed or assumes too much responsibility. Sarah may have started to exploit her father financially to fill the void she felt after losing her marriage and job, or as a result of past family dynamics that she may have resented. She may have felt burdened, rather than proud of herself for caring for her father out of compassion. Although caregiving can bring people closer together, this case may not have been one simply of an independent daughter caring for her father, but rather a complicated dynamic of interdependence coupled with grief and loss.

Capacity and Risk Assessment

In elder abuse and neglect cases, adults can decide whether they want intervention unless they are incapacitated or at risk of undue influence and harm. In this case, the APS worker determined that John did have the capacity to understand his situation and make decisions. The worker determined that he was not at enough risk for professionals to ignore his stated wishes and intervene on his behalf.

Legal obligations would shift, however, if John had dementia or a similarly incapacitating condition. If Kathy were to file a guardianship petition, a probate judge (or a jury) would determine whether John was incapacitated as defined by state law. The judge could order a guardian to provide "care of the person" or a conservator to take control over John's finances.

Community Support

Community support issues emerged in this case as well. One such issue was that of how much involvement individuals outside of the family should have in family affairs. For example, should Kathy have stayed out of family business, or did she have a responsibility to refer this case? How was this case more than one of simply a father and daughter?

Evidence suggests that concern was warranted. Sarah had isolated her father by refusing help and leaving him alone while she went out to take a break from her troubles. She assumed her father did not need a doctor unless there was some obvious crisis. She accepted health changes as normal, something that requires no professional attention. She was also taking more and more money from her father, rationalizing to herself that she should be compensated for offering care and that this money was ultimately family money anyway. And yet, she also relied on her father to offer free babysitting and a place to stay.

These major case points help provide a framework for describing the skills used by both social work and restorative justice within this case example. Both disciplines focus on safety and resource issues. Using the key points as a framework, social work and restorative justice skills will be applied to the Schneider family situation.

SKILL BUILDING

Social Work Skills

The overall goal in a situation of alleged elder maltreatment is to decrease risk and increase the safety of the older adult. With the case of John, a social worker might have focusd on issues of possible financial exploitation, but also the signs of geriatric depression. In addition, there are ethical issues in dealing with conditions of maltreatment with older adults. Unless the older adult is assessed as incapable of competent decision making, the person may choose to remain in a situation that could result in harm. Social workers need to have well-refined assessment skills, and to be able to establish trusting relationships with these older adults, even in a short period of time. In the Schneider case, the practitioner would evaluate whether the social isolation and withdrawal was a consequence of his grief and loss, or complicated by the dynamics with his daughter. Clearly, these are subjects that require interpersonal skills, in order to interview older adults about these sensitive personal issues.

In order to accurately evaluate potential maltreatment conditions, social workers who practice with older adults need to be knowledgeable about geriatric conditions and functioning. In particular, older adults need to be assessed to determine if they are capable of making judgments and decisions, as dementia and other organic conditions may limit the older person's abilities. For example, was there evidence that John did not have competence to make reasonable decisions in his financial dealings? In family situations where a spouse or partner has acted as a buffer for decreased competence, a death may herald a precipitous decline in functioning for the older adult. In addition, social changes may reflect a situation where an older adult is being maltreated such as the case example. Although John had experienced a significant loss, his social withdrawal was extreme and needed to be investigated.

Within the area of elder maltreatment, the social worker needs to have good case management skills. As a case manager, the practitioner needs to possess thorough knowledge of resources within the community that can be involved to support the older adult, such as alternative living arrangements, healthcare resources, and financial assistance. In the Schneider case, a case manager may have needed to find resources to help the family cope, such as a program to help John reengage with the community. If part of the issue is caregiver stress, community resources to give John an alternate social outlet and to help Sarah with the emotional aspects of care could help the family function more effectively.

As the case study suggests, interpersonal and family dynamics are an important part of understanding elder abuse and neglect. Caregiver burden is a significant predictor of maltreatment (Beach et al., 2005; Gordon & Brill, 2001). With the aging of the population, increasing numbers of families will have responsibility for assisting an older individual. Social workers need to assess the level of caregiving stress that exists within a family and assist with getting caregivers support for their tasks of care. Several types of intervention protocols have demonstrated efficacy in helping reduce burden, such as psychoeducational and support groups, skill-building programs, and respite care (Cassie & Sanders, 2009).

Restorative Justice Skills

As in other restorative justice practices, this case focused on the question of harm as well as how to repair the relationship between John and Sarah. Within this discussion, John and Sarah's needs were identified, as were as resources that could provide support. This case began with referral by Kathy. The first skill a practitioner needs is how to sensitively contact interested parties. John had already refused intervention, and might have been wary or embarrassed to have an outsider know of his situation. Through discussion and interviews with John and Sarah, the next question was, what additional parties should be contacted, given permission from John? Additional family members might have been contacted, particularly John's other children and any close friends or family. Additional church members might have been contacted also, again with the knowledge and permission of John. The practitioner needs to establish the trust and confidence to allow slow disclosure of this issue as interested parties are contacted and consulted for their input.

The next skill is how to explain the restorative justice process and work with the family to determine who should attend the meeting. In this case, John and Sarah might have been more comfortable talking alone before additional members were invited to additional meetings. Or, to address concern about abuse, it may have helped to have additional family members present, or an elder advocate who could help lessen any power imbalance between John and Sarah. Participation had to be voluntary, and Sarah had to be willing to be held accountable for her actions. Accommodations for older adults can include holding meetings at their home for convenience and privacy, conducting meetings at the time of day when they are most rested and alert, and taking frequent breaks. In related programs of elder mediation, practitioners may conduct a capacity assessment to ensure that the older adult can participate in discussion and decision making.

The third skill is facilitation of the meeting. Facilitators follow a basic format of introductions, determining ground rules, sharing, discussion, and decision making. More important, however, are skills in demonstrating respect and compassion for all participants and the process so that the group can work effectively to identify problems and solutions. As explained by Groh (2003),

> It is essential that facilitators understand and are sensitive to the complex issues of elder abuse. At the same time, they need to ensure that sensitivity does not express itself in an attempt to rescue the older adult. . . . Facilitators contribute to a sensitive, responsive restorative justice approach when they: help the group stay focused and productive by asking the right questions, ensure everyone present is heard, make sure the final agreement addresses relevant needs and is workable, ensure that individuals in the group, while denouncing the offending behavior, show support of the person who offended, balancing an ethic of care and an ethic of justice. (p. 7)

In this process, more than one meeting may be necessary. This is especially true with older adults, who might have less stamina than younger participants. In addition, facilitators may follow up with parties to see if they would like additional meetings or to be connected with additional resources. This is not necessarily case management (Holkup et al., 2007). Instead, the practitioner ensures that families are aware of available resources and how to make the most use of them.

This general description of a program may be modified in working with indigenous populations and communities of color. Social workers may take a more passive role as coordinator of meetings and care plans, rather than that of initiator or even facilitator, so that the family and community are the decision makers. In the Family Care Conference program, for example, the facilitators are middle-aged and older members of the community who are well-known and widely respected (Holkup et al., 2007). They do not directly handle cases in their own families but do meet to discuss cases. Food is brought by the facilitator, shared during the meeting, and given to participants to take home. A spiritual leader is invited to open and close the meeting in prayer. After sharing initial information, the facilitator leaves the room so that the family may deliberate in private.

SOCIAL WORK AND RESTORATIVE JUSTICE: COMPARISON OF PRACTICE AND LIMITATIONS

As a case of alleged abuse and neglect, both social work and restorative justice use similar skills to sensitively interview interested parties and assess John's risk of harm. Both include the importance of elder empowerment and preserving or promoting autonomy. Outcomes from either approach could include identifying resources that might improve the caregiving context and better meet John's needs.

One assessment difference is that the case in geriatric social work is considered as one of John as an older adult, while the case in restorative justice is one focused on the caregiving relationship and context. This means that social workers are more likely to have extensive training in assessing John's health and mental health needs and abilities as part of his aging process. His relationships with Sarah and Kathy are only important as a source of caregiving which can also be assessed and strengthened. Sarah's health and mental health needs, for example, are a factor only as they impact her ability to care for John. Church members may not be consulted beyond the referral process, unless they are identified as part of John's caregiving network.

In restorative justice, however, the focus on relationships, process, and context means that more emphasis might be placed on holding Sarah accountable for her actions and also identifying her needs and concerns. In this way, John's situation is not located solely within his abilities but is intimately connected to his social environment. Through understanding of victimology, practitioners address how John's vulnerability may be caused by dynamics between him and his daughter.

Both approaches share limitations. One is that both require participants who are voluntary and neither can fully address abuse cases of violence or severe power imbalance. These cases are typically referred to the criminal or civil justice system. Otherwise, John's situation could be exacerbated if Sarah was able to impose her will on the process and outcomes, or if she felt threatened and retaliated.

An additional question in both approaches is how to intervene if John did not have the capacity to understand his situation, identify his needs, and make decisions. Asking John to participate in development of a care plan or in a restorative justice meeting might not have been be appropriate. These cases might be referred to probate court as an adult guardianship case, or a family member might be identified who could become the legal or healthcare decision-maker on behalf of John (Crampton, 2004).

Limitations of A Geriatric Social Work Approach

Geriatric social work is still a relatively new area of practice. Although more social workers are working with older adults and their families, few practitioners report that they have adequate preparation for working with the geriatric population (Scharlach, Damron-Rodriquez, Robinson, & Feldman, 2000). As a result, social workers are unaware of how issues of aging are key aspects of various client situations. For example, the person and environment configuration is a basic premise of social work practice. Yet, practice tends to focus on older adults as individuals first, and then expand to include the social environment. In the Schneider case, the grief and loss that John experienced after Martha's death was real. However, Martha also seemed to serve as a social conduit for John and after her death, he lost a partner who had helped him connect to others. Practitioners who have limited knowledge of aging may not understand the intricate balance between older persons and their environment. When problems occur, the paradoxical impact can be to blame the older adult or label the older person as resistant to receiving help. A great example is when older adults resist admitting abuse due to a fear that they will be forced out of their home, or that the abuser will retaliate and create a greater hardship for them.

The case example also highlights another limitation in geriatric social work practice. Although a vitally important area of practice, elder maltreatment has not gotten the attention of either child abuse and neglect or domestic violence. Because of the greater research and practice emphasis in those areas to date, social work training would benefit from incorporating insights from domestic violence—such as awareness of how power dynamics influence age-identified vulnerability and risk. Current interventions reinforce the concept that old age results in separation from community. While interventions are used to help older adults to remain at home and in communities as long as possible, a common assumption is that old age ultimately results in removal from community to a nursing home or hospital. Therefore, later life is a problem of the individual person rather than a community and justice issue.

Finally, social workers in general need to increase their awareness of the potential of older adults as resources within their communities. As the restorative justice practices demonstrate, many cultures include community elders as key members of the process. For example, Braithwaite (2002) described the importance of older adults in various cultures: "Maori, North American, and Australian Aboriginal peoples tend to think it important to have elders with special gifts of spirituality, what Maori call *mana* attend restorative justice processes" (p. 53). Overall, the skills, wisdom, and experience of older adults have been neglected resources within families and communities. As a result, the older population is viewed as a drain or burden on society, rather than as a valued resource or asset.

Limitations of A Restorative Justice Approach

Despite rhetoric about the importance of process and context, many restorative justice programs are institutionalized within court systems that limit the scope of intervention. For example, pressure for efficient case management may mean a limited number of meetings are typically scheduled within the same court date of case referral. Families are then caught off guard, particularly when they had turned to the courts for a decision. In addition, scheduling family meetings outside of these constrictions can be equally difficult. Family members are likely to be busy and geographically dispersed. Community-based programs have to be well known and trusted as a referral source. Given these challenges, it would be even more difficult to try to include community members, such as members of John's church.

A second limitation can be a focus on repairing relationships, resolving conflict, and reaching agreements. Older adults may be reluctant to fully voice or even admit how they have felt marginalized and threatened, not only by familial relationships, but also by losses associated with growing older. John may feel embarrassed that his situation has attracted outside attention, and therefore wish to avoid painful discussion. He may refuse to admit there are conflicts, making conflict resolution much more difficult. Additional pressure to reach agreement can come from project evaluators, who measure success by how many meetings yield such agreements. In these ways, an intervention nominally focused on John's needs becomes a program for managing John himself as a problem.

A third limitation is that practice for addressing elder abuse and neglect has been modeled on Child Protective Services. Infantilization of older adults through intervention, therefore, is a frequent criticism. By framing the case as one of elder abuse or neglect, the strengths developed by John, for example, over his lifetime may be overlooked. In addition, practitioners may not be fully trained in the process of aging. They may unconsciously hold common ageist assumptions about the inevitability of elder frailty and vulnerability. In working with families, they may not try to learn more about how complex dynamics have developed over generations, rather than suddenly surfaced in the midst of an elder care crisis.

NEXT STEPS

Gerontologists like to point out the relevance of our work by emphasizing how aging is a lifelong process rather than an event that is attained at a certain birthday.

However, the focus in geriatric practice has been primarily on older adults who become frail, dependent, and vulnerable. One important lesson from restorative justice practice as learned in African-American, Latino, and indigenous communities is that one might develop positive roles only through lifetime maturity. A second lesson is how our frailties and vulnerabilities are not only questions of personal autonomy, but also realities of interdependence negotiated through familial relationships and community contexts.

One exciting possibility for integrating geriatric social work and restorative justice is to address aging as part of community capacity building. The removal of older adults from homes and communities and placing them in institutions can be culturally inappropriate and is actively avoided by most older adults. What if the challenges and vulnerabilities of aging were located not in individuals but as part of everyday life? As a shared experience, we are each affected by our own aging process and those of others. The risk of elder abuse and neglect is one that can be experienced in any ethnic group or social class. When John's case was discovered, the problem seemed to be maltreatment committed by one person. However, the case could also be approached as one of family isolation and community ignorance of their responsibility. As Hubert Humphrey said, the "true measure of society is in how it treats its most vulnerable members." As a social reality rather than individual liability, Mom or Dad's increasing dependence and isolation becomes a loss shared with family, neighbors, and other community members. Everyone is affected and therefore has a stake in a solution. The process of helping can strengthen rather than weaken social ties, particularly if we see in these older adults a bit of our future selves.

In youth-oriented American culture, aging is treated as something to be avoided. Popular media and advertising continually remind us that healthy people are young and that all effort should be made to avoid old age. Yet, the reality is that most of us will grow older and rely upon our family networks for care. Improved public health and medical technology has increased longevity across racial, ethnic, and social classes. The question is how age-related changes can be negotiated through interdependent relationships across generations and within family and community. In some traditional societies, an ethic of reciprocity is important. As an African proverb states, "just as the elder helped you to cut your first teeth, so you must help them as they lose theirs." A restorative justice approach to aging could incorporate both moral responsibility toward the vulnerable of society and a norm of reciprocity in relationships.

How might this be achieved? In John's case, intervention could be expanded from focus on the dyad of John and Sarah to a family- and community-based discussion. One community justice program trains professionals such as police and hospital workers to identify signs of abuse and neglect. More importantly, a restorative justice approach suggests a need for preventive work and early intervention. Waiting until a crime or intense conflict arises can make successful intervention more difficult. In some areas, community-based work is challenging due to frequent moves and the geographical separation of family. However, the Aging Network provides national, state, and local services that could include basic education about aging as well as how to intervene in cases of abuse and neglect. Professionals in the network could begin identifying local leaders who could be trained to facilitate meetings and who might be more welcomed into the private lives of older adults. These leaders may be senior members of their community as well. Above all, recognizing aging as a social, as much as an individual, issue might reduce the stigma that keeps many older adults from seeking and accepting resources.

NOTE

i Within this chapter, the term "geriatric social work" is used. For the authors' purpose, this terminology is synonymous with "gerontological social work."

REFERENCES

Adamek, M. (2003). Late life depression in nursing home residents: Social work opportunities to prevent, educate, and alleviate. In B. Berkman & S. D'Ambruoso (Eds.), *Handbook of social work in health and aging* (pp. 149–161). New York: Oxford.

Adamek, M., & Slater, G. Y. (2009). Depression and anxiety. In S. M. Cummings & N. P. Kropf (Eds.), *Handbook of psychosocial interventions with older adults: Evidence-based approaches* (pp. 146–181). London: Routledge.

Austin, C. D., Des Camp, E., Flux, D., McClelland, R. W., & Sieppert, J. (2005). Community development with older adults in their neighborhoods: The elder friendly communities program. *Families in Society, 86*, 401–409.

Bazemore, G. (1999). The fork in the road to juvenile court reform. *Annals of the American Academy of Political and Social Science, 564*, 81–108.

Beach, S. R., Schulz, R., Williamson, G. M., Miller, S., Weiner, M. F., & Lance, C. E. (2005). Risk factors for potentially harmful informal caregiver behavior. *Journal of the American Geriatrics Society, 53*(2), 255–261.

Boat, B. W., & Knight, J. C. (2000). Experiences and needs of Adult Protective Services case managers when assisting clients who have companion animals. *Journal of Elder Abuse and Neglect, 12*(3–4), 145–155.

Botsford, A. L., & Rule, D. (2004). Evaluation of a group intervention to assist aging parents with permanency planning for an adult offspring with special needs. *Social Work, 49*(3), 423–431.

Bradford, W. (2002–2003). "With a very great blame in our hearts:" Reparations, reconciliation, and an American Indian plea for peace with justice. *American Indian Law Review, 27*,(1), 1–175.

Braithwaite, J. (2002). *Restorative justice and responsive regulation.* New York: Oxford University Press.

Brandl, B., Dyer, C. B., Heisler, C. J., Otto, J. M., Stiegel, L. A., & Thomas, R. W. (2007). *Elder abuse detection and intervention.* New York: Springer.

Butterwick, S., & Hommel, P. (2001). *Evaluating mediation as a means of resolving adult guardianship cases*. Ann Arbor, MI: The Center for Social Gerontology.

Cassie, K. M., & Sanders, S. (2009). Familial caregivers of older adults. In S. M. Cummings & N. P. Kropf (Eds.), *Handbook of psychosocial interventions with older adults: Evidence-based approaches* (pp. 280–307). London: Routledge.

Crampton, A. (2004). The importance of adult guardianship for social work practice. *Journal of Gerontological Social Work, 43*, 117–129.

Crampton, A. (2009). Global aging: Development success or policy crisis? *Pardee Center Working Paper Series, 6*, 1–28.

Dubble, C. (2006). A policy perspective on elder justice through APS and law enforcement collaboration. *Journal of Gerontological Social Work, 46*(3), 35–55.

Federal Interagency Forum on Aging Related Statistics. (2008). *Older Americans 2008: Key indicators of well being*. Hyattsville, MD: Author.

Gordon, R. M., & Brill, D. (2001). Abuse and neglect of the elderly. *International Journal of Law and Psychiatry, 24* (2–3), 183–197.

Greenberg, J., Seltzer, M., & Brewer, E. (2006). Caregivers to older adults. In B. Berkman & S. D'Ambruoso (Eds.), *Handbook of Social Work in Aging* (pp. 339–354). New York: Oxford University Press.

Greene, R. R. (2008). *Social work with the aged and their families* (3rd ed.). New Brunswick, NJ: Aldine Transaction.

Groh, A. (2003). *A healing approach to elder abuse and mistreatment: The Restorative approaches to elder abuse project*. Kitchner, ON: Community Care Access Centre of Waterloo Region. Retrieved April 20, 2010, from http://www.sfu.ca/cfrj/fulltext/groh.pdf

Holkup, P., Salois, E., Tripp-Reimer, T., & Weinert, C. (2007). Drawing on wisdom from the past: An elder abuse intervention with tribal communities. *The Gerontologist, 47*(2), 248–254.

Hooyman, N. (2008). Aging. In T. Mizrahi & L. E. Davis (Eds.), *The encyclopedia of social work* (20th ed.): Vol 1. (pp. 88–96). New York: NASW & Oxford University Press.

Hurdle, D. (2002). Native Hawaiian traditional healing: Culturally based interventions for social work practice. *Social Work, 47*(2), 183–192.

Linzer, N. (2004). An ethical dilemma in elder abuse. *Journal of Gerontological Social Work, 43*(2/3), 165–173.

McCallion, P., & Nickles, T. (2009). Individuals with developmental disabilities and their caregivers. In S. Cummings & N. P. Kropf (Eds.), *Handbook of psychosocial interventions with older adults: Evidence-based approaches* (pp. 234–254). London: Routledge.

Murphy, S. Y., Hunter, A. G., & Johnson, D. J. (2008). Transforming caregiving: African American custodial grandmothers and the child welfare system. *Journal of Sociology and Social Welfare, 35*(2), 67–89.

Myers, L. L., Kropf, N. P., & Robinson, M. M. (2002). Grandparents raising grandchildren: Case management in a rural setting. *Journal of Human Behavior in the Social Environment, 5*(1), 53–71.

National Center for Health Statistics. (2009). *Health, United States, 2009*. Hyattsville, MD: Retrieved April 20, 2010, from http://www.cdc.gov/nchs/hus.htm

Nerenberg, L. (2008). *Elder abuse prevention: Emerging trends and promising strategies*. New York: Springer.

Nerenberg, L., Baldridge, D., & Benson, W. (2004 June). *Preventing and responding to abuse of elders in Indian Country.* Washington D.C.: National Council on Indian Aging for the National Center on Elder Abuse. Retrieved April 20, 2010, from http://www.nicoa.org/Elder_Abuse/elderabusereport.pdf

Oppong, C. (2004). Gendered family strategies and responsibilities of grandparents in subsaharan Africa. *University of Ghana Institute for African Studies Occasional Research Paper Series 2004 No. 6,* 1–51.

Putnam, M., & Stark, S. (2006). Aging and functional disability. In B. Berkman & S. D'Ambruoso (Eds.), *Handbook of social work in aging* (pp. 79–90). New York: Oxford University Press.

Ragland, D. R., Satariano, W. A., & MacLeod, K. E. (2005). Driving cessation and increased depressive symptoms. *Journals of Gerontology: Series A: Biological Sciences and Medical Sciences, 60A*(3), 399–403.

Scharlach, A., Damron-Rodriquez, J., Robinson, B., & Feldman, R. (2000). Educating social workers for an aging society: A vision for the 21st century. *Journal of Social Work Education, 36*(3), 521–538.

Schulz, R., & Beach, S. R. (1999). Caregiving as a risk factor for mortality: The caregiver health effects study. *Journal of the American Medical Association, 282,* 2215–2219.

Siebert, D. C., Mutran, E. J., & Reitzes, D. C. (1999). Friendship and social support: The importance of role identity to older adults. *Social Work, 44,* 522–533.

Stewart, M., Craig, D., MacPherson, K., & Alexander, S. (2001). Promoting positive affect and diminishing loneliness of widowed seniors through a support intervention. *Public Health Nursing, 18*(1), 54–63.

Sullivan, D., & Tifft, L. (Eds.). (2006). *Handbook of restorative justice.* London: Routledge.

United Nations, Department of Economic and Social Affairs, Population Division. (2009). *World population prospects: The 2008 revision highlights.* New York: United Nations. Retrieved April 20, 2010, from www.un.org/esa/population/publications/wpp2008/wpp2008_highlights.pdf

Waites, C., Macgowan, M., Pennell, J., Carlton-LaNey, I., and Weil, M. (2004). Increasing the cultural responsiveness of family group conferencing. *Social Work, 49*(2), 291–300.

Wilhelmus, M. (1998). Mediation in kinship care: Another step in the provision of culturally relevant child welfare services. *Social Work, 43*(2), 117–126.

Wolf, R. S. (2000). The nature and scope of elder abuse. *Generations, 24*(11), 6–12.

Zodikoff, B. D. (2006). Community services for lesbian, gay, bisexual and transgender older adults. In B. Berkman & S. D'Ambruoso (Eds.), *Handbook of social work in health and aging* (pp. 569–575). New York: Oxford.

Chapter Thirteen

Concluding Thoughts and Next Steps

ELIZABETH BECK, NANCY P. KROPF AND

PAMELA BLUME LEONARD

CROSSING THE LINE: THE TAMMY GIBSON STORY

Tammy Gibson's stepbrother killed her father and her stepmother. Heartbroken and full of rage, sadness, and resentment toward her stepbrother, Bobby, Tammy listened to the prosecutor's advice. At Bobby's trial, Tammy supported the state's efforts to obtain justice for her father and stepmother, and she sat behind him on the "prosecution side" of the courtroom throughout the trial.

Bobby was sentenced to death. Tammy hoped this would mean that she could forget about the terrible deaths of her father and stepmother, resume her life, and mostly forget about Bobby. Yet three years after the murders, Tammy's sister had died from ovarian cancer and Tammy felt orphaned and alone.

For several years into Bobby's death sentence, Tammy remained an advocate for the death penalty. She determined that she would avoid the film *Dead Man Walking*, which focuses on the relationship between death row inmate Matthew Poncelet[i] and his spiritual advisor Sister Helen Prejean. However, one night when she could not sleep, Tammy turned on the TV and began watching the film. Despite her resistance, Tammy was touched by Matthew Poncelet's humanity. The following day she noticed that Sister Helen was speaking in her community. Tammy resolved not to attend, but through a series of coincidences she ended up at the lecture. Following the talk, Tammy approached Sister Helen and began to share her story. According to Tammy, Sister Helen "talked through my anger, and I began to see how it burdened me."

Shortly thereafter, Tammy decided that it was time to visit Bobby, whom she had not seen for 14 years. She took a bible to him and the two interacted as siblings often do, with love and care. "We spoke, we cried, we connected, we shared stories from our childhood . . . I told him that I loved him," Tammy said. Over time Tammy began to understand Bobby and the burdens he had carried as a child. Though Tammy never made excuses for Bobby's behavior, it was important to her to learn that Bobby was deeply remorseful for his actions and that he had tried to call but was unable to reach his sponsor at Alcoholics Anonymous just before the murders occurred.

Tammy continued to visit Bobby and when he received an execution date, Tammy asked the parole board to spare his life. Tammy describes this experience as "crossing the line." To Tammy, a courtroom has a line down the middle, with one side for victims and the other side for defendants, and "no matter what, you do not cross the line." And once you choose sides, you never look back. But as Tammy reached out to Bobby, she found the relationship they had developed brought her much joy. For Tammy, crossing the line provided an opportunity for her to grow and eventually heal. Reflecting on her first visit with Bobby, Tammy said, "I grew on that day. I knew that day that I could go down any road and face anything, and I would be okay."

There is no line between social work and restorative justice as there is in a court of law, but what Tammy modeled holds merit for social workers and restorative justice practitioners.

First and foremost, Tammy allowed herself to leave what she knew—her comfort zone, if you will—and she did so in both physical and cognitive ways. Before visiting Bobby, Tammy could not have imagined herself in an environment as foreign as a prison visiting room. Her worldview changed when she recognized that the framework—the paradigm—she had been using to understand the justice system and the death penalty was not holding up. Tammy admitted to herself that, rather than receiving the closure she was promised from the criminal justice system, she was left with many unanswered questions. The need for answers led her to take in new knowledge and information, and eventually admit to herself that this new way of seeing resonated with her. She built on her strengths to determine the most appropriate path to take for her healing. Ultimately, Tammy chose to forgive Bobby, and she continues to reflect on the importance of that decision for her own life. Tammy's view of forgiveness—namely, that it is a personal decision—is shared by many restorative justice practitioners. Relying on her own inner wisdom and strength, Tammy empowered herself to take action by visiting Bobby. Later, as Bobby's execution drew near, she and three of her siblings asked to meet with the governor to encourage him to support clemency to save Bobby's life. The meeting with the governor was not granted, so Tammy expressed her wishes to the court. Tammy's shift from being a victim to becoming a victim–survivor is strong evidence of her resilience.

THE FIT: SOCIAL WORK, RESTORATIVE JUSTICE, AND TAMMY GIBSON

Tammy's story crossed into five areas of significant fit between social work and restorative justice: the strengths perspective and resilience, empowerment, well-being and healing, cultural competence, and social justice. While arguments regarding the fit between social work and restorative justice are not plentiful in the literature, they are powerful (see Gumz & Grant, 2009; van Wormer, 2004; 2006).

Strengths Perspective

van Wormer (2004) elegantly summed up the link that the strengths perspective forms between social work and restorative justice when she wrote, "Restorative justice is a process designed to bring out the best in people, regardless of what they have done, or the worst of what they have done, and so is social work's strengths perspective" (p. 220). In social work, the strengths perspective is used in practice fields as divergent as clinical work with an individual, and capacity building in community work. In both cases, the assets of clients or communities are identified and bolstered so that these strengths serve as a foundation for change (Kretman & McKnight, 1993; Saleeby, 1992). In this regard, the strengths of individuals and communities, as well as other systems, are capitalized on to promote resilience.

The strengths perspective is crucial to achieving the potential of restorative processes. Otherwise, how could individuals engage with each other in a respectful way when one has harmed the other, perhaps profoundly (Daly, 2008; Pranis, 2005; 2007)? At the same time, an important benefit of engaging in a restorative encounter is resilience, which includes the ability to form a new level of identity based on the incorporation of painful and important experiences (Greene, 2008).

Empowerment

Barton (2003) argued that empowering individuals and communities is an unstated assumption in restorative justice. His statement resonates with an important tenet of the modern restorative justice movement, which is based in Nils Christie's seminal article, *Conflicts as Property* (1976). Christie maintained that in our effort to resolve conflict, we have taken conflicts away from those who are directly involved, so their conflicts become other people's property. Christie explained that victims become double losers, because they experience the original loss associated with the crime and the loss of the case to the state as well.

Restorative justice promotes empowerment by seeking to return, at least in part, the conflict to those who were directly involved by giving voice to victims, offenders, and communities following crime. Zehr and others support the notion that restorative processes can provide healing in this regard. For example, in Victim–Offender Dialogues, the victim is able to ask the offender critical questions such as, "Why my house?" "Why my daughter?" "What did she say at the end?" Having an opportunity to ask these kinds of questions and getting answers to them can help restore victims' sense of safety and power.

Empowerment in social work is a goal found in community and direct practice. The community-practice perspective is rooted in social work's history of seeking to end oppression (van Wormer, 2004). One goal of community practice is to redistribute power and resources from traditional power holders to under-resourced communities. Bazemore, Gordon, and Schiff (2001) and Pranis (2005, 2007) are just a few who have demonstrated the usefulness of restorative justice in shifting power from the state to the community.

Cultural Competence

Both restorative justice and social work value cultural competence, and each struggles to make sure that its practices reflect this ideal. In social work, cultural competence is defined as the ability to provide service and function effectively "in the context of cultural difference" (Cross, 2008 p. 487). Combined with strengths-based values, cultural competence in social work includes the development of practice models based on the strengths and experiences of specific cultures. Because so much of it has been informed by indigenous cultures, restorative justice can hold a great deal of cultural relevancy, particularly for First Nations people. In fact, MacRae and Zehr (2003) cite cultural appropriateness (defined as adapting to the cultural perspectives of the participants) as one of the seven goals of the New Zealand Children, Young Persons and Their Families Act, which revamped New Zealand's juvenile justice system into a restorative model. Additionally, a number of restorative justice practices include space for specific cultural rituals. While both restorative justice and social work hold cultural relevance as an important practice principle—and, indeed, as an ethical standard—both restorative justice and social work acknowledge that more needs to be done by each discipline to address the structures of oppression (Daly, 2008).

Well-Being

The preamble to the National Association of Social Workers code of ethics states that the primary mission of social work is to enhance human well-being. Human well-being is of primary importance to restorative justice, as well. Howard Zehr (2002) outlined three pillars of support that are necessary for individual well being following crime: autonomy, order/safety, and relatedness. Restorative justice practice seeks to strengthen each of these pillars.

Dennis Sullivan and Larry Tifft (2001) see restorative justice as a strategy that not only supports healing following crime, but also has the potential to heal "the foundations of our everyday life" (p. 1). Sullivan and Tifft argue that, because restorative justice is an approach based on needs and relationships, it includes principles and practices that have the potential to transform interactions and power dynamics. In 2006, they added that because restorative justice responds to harm by the use of nonviolence and because restorative ideals view the pain and suffering of all as worthy of repair, the movement is seen by the state as subversive, something that needs to be contained. Likewise, from the settlement house movement in the early twentieth century to its role in supporting health care reform, social work has a long history of challenging the power of the state as it works to enhance human well-being and support social and economic justice.

Social Justice

Social justice is an important hallmark of social work. While restorative justice may be viewed as an international social movement, David Gil (2008), social worker and professor of social policy, notes that it does not generally aim to "transform structurally violent, unjust societies into structurally non violent ones" (p. 499). In this regard, Gil suggests it falls short in meeting its potential to support social justice.

Gil is correct; these issues must be addressed. We, the editors of this book, see social work, with its rich history in advocacy, as an important partner in transforming society. We also take a strong person-in-the-environment approach in that we acknowledge that individual well-being and social change need to coexist. In addition to advocating the type of structural change that Gil supports, we also believe that social workers can use their advocacy tradition to promote restorative justice in the criminal justice system and restorative practices in myriad settings.

As for strengthening the fit between restorative justice and social work, what's next? We will look at three areas: practice skills, research, and systems change.

NEXT STEPS: EXAMINING THE FIT

Remaining Questions

Our book presents numerous settings in which practitioners have drawn from and, in some cases, melded the fields of social work and restorative justice. However, none of our case studies definitively address questions we raised in the introduction about the feasibility and outcomes of a formal collaboration of the sort we authors suggest between social work and restorative justice. It will take additional programs, including training, experience, and research, and ongoing rigorous debate to evaluate the benefits, drawbacks, and unintended consequences of an alliance that almost certainly will result in greater institutionalization of restorative justice.

Further, even though a major portion of this book is devoted to describing and analyzing restorative justice practice skills, that is only a first step in building a partnership. After all, if that were the extent of our intent, restorative justice practitioners soon would be obsolete. We acknowledge that a tremendous amount of thinking, debating, planning, and negotiating remains to be undertaken in building a mutually beneficial relationship between social work and restorative justice.

At the same time, we authors believe there is a need *right now* for restorative justice to resist the dominance of our exclusive institutions, particularly criminal justice. The case studies in this book show that social work offers some insight into how to mitigate the effect of what Mackay (2006) calls the "legal centralism" (p. 85) that has overtaken many restorative justice initiatives. Likewise, restorative justice offers social work a burst of new and creative modalities not only to meet the needs of their clients, but to enrich their capacity for healing and transformation. In short, we believe that by joining together, social workers and restorative justice practitioners become stronger advocates of a more inclusive, healing, and restorative culture.

Practice Skills

Common Processes

Restorative justice and social work follow a common structure in their practice processes. In the *assessment* phase, the practitioner gathers information about the client or involved parties in a way that gives meaning to the context for interventions. In addition, the practitioner needs self awareness, to determine if she or he has the necessary skill set, knowledge, and experience to be effective in a particular situation. In the *intervention* phase, the practitioner uses his or her skills to effectively change the situation. The final phase of practice, *evaluation,* typically involves concluding the intervention and determining whether the outcome has been helpful and, if so, to what degree. Evaluation might also involve decisions about extending the process if satisfactory change has not been achieved. While this practice process structure is common to both restorative justice and social work approaches, there are important differences in the methods and expected outcomes of each.

In assessment, the practitioner collects information about the specific situation and "makes sense" of it by integrating the information with theory. Throughout the chapters in this book, the various authors have provided examples of how assessments help each set of practitioners individualize situations and provide a context for intervening. In the child welfare and family violence chapters, assessment involved learning more about functioning within the family, relationships between the family members, and relationships with external resources and sources of support, as well as individual functioning and development. Other chapters provide evidence of collecting information about other systems such as neighborhood cohesion (in the community chapter) and political and social functioning on a national level (in the international chapter). Practitioners of both restorative justice and social work need to be skilled in collecting relevant assessment data and have the theoretical foundations to use this information to predict and explain behavior and functioning.

While assessment is focused on learning about the clients' or affected parties' situation(s), the assessment process also includes reflection about the practitioner's readiness and ability to be involved. That is because in addition to understanding the situation, both types of practitioners—as part of the process of change—must also understand themselves. In both social work and restorative justice, many situations involve trauma, pain, and wounding. Practitioners who are inexperienced or whose unresolved personal issues may get in the way of effective helping need to seek the advice and support of a supervisor or mentor. (For information about preparing to address trauma, see the chapter on severe violence, where Dave Gustafson wrote about how he and his partner Sandi Berger prepared themselves.)

Practice Skills

Throughout this book, the roles of both restorative justice and social work practitioners have been outlined and how intervention skills were applied have been illustrated by case studies. As we have seen, both approaches share common skills. In social work and restorative justice, practitioners need strong communication skills, both in active listening and in dialogue. In addition, management of conflict is crucial to professionals in both areas. Part of this process is creating a safe environment where individuals of different statuses and roles can interact and hear each other's perspectives. Acknowledging and building on these common skill areas are crucial in facilitating change in both restorative justice and social work.

However, there also are differences in practice skills. While both types of practitioners focus on the relationships with involved parties, social work practitioners often have ongoing relationships with the clients they serve, and these interactions are guided by a code of ethics. While restorative justice is based on values and principles, as yet there is not a process of accreditation or even a code of ethics guiding practice. This is particularly sobering, given the enormity of issues that restorative justice practitioners address, and thus it is not surprising that restorative justice can be conceptualized as a "bushel of hope containing a bundle of risks."

In addition to having knowledge and skills, practitioners have to know how and when to marshal them effectively—what singer/songwriter Mary Chapin Carpenter described in "The Hard Way" as "the knack for knowing when and the gift for knowing how." This means finding resources to provide the safety and preparation that participants need. It also means eschewing assumptions, expectations, and formulas when interacting with people in the context of restorative justice. Because the process of restorative encounters is victim-centered, experienced practitioners will tell you that the restorative approach to working with conflict and harm does not fit the rigid structures of most institutions. As Good and Gustafson (2009) put it, restorative justice does not get done within "the clinical hour," and practitioners may find themselves seeking support not from textbooks or university-based mentors, but from community elders.

In evaluation, the critical issue for both types of practitioners is whether the involved individuals have changed. Some social work situations have clear and defined outcomes, such as a client's achieving a certain level of competency as measured by a standardized instrument (e.g., a parenting scale). In other situations, the end of an intervention may not be focused on a particular outcome having been achieved (e.g., a certain level of competency), but rather on whether a client is eligible to continue to receive services. Unfortunately, this can mean service is terminated even when a satisfactory outcome is not yet accomplished. An example would be when a woman has to leave a domestic violence shelter because she has stayed the maximum length of time, instead of when she has found a safe alternative living arrangement.

In restorative justice, evaluation takes different forms. Evaluation includes assessing the process itself and determining whether the involved parties have been able to voice their perspectives. In addition, a goal of restorative justice is that the involved parties come up with a plan for adequately handling the conflict or harm that is acceptable to all of them. The chapter case studies provided excellent examples of how evaluation is determined for both process and outcome.

Clearly, both social work and restorative justice can learn from the practice processes used within the other discipline, and these areas of similarity provide ways to integrate the disciplines and work effectively and collaboratively. In addition, answering empirical questions about the effectiveness of combined restorative justice and social work outcomes is critical.

Research

Theory undergirds research. This is true whether the research objective is to test a hypothesis or to develop a theory. As evidenced by the chapters in this book, neither social work nor restorative justice has a unique or definitive theory base. Instead, the chapters cover various levels of theories, from those dealing with individual functioning to more pervasive perspectives on social justice. The theoretical content is extracted from various disciplines, including criminal justice, sociology, psychology, and anthropology.

Both social work and restorative justice have orienting theory. In social work's case, efforts have been made at employing metatheories, such as system theory or the ecological perspective, but these metatheories have met with various levels of criticism concerning their abilities to predict and explain human functioning (Wakefield, 1996). Developing a metatheory for restorative justice would be particularly difficult because, as we saw in Chapter 3, the definition and goals of restorative justice mean different things to different audiences, stakeholders, practitioners, and researchers.

Rather than common metatheories, social work and restorative justice each hold important and distinct orienting theories. Social work historically has made use of theories that seek to guide professional interventions, such as Germain and Gitterman's Life Model (1996), Reid and Epstein's Task Centered Model (1972), or Robert's Crisis Intervention Model (2000). The purpose of this level of theory is to provide a representation of how social workers can understand clients, make decisions about practice roles and interventions, and evaluate effectiveness with clients. Although there is not a single best-practice model within social work, practice models that include assessment, intervention, and evaluation are helpful for teaching and implementing various approaches to solving problems in functioning.

Restorative justice makes use of several theories to explain why the practice might work. Some significant theory comes from the Tomkins Institute, its founder Silvan Tomkins, who examined the role of human emotion as a motivator for behavior, and its present director, Donald Nathenson, who has created a significant body of work on shame and violence. Braithwaite's view of reintegrative shaming also provides a significant theoretical context for why restorative justice works. However, these theories focus on the individual level—specifically, what impacts and motivates individual change.

We have identified three lines of inquiry as a constructive way to integrate and expand restorative justice and social work theory and gain empirical knowledge: 1) using intervention research to construct and evaluate practice theories and support theory development while gaining greater insight into lingering issues within each field; 2) learning from others, which includes exploring established partnerships among practitioners; and 3) creating opportunities for interactions.

Intervention Research

Social worker and restorative justice practitioner Mark Umbreit's work provides a model for intervention research. He has examined a specific intervention, Victim–Offender Dialogue, which holds the specific aim in the area of well-being. At present, numerous restorative justice practices are in need of rigorous evaluation. A starting point might be examining the four operational values of restorative justice as identified by van Ness and Strong (2006). These cornerstones, detailed in chapter 3, involve encounter, amends, reintegration, and inclusion. Specifically, it would be important to know if and how these values affect the goals of restorative justice, such as fostering individual well-being. Additional questions can be asked: Does the use of Circles in school programs support enhanced decision making for adolescents? What is the relationship between recidivism and restorative practices? Does victim–offender interaction support individual well-being?

While studies need to explore issues like outcomes and well-being, there are important research gaps in the restorative justice literature that need to be addressed in the research model. Lacking an accredited PhD program and having a short practice history, restorative justice practice has relied on anecdotal evidence based more on the experiences and judgment of individual practitioners or programs than upon empirical evidence gathered from a variety of programs. Some comprehensive studies have been meta-analyses of existing literature; studies designed to address the efficacy of restorative justice theory (in whole or in part) have hardly begun. As a result, the scope of unanswered questions about restorative justice is both deep and wide. To remedy this, studies must seek to answer basic questions about restorative practices, including:

- how race, gender, age, community of residence, and social status of restorative justice facilitators affect outcomes;
- whether there have been unintended negative consequences as a result of restorative justice initiatives (e.g., intra-family disputes regarding participation, process, or outcome; increase or complication of grief);
- the durability and transferability of positive (and negative) effects for victims and offenders;
- which elements of programs, practices, and characteristics of practitioners are more and less effective; and
- how the community is integrated into the practice.

Clearly, what is needed is a body of empirically based intervention strategies, and this requires funding. Our assumption is that restorative processes have the ability to meet social work and societal goals such as stemming violence, enhancing self-esteem, and supporting individual growth and development. We need to be able to test these assumptions through rigorous evaluations, and then we need to use those findings to influence system change.

Learning from Others
A second important line of research involves the interaction between social work and restorative justice practitioners. We believe there are important lessons to be learned from the experiences of people in countries that utilize social workers and have experiences with restorative justice and restorative processes. As we saw in Liberia, for example, there is a significant relationship and interaction between the two fields. A research agenda that uses experiences from across the globe to explore the ways in which social workers and restorative justice practitioners have partnered can yield important insights regarding best practices and help navigate obstacles that can arise in collaborations.

While countries like New Zealand and Australia offer an important starting point for gleaning such research, it would also be helpful to explore American examples. One possible interaction to be explored might be the Minnesota Department of Corrections, which created the position of Restorative Justice Planner to apply principles of restorative justice to corrections, courts, law enforcement, education, and communities. Qualitative and survey data on the nature of the collaboration between social work and restorative justice could yield important insights, and promote the growth of each field.

Moreover, this line of research would explore tensions between the fields. For example (as mentioned previously), restorative justice practice sometimes occurs outside of institutional boundaries. It also has a decreasing reliance on professionals and experts. Additionally, restorative justice practitioners often find themselves balancing the needs of offenders and victims; social workers tend to have one identified client.

There also are areas where restorative justice and social work need to push or encourage each other. One example is the area of cultural competency. Certainly cultural competency is addressed in the restorative justice literature; restorative values and practices borrow from and affirm many indigenous cultures, most famously First Nations in North America and the Maori in New Zealand. Acknowledging the debt owed to these cultures is appropriate but not sufficient to address deeper issues of race, gender, and privilege. However, in the restorative justice literature cultural competency is generally geared to adjusting communication skills rather than addressing issues of structural violence or privilege. While social work supports that cultural competency includes attention to deeper structural issues, practitioners in both fields (and, sadly, most of the contributors to this book) are predominantly white. Shedding tendencies toward exclusivity is more than a recruitment challenge for restorative justice advocates and social workers—it is a test of the credibility of the values and principles of each.

A second part of learning from others to support research and practice would include focused meetings and interactions between practitioners and researchers. Though interdisciplinary collaboration on a large scale presents several difficulties, one of particular note stems from limited cross-pollination among conferences and opportunities for professional growth. A funded symposium would provide an important avenue for such collaboration. In addition to exploring the interaction between fields, adding a practice institute would allow participants to gain skills.

Systems Change

Social work's track record in affecting systems change at the local, state, and federal levels has resulted in a tremendous expansion of service provision and policies that support human service and social justice, dating back to the settlement house movement. As noted in chapter 2, settlement house workers linked social and neighborhood problems with the direct service needs of the individuals who participated in settlement house programs. In this way the workers engaged in what has been termed the "three-R" strategy: residence, research, and reform. Today social workers use the same model to support both populations they serve and the profession, although the terms have changed to: practice, research, and advocacy. One example is the efforts of the National Association of Social Workers (NASW) to pass the Dorothy I. Height and Whitney M. Young, Jr. Social Work Reinvestment Act, which seeks to secure "federal and state investments, related to recruitment, training, retention and research, that strengthen the professions and the communities it serves." The three-R model was used in the development and advocacy of the Reinvestment Act. Specifically, as a professional organization, NASW knew from its members that social work experienced problems in the areas of recruitment and retention of a committed workforce. Research showed that educational debt, low salaries, and safety concerns associated with the profession were some of the barriers to recruitment and retention. As a response, the bill was written, cosponsors were organized, and an advocacy campaign involving 56 chapters of the NASW and a national presence in the halls of Congress and at the White House was launched.

If the implementation of restorative justice is going to be expanded in cases of criminal justice and in additional venues, systems change is necessary to insure that practitioners receive effective training, supervision, and evaluation of programs and practitioners. In this regard, social work can be an important partner. The three-R model used by social workers to promote change, and the skills that social workers have gained by implementing it, provide important tools for the field of restorative justice as it seeks to strengthen its practice reach and growth as a profession.

Evidence of the partnership between restorative justice and social work for affecting systems change can be found within the multiple child-protective service agencies in the United States that now use restorative strategies. While this book has not examined the integration of restorative processes into child welfare offices across the country, that information would make an important contribution to the literature.

Daily Life and Ethos

We end this book with wisdom collected by Barb Toews, a restorative justice researcher, theorist, and practitioner and PhD student at Bryn Mawr College's Graduate School of Social Work and Social Research. Toews has provided some suggestions for what she calls daily life and ethos, which we share to support social workers, restorative justice practitioners, and those of us who are both:

- Remember others' humanity and worth.
- Live nonviolently.
- Walk with the victims and offenders among us.
- Listen more, talk less.
- Be good to yourself.
- Acknowledge when you hurt someone you love.
- Value and promote trust.

The three of us who brought this book project together each have gained from the intersection of our own field with the other: Elizabeth Beck and Nancy Kropf from social work to restorative justice, and Pamela Leonard from restorative justice to social work. We learned a tremendous amount from the chapter authors, who are experts and leaders in their respective fields of practice, and we are confident that you will benefit as well. We believe strongly in the efficacy and practice of each field, and we are very hopeful that together social work and restorative justice practitioners will further dialogue, peacemaking, and reconciliation.

NOTES

i Poncelet was a fictional character based on Patrick Sonnier and Robert Lee Willie, two men on death row in Louisiana who received spiritual counseling from Helen Prejean.

REFERENCES

Barton. (2003). *Restorative justice: The empowerment model.* Sydney, Australia: Hawkins Press.

Bazemore, G. & Schiff, M. (2001). Understanding restorative community justice: What and why now? In Bazemore, G. & Schiff, M. (Eds.), *Restorative community justice: Repairing harm and transforming communities* (pp. 21–46). Cincinnati, OH: Anderson Publishing Co.

Braithwaite, J. (1989). *Crime, shame, and reintegration.* Cambridge, UK: Cambridge University Press.

Christie, N. (1977). Conflicts as property. *The British Journal of Criminology, 17,* 1–15.

Cross, T. L. Cultural competence. In T. Mizrahi & L. E. Davis (Eds.), *Encyclopedia of social work* Vol 1. (pp. 487–491). New York: Oxford University Press.

Daly, K. (2008). The limits of restorative justice. In Sullivan, D. & Tifft, L. (Eds.), *Handbook of restorative justice.* (pp. 134–146). London: Routledge.

Germain, C. B. & Gitterman. A. (1996). *Life model of social work practice: Advances in theory and practice.* New York: Columbia Univesity Press.

Gil, D. (2008). Toward a 'radical' paradigm of restorative justice. In D. Sullivan, & L. Tifft. (Eds.), *Handbook of restorative justice* (pp. 499–511). New York: Routledge International Hanbooks.

Good & Gustafson. (2010). Coming together after violence: Social work and restorative practices. In Beck, E., Kropf, N., & Leonard, P. B. (Eds.), *Social work and restorative justice: Skills for dialogue, peacemaking, and reconciliation* (pp. 356–401). New York: Oxford University Press.

Greene. R. R. (2008). *Human behavior theory and social work practice.* New Brunswick, NJ: Aldine Transaction.

Gumz, E. & Grant, C. (2009). Restorative justice: A systematic review of the social work literature. *Families in Society, 90*(1), 119–126.

Kretman, J. P. & McKnight J. L. (1993). *Building Communities from the Inside Out: A Path Toward Finding and Mobilizing a Community's Assets.* Chicago, IL: ACTA Publications.

Mackay, R. E. (2006). The institutionalization of principles in restorative justice—a case study from the UK. In I. Aertsen, T. Daems, & L. Robert (Eds.), *Institutionalizing restorative justice* (pp. 194–215). Cullumpton, Devon, UK: Willan Publishing.

MacRae, A. & Zehr, H. (2004). *The little book of family group conferences – New Zealand Style.* Intercourse, PA: Good Books.

Nathenson, D. (1992). *Shame and Pride: Affect, Sex and the Birth of the Self.* New York: Norton.

Pranis, K. (2005). *The little book of circle processes: A new/old approach to peacemaking.* Intercourse, PA: Good Books.

Pranis, K. (2007). Restorative values. In G. Johnstone and D. W. Van Ness (Eds.), *Handbook of restorative justice* (pp. 59–74). Cullumpton, Devon, UK: Willan Publishing.

Pranis, K., Stuart B. & Wedge, M. (2003). *Peacemaking circles: From crime to community.* St. Paul, MN: Living Justice Press.

Reid W. J. & Epstein.L. (1972). *Task-centered casework.* NY: Columbia University Press.

Robert, A. (2000). (Ed.). *Crisis intervention handbook : Assessment, treatment, and research.* New York: Oxford University Press.

Saleeby, D. (1992). *The strengths perspective in social work practice.* New York: Longman.

Sullivan, D. & Tifft, L. (2005). *Restorative justice: Healing the foundations of our everyday lives.* (2nd ed.). Monsey, New York: Willow Tree Press.

Tomkins Institute. Retrieved March 13, 2010 from http://www.tomkins.org/

Tomkins, S. (1962). *Affect Imagery Consciousness: Volume I, The Positive Affects.* London.

Umbreit, M. (2001). *The handbook of victim offender mediation.* San Francisco, CA: Josey-Bass.

Van Ness, D. W., & Strong, K. H. (2006). *Restoring justice: An introduction to restorative justice* (3rd ed.). Cincinnati, OH: Anderson Publishing Co.

Sullivan, D. & Tifft, L. (2005). *Restorative justice: Healing the foundations of our everyday lives.* (2nd ed.). Monsey, New York: Willow Tree Press.

van Wormer, K. (2004). *Confronting oppression, restoring justice: From policy analysis to social action.* Alexandria, VA: Council of Social Work Education.

van Wormer, K. (2006). A case for restorative justice: A critical adjunct to the social work curriculum. *Journal of Teaching Social Work, 26*(3/4), 57–69.

Wakefield, J. C. (1996). Does social work need the eco-systems perspective? *Social Service Review,* 70(2), 213–243.

Zehr, H. (2002). *Little book of restorative justice.* Intercourse, PA: Good Books.

Afterword

The field that has come to be known as restorative justice was born in experiment and practice rather than theory; the term "restorative justice" and the conceptual framework came later. Although it did not directly emerge from the field of social work, restorative justice was born in a context and era much influenced by social work. It is appropriate, then, that the fields of restorative justice and social work are again converging, as the authors in this volume so convincingly argue.

We acknowledge deep historical roots for the field of restorative justice; many indigenous traditions were essentially restorative, though with different terminology. However, the first practical programs grew out of juvenile probation in the 1970s, in an era when probation was more social work than surveillance. In fact, it was common for probation officers of this era to have social work backgrounds. Steve Miller was the chief juvenile probation officer under whom the first U.S. "victim offender reconciliation program" or VORP was developed (in Elkhart, Indiana, in the mid 1970s). Although he had graduated with a B.A. in sociology, he had taken a variety of social work courses that he says were foundational to his work. Mark Yantzi, the Canadian probation officer who, with Dave Worth, in 1974 conducted what is considered the first VORP case, similarly had a sociology degree with a focus on human services. Yantzi later did a Masters of Applied Science in Human Relations and Counseling, his thesis focusing on "the role of the third party in the victim-offender conflict."

Following the misguided discrediting of the "liberal" strategies of the 1960's that focused on rehabilitation and jobs, the 1970's and 80s reflected a more conservative emphasis that called for "just deserts" and more punitive sentencing. Although this emphasis was most pronounced in adult justice, juvenile justice was affected as well. This was not an environment that fit well with social work and as the authors here describe, social work began to move away from courts and corrections. Meanwhile, in this punitive environment, restorative justice developed as an ongoing attempt to provide justice theory and practices that were more human and service-centered for both victim and offender. As it has matured, its links with social work – actual as well as potential – have grown increasingly important. We echo the chorus of voices in this book calling for stronger bonds.

One of the most evident intersections of restorative justice and social work is in the foundational issue of values. Moreover, their ultimate goal is similar: to help build and maintain healthy individuals, relationships and communities. Restorative justice offers a framework and a set of practices to repair, to the extent possible, relationships that have been damaged, focusing especially on human needs and obligations. These practices and concepts have greatly benefited by the skills and framework offered by social work. This is exemplified in our own collaboration over the past three decades.

Both of us – Lorraine and Howard – have been with the field of restorative justice since its early years. Howard was director of the first VORP in the U.S., in Elkhart, Indiana, and is considered one of the developers of the conceptual framework. He has played a significant role in the spread of the field internationally. His work has largely been in the criminal justice arena. Lorraine has often credited her degree in social work as the beginning of her work in the area of crime and justice. During her junior year in college, she did a year-long practicum in a pre-trial diversion agency which peaked her interest in the area of juvenile justice. She then began her career in the Elkhart VORP as well and has since concentrated especially on practice and training of practitioners. Following a number of years of practice, she received her Masters in Social Work and was heartened to see the excitement growing in the field in the area of criminal justice. She has found it especially significant that the *Encyclopedia of Social Work* discusses the importance of not only social workers within the field of criminal justice and also that there is a growing trend toward restorative justice in social work.

As the two of us have worked together throughout most of these years, often collaborating on projects, trainings and cases, we have certainly experienced the benefits of the knowledge both fields have to offer. Our latest collaboration, for example, has resulted in a book entitled *What Will Happen to Me* highlighting photographic portraits and quotes from some of the hidden victims of crime – children who have parents in prison. Intended in part for caregivers of these children such as grandparents, teachers – and social workers - the project is informed by some key restorative justice values or goals: to help us address the needs of "stakeholders" in justice, to reduce the "othering" of people who are marginalized by society, to create dialogue around these issues. The project was inspired by Lorraine's MSW thesis that focused on the issues these children face. The first phase of this project was an exhibit that features photographic portraits by Howard as well as interviews with children of incarcerated parents as a way to give a voice to those children who are not heard through the justice process.

Restorative justice arose as an effort to address some of the deficiencies in the criminal justice system: its neglect of victims, its failure to hold those who offend accountable in a meaningful way, its disempowerment of the community, its tendency to heighten rather than reduce social conflict. This application of restorative justice within criminal justice continues to expand throughout the world. However, because the values, principles and practices of these two approaches are often at such odds, the relationship continues to be an uneasy one.

In spite of its deficiencies, the criminal justice system has some crucial functions: at its best it provides a way to sort out at least a semblance of "truth" when people are in denial, to uphold due process and the rule of law, to draw boundaries on unacceptable behavior. Unfortunately, though, it does so in a way that is largely negative. Its basic message is: if you harm others, we will harm you in return. This tends to reinforce the tit-for-tat concept of justice that drives much wrongdoing. Moreover, the conceptual framework is largely negative. Thus it is necessary to bring other values from "outside" into play in order to mitigate this negativity. Probation or correctional officers' jobs are primarily to contain bad behavior so in order to create humane conditions, we have to impose other values and guidelines that humanize their roles. A vision of how we as human beings want to live together is not inherent in these roles, in short, so we provide behavioral guidelines and consequences to insure that the roles are done humanely.

Unlike the criminal justice framework, we argue that restorative justice and social work contain within them a vision of how we want to live together in our communities. The values and practices that are required to maintain healthy individuals and relationships are inherent in the conceptual and value frameworks themselves. The two fields also share an inherent vision to address the critical issues within both areas: systemic issues of oppression that have often been pushed to the back burner in the interests of meeting human need in the here and now. Arguably, therefore, there is a much stronger natural affinity between restorative justice and social work than between criminal justice and restorative justice. This is just one more reason that we are so appreciative of the editors and authors of this book.

As this book makes clear, restorative justice's applications go far beyond the justice system. Schools, for example, are an area of considerable growth; whole school approaches seek not only to respond to wrongdoing restoratively but also to build climates of safety and care within the classroom and community. University conduct and workplace harms are other areas of growth. Child welfare is an arena in which restorative justice is making significant inroads and where social workers play essential roles; the relationship between case coordinators for family group conferences/decision-making and case social workers is essential. While there may be current tensions between what is seen as restorative justice processes (family group conferences) and social services (child welfare cases) because of limited available funding for social services, our hope is that the clear benefit to families and communities of these overlapping models will lead to more interaction between these fields.

Social work and restorative justice have much to gain from each other. Indeed, we need each other! This book makes a significant contribution to an essential dialogue and collaboration.

Index

CPSIA information can be obtained
at www.ICGtesting.com
Printed in the USA
BVOW06*0211070218
507432BV00005B/86/P